Archives of War

This book offers a comparative analysis of British Army Unit War Diaries in the two World Wars, to reveal the role played by previously unnoticed technologies in shaping the archival records of war.

Despite thriving scholarship on the history of war, the history of Operational Record Keeping in the British Army remains unexplored. Since the First World War, the British Army has maintained daily records of its operations. These records, Unit War Diaries, are the first official draft of events on the battlefield. They are vital for the army's operational effectiveness and fundamental to the histories of British conflict, yet the material history of their own production and development has been widely ignored. This book is the first to consider Unit War Diaries as mediated, material artefacts with their own history. Through a unique comparative analysis of the Unit War Diaries of the First and Second World Wars, this book uncovers the mediated processes involved in the practice of operational reporting and reveals how hidden technologies and ideologies have shaped the official record of warfare. Tracking the records into The National Archives in Kew (U.K.), where they are now held, the book interrogates how they are re-presented and re-interpreted through the archive. It investigates how the individuals, institutions and technologies involved in the production and uses of unit diaries from battlefield to archive have influenced how modern war is understood and, more importantly, waged.

This book will be of much interest to students of media and communication studies, military history, archive studies and British history.

Debra Ramsay lectures in Film and Television Studies at the University of Exeter, U.K., and is the author of *American Media and the Memory of World War II* (2015).

Media, War and Security

Series Editors: Andrew Hoskins, University of Glasgow and Oliver Boyd-Barrett, Bowling Green State University

This series interrogates and illuminates the mutually shaping relationship between war and media as transformative of contemporary society, politics and culture.

Violence and War in Culture and the Media
Athina Karatzogianni

Military Media Management
Negotiating the 'front' line in mediatized war
Sarah Maltby

Icons of War and Terror
Media images in an age of international risk
Edited by John Tulloch and R. Warwick Blood

Memory, Conflict and New Media
Web wars in post-socialist states
Edited by Julie Fedor, Ellen Rutten and Vera Zvereva

Violent Extremism Online
New perspectives on terrorism and the internet
Edited by Anne Aly, Stuart Macdonald, Lee Jarvis and Thomas M. Chen

Western Mainstream Media and the Ukraine Crisis
A study in conflict propaganda
Oliver Boyd-Barrett

European Foreign Conflict Reporting
A Comparative Analysis of Public News Providers
Emma Heywood

Archives of War
Technology, Emotion and History
Debra Ramsay

Archives of War
Technology, Emotion and History

Debra Ramsay

LONDON AND NEW YORK

First published 2024
by Routledge
4 Park Square, Milton Park, Abingdon, Oxon OX14 4RN

and by Routledge
605 Third Avenue, New York, NY 10158

Routledge is an imprint of the Taylor & Francis Group, an informa business

© 2024 Debra Ramsay

The right of Debra Ramsay to be identified as author of this work has been asserted in accordance with sections 77 and 78 of the Copyright, Designs and Patents Act 1988.

All rights reserved. No part of this book may be reprinted or reproduced or utilised in any form or by any electronic, mechanical, or other means, now known or hereafter invented, including photocopying and recording, or in any information storage or retrieval system, without permission in writing from the publishers.

Trademark notice: Product or corporate names may be trademarks or registered trademarks, and are used only for identification and explanation without intent to infringe.

British Library Cataloguing in Publication Data
A catalogue record for this book is available from the British Library

ISBN: 978-0-367-77610-7 (hbk)
ISBN: 978-0-367-77616-9 (pbk)
ISBN: 978-1-003-17210-9 (ebk)

DOI: 10.4324/9781003172109

Typeset in Bembo
by Taylor & Francis Books

To A.J. Mouton. Captain in the South African Airforce, and my father.

Contents

List of illustrations viii
Acknowledgements ix

Introduction: From battlefield to archive 1

1 "Scribbled hastily in pencil": Unit war diaries in the First World War 23

2 The typeset war: Unit war diaries in the Second World War 73

3 The matter of materials and archives 136

Conclusion: From the age of information to information overload 192

Bibliography 216
Index 233

Illustrations

Figures

1.1 8th Battalion North Staffordshire Regiment, March 1918, WO 95-2082-1, TNA, Kew   35
1.2 1 Battalion North Staffordshire Regiment, 25 December 1914, WO 95-1613-3, TNA, Kew   55
2.1 1 Staffordshire Regiment, "Introductory Notes to the War Diary 1st Bn The South Staffordshire Regiment for the Period March–July 44," WO 172-4920   106
2.2 2 Welsh Guards, "The Nijmegen Nuisance," WO 171-1260, TNA, Kew   122

Box

3.1 "War Diaries transcription notes" by Stevie Docherty   171

Acknowledgements

This is a book that investigates processes and practices, including those involved in writing a book like this, so I want to draw attention here to the fact that acknowledgements are often overlooked, and go unread, but the people mentioned here are even more significant than all the references listed in this book, as without many of them, this book would not have happened.

So here I acknowledge the colleagues and friends who have spent time talking with me about this book, and read pieces of it, providing ideas and feedback. Dr Tricia Zakreski, for astute and insightful comments and feedback. Dr Benedict Morrison and Dr Ranita Chatterjee for support and conversations about this book and so much more. Professor Andrew Hoskins, who worked his magic on the title. Professor Roberta Pearson, for endless support. William Spencer, Falklands veteran and military specialist at TNA who patiently provided advice and answered questions. Catherine Garrod, for accommodation during visits to the archive, and for her cheerleading of this project and so much else. And Ash Vanstone, for the love and laughter that kept me going.

The non-humans in my life are as important to this book. Marmalade saw the start, but not the end. Onyx and Whisper were there at the end, but not at the beginning. And special thanks must go to a certain Mr Alfie Mount, a sprocker spaniel who got me out of the house every Saturday morning, and who showed me how to value, as only a spaniel can, space and light and air.

And finally, thanks must go to Winsome Mouton and Darrian Churchill, my mother and brother who always believe. And to my husband, Warwick Ramsay, without whom this book would not have happened and in whose eyes the sun continues to rise, every day.

Notes on Transcription in Chapter 3 were compiled by Stevie Docherty, and appear here with her permission.

A portion of Chapter 1 appeared as an article, "'Scribbled Hastily in Pencil': The Mediation of World War I Unit War Diaries," in the *Media, War & Conflict* Journal, on the 2 August 2021, https://doi.org/10.1177/17506352211033210.

Introduction
From battlefield to archive

At first, it may appear that the spaces of the war and those of the archive are totally at odds. Archives conjure up ideas of hushed rooms with carefully catalogued material on dusty shelves. The kind of place, in the words of Carolyn Steedman, that

> is to do with longing and appropriation. It is to do with wanting things that are put together, collected, collated, named in lists and indices; a place where a whole world, a social order, may be imagined by the recurrence of a name in a register, through a scrap of paper, or some other little piece of flotsam.[1]

The reading rooms of archives are thought of as spaces in which the flotsam of the past washes up, where it can be carefully picked through and sorted, to construct both memory and history. The spaces of war, in contrast, are defined by what World War II veteran and philosopher J. Glenn Gray called "the tyranny of the present"[2] – spaces in which past and present are subsumed in the extreme urgency of armed combat. But wars, and especially industrial wars, are not waged without producing an abundance of documentation – casualty lists, standing orders, leave registers, daily reports, after-action reports. Some of this mass of official paperwork makes its way into archives, where it provides essential primary source material for the histories of conflict. This book is about two specific sets of records – British Army Unit War Diaries from the two World Wars. It is about why these records were created, how they took shape on the battlefields of the First and Second World Wars, and what they allow us to understand about those conflicts. It is also about The National Archives of England and Wales, where these records do not simply appear like flotsam on a beach, but where they are organised, re-presented and reconfigured through the structures and technologies of archival practice.

In the early 1900s, in part because of lessons learned in the South African War (1899–1902) but also because of broader organisational changes, the British Army's *Field Service Regulations* (*FSR*) instituted a practice of operational reporting by instructing every unit and formation in active service to keep a "concise and accurate record" of their daily activities.[3] These records had two

DOI: 10.4324/9781003172109-1

2 Introduction

purposes. As listed in order, the first was to furnish accurate source material for future histories of conflict, and the second was to provide information to allow the Army to wage war more effectively. In trenches, dimly lit rooms or bombed-out ruins, in field offices, jungles, deserts and mountains, sometimes as events unfolded, sometimes afterwards, with indelible pencils, pens or typewriters, junior officers, intelligence officers and/or clerks of the British Army from fighting units to headquarters, committed to paper the events and experiences of their units. Much of the writing about war – memoirs, histories, novels – is produced away from the battlefield and in the aftermath of conflict. Most Unit War Diaries, in contrast, were produced in or near the spaces of conflict, and generally during wartime, making them the first official representations of war. They were considered essential to systems of command, control and communication during wartime, and afterwards became the Army's de facto source of evidence and historical information. They were crucial for the writing of the Official Histories of both World Wars. Today in the public domain in The National Archives in Kew, they constitute a prodigious stockpile of material for academics, family historians and anyone with an interest in military history. They feature in bestselling accounts of conflict,[4] and are essential sources in the recent trend towards investigating the significance of the Army's organisational systems and technologies of information management in waging war.[5] Yet despite their significance to the Army's operational effectiveness and to historiography, Unit War Diaries of the First and Second World Wars have never been recognised as mediated, material objects with their own history.

Representations of war in general in media are the subject of a great deal of analysis and attention both within and outside of academia. The ways in which the two World Wars in particular have played out in news media, novels, poetry, films, television series and digital games have been scrutinised at great length and depth, including in my own work.[6] But as Lisa Gitelman reminds us, media are not only comprised of the categories – film, television, news media – usually associated with the rather vague catch-all term "the Media," but are also constituted in forms and technologies often so overlooked they have acquired a kind of invisibility.[7] The representation of warfare in official documents, through technologies of media such as pens, pencils and typewriters, has not had much attention in the vast body of literature on media and war.

Unit War Diaries are not the reports of journalists, the reflections of novelists, poets or scriptwriters, nor are they the memoirs of great military or political leaders. They are official documents composed using technologies provided by the Army and in response to the Army's instructions and needs. Yet they are also the highly individual responses and thoughts of soldiers attempting to process the experiences of two unprecedented conflicts through the medium of official military documents. Unit War Diaries are therefore more than components of command, control and communication, and more than information, data or raw material for historiography. Just as documentation has been overlooked in literature on media and war, processes of mediation have been neglected in research into the significance of information and organisational management in the British Army in the two World Wars. The production and circulation of information through various practices and technologies in the British Army and other military forces has been examined,[8] but the question of how, or even if, information might have been shaped by those very practices and technologies has not been raised.

The lack of attention to documentation in discourse on war and media, and of mediation in information management in warfare, raises the following questions around Unit War Diaries that this book sets out to investigate:

> How do the material records of the British Army represent the two World Wars?
> How have cultural and technological shifts in the production, storage and circulation of Unit War Diaries shaped the material records of the two World Wars?
> How have the individuals, institutions and technologies involved in the production of Unit War Diaries influenced how war is understood and waged?

Addressing these questions involves tracking Unit War Diaries from the writing spaces of the two World Wars to the reading spaces of The National Archives.[9] To fully investigate the trajectory of Unit War Diaries from battlefield to archive, and to reveal what happens to the record of war as it cycles through different technologies and institutions, this book integrates research into the British Army's evolution and its organisational practices with insights from the fields of information, documentation and archival studies. But this book is not only an investigation of the hitherto neglected history of the strategies and ideologies of operational reporting and of Unit War Diaries as material artefacts. It also draws on research into war, media and emotion, and adopts techniques from textual analysis, to explore Unit War Diaries as mediated representations of conflict. These combined approaches allow this book to interrogate Unit War Diaries as the product and expression of the historically situated interplay between individuals, institutions, war and technologies of media, with an overarching goal of revealing how these elements have shaped the record, and therefore the understanding, of war.

"One way to think about records," writes Margaret Hedstrom of archival records, "is to move back from the thing – the inscription – to the act of its becoming."[10] The process of how Unit War Diaries came into being is a large part of this book's focus, and it begins long before any soldier put pen or pencil to paper in the trenches of the First World War. Unpicking some of the complexity of the entanglements between individuals, institutions and technologies of media begins by taking a step back from the records to have a very broad look at shifts and developments throughout the Nineteenth Century, a subject covered in more detail in Chapter 1, but one which it is useful to cover briefly here to illustrate how Unit War Diaries came into being, and to provide a context for their trajectory from battlefield to archive.

4 Introduction

Bureaucracy and paperwork in the Nineteenth Century

The Nineteenth Century is often conceptualised as an age of revolutions, and not only because of the revolts against established regimes or struggles for independence that spread around the world during this century (in France, Austria, Prussia, parts of Italy, Bulgaria, Mexico and India, to name a few), but also because of the social changes and ideas that attended them (such as the rise of cultural nationalism and Romanticism). The Nineteenth Century was also the age in which changes initiated by the Industrial Revolution began to take hold across all areas of life in Britain. Institutions and individuals faced new challenges as technological changes, especially those related to steam, such as the steam engine and printing press, facilitated the rapid production and circulation of goods, capital and information around the world. While for most individuals, the world of work was transformed during this century, institutions from governments through commercial enterprises to militaries responded by reorganising themselves to meet new standards of efficiency and speed. Bureaucratic systems of organisation were perfectly suited to meet the demands of the age, based as they are on hierarchical systems of control, the division and specialisation of labour, standardisation and scientific measurements of gains and losses. The British Army was among those institutions that adopted bureaucratic structures and principles, part of which included the implementation of Unit War Diaries.[11]

The Nineteenth Century was the age in which "information" evolved as a concept to become thought of as something separate from individual knowledge.[12] Information became increasingly associated with its material forms, especially with documents or the printed text, rather than with knowledge held and imparted by individuals. Print enabled the circulation of an unprecedented range of textual materials, increasing the availability of information on topics as varied as style manuals for handwriting to scientific treatises on war. Information acquired an importance like that of any other commodity circulating in the Nineteenth Century's commercial and political systems. Documentation, in turn, requires managing, leading to systems of classification, indexing, and of course, storage. Even the humble cardboard box (discussed in more detail in Chapter 3) has its origins in the late Nineteenth Century. The welter of paperwork produced by government institutions, considered as evidence of State activities and decisions, required preservation.

State archives, such as the Public Record Office in the U.K., had new demands placed upon them as a result, and were themselves shaped by the challenges and responsibilities of managing and organising government documentation, giving rise to specialist systems of selection, cataloguing and description. Documentation increasingly gained authority, augmented through archival processes, as authentic records of past events. An ouroboric relationship emerged in the Nineteenth Century and has continued since between information, documentation and institutions of power and control, in which each lent the other authenticity and weight. The document became the raw material for the new profession of history. History as a profession emerged in the latter half of the Nineteenth Century and aligned itself with the sciences at least in part because its practice involved supposedly objective reporting on the empirically verifiable and stable facts gleaned from primary textual sources. The idea of objective, scientific rationalism had in turn gained ground throughout the 1900s as one of the core ideological frameworks through which the world was viewed and understood.

Operational reporting in the British Army, in the form of Unit War Diaries, thus came into being at a critical juncture in which State institutions, including the Army, had reorganised themselves along bureaucratic lines, documentation had taken on new significance, and both history and archiving were developing practices that would define them as professions. These organisational practices and processes evolved in response to the challenges and opportunities posed by industrialisation but were also bolstered by the rapid spread of corporate capitalism, which was in turn fuelled by the resources and reach of the European Colonial empires. Unit War Diaries are both product and expression of the efficiency of bureaucratic systems of organisation and the apparent success of principles of objective methods as a mode of understanding the world, and one of the core concerns of this book is in investigating what implications there are for the representation of war through these methods and modes.

Yet precisely at this moment in which so much investment, both literal and figurative, was placed into rational forms of organisation and thinking, war was evolving into a phenomenon that could obliterate lives, create destruction on an unprecedented scale, disrupt and devastate societies, and ultimately present a threat to the world itself. But even the vast, complex and sometimes chaotic phenomenon of industrial warfare, as this book will show, was believed to be controllable and explicable through rational, 'scientific' principles. Michel Foucault questions the impulse towards subjecting almost everything to scientific practices by asking what "types of knowledge" are disqualified in the process, together with "what speaking subject, what discursive subject, what subject of experience and knowledge" might be minimised in the process of adopting scientific modes of discourse.[13] Prompted by Foucault's question, this book investigates what types of knowledge or experiences related to war might be squeezed out of Unit War Diaries by the bureaucratic structures and the rational systems of order and control underpinning the construction of operational reporting. To reveal and interrogate the principles, practices and technologies through which information is generated and mediated in Unit War Diaries, this book draws on information and documentation studies, as well as on perspectives from media studies.

Information, documentation, mediation

Information sometimes takes on a kind of neutral quality in discussions of practices of information management in the military, as if it were a thing to be communicated, consumed and utilised – a position that itself reflects the separation of information into a discrete category that occurred in the Nineteenth Century. Emily Goldman, for example, defines information as data, consisting of "the words, numbers, images and voices that are flowing from one point to another in an orderly fashion, that impart meaning, that inform the information consumer, and that have the potential for influencing the future state of affairs."[14] Once this data is processed, according to Goldman, it becomes knowledge.[15] Similarly, Brian Hall argues that information is only meaningful when it has been "analysed and interpreted. Once processed and understood, information becomes knowledge."[16] Jon Lindsay, however, argues that we need to move beyond conceptualising information as facts or figures, or in the digital world, as "bits and bytes," to understand it instead "as a system of pragmatic relationships (between representations and referents, format and meaning, text and context, humans and computers, users and designers, allies and enemies, etc.)."[17] In this book, I am interested in investigating the relationships and technologies involved in the practices of record keeping in the British Army during the two World Wars that defined what kind of information about conflict was important in the first place, and that in the second, shaped the ways in which war was understood and waged. My approach thus follows Luke Tredinnick's exhortation to those writing on information history to investigate how information "as a product of particular social and cultural contexts, mediated by particular institutions such as the archive or library, and embedded with particular historically situated social processes comes to influence the ways in which we frame our understanding of the past."[18] This book addresses a critical gap in many of the discussions of information by revealing the role played by documentation and technologies of media in configuring, structuring and giving meaning to information long before it is analysed and reconstituted as knowledge.

Those writing on documentation have gone some way towards addressing the relationship between technologies and the quality and nature of information. Ethnographic and sociological studies of organisations have looked into how the formal and material qualities of documents influence interactions between individuals and organisations and shape the nature of organisational information and knowledge. Annelise Riles, for example, examines how the aesthetic qualities and practices of networked, bureaucratic institutional life, including the production and sharing of documents, shape information and knowledge to the extent that they "generate the effects of their own reality by reflecting on themselves."[19] David Dery makes a similar argument around the concept of "papereality" – the idea that records, rather than the knowledge of individuals, are the "binding picture of reality" for organisations; one which can only be significantly disrupted by other recorded versions of events.[20] The ways in which documents mediate between individuals and institutions, as well as the version of reality that is constructed in records of war, are key concerns of this book, although my approach is not based in ethnography or in organisational studies. Instead, this book is oriented more towards the space opened by Lisa Gitelman's work on documents from pre-printed forms to the Portable

Document Format (PDF) to create "a better, richer media studies."[21] More specifically, my aim is to expand the study of media and war to include official documents and technologies of writing.

While much work on documentation (including Gitelman's) focuses on the documents produced by corporate and/or state bureaucracies, my interest lies in investigating what happens when practices of documentation more usually associated with office spaces are implemented on battlefields. Gitelman identifies the pre-printed, blank form as particularly significant to the operation of bureaucratic organisations, arguing that "blanks make bureaucracy, directing and delimiting fill-in entries that form the incremental expressions of the modern, bureaucratic self."[22] Chapter 1, which focuses on the records of the First World War, includes an analysis of how Army Form C.2118, the pre-printed blank form designed for the completion of Unit War Diaries in both World Wars, delimits and directs the information about conflict. Gitelman argues that "because blank forms help routinise, they dehumanise,"[23] but in both Chapters 1 and 2 (which focuses on the Second World War) this book investigates if, or how, the individuals completing these forms pushed back against the structure of the official document, whether deliberately or inadvertently, and whether by doing so, they reveal something of the human being behind the form. The C.2118 form is the document through which individuals recorded sometimes unprecedented and horrific events. These pre-printed forms therefore represent not just the expression of the self in relation to institutional bureaucracy, but expressions of the self in relation to industrial warfare. This book reveals how the C.2118 form mediates between individual, institution, and events in war.

Examining documentation broadens perspectives of what comprises the 'media' in 'media studies' but investigating the production of documents also involves attending to technologies that are sometimes overlooked in discussions of media. Much early scholarship on media was concerned, understandably, with mass media, and particularly on the content, composition and possible effects, of media texts. Theorists such as Marshal McLuhan and Friedrich Kittler were pivotal in shifting attention off media texts and onto the technologies through which these texts were communicated and received, but their work became part of a trend that identified technology as the sole source and driver of social and cultural change. The rise and spread of digital media and technologies initiated a re-evaluation of 'old' media forms in response to challenges posed by 'new' media on established thinking and models. The very ubiquity of digital technologies and their infiltration into almost every aspect of daily life pushed thinking about them beyond either technological determinism or ideas of neutrality to consider more nuanced interpretations of media technologies as "complex, sociomaterial phenomena."[24] Regardless of disciplinary orientation, most contemporary scholarship, and this includes the approach I adopt here, understands technologies of media as "the product of distinct human and institutional efforts" and as social and cultural "constructs richly etched with the politics, presumptions, and worldviews of their designers."[25]

8 Introduction

This book draws on contemporary understandings of media technologies as embedded in, and expressions of, culture and society to analyse the technologies of writing commonly used to complete Unit War Diaries – specifically the indelible pencil and the typewriter. Compared to the vast body of literature on the relationship between the camera and war, and war and visual media in general, there is almost nothing on how war is represented in official documents. Yet these documents are as much mediated representations of warfare as photographs or films and are also created using technologies of media. Although the typewriter was available during the First World War, for reasons that will become clear in Chapter 1 the indelible pencil was used extensively throughout the British Expeditionary Forces. While some attention has been given to the impact of the typewriter in the First World War,[26] the indelible pencil has remained relatively unnoticed, yet it is as much a product of industrial manufacturing as the typewriter and was a significant writing technology used to complete Unit War Diaries. Chapter 1 therefore focuses on handwritten diaries, and on the cultural importance of handwriting and its relationship to official documentation. Chapter 2 turns to the typewriter, which by the Second World War had become intrinsic to the processes of waging war, to investigate the role played by this media technology in shaping the representation of war.

But a comprehensive understanding of Unit War Diaries requires not only an appreciation of how they are embedded in historically contingent perspectives of information, or of their formal qualities as documents shaped by specific technologies of media, but also an analysis of them as mediated texts. At the beginning of this Introduction, I mentioned that Unit War Diaries were official documents, but that they also contain (quite literally, as will become apparent as the book progresses) the responses of the individuals who completed them. Something of the ambiguity of these reports is evident in their very title as 'diaries' of war. The diary has an "'uncertain' nature between literary and historical writing, between fictional and documentary, spontaneous and reflected narrative" that has challenged both literary scholars and historians.[27] Because Unit War Diaries were implemented to meet the needs of future historians and of the Army, they were not intended to take the form of subjective, personal testimony, but to represent the experiences of groups in the British Army's formations, from Headquarters to Battalion, in precise, objective terms. Those terms were governed, as this book will show, by rules and regulations designed as part of a general military approach that, according to John Keegan, enabled the officer to "describe events and situations in terms of an instantly recognisable and universally comprehensible vocabulary, and to arrange what he has to say about them in a highly formalised sequence of 'observations', 'conclusions' and 'intentions'."[28] Consequently, official records are often critiqued as sanitised and emotionless versions of events in war. Roger Beaumont, for example, comments on how official accounts can be "mechanistic" and have been broadly characterised as "spare in style and content, flat and unidimensional."[29]

But despite the controls and restrictions imposed by official structures and regulations on Unit War Diaries, and the significant influences they had on the record of war, uniformity and unidimensionality could not be easily imposed on the thousands of men who completed them over the course of the two World Wars. Through identifying the trace marks of individual handwriting, breaks in reporting protocols, the construction of narratives embellished with literary and historical flourishes, philosophical observations, the use of excessive punctuation, and even spelling and typing errors, this book will argue that individuality pushes its way into the texts of the C.2118 forms and after-action accounts and brings these documents closer to the personal diary and further away from the concise and controlled format of official reporting. These kinds of ruptures in the official stream of information and the subjectivity of some of the reports undermine the authority of Unit War Diaries for some historians, including, as Chapter 1 details, those responsible for the Official Histories of the First World War. This book, however, hones in on those moments and instances that break through the controlled veneer of the texts of Unit War Diaries, because it is through them that the presence of individual affective and embodied responses to warfare are revealed.

Recognising these moments as affective and embodied responses to war moves beyond thinking about Unit War Diaries in terms of 'information' assessed primarily in terms of its utility. It shifts attention off what Sally Swartz refers to as the "fiction of accuracy" found in the things that are measurable, countable, or trackable (all valued in bureaucratic systems), and onto another dimension of warfare.[30]

Emotion in the writing spaces of war

"War," according to Christine Sylvester, "cannot be fully apprehended unless it is studied up from people and not only studied down from places that sweep blood, tears and laughter away, or assign those things to some other field to look into."[31] Memoirs, personal diaries, as well as fictional accounts of war in literature, plays, films and television series are privileged as the appropriate arenas for engaging with 'blood, tears and laughter,' i.e. the emotional dimension of warfare. In contrast, military history has long tended to avoid including emotion in its "inventory of assumptions, and usages through which the historian makes his professional approach to the past."[32] Both Keegan and Roger Beaumont attribute the tendency to avoid or downplay emotion in military history to its dependence on documentation as the primary form of evidence for events in war, which Beaumont describes as "a degree of reliance that approaches fixation," even if it is, to a certain degree, understandable.[33] There is after all a long history in Western philosophical thought of separating emotion from reason, and of seeing it as muddying the processes of rational observation and decision-making believed essential for scientific method. Ignoring or downplaying emotion in history in general and in the history of warfare in particular can be traced back to this tradition, as well as to the rationalist roots of the discipline as it emerged towards the end of the Nineteenth Century. *Archives of War* is not a military history, but it investigates the material upon which much military history is based to provide greater insight into how these records attempt to eliminate emotion, what elements push through regardless of those attempts, and what these records reveal about how this dimension of warfare was negotiated by both the British Army and by individuals.

There has been increasing recognition of war as an embodied, individual experience involving physical and emotional responses. Joanna Bourke, who has written amongst other things on the relationship between the male body and conflict in the First World War, on the act of killing in Twentieth Century Warfare and on the role of fear in the two World Wars,[34] has been especially influential in locating and revealing the significance of the "language of emotions" in war, as opposed to the "cool calculation of many war writings."[35] There are movements towards addressing emotion and conflict in Strategic Studies,[36] and in the field of International Relations and Security,[37] where it is increasingly recognised as "essential to the way in which conflicts are both thought and fought."[38] But emotions are, as Bourke points out, "nebulous, contradictory and complex."[39] In addition to being individual and embodied, they are also historically, culturally and socially contingent.[40] While emotions can be tricky to study in everyday life, they are even more difficult to identify and address in the spaces of war, especially during armed combat, which might arouse a stormy spectrum of intense, messy and unpredictable emotions in the participants. Like Stephanie Downes, Andrew Lynch and Katrina O'Loughlin, this book adopts an approach to emotion in war built on Monique Scheer's conceptualisation of emotion as a 'cultural practice.'[41] Scheer draws on Pierre Bourdieu to argue that emotions are constituted in a specific *habitus* that "specifies what is 'feelable' in a specific setting, orients the mind/body in a certain direction without making the outcome fully predictable."[42] As a cultural practice, emotion requires a medium for its expression, through actions that include bodily expressions, spoken and written words, or the use of material objects.[43] Emotional practices from the past can thus be identified through the "traces of observable action" in various forms of media used for expression, including written texts.[44] This book extends existing work on war and emotion by identifying how observable traces of emotional practices are mediated by and through the medium of official documentation.

Tracking observable traces of emotion in the Unit War Diaries avoids the impossible problem of attempting to verify the nature or even the 'truth' of what individuals might have been feeling at the time and focusses instead on the material traces of their emotional practices on the page. Emotives are an important component of emotional practice, and possibly the most obvious in terms of material traces. As conceptualised by William Reddy, emotives are overt references to emotion in language, and I use linguistic analysis to identify them in Unit War Diaries and to map trends in their overall usage across the reports of both wars.[45] Emotives, although significant, provide insight only into how language might be used as part of the practice of the *performance* of emotion – to intensify, explain, provoke or even hide emotion. But the embodied experience of war also includes affective responses. Affect is sometimes used interchangeably with emotion, but I am using it here and throughout this book as it is understood by Brian Massumi – as something that precedes and/or exceeds emotion, but that also resists conscious apprehension and therefore easy translation into language.[46] Affective responses also leave observable traces, such as the use of specific forms of punctuation, often ignored in analysis of emotional practices in written work. This book uses linguistic analysis to track these observable traces too, as well as to plot the errors that disrupt the authoritative veneer of official documents.

Linguistic analysis is valuable in identifying overarching trends in emotional practice across the Unit War Diaries of both World Wars, but for a more nuanced understanding of the intersections between individuals, conflict, and the Army as institution, analysis of a different kind is required. This book will argue that the regulations and the formal qualities of the official Army form create a framework that attempts to shape the way in which information is delivered and to strip it of narrative, especially in the records of the First World War, but there are instances in which narratives evolve in ways that push back at those structures. These narratives are also a form of emotional practice. By employing close reading, a technique more usually associated with the reading of literature, this book confronts, rather than ignores, the sometimes slippery nature of Unit War Diaries as both official documents and personal accounts, and helps to reveal how and why these narratives were articulated, instead of being concerned what they might omit or obscure in terms of the facts about particular events. Close reading, according to Annette Federico, involves

> the cultivation of self-consciousness about the reading experience, a desire for more awareness of what's going on – the kind of reading that opens the door to a deeper, more critical understanding of the *particular* work being read, and of the *experience* of reading as a whole.[47]

It is a technique more usually applied to works of fiction, poetry and drama, but Federico suggests it could equally be applied to other forms of writing and also other forms of media, such as films. But it is not often, if ever, a technique applied to official documentation. I apply this technique to Unit War Diaries to deepen the understanding of how these records were written, and what the experience of reading them reveals. Whereas Downes, Lynch and O'Loughlin identify literature on war as having a "particular power to take the emotional understanding of war beyond the limits and disguises of 'official' languages,"[48] this book's analysis of the material traces of observable actions of emotional practice in Unit War Diaries opens them up as spaces in which emotion is performed and used to process events in war, and occasionally even becomes a form of resistance against both bureaucratic structures and war itself. Understanding Unit War Diaries as a form of emotional practice, and not just an institutional process of communication and control, enables a much richer understanding of the relationship between individuals and the British Army in the two World Wars, and it uncovers a hitherto hidden, or ignored, emotional dimension to the process of operational reporting and the official records of war.

Jay David Bolter's concept of the "writing space" is a useful one in understanding how the factors I have mapped out so far converge in Unit War Diaries. Bolter defines a writing space as:

> a material and visual field, whose properties are determined by a writing technology and the uses to which that technology is put by a culture of readers and writers. A writing space is generated by the interaction of material properties and cultural choices and practices [...] Each fosters a particular understanding both of the act of writing and of the product, the written text...[49]

From the immaterial forces of social and institutional cultures to the material technologies used to complete the documents and the choices made by individuals in terms of what to include or exclude from their accounts, each of the elements at work in the writing spaces of the First and Second World Wars has left an imprint on the record of war. Both chapters on the two World Wars, therefore, begin by establishing the forces at work in both British society and the British Army that influenced the Army's procedures for generating and controlling information, as well as its understanding and approaches to emotion on the battlefield. Each chapter investigates the cultural and institutional significance of the technologies used in the writing spaces of each war used to complete Army Form C.2118, focussing particularly on the indelible pencil in the First World War, and the typewriter in the Second. Each chapter on the World Wars undertakes linguistic and close textual analysis of the records to reveal what emerges in the accounts of individuals from the convergence of all these elements in the writing spaces of war.

But all of that is only half of the story of the records of war.

This book extends the concept of the writing space to consider how similar forces operate in the reading spaces in which Unit War Diaries are accessed. Bolter argues that "each culture and period has its own complex economy of writing, a dynamic relationship among materials, techniques, genres and cultural attitudes and uses,"[50] but unless we also examine how similar relationships play out in the spaces in which materials are read, we risk a partial understanding of what happens to texts after they have been produced. Acts of reading, like acts of writing, are also historically situated and shaped by interactions of cultural practices, choices and materials, especially when they are mediated via institutional spaces like archives.

Archives of war

While the first two chapters of this book deal with the production of Unit War Diaries in the two World Wars, Chapter 3 turns to The National Archives of England and Wales, which is responsible for the curation, preservation and presentation of these records once they enter the public domain. In its early history, the archive was thought of as a neutral space in which records were stored. Hilary Jenkinson, an influential and controversial figure in English archives, was well-known for his unwavering conviction that the archivist's role was "simply to conserve intact every scrap of evidence which not only the contents of the documents but their form, makeup, provenance, and position in relation to other documents have to offer," without necessarily understanding them (in fact, Jenkinson argued that it might even be preferable not to have a knowledge of the contents), and definitely without becoming involved in decisions around their selection.[51] But just as history is no longer thought of as a process of representing an essential and totalising 'truth' of the past gleaned from primary documents, archival practices have become recognised as closely connected to, and implicated in, systems of power. Jacques Derrida's well-known interrogation of the concept of the archive, beginning with the etymology of the word itself, identified the close connection between archives, power, and the force of law:

> it keeps, it puts in reserve, it saves, but in an unnatural fashion, that is to say in making the law (*nomos*) or in making people respect the law [...] It has the force of law, of a law which is the law of the house (*oikos*), of the house as place, domicile, family, lineage, or institution.[52]

For Derrida, the archive was both private and public, and it was controlled by those who held political power. Although Derrida does not, as Francis Blouin, Jr. and William Rosenberg point out, address the role of archivists themselves in his analysis,[53] archival processes have been increasingly recognised as "neither natural nor neutral."[54] Archival institutions continue to be investigated, especially by those interested in the voices that might be silenced or excluded in archival records, as "loaded sites that produce realities as much as they document them."[55] Most archivists and historians today would agree at least that archives "house not what is left but what has been *kept*, and organise these calcified writings into hierarchical families which limit and shape the range of possible interpretations."[56] Through the concept of the reading space, this book builds on such approaches to address the archive as a physical and a virtual space, as an institution with a distinct and evolving cultural identity, and as a set of practices and media technologies, all of which converge to shape the encounters with Unit War Diaries of the two World Wars and the ways in which they are understood.

Chapter 3 will reveal how the story of the state archive in the U.K. is entangled with Britain's wars, and of how the profusion of records produced

14 *Introduction*

during conflicts contributed to the evolution of the archive as institution. The third chapter examines how the development of the state archive and of archiving as a profession was caught up in the spread and influence of industrial technologies and practices throughout life in the Nineteenth Century and into the early Twentieth Century. At the end of the Twentieth Century and into the Twenty-first, however, archives and archival practices are in the process of responding to the spread of digital technologies and a series of shifts in everyday practices that are as pervasive and profound as those that emerged during the industrial era. The transformations initiated by digital technologies to the practices of producing documentation, and therefore to the ways in which archives need to adapt to selecting, preserving, and making them accessible, are topics of much interest and attention not only in academic spheres, but also for archives and the state institutions with which they are involved. For example, just as this chapter is concerned with identifying historical entanglements between past conflicts and archives, Daniela Agostinho, Solveig Gade, Nanna Thystrup and Kristin Veel argue that "in order to understand the rationale of contemporary wars, we need to investigate the increasingly structuring role played by digitisation and digital archives within warfare" in their introduction to a series of compelling essays that do exactly that.[57] *(W)Archives* brings together a collection of perspectives interrogating "the ways in which archives are deployed to an ever-greater extent as technologies of warfare, venues for dissent, and demands for accountability" in the digital age.[58]

The transition to digital formats has been high on the list of priorities for The National Archives since the 1990s. The Public Record Office (which later fused with other organisations to become The National Archives), identified helping government departments with the "move from paper to electronic record-keeping" and with ensuring that their collections are made available "electronically" as part of its key strategies in the late 1990s.[59] Accessing Unit War Diaries in the reading spaces of The National Archives involves engaging with a range of technologies, analog and digital. Wolfgang Ernst identifies a diffusion of the archive into networked life through "an economy of circulation: permanent transformations and updating" in which archives "are no longer final destinations but turn into frequently accessed sites. Archives become cybernetic systems. The aesthetics of fixed order is being replaced by permanent reconfigurability."[60] The first two chapters examine the significance of technologies of writing to the formation of Unit War Diaries, but the final chapter investigates some of the implications of the development of the "economy of circulation" that Ernst identifies in the transformation of the First World War Unit War Diaries into digital formats by The National Archives, as well as the transformations and reconfigurations of Unit War Diaries into various digital forms for the purpose of researching this book.

In analysing the writing spaces of the two World Wars, this book is concerned not only with cultural and institutional forces and technologies of media, but also with the human beings operating at the intersection of these elements. In considering the reading spaces of the archive, therefore, this book by necessity must address "the missing researcher in the research."[61] This is a book that draws attention to the strategies and processes involved in the mediation of textual traces of the past and examines their implications for the understanding and writing of history. I am not unaware of the trickiness of writing an analysis of the process and technologies involved in producing mediated texts and their uses in a form that is itself a mediated text. The question posed by Gitelman – "How are media the subjects of history when doing history depends on so many tacit conditions of mediation?" – demands a self-reflexive examination of my own interactions and responses to the archive as space and institution and to the materials and technologies that shape interactions with the records in order to make those conditions of mediation, and their implications, explicit.[62]

By undertaking the analysis of the archive from a self-reflexive perspective I am following the contours of a path already trodden by, amongst others, Arlette Farge and Carolyn Steedman. Farge eloquently details the physical, emotional, and intellectual experiences of interacting with judicial records of Eighteenth Century France, from the moment of entering the archive to collecting material and the eventual process of writing. She describes interacting with the architecture, systems and staff of the archive, including silent but intense battles between regular visitors for the best seats in the reading room.[63] But most of Farge's analysis is devoted to interactions with the records – unfolding the documents, the seduction and challenge for the researcher of the "feeling of being in contact with the real" that comes from physical interactions with the materials and even the painstaking process of copying texts by hand.[64] Like Farge, Carolyn Steedman describes physical and emotional aspects of researching in archives, in this case the Public Records Office (TNA's organisational predecessor):

> You scarcely move, partly to conserve body heat, but mainly because you want to finish, and not to have to come back, because the PRO is so far away, so difficult to get to. That is the immediate ambition that excites you: to leave; though there exist of course the wider passions, of finding it (whatever it is you are searching for), and writing the article or book, writing history.[65]

Steedman's focus is also primarily with the materiality of the records, and she connects Derrida's largely figurative 'archive fever' to the actual health conditions caused by inhaling archival dust loaded with toxins from historical processes of producing parchment, ink and glue. This book diverts from the path laid down by Farge and Steedman by analysing how interactions with The National Archives as institution, as physical and virtual space, as well as with the practices of archival description generate meanings that inflect the reading and understanding of the records before a single box or digital file has been opened. However, the significance of the technologies involved in accessing

16 *Introduction*

the records is not overlooked, and I track what was lost, or gained, as Unit War Diaries cycle through older forms of technology and materials such as paper, boxes and files, to digital formats such as PDF, digital images and .txt files. In doing so, my aim is to map and engage with the "sensorial affective response[s]" to the records of past conflicts created by and through the reading spaces of the archive.[66]

Notes on approach

One of the primary challenges of working with some forms of archival records is their sheer bulk. Farge draws on metaphors relating to water to describe the scale of the material traces of the past in state archives. She writes that the contents of an archive can be "excessive and overwhelming, like a spring tide, an avalanche, or a flood."[67] Similarly, Swartz argues that "an archive can never be fully known" but that we can only pick out the "flotsam and jetsam, offered up by the archive-sea."[68] While both Farge and Swartz are alert to the qualities of the materials they deal with, these kinds of metaphors encourage a sense of the records as natural, raw materials for history, a perspective that this book challenges through its interrogation of the institutional practices and technologies that mediate the records of war. But such metaphors are evocative in describing both the scale of records and the overwhelming feelings they might generate in those dealing with them. With every unit of the British Army producing daily accounts during two global conflicts, the Unit War Diaries are a formidable set of records.

WO 95, the series that contains the War Diaries for the British and Colonial units serving in theatres of operations and as armies of occupation between 1914 to 1922, consists of 5,500 pieces and extends to an estimated 3 to 4 million pages. The Second World War Unit War Diaries are not contained in a single series but in fourteen (WO 166–179), arranged by theatre of operations. These consist of a total of 88,244 pieces. For those unfamiliar with archival description (and Chapter 3 will examine this topic in much more detail), a series refers to a grouping of records with the same provenance and generally with a shared function. A 'piece' is the term used by TNA to refer to "the deliverable unit" of the record, in either paper or digital format, which can be a box, a file or a bundle of records.[69] Each box, file or bundle in the Unit War Diaries series typically contains the daily operational reports, generally (but not always) recorded using Army Form C.2118, and also generally (but not always) for a calendar year. Although the format of the C.2118 form remains relatively uniform, the content varies widely, from concise entries, through detailed, hour-by-hour accounts, or long, expanded narratives. In addition to the C.2118 forms, the boxes or files might also include any number of appendices – everything from hand-drawn maps, messages exchanged during fighting, orders of battle, casualty lists and letters, after-action reports, telegrams of congratulations, descriptions of training exercises, parades and records of sports days. The sheer scale and diversity of this material presents such a prodigious challenge that even an entire team of researchers, with unlimited time and resources, would struggle to meet it.

Farge is certainly correct in her observation that working with large sets of records like these can feel a little like drowning.[70] However, such metaphors can also obscure the painstaking process of selecting a body of material for analysis. By necessity, this book is based on a limited selection of the overall set of records that constitute the Unit War Diaries of the two World Wars. Given that much of this book is concerned with unravelling the practices and processes that led to the mediation of the records of war, as well as their representation through the archive, it is also important to be transparent about my own process of the selection of records for analysis, which was not quite as organic as picking flotsam and jetsam out of the sea.

As Chapter 1 makes clear, from the First World War onwards, the process of waging war was subject to the same bureaucratic processes of rationalisation and organisation that were applied to commercial industrial enterprises. War, in other words, became work. The production of documentation was an essential part of the labour of war. Producing documents on the home front or in Headquarters away from the field of battle was in many ways like producing documents in offices of any other organisation, even if the stakes and pressure were higher. But it is in battle zones during ground combat, one of the most complex arenas of mechanised warfare, that the practice of reporting on war was most urgent and most challenging. The records produced by those Units actually involved in fighting on the ground reveal the real consequences of porting the processes and tools of bureaucratic management from offices onto battlefields. These reports are the most critical in providing insight into what happens when war is conceptualised as another form of industrial labour and is mediated via official forms and structures. The first step in narrowing down the vast body of material, then, was the decision to concentrate on reports at the 'sharp end' of war, at Battalion level, rather than records produced in the higher echelons.

The records of the following regiments were selected for analysis: the Cheshire Regiment, the North and South Staffordshire Regiments, the Sherwood Foresters (Nottingham and Derbyshire Regiment), Welsh Guards, Worcestershire Regiment and the Parachute Regiment. The records of these regiments include the experiences of foot soldiers, armoured and mechanised forces and elite airborne troops. Focusing on the records of these regiments, which, with the exception of the Parachute Regiment, fought in both wars, created continuity across the records of the two World Wars, and facilitated comparative analysis between them. For the records of the First World War, 31 pieces (to use TNA's terminology), consisting of 2,400 pages, were selected. From these, a further sample of 430 pages of the C.2118 forms was transcribed, forming a final corpus of 58,137 words. For the records of the Second World War, 58 pieces were selected (because these are not digital but paper files, a page count is not available), from which 1,670 pages in total were transcribed, forming a corpus of 225,212 words, a larger corpus because it includes both C.2118 forms and appendices. Transcription of the records was necessary to transform the records into a format (plain text files) that could be used with software for linguistic analysis. While Optical Character Recognition software could be used on typed records, results were extremely patchy due to the varied nature and state of the pages, and a great deal of manual correction was required. All handwritten records (the sampled records of the First World War were handwritten) had to be transcribed manually. The final chapter describes these processes in much more detail, but I note them here because the challenges of transcription are inevitably part of the process of determining the final size of the sample of records for analysis.

The size of the sample was additionally shaped by the fact that it needed to be large enough for linguistic analysis, but still small enough to enable meaningful close reading of the texts.[71] The general inclination when working with such a large set of records is to control them by organising them into a form that allows them to be mined them for data, which is exactly what The National Archives did with the First World War records in a project called Operation War Diary, discussed in more detail in Chapter 3. But mining them for data such as weather conditions, casualty figures, time spent by units in various locations, while useful, can only ever provide a partial picture of war. That picture reinforces the rational and bureaucratic principles that only these kinds of data (the measurable and calculable) about war are significant. In such approaches, it is difficult to identify how these data points might be situated within specific social and cultural contexts, and how they are mediated through the technologies that produce them. A smaller sample size, however, enables a granular reading of the content of the diaries, revealing those things not usually captured in neat nets of data – signs of individuality, the slipperiness of emotion, and the messiness of war. I am aware of the dangers, in selecting and working with a selected sample of a much larger set of records, of what Swartz calls "a wish to mistake the part for the whole."[72] My intention is not to extrapolate conclusions about all the series of Unit War Diaries from the two World Wars, but to uncover the history of operational reporting and to leverage the possibility of different perspectives of the official records of war, with the goal of raising questions that could perhaps be explored in the future using larger samples, or when technology and resources allow, perhaps the entire set.

In no small part, this book was prompted by a desire to understand what Roger Beaumont calls the "chronic divergence" between official accounts of war and the "individual human experiences of war found in diaries, letters or clinical accounts."[73] This book sets out to uncover the origins and implications of that divergence in the records of the British Army. It addresses a fundamental gap in the historiography of Britain's wars by investigating the technologies, institutions and individuals that have influenced the official records, and therefore the history and understanding, of the two World Wars. By interrogating operational reporting as a mediated process, it uncovers the role played by documentation and hitherto unnoticed media technologies – the indelible pencil, the typewriter – in crafting versions of events in war that conform to bureaucratic and rationalist principles. It will reveal that operational reporting is not a neutral system for producing and communicating information about war, but an ideological and technological framework that shapes what information about war actually *is*. It will also argue that the archival systems and structures through which those records are later accessed augment the notion that war can be contained, both literally and figuratively, through linear and rational systems of organisation. But this book is also about how the human experience of war sometimes disrupts those systems of containment and control and surfaces in unexpected ways to leave material traces of affective and emotional responses across the official record of war. Ultimately, this book interrogates Unit War Diaries as a dynamic and shifting "site of mediated exchange" between events in war, the technologies used to record them, the soldiers involved in combat, the Army and the archive, and those who eventually come to use these records.[74] In doing so, my goal is to not only provide fresh insights into official records and their uses and the history and experiences of the two World Wars, but also to reveal the influence of these practices on the way in which conflict is understood and waged today.

Notes

1 Carolyn Steedman, *Dust* (Manchester: Manchester University Press, 2001), 81.
2 J. Glenn Gray, *The Warriors: Reflections of Men in Combat*. 2nd ed. (1959, Lincoln NE: University of Nebraska Press, 1998), 28.
3 General Staff, *Field Service Regulations, Part II: Organisation and Administration*, 1909 (London: HMSO, Reprinted, with Amendments, 1913), 176.
4 For example, Antony Beevor, *D-Day: The Battle for Normandy* (London: Random House, 2009) and David Saul, *100 Days to Victory: How the Great War was Fought and Won* (London: Hodder and Stoughton, 2013).
5 For example, see Simon Godfrey, *British Army Communications in the Second World War: Lifting the Fog of Battle* (London: Bloomsbury, 2013); Aimée Fox, *Learning to Fight: Military Innovation and Change in the British Army, 1914–1918* (Cambridge: Cambridge University Press, 2017) and Brian Hall, *Communication and British Operations on the Western Front* (Cambridge: Cambridge University Press, 2017).
6 Debra Ramsay, *American Media and the Memory of World War II* (New York: Routledge, 2015); Debra Ramsay, "Liminality and the Smearing of War and Play in Battlefield I," *Games Studies: International Journal of Computer Games Research* 20, no. 1 (2020).
7 Lisa Gitelman, *Paper Knowledge: Toward a Media History of Documents* (Durham NC and London: Duke University Press, 2014), 19.
8 See, for example, Geoffrey L Herrera, "Inventing the Railroad and Rifle Revolution: Information, Military Innovation and the Rise of Germany," *Journal of Strategic Studies* 27, no. 2 (2004): 243–271; David French, "Doctrine and Organization in the British Army, 1919–1932," *The Historical Journal* 44, no. 2 (2001): 497–515; Dennis E. Showalter, "Information Capabilities and Military Revolutions: The Nineteenth-Century Experience," *Journal of Strategic Studies* 27, no. 2 (2004): 220–242; Brian N. Hall, "The British Army, Information Management and the First World War: Revolution in Military Affairs," *Journal of Strategic Studies* 41, no. 7 (2018): 1001–1030; and Hall, *Communication and British Operations*.

20 Introduction

9 Jay David Bolter, *Writing Space: Computers, Hypertext, and the Remediation of Print*, 2nd ed. (Mahwah, NJ: Lawrence Erlbaum Associates, 2000).
10 Margaret Hedstrom, "Archives, Memory, and Interfaces with the Past," *Archival Science*, 2 (2002): 25.
11 For a general discussion on the implementation of bureaucratic structures in military organisations at the turn of the Nineteenth Century, see Christopher Dandeker, *Surveillance, Power and Modernity: Bureaucracy and Discipline from 1700 to the Present Day* (Cambridge: Polity Press, 1990), 66–110. For a discussion focussed on the formation of the General Staff and its significance to the British Army, see Paul Harris, *The Men Who Planned the War: A Study of the Staff of the British Army on the Western Front, 1914–1918* (Abingdon: Routledge, 2016).
12 Craig Robertson, *The Filing Cabinet: A Vertical History of Information* (University of Minnesota Press, 2021), 4; Toni Weller, "Introduction: Information History," in *Information History in the Modern World: Histories of the Information Age*, ed. Toni Weller (New York: Palgrave McMillan, 2011), 5.
13 Michel Foucault, *Society Must be Defended: Lectures at the Collége de France, 1975–76*, English Series ed. Arnold I. Davidson, trans. David Macey (New York: Picador, 2003), 10.
14 Emily Goldman, "Introduction: Information Resources and Military Performance," *Journal of Strategic Studies* 27, no. 2 (2004): 196.
15 Goldman, "Introduction," 200.
16 Hall, *Communication and British Operations*, 13.
17 John R. Lindsay, *Information Technology and Military Power* (Ithaca NY and London: Cornell Scholarship Online, 2021), 7.
18 Luke Tredinnick, "Rewriting History: The Information Age and the Knowable Past," in Weller, *Information History*, 177.
19 Annelise Riles, *The Network Inside Out* (Ann Arbor: University of Michigan Press, 2001), 3.
20 David Dery, "'Papereality' and Learning in Bureaucratic Organizations," *Administration and Society* 29, no. 6 (1998): 678.
21 Gitelman, *Paper Knowledge*, 6.
22 Gitelman, *Paper Knowledge*, 30.
23 Gitelman, *Paper Knowledge*, 31.
24 Tarleton Gillespie, Pablo J. Boczkowski, and Kirsten A. Foot, "Introduction," in *Media Technologies: Essays on Communication, Materiality, and Society*, eds. Tarleton Gillespie, Pablo J. Boczkowski, and Kirsten A. Foot (Cambridge MA: MIT Press Scholarship Online, 2014).
25 Gillespie, Boczkowski and Foot, "Introduction."
26 See Hall, "The British Army," for example.
27 Jochen Hellbeck, "The Diary between Literature and History: A Historian's Critical Response," *The Russian Review* 63, no. 4 (2004): 621.
28 John Keegan, *The Face of Battle: A Study of Agincourt, Waterloo and the Somme* (London: Penguin, 1978), 18–19.
29 Roger Beaumont, *War, Chaos and History* (Westport CT: Praeger, 1994), 22.
30 Sally Swartz, "Asylum Case Records: Fact and Fiction," *Rethinking History* 22, no. 3 (2018): 291.
31 Christine Sylvester, "War Experiences/War Practices/War Theory," *Millennium: Journal of International Studies* 40, no. 3 (2012): 484.
32 Keegan, *Face of Battle*, 35.
33 Beaumont, *War*, 20.
34 Joanna Bourke, *Dismembering the Male: Men's Bodies, Britain and the Great War* (London: Reaktion Books, 1996); *An Intimate History of Killing: Face-to-Face Killing in Twentieth Century Warfare* (London: Granta Books, 2000); "The Emotions in

War: Fear and the British and American Military, 1914–45," *Historical Research* 74, no. 185 (2001): 314–330.
35 Bourke "Emotions in War," 314.
36 Samuel Žilinčík, "Strategy and the Instrumental Role of Emotions," *Real Clear Defense: The Strategy Bridge* (25 September 2018).
37 Christine Sylvester, *War as Experience: Contributions from International Relations and Feminist Analysis* (London: Routledge, 2013).
38 Linda Åhäll and Thomas Gregory, "Introduction: Mapping Emotions, Politics and War," in *Emotions, Politics and War*, eds. Linda Åhäll and Thomas Gregory (London and New York: Routledge, 2016), 2.
39 Bourke, "Emotions in War," 315.
40 Anna Wierzbicka, "Talking about Emotions: Semantics, Culture, and Cognition," *Cognition and Emotion* 6, no. 3–4 (1992): 285–319; Barbara H. Rosenwein, "Worrying about Emotions in History," *The American Historical Review* 107, no. 3 (2002): 821–845: Paul Griffiths and Andrea Scarantino, "Emotions in the Wild: The Situated Perspective on Emotion," in *Cambridge Handbook of Situated Cognition*, eds. Philip Robbins and Murat Aydede (Cambridge: Cambridge University Press, 2008), 437–453; Monique Scheer, "Are Emotions a Kind of Practice (and is That What Makes Them Have a History?)? A Bourdieuian Approach to Understanding Emotion," *History and Theory* 51, no. 2 (2012): 193–220.
41 Stephanie Downes, Andrew Lynch, and Katrina O'Loughlin, "Introduction – War as Emotion: Cultural Fields of Conflict and Feeling," in *Emotions and War: Medieval to Romantic Literature*, eds. Stephanie Downes, Andrew Lynch, and Katrina O'Loughlin (New York: Palgrave Macmillan, 2015), 3–4; Scheer, "Are Emotions a Kind of Practice," 205.
42 Scheer, "Are Emotions a Kind of Practice," 205.
43 Scheer, "Are Emotions a Kind of Practice," 219.
44 Scheer, "Are Emotions a Kind of Practice," 218.
45 William Reddy, *The Navigation of Feeling: A Framework* (Cambridge: Cambridge University Press, 2001).
46 Brian Massumi, *Parables for the Virtual: Movement, Affect, Sensation* (Durham NC and London: Duke University Press, 2002), 32.
47 Annette Federico, *Engagements with Close Reading* (New York: Routledge, 2016), 9.
48 Downes, Lynch, and O'Loughlin, "Introduction," 10.
49 Bolter, *Writing Space*, 12.
50 Bolter, *Writing Space*, 21.
51 Hilary Jenkinson, "British Archives and the War," *The American Archivist* VII, no. 1 (January 1944): 16.
52 Derrida, Jacques, "Archive Fever: A Freudian Impression," *Diacritics* 25, no. 2 (Summer, 1995): 12.
53 Francis X. Blouin, Jr. and William G. Rosenberg, *Processing the Past: Contesting Authorities in History and the Archives* (Online Edition, Oxford Academic Online, 2011), 141.
54 Hedstrom, "Archives, Memory," 26.
55 Caroline Elkins, "Looking beyond Mau Mau: Archiving Violence in the Era of Decolonization," *The American Historical Review* 120, no. 3 (2015): 853.
56 Barbara Brookes and James Dunk, "Introduction: Bureaucracy, Archive Files, and the Making of Knowledge," *Rethinking History* 22, no. 3 (2018): 281. Emphasis in original.
57 Daniela Agostinho, Sovleig Gade, Nanna Bonde Thystrup, and Kristin Veel, "Introduction: Materialities of War, Digital Archiving, and Artistic Engagements," in *(W)Archives: Archival Imaginaries, War, and Contemporary Art*, eds. Daniela Agostinho, Sovleig Gade, Nanna Bonde Thystrup, and Kristin Veel (London: Stenberg Press, 2021), ix.

22 *Introduction*

58 Agostinho et al., "Introduction," ix.
59 The Fortieth Annual Report of the Keeper of Public Records on the Work of the Public Record Office and the Fortieth Report of the Advisory Council on Public Records, 1998, HC 615, 2.
60 Wolfgang Ernst, "Archives in Transition: Dynamic Media Memories," in *Digital Memory and the Archive*, Wolfgang Ernst, ed. Jussi Parikka (Minneapolis MN: University of Minnesota Press, 2012), 99.
61 Sylvester, *War as Experience*, 93.
62 Lisa Gitelman, *Always Already New: Media, History and the Data of Culture* (Cambridge MA: MIT Press, 2006), 127.
63 Arlette Farge, *The Allure of the Archives*, trans. Thomas Scott-Railton (New Haven CT: Yale University Press, 2013), 18–23.
64 Farge, *Allure of Archives*, 10.
65 Steedman, *Dust*, 29.
66 Agostinho et al., "Introduction," ix.
67 Farge, *Allure of Archives*, 5.
68 Swartz, "Asylum Case Records," 294.
69 The National Archives, "Digital Cataloguing Practices at The National Archives" (March 2017), 11.
70 Farge, *Allure of Archives*, 5.
71 I recognise that for those working in the field of linguistics, the sample size might be considered small.
   However, this is not intended as the kind of linguistic analysis that is concerned with morphology or syntax, or other structural features of language. My use of linguistic methods is more closely related to the social use of language, in identifying the deployment of emotives and the use of punctuation in specific social, cultural and institutional contexts.
72 Swartz, "Asylum Case Records," 295.
73 Beaumont, *War*, 11.
74 Paul Stiff, Paul Dobraszczyk, and Mike Esbester, "Designing and Gathering Information: Perspectives on Nineteenth-Century Forms," in Weller, *Information History*, 83.

1 "Scribbled hastily in pencil"
Unit war diaries in the First World War

Introduction – The work of war

"Our work is killing," wrote Ernst Jünger of the soldier's role in the First World War, "and it is our duty to do this work well and completely ... for every age expresses itself not only in practical life, in love, in science and in art, but also in the frightful."[1] All the expressions of the age in which the First World War (1914–1918) occurred – from the everyday to science and the arts – were profoundly impacted by the effects of industrialisation. War was no exception. The First World War was not only the first global conflict, it was also the first conflict waged at an industrial level. Just as the speed of production and transportation initiated what James Beniger refers to as a "crisis of control" in industry and commerce toward the end of the Nineteenth Century the application of industrial processes and technologies to the battlefield, as well as the unprecedented scale of the conflict itself, triggered a similar crisis for military organisations.[2] Industrial manufacturing increased the scale of the production of munitions, and the marriage of industry and science introduced weapons the like of which had never been seen before.[3] This was the first conflict to see the use of the tank, the flamethrower and chemical weapons such as mustard gas, all of which demanded new approaches to waging war.[4] The steam train, which had transformed the pace and scope of industry and daily life, similarly transformed warfare by moving weapons, matériel and men rapidly across battlefields, necessitating new approaches to strategy and communications.[5] Industrialisation also boosted the production and circulation of information. This was the first war in which telecommunications were used extensively, connecting the home front to the war front in unprecedented ways, and necessitating rapid decision-making by those far from events.[6] As in the commercial sphere, information in war became an asset requiring 'management,' most usually through written records.

The First World War was the first conflict in which the British Army implemented daily record keeping by every branch of staff from general headquarters to all "subordinate commands, including garrisons and posts."[7] The purpose of these records was twofold:

DOI: 10.4324/9781003172109-2

1   To furnish an accurate record of the operations from which the history of the war can subsequently be prepared.
2   To collect information for future reference with a view to effecting improvements in the organisation, education, training, equipment and administration of the Army for war.[8]

At the point of their inception and into the two World Wars, these reports were termed Unit War Diaries. From a broader perspective, the increase in paperwork was itself, as Paddy Griffith points out, a "very modern 'management response' to the problem of battle, since it helped to define the problem in a manageable way, at the same time as it reduced the bafflement felt by commanders and increased their ability to control events."[9] Paper records, and the information they contained, were thus critical to processes of command and control, but also, and perhaps less obviously, they were crucial to maintaining the sense that new and sometimes overwhelming conditions on industrial battlefields could be contained and understood. The production and circulation of information facilitated decision making and operations in a war that exceeded all previous understandings of conflict. If war had become work, paperwork was now an essential part of that labour – a practical approach to managing and controlling the frightful nature of industrial warfare through an increasing proliferation of messages, orders, dispatches, debriefs, questionnaires, and daily reports like the Unit War Diaries.

Industrialisation impacted not only how war was waged, but also how it was organised. The systems through which paperwork circulated have been examined in work that focuses on how industrial technologies influenced the organisation of warfare, especially with regards to the significance of Information Management (IM) in the British Expeditionary Force (BEF) and the militaries of other combatant nations. Dennis Showalter, for example, places the "print information revolution" at the heart of the reorganisation of military institutions and of a transition to systematic standardisation in their practices before the outbreak of the First World War.[10] Brian Hall's work is crucial in revealing the significance of the BEF's systems and procedures of IM and communication to the evolution of a 'Modern Style of Warfare' in the First World War.[11] This kind of research has provided critical insight into the significance of IM for the operational effectiveness of command, control and communication in the BEF and other militaries, but the fundamental question of how information about war takes shape in specific conditions and how it is formulated through particular technologies has not been widely considered.

Information is both understood and generated through a series of historically situated actions governed by institutional needs and expressed via specific technologies – in other words, through practices of mediation. Despite their significance for the Army's operational effectiveness and for historiography, the history of Unit War Diaries as material, mediated artefacts has been largely overlooked, raising the following questions that this chapter sets out to address:

What role did technologies of operational reporting and writing play in determining what was considered as information in the first place by the BEF in the First World War, and in what ways might they have shaped its composition?

More broadly, what happens to the record of conflict when war is considered not just as 'work', but as a specific kind of commercial and industrial labour subject to similar bureaucratic principles of organisation and control?

To answer these questions, this chapter investigates a selection of First World War Unit War Diaries as mediated artefacts that are both embedded in, and expressions of, the historically situated interplay between broader culture, the Army's institutional needs, technologies of writing and the individuals caught in the intersection of these forces. Moving beyond perceptions of these records as mere conduits for information, this chapter will reveal how Unit War Diaries are imbricated in practices that have delimited and structured the understanding of war.

Although the investigation of the historical context for Unit War Diaries and the analysis of specific technologies of writing have been separated in the first two sections of this chapter for the sake of clarity, they should be understood as integrally related. Technologies are not neutral but are products and agents of their historically situated cultures. If, as Palazzo argues, "culture played a particularly important role in the British Army, for it was culture, rather than doctrine, that determined the British method of war-making,"[12] then a brief investigation of the broader cultural relationship between bureaucracy, information, paperwork and war in the first section of this chapter provides a vital context for the British Army's approach to developing procedures for generating and controlling information, as expressed within the *Field Service Regulations* (*FSR*) Parts I and II. The rules governing the implementation of War Diaries were established in the *FSR*, and a close analysis of these regulations reveals the evolution of the institutional discourse and ideological framework in which the War Diaries were situated. This chapter interrogates the British Army's regulations governing the keeping of records to reveal firstly what the Army identified at this stage in its development *as* information, and secondly how that information was corralled into document form. Following Jennifer Slack, David Miller and Jeffrey Doak, I argue that we need to move past the notion that "the goal of communication is always clarity and brevity" to an understanding of how organisational practices and cultures shape and delimit information in official records.[13]

The next section of the chapter moves on to an investigation of the pre-printed Army Form C.2118, and the indelible pencil. The C.2118 form has been generally treated as transparent in discussions of IM and command, control and communications, but this chapter will argue that this document plays a critical role not only in mediating information about events in conflict, but also in mediating the relationship between individuals and the Army as an institution. Although there are a range of different documents other than the C.2118 form included in the First World War Unit War Diaries, such as letters or reports about events after they had occurred, messages of congratulations, maps, etc., this chapter focusses on the C.2118 form, as it is the first time that this form was used extensively to record the events of war.

Similarly, although technologies such as the telegraph and typewriter have been investigated in studies of IM and the First World War,[14] the indelible pencil has been ignored, yet it is as much an industrial technology as any other from the period. The indelible pencil was common in the BEF, to the extent that The National Archives, which now houses Unit War Diaries, describes them in their online research guides as "scribbled hastily in pencil."[15] This chapter remedies the oversight of this technology of writing by focussing on handwritten diaries, rather than typed records, and investigating the cultural cache afforded to writing and to the indelible pencil in the 'work' of war. It investigates the significance of hasty scribbles, and of handwriting in general, in leveraging space for individuality through the C.2118 form into bureaucratic processes. The unique writing spaces of the Western Front form the focus of this chapter, not least because of the unprecedented nature of trench warfare and its significance in this conflict. As mentioned in the Introduction, to better understand the pressures of producing records in the field, as opposed to the more routine production of records in the offices of Headquarters away from the action, this chapter focuses on diaries produced at Battalion level, as these were involved directly in fighting.

The First World War Unit War Diaries are not the reflections of poets, nor the memoirs of prominent military or political leaders, but the responses of ordinary men (generally the regimental adjutant or nominated junior officer, but sometimes also intelligence officers) attempting to parse the experiences of an unprecedented war through the medium of official military documents. Yet moments of subjectivity and/or emotion in Unit War Diaries are often ignored or marginalised in favour of accounts that are "meticulous and concise."[16] In contrast, the vast body of the literature and poetry of the First World War is considered as having a "particular power to take the emotional understanding of war beyond the limits and disguises of 'official' languages."[17] But by investigating Unit War Diaries as a form of "emotional practice" this chapter's final section breaks through the apparent disguises of official documents to reveal how Unit War Diaries offer unique insights into the individual, embodied experience of modern warfare.[18] Through a combination of linguistic analysis and close textual reading, the final section investigates collisions between individual affective responses and bureaucratic systems of control within the official structures of the War Diaries. The chapter ends by briefly considering the implications of the controls and systems on Unit War Diaries on the understanding of warfare, particularly its emotional impact and its unpredictability, in the Official Histories of the First World War.

Industrialisation, bureaucracy, and the British Army

The Nineteenth Century is well-documented as an age of revolutions – industrial, cultural, political – but it is also a period in which bureaucracy emerged as the principal organisational structure in political, martial and economic spheres of society. Although bureaucracy predates the industrial era, it was uniquely suited to the demands of the age because it offered mechanistic systems of organisation that facilitated "[p]recision, speed, clarity, accessibility of files, continuity, discretion, unity, strict subordination, avoidance of friction and material and personal expenses."[19] There are symbiotic and synergistic entanglements between the rise of bureaucracy and industrialisation, capitalism, the military and the nation-state, much of which falls outside my remit here,[20] but a brief overview provides a crucial context for understanding why the British Army began to identify specific kinds of information as critical to its functioning and to adopt new systems and technologies for its management.

Increased production and the rapid distribution of goods as well as capital around the world during industrialisation pressurised a range of institutions, from the state to commercial enterprises and the military, into developing infrastructures based around routinisation, hierarchical structures and the specialist division of labour. The division of labour and specialisation in all bureaucratic organisations means that individual leadership, knowledge and/or tradition are no longer enough to support operations.[21] Instead, information about processes must be stored within the organisation itself, lending new importance to the production, storage and "accessibility of files."[22] Max Weber identifies the "modern means of communication" as especially significant in allowing bureaucratic organisations to operate with optimal speed and efficiency.[23] New communication technologies, together with an intensified significance of information for the operation of bureaucratic organisations central to society, were instrumental in engendering what Ronald Day calls a "culture of information" in the Nineteenth Century.[24]

Print played a significant role in the development of an information culture. The introduction of the steam-driven printing press in the early decades of the 1800s revolutionised printing and contributed to a rapid expansion of print media such as newspapers, periodicals, books, self-help and how-to guides, all produced on a hitherto unprecedented scale. Both the significance and authority of the written word, which had already become associated with work and knowledge over the course of early modernity,[25] were amplified in broader culture, largely because of the spread of the printed text. In wider culture as well as in the specific practices of acquiring, producing, circulating and managing information in bureaucratic organisations, the document, most often in the form of the printed text, acquired an apparent objectivity and stability that made possible "separating the *known* from the *knower*."[26] The idea of information as a source of power or as a resource to be managed and organised illustrates that, as Toni Weller argues, it was no longer understood as a "'rhetorical instrument' used to convince, persuade or inform, but instead became divorced from content and specific purpose."[27] As Weller points out, it was not just that there was more information circulating in society in the Nineteenth Century, or that much of it was new, there was also a "profound shift" in the understanding of the concept itself, as "for the first time people began to view information as a category in its own right."[28] As information circulated through organisations and society, not only was it separated from its source and its contextual framework, it was increasingly conflated with its material forms. The document itself became understood *as* information, which in turn became "a commodity, a 'thing' desirable in itself."[29]

The identification of information as a commodity and its segregation from source and context was (and still is) actively managed in most bureaucratic organisations. After all, "[t]o classify, process, store, retrieve, or transmit information quickly or with less cost and effort, it must be compressed, codified, and organised in a systemic fashion. In the process, narrative, descriptive, or decorative information is turned into *data*."[30] In other words, information in bureaucratic organisations is ideally "storyless," to borrow a term from Neil Postman.[31] Attempts to render information into data that are not embellished by narrative or tainted by emotion are characteristic of bureaucratic processes, which, according to Weber, insist on "the successful exclusion of love, hate, and all purely personal, irrational, and emotional elements, to which calculation is alien, from the process of discharging official business."[32] Bureaucratic operations are predicated on the application of rationalism, which by the Nineteenth Century was situated in direct opposition to emotion.[33] Scientific rationalism was celebrated within the broader cultural milieu in which bureaucratic systems of organisation evolved as the ultimate methodological approach and mode of thinking that would supposedly bring the world and its mysteries under control and subjugation.

Bureaucracy is therefore more than a system of structuring organisations and of ordering information. It is an ideology centred on the increasing dehumanisation of operations in organisations to perfect systems of routinisation and rationalisation, maximise efficiencies and enable their continuous 'objective' measurement through calculations of costs, benefits and losses. The construction of storyless information, or the reduction of details about events to calculable facts and figures is thus not a neutral process, but "a crucial control mechanism [through which] organisations engage in the construction and privileging of views of the world that become the world."[34] Decision making and operations within bureaucratic organisations consequently in the main do not stem from direct knowledge of events, but from *documented interpretations* of those events shaped by organisational control mechanisms, generating what Lisa Gitelman calls "paper knowledge" and David Dery refers to as "papereality."[35] The British Army established a set of specific guidelines for the nature and production of its own version of 'papereality' in the *Field Service Regulations* in the early 1900s.

By the turn of the century, whereas war had once been regarded as an art practiced by individuals, it had become an industrial endeavour conducted on a scale that exceeded the grasp of any single individual. Even before the First World War, Britain's almost continuous involvement in skirmishes and 'small wars' throughout its Empire during the Nineteenth Century had already made clear that

> the great increase in the range of firearms, in the extension of troops, and in the size of armies renders it more and more impossible for any one man, be he commander-in-chief or war correspondent, or even for a large staff to follow at the time with any accuracy the detailed movements of units in action.[36]

Although still drawn from the wealthy classes, officers were no longer restricted to the aristocracy, and martial proficiency became understood as a distinct discipline that could be learned, rather than an individual innate talent. Following the Esher Report in 1904, the British Army's organisational structure was overhauled and rationalised into structures further facilitating this kind of professionalisation and the division of labour along increasingly specialised lines. Those with expertise in waging war were separated from a growing administrative staff responsible for logistics, procurement, supplies and communications. The industrialisation of war thus involves not only the use of industrial weapons and technologies, but a concomitant transformation of the military along bureaucratic lines. As the military became professionalised, war itself became identified as an object of scientific study.

The increased circulation of military journals and other publications, together with the rise of military think tanks such as the Royal United Services Institute (established by the Duke of Wellington in 1831) and the development of training facilities for officers such as the Staff College at Camberley, are all indications of a trend not only towards the professionalisation of expertise in the British Army, but also toward subjecting war to 'scientific' analysis. The apparent success of science's ability to reliably predict events and thereby increase control over them made its approaches "highly attractive to military thinkers and practitioners" in the long struggle to impose order on warfare.[37] Military professionals and writers such as Colonel G.F.R. Henderson began to identify war as "a science most carefully studied, both by statesmen and soldiers."[38] There was also an increasing recognition of the significance of military history as an essential component of the 'scientific' study of war that would provide essential knowledge for commanders in the absence of experience. At the same time, much-publicised failures of command and control in the South African wars led to calls for "mechanical" systems of organisation intended to impose order on the "turmoil" of war and to "mitigate confusion."[39]

For European Armies, most notably the Prussian and French, problems of command and control and the preservation of institutional knowledge were addressed by formalising philosophies and principles as guides for action — through the development of doctrine, in other words. The British Army's experience of fighting numerous 'small wars' across the Empire in vastly different circumstances, however, made for an understandable resistance to the application of a centralised, 'one-size-fits-all' doctrine for a military that required and valued flexibility above authoritarianism.[40] Instead, the General Staff at the War Office, via the leadership of Douglas Haig (appointed as Director of Military Training in 1906) opted for a much looser set of guidelines principally articulated through the *Field Service Regulations*, published in two parts in 1909. *FSRI* deals with operations, outlining the "General Principles which govern the leading in war of the Army."[41] *FSRII* focusses on the "organisation and administration of the Army."[42] The division between principles for operations and administration in these two sets of regulations is a material illustration of the bureaucratic segregation of specialist roles in military organisations described earlier.

Field Service Regulations: Instructions for 'storyless' information

There is no sense of a "a uniform doctrine" in either *FSRI* or *II*.[43] The tenets supposedly governing operations in *FSRI* are never clearly defined, and the emphasis throughout is on individual initiative in "the application of principles to circumstances."[44] The significance attributed to individual knowledge of local conditions is a clear indication of the influence of the Army's experience in fighting Colonial wars, but *FSRI* was also created with the possibility of a major continental war in mind, and indeed it was used throughout the First World War.[45] It was not framed or understood this way at the time, but the struggle evident in *FSRI* between attempts to foster flexibility alongside ways of establishing order and maintaining control reveals a military reluctant to surrender the autonomy of the individual to the bureaucratic emphasis on process, and suggests that the implementation of bureaucracy in the British Army was not without resistance.

The tension between process and individuality is evident in *FSRI*'s guidelines for communications in the field, defined in *FSRI* as "orders, reports, and messages."[46] While *FSRI* acknowledges that circumstances might dictate whether communication is verbal or written, the general rule is that an attempt should be made to put things in writing "whenever it is practicable to do so."[47] Reflecting the increasing emphasis on paper records in all spheres of life by the turn of the Nineteenth Century, written forms of communication are thus accorded a stability lacking in verbal forms, which the *FSRI* identifies as being prone to being "incorrectly delivered or misunderstood, especially in the excitement of engagement."[48] *FSRI* identifies writing as the medium of choice for communications in part because of its perceived capacity to minimise the emotional impact of warfare, and the rules very clearly delineate its composition. *FSRI* insists that all forms of communication and orders should be "as concise as possible, consistent with clearness."[49] Clarity and simplicity are valued above "literary form," and any indeterminate language is to be avoided.[50] *FSRI* therefore advocates a style of written communication that squeezes out emotion and restricts narrative, effectively filtering information about events through a prism of rationalism. These rules apply not only to orders and messages, but also to reports of events in the War Diaries as addressed in *FSRII*.

FSRII clearly identifies the significance of written material generated during operations for future histories. Chapter XVI, which deals with general procedures for the administration of (among other things) office work, despatches and the War Diaries, establishes the rules for how files are to be managed in the field in the first few paragraphs.[51] Documents containing "anything of a nature likely to prove useful when the history of the campaign is written" should be preserved in files marked with "R" (for Record) and sent to the Adjutant General's office.[52] There are no rules provided for the selection of material for preservation or destruction, nor any real indication of who should make such decisions, but the written record is identified as of primary importance in generating a sense of how events occurred for future histories. In all likelihood with the memory of the numerous and conflicting histories of the South African wars in mind (some of which led to fierce critiques of the military),[53] the architects of *FSRII* make it clear that the daily records of activities, the War Diaries, are specifically intended as the foundation for future histories of warfare by identifying this as the first reason for their maintenance: "To furnish an accurate record of the operations from which the history of the war can subsequently be prepared."[54] Unit War Diaries are thus imprinted with authenticity and pre-loaded with the weight of history from the outset. The *FSRII* specifically identify Unit War Diaries as primary source material providing evidence of a usable, knowable past. Both volumes of the *FSR* are thus part of "discursive and institutional systems" in which the War Diaries are situated,[55] and which identify them as 'accurate' records that detail *what has actually taken place*. By establishing controls over the collection and composition of "accurate" information, the principles governing the writing of the Diaries ultimately effect a measure of control over the future history of warfare.

The second reason behind the implementation of the War Diaries as outlined within the *FSRII* is "to collect information for future reference with a view to effecting improvements in the organisation, education, training, equipment and administration of the Army for war."[56] This objective reveals the British Army as a learning organisation – defined by Margaret Dale as one that "takes action to help its members develop skills of managing in uncertain and ambiguous conditions."[57] The capacity of the Army to learn in the field would be tested to its limits in the First World War, but the decision to introduce the Diaries is indicative of the Army's recognition of information as critical not only to its ability to function effectively, but also to its ability as a bureaucratic organisation to measure its operational successes or failures. The *FSRs* provide evidence of the British Army's early adoption of some of the strategies of what would later become known as Information Management. They corroborate Hall's argument that "the BEF had a greater awareness of, and appreciation for, IM than historians have recognised."[58] *FSRII* follows on from *FSRI* in outlining principles that attempt to eliminate, or at least minimise, the subjective and the personal in collecting information and writing reports through implementing routinisation and standardisation, thereby lending the text a kind of scientific rigor and detachment that augments its authority as a primary source for historiography and for the Army's organisational knowledge.

From the first day of mobilisation, diaries were to be kept daily, in duplicate (using carbon paper), with the original forwarded to the Adjutant General's office on the last day of each month. The composition of the Diaries is standardised – they are to be written on one side of the page only, following certain conventions in naming and spelling – with guidance for the kinds of information required.[59] In addition to information on weather, field works, casualties, terrain and other elements involved in a campaign, the Diaries should include "all important" orders and decisions, "all important matters relating to" duties and administration, as well as a summary of "information received and of all matters of importance, military or political, which may occur from day to day" and reports on how well organisational systems are standing up to the "test of war."[60] A "detailed account of all operations" is also required.[61] A footnote to this point indicates that in the event of "important actions, of which a detailed account may cover much space," a short note in the Diary will suffice until a more complete report on the action can be included in the appendices.[62] Like much in the regulations overall, the rules governing the War Diaries are simultaneously extremely specific and very general. Yet despite the continued tension between individuality and control, the *FSR* establish a rational, routinised and standardised filter for sifting through events in war and identifying what might be important and what should be excluded, thereby potentially shaping how those events are rendered down in writing to usable chunks of information. The *FSR* formalise writing practices and record keeping and leverage them into the act of waging war as part of a self-conscious and deliberate strategy to provide empirical source material not only (or even primarily) for the Army's operational effectiveness, but for the future histories of warfare.

From one perspective, it might seem perfectly logical that military communications, especially in a time of war, should be as clear and as brief as possible. However, couched in the guidelines of both sets of regulations is the assumption that it is possible to transform the chaos of combat into manageable forms of communication that are precise and accurate, creating chunks of storyless information that rationalise warfare and mute its affective power. There is therefore more than a struggle between "standardisation versus flexibility" evident in the Field Service Regulations.[63] There is also a battle between the control mechanisms of bureaucracy and the chaos of modern warfare. *FSRI* and *II* do more than provide the guidelines for how information should be communicated. They initiate a procedural framework that determines what information about war actually *is* – dates, times, weather conditions, casualty numbers, etc. – all transcribed into written form and organised through principles of rationalisation, routinisation and standardisation. They rehearse a specific version of the reality of war as understood through calculable data points measuring gains and losses. The principles outlined in the *FSR* thus attempt to remove from modern combat, one of the most extreme and complex phenomena in the world, any sense of violence or suffering, any sense of wrongness, and ultimately any sense of humanity. The memoirs of a General Staff Officer in the BEF bear testament to the specific kind of reality crafted through these kinds of processes:

> We ate, drank, slept, played a little and talked, very much as if we were workers in some commercial house directing coffee from a plantation to a warehouse and then to a breakfast table, instead of dealing in blood and tears [...] It is well that Imagination went to sleep, or was lacking. For so the work could be done.[64]

The tendency of bureaucratic processes to erase emotion and imagination in general takes on a new resonance when applied to war. By rationalising warfare, it becomes possible to think about it as no more than another iteration of industrialised labour, subject to the same principles of organisation, and perhaps even more importantly, to similar processes of normalisation in the modern world.

Pre-printed blank forms were as essential for the implementation of the Army's bureaucratic processes as they were for any other commercial enterprise. The tensions in the *FSR* between the tendency in bureaucratic processes to dehumanise through standardisation and the British Army's belief in the autonomy of the individual coalesce in the pre-printed form provided for the War Diaries – C.2118. The pre-printed blank form has acquired a kind of invisibility in studies of IM in the BEF, as if it functions as a neutral, stable containment space for its content. In the next section, applying the notion of the official form as a "site of mediated exchange" to the C.2118 and the writing technology used to complete it offers a richer perspective on how this document shapes information, and mediates relationships between culture, institution and individuals.[65]

Technologies of writing: The C.2118 form and the pencil

The daily "detailed account of operations" required by the *FSRII* was to be provided on a preprinted, blank form – Army Form C.2118. C.2118 is one of a plethora of over 1,000 pre-printed blank forms designed to mediate the Army's bureaucratic processes, from court martials and casualty notices to receipts and requisitions. These forms proliferated over the course of the First World War, as noted the Director of the Army's Printing and Stationery Services (APSS) in December 1917, who described "the extravagance and multiplication" of forms and documents in various divisions and Departments.[66] Preprinted blank forms are a symptom of bureaucratic organisations, and they were as endemic in broader society as they were in the Army by the start of the Twentieth Century. Tax forms, census forms, warrants, marriage and death certificates and other documents allowed the bureaucratic state to collect and classify information on its subjects. The transactions and functions of businesses also became increasingly dependent on a range of printed forms and books. The preprinted blank form, with its standardised structure and/or set questions designed to gather specific information, is a crucial tool within the "repertoire of techniques through which bureaucracies come to know."[67] Implicit in the purpose of the blank form is that its primary function is to serve the needs of the bureaucratic organisation, and its structure organises information accordingly. In turn, forms themselves create more bureaucratic processes and institutional structures. The Director of the Army's Printing and Stationery Services (APSS) noted that "on many occasions the mere fact of approval of a new form introduces an Office system which appears to be designed to justify its existence by reprinting numbers of the form in question."[68] He goes on to observe that those structures were sometimes fiercely defended, with the proposed removal of a form in the Army being "regarded by some Directorates as tantamount to an attack on their organisations."[69] Blank forms are thus expressions of organisational identities as much as they are part of information systems.

The preprinted blank form is identified through its material properties – paradoxically, as Gitelman points out, it is the print that makes "most blanks blank."[70] The print provides parameters for where the text should be located and how it should be structured, while the cultural and institutional practices associated with the form attempt to shape and delimit the production of content. C.2118 is in landscape orientation, with the length of the form being longer than its height. The document is titled "War Diary or Intelligence Summary," with the instructions to erase the heading not required beneath it. On the top left-hand side are references to the *FSRII* and the Staff Manual for instructions on how to complete the form. The title of the form itself is on the top right-hand corner. The form is divided into three columns, the first for "Hour, Date, Place," the second and largest column is for the "Summary of Events and Information" and the third column is headed "Remarks and references to Appendices." Far from being a neutral space for writing, C.2118 is a physical framework that reinforces the directives of the *FSR*. The form attempts to order events by time and space (Column 1), and to ensure they are expressed succinctly through summaries (Column 2) and connected by annotations identifying a discursive network of appendices, other official forms, notes and letters (Column 3).

C.2118 is defined not only by these material properties, but also by the cultures and practices of the Army as an institution. It is, in other words, an essential component of a "writing space" operating within an historically contingent "dynamic relationship among materials, techniques, genres, and cultural attitudes and uses."[71] Understood as an element of a writing space, C.2118 can be situated within the broader culture of information in which the

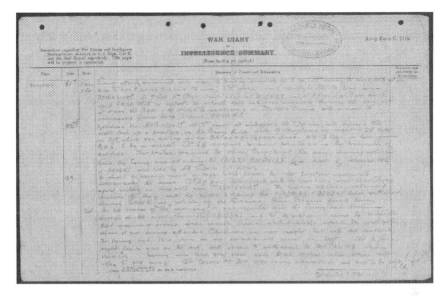

Figure 1.1 8th Battalion North Staffordshire Regiment, March 1918, WO 95-2082-1, TNA, Kew

document holds an authoritative status as information, but it is also located more specifically within the culture of the British Army, where it mediates the relationships between individuals and the Army as an institution, in addition to mediating the experiences of conflict. C.2118 is preloaded with the authority of the Army's hierarchical structures and bureaucratic systems and it situates those who are required to complete the form in relationship to those structures and systems. C.2118, like other preprinted blank forms, thus "triangulate[s] the modern self in relation to authority: the authority of printedness, on the one hand, and the authority of specific social subsystems and bureaucracies on the other hand."[72] It requires its bureaucratic subjects to comply with its directives and attempts to subordinate individuality to the Army's organisational needs and requirements.

Inherent in the instructions for the completion of the War Diaries and in the very structure of C.2118 itself is the notion that all that is required of those completing them is to filter and convert events from an external and objectively verifiable reality into data. Slack, Miller and Doak's analysis of technical writing provides a useful model to apply to the C.2118 form.[73] As in technical writing, the information contained in the forms is not so much as authored as re-presented. As Slack, Miller and Doak point out, Unit War Diaries thus fall into the category of those documents that Foucault excludes from those we conceive of as being "authored," such as letters and contracts.[74] The authority of C.2118 resides in the idea of factual information and in the form itself, and not in the authority of the individual who has completed it. The instructions and the structure of the form attempt to render the writer invisible by shifting emphasis away from the person responsible for constructing the report and onto the information that the organisation needs to know. From one perspective, then, the C.2118 form dehumanises war through its very structure. From another, however, it is a contested space in which individual expression collides with bureaucratic systems of containment and control.

The basic material properties of the completed forms provide evidence of that struggle, especially those that are handwritten. Technologies of writing play a critical role in the constitution of writing spaces. By the start of the First World War, the typewriter was indispensable in commercial spheres where it met demands for speed and standardisation. As will be discussed in more detail in the next chapter (Chapter 2), the typewriter was emblematic of industrial progress and modern efficiency and was a highly sought-after machine for the staff of the BEF during the First World War. "A reliable typewriting machine has arrived at last to the relief of our excellent brigade clerk, Sergeant Hodgkinson," wrote General Jack in 1914.[75] Up until that point Sgt Hodgkinson had been producing most of the brigade's reports by hand. Not all clerks were as lucky as Hodgkinson, however. The distribution of typewriters was strictly controlled by Captain S.G. Partridge, Director of the Army's Printing and Stationery Services, which also produced and disseminated manuals, pamphlets and other documents crucial to the BEF's activities. Requests for typewriters had to be made through the APSS, and Partridge was given authority to refuse them by the Quartermaster General, Brigadier General Dawkins. Dawkins was of the opinion that "people write too much already" and should not be encouraged to produce more paperwork.[76] Partridge appears to have wholeheartedly adopted Dawkins' position, and routinely refused requests for typewriters, although the expense of the machines and the difficulties of maintaining them in the field undoubtedly also played a part in his decisions. In the first half of 1915, for example, he refused around 32 requests from engineering units, as well as artillery and infantry brigades.[77] He seemed especially reluctant to allocate the machines to the infantry, due to the concern that "once the Army is on the move, machines are likely to be knocked about or lost."[78] While there is no evidence to show exactly how many typewriters were used by the BEF, in 1918 Partridge asserted that there were "5,000 or so machines" in France.[79] The relative scarcity of typewritten reports in the First World War Unit War Diaries suggests that most machines were reserved for use higher up the command chain, rather than for frontline troops. But while the introduction of the typewriter has been discussed as part of the BEF's adoption of modern (and commercial) methods and technologies of producing and managing information, the technologies involved in producing handwritten reports were no less products of the industrial era. The writing spaces of Unit War Diaries involved a confluence of technologies, and they illustrate that even in the age of print and the mechanisation of writing and of warfare, handwriting was still an important aspect of daily life.

The handwritten War Diaries are, as Jay David Bolter argues of manuscripts in the Middle Ages, the product of "the relatively leisured pace of the writing hand, not the insistent rhythm of the machine,"[80] yet they were written during a war that was transformed by the pace and power of industrial machinery. The act of writing, like the act of reading, has not always been undertaken or understood in the same way through different times and in different spaces.[81] Writing by hand, as Bolter points out, is "no more natural, no less technological" than writing with a typewriter or digital keyboard.[82] Before the typewriter gained a firm foothold, the gradual replacement of the feathered quill by the steel pen (itself a product of industrial innovations in manufacturing techniques) in the Eighteenth Century facilitated quicker handwriting, meeting new demands for productivity in the modern age. The rise of bureaucratic institutions was dependent on a growing pool of clerks in both commerce and government, all of whom were meant to produce reams of legible, neat and uniform paperwork, aided by the steel pen, and by the many copy books and print manuals promoting particular styles of writing believed to be suitable for commercial purposes. Late in the 1800s, the steel pen met competition in the form of the fountain pen, or the reservoir pen, which did away with the need for messy and awkward inkwells and which remained the pen of choice until the development of the ballpoint pen well into the 1940s. The prevalence of manuals for handwriting in the 'how-to' guides that proliferated at the turn of the century indicate how learning to write was itself transformed into a "consumer activity."[83] I want to spend a moment examining some of the choices available to consumers at the time, in order to shed light on how the activity of writing was valued and understood.

In a very similar way to today's choices between Apple and Android phones, or brands of laptops, "the choice of a pen was as much representing an aspiration, belief, or value, as it was a desire to buy a serviceable pen."[84] During the First World War, pen manufacturers linked these aspirations, beliefs and values to the conflict. Waterman advertised a "Super-pen for our Super-Men" as the ideal pen for anyone serving in the military, with a number of "endorsements" from those in the field, including "a Lieutenant" who refers to his pen as "my never failing friend" throughout a gruelling spell of active service.[85] Onoto adverts proclaimed it as "the BRITISH PEN" and accused those who bought "foreign" makes of pen of "[weakening] our power in the war."[86] The makers of Swan "fountpens" continually emphasised their "pre-war" pricing, in order to provide "every officer [with] a good fountain pen for signing orders, vouchers, receipts, messages and for writing home."[87] It is impossible to gauge how many men carried such pens with them into war, but these adverts are a reminder of the cultural weight specific to the Nineteenth and early Twentieth Centuries accorded to writing by hand and its associated technologies. In an era characterised by the emergence of monumental, impersonal forces, handwriting was a personal medium, "a medium of the self," as Tamara Plakins Thornton refers to it, which enabled personal expression not only through meaning-making in the text, but also through the act of constructing words on the page and through the choice of the technologies used in that process.[88] Handwriting became a form of agency that quite literally allowed the individual to "inscribe [their] place" in increasingly depersonalised and bureaucratic systems.[89]

Despite pen-makers' claims of reliability and durability and the development of tablets rather than liquid ink, fountain and steel pens were fiddly and difficult to manage on the Front Line. Soldiers, clerks and officers in the BEF were far more likely to use pencils, rather than pens, to produce official documents. As with the steel pen, innovations in production during the Eighteenth Century led to the increasing manufacture of pencils, in particular the copying or indelible pencil. The copying pencil was a neater and cheaper alternative to using ink pens and dispensed with the need for inkwells or ink tablets. Not only was it indelible, when dampened it could create a mirror-image transfer that could be easily used as document copy, and later, because it could be used with firm pressure (unlike fountain pens), it was used in conjunction with carbon paper – important for the War Diaries, which had to be produced in duplicate. An early forerunner of the ballpoint pen, its cheapness and convenience led to the widespread distribution of American-made copying pencils among the BEF.[90]

The copying pencil resembles both the ordinary pencil and, when dampened, the fountain pen, making its traces difficult to identify with any certainty, but its widespread distribution within the BEF and use with carbon paper strongly suggest that this was one of the primary writing technologies used to compose the War Diaries – hence TNA's description of them as "scribbled hastily in pencil."[91] In today's writing spaces, pencil is often used for scribbles that can be erased and are not intended to be permanent. But the pencils used in the early 1900s had a very different functionality; one associated with contemporary standards of efficiency and productivity and related to copying and preservation. While there is no doubt that some of the Diaries were written hurriedly and grudgingly in the midst of the pressures of fighting, the cultural weight accorded to handwriting at the time should not be underestimated, nor should the significance of individual responses to the institutional demands of the pre-printed form.

In many cases it is impossible to know who produced the reports in the Diaries. The completion of War Diaries was the responsibility of unit commanders, but they were often written by the regimental adjutant or other junior officers, whose names never appear. They are ghost-writers, standing in for their commanding officers and conveying the experiences of their unit through the scientific approach outlined by the *FSR* and framed by the printed form. Yet despite the attempt to erase the individual via the authority given to rational, de-narrativised information, and the hierarchical structure of the Army, the uniqueness of each writer is evident in the singular nature of their scripts. Ranging across the repeated structure of the pre-printed blank form is a huge variety of different forms of handwriting, almost all of it in cursive. From the neat and elegant penmanship evident in many of the Diaries of the Cheshire Regiment through the small but slightly messier hand in the reports of the Notts and Derby Regiment and Sherwood Foresters to the absolutely appalling script of the reports signed by Lt Colonel Murray Thriepland in the Unit War Diaries of the Welsh Guards, the completed C.2118 forms bear evidence of individuality and unpredictability in a system attempting to minimise exactly those things.[92] The very illegibility of some of the handwriting (Lt. Col. Thriepland's reports are a good example) confounds bureaucratic impulses of order and standardisation long before content is evaluated. 2.6% of the sample of the reports of the 1st Bn Welsh Guards from 1916 (which constitutes just over 9,000 words) is illegible, but that figure does not fully convey the loss of meaning in these records. This entry for the 16 September 1916 gives some indication of how Thriepland's handwriting confounds understanding and obscures details:

> It took me till 3am to understand operation orders, with a final complicated system of barrages to [illegible][illegible] time, [illegible] Bn orders, confer with 1 Bn from Gds C.O. who was to [illegible] in with me, explain [illegible] to Coy Commanders etc. etc. It was raining hard & I was in a shelled hole which did not expedite matters.[93]

Thriepland's individual handwriting fragments information, rendering some of it unusable, but it also imprints a sense of human individuality into the material structure of the C.2118 form.

Thriepland's entry additionally provides an indication of the challenges of attempting to read and write messages and orders in the spaces of war. The haste and messiness evident in some of the reports are indications that the structure of C.2118 and the principles governing its completion, while significant in understanding the construction of the reports, are nevertheless only two facets of an intricate concatenation of elements that constitute the writing spaces of war. Much writing about war — memoirs, histories, novels — is produced in its aftermath. In contrast, Unit War Diaries were produced in or near the spaces of conflict, sometimes as events unfolded. The writing and reading spaces of the reports of war are spaces of the battlefield, which creates a unique set of pressures. General Jack's diary describes some of the difficulties of attempting to conduct administrative tasks in the spaces of war: "Out here much of our reading and writing has to be performed in ill-lit rooms, cellars or windowless shelters — in the two last-named by the rays from a candle-stump" often in the midst of "the drum of our cannonade" and "counter-bombardment" from the Germans.[94] It is no wonder that so many of Lt Col Thriepland's accounts are illegible, considering the conditions under which some of them may have been written.

The effects of writing reports while units are involved in active combat are also evident in the notes taken while events unfolded. The almost hour-by-hour account of the Notts and Derby Regiment's experiences from mid- to late September 1916, for example, bear evidence of haste in errors and occasionally messy scrawls in the otherwise neat handwriting.[95] Perhaps revealing even more about the pressures of writing about war whilst waging it are the gaps in some reports. In some instances, fighting was so intense it made reporting impossible, and the Diaries contain only a line or two at most, with after-action reports filling in for real-time observations. For instance, a successful raid carried out on 20th March 1916 by the North Staffordshire regiment warrants only a few lines in the actual Diary entry, but an expanded, typed, five page Appendix (A), gives much more detail on the operation in what is effectively an after-action report.[96] The inclusion of after-action accounts, sometimes compiled years after the events (as in T.F.C. Downman's explanation of events in the battle of Gommecourt two years after the action) suggest that the formal qualities of the C.2118 forms and the regulations governing them constrained the nature of the information they contained, leading to the need for supplementary narratives and explanation.[97] This chapter focusses on the handwritten C.2118 form, but the presence of these kinds of after-action accounts also demonstrates that the very nature of conflict itself sometimes challenged the practice of keeping the diaries in the very moments when information about what had happened was most urgently needed. In their introduction to a collection of essays examining emotions and war in literature, Downes et al argue that war literature is "not simply *about* the historical and bodily emotional experience of war, but *of* it."[98] If this is true of the retrospective writing of fiction and history about war, then it is even more true of the C.2118 forms, which are not only reports about conflict, but are products of it. Hurried, messy notes as well as absences in the reports are direct consequences of the physical effect of combat on the writers, and bear testament to the embodied experience of war.

Acknowledging that the Unit War Diaries are products of the embodied experience of conflict opens them up as more than "information" about the past, and reveals the vital, but often obscured, role played by emotion in both the waging and reporting of war. Rather than dismiss moments of emotional expression as unreliable or as aberrations in the overall flow of information, the next section undertakes linguistic and close analysis of the corpus of C.2118 forms to identify how individual affective responses interact with the framework of organisational principles of operational reporting. Thus far we have investigated intersections between culture, institutional practices and technologies in the writing spaces of war, but it is crucial that we also acknowledge the presence of the human beings in the midst of these intersections. Investigating how War Diaries function as emotional practices allows us to interrogate how individuals responded to the pressures and tensions generated by the various factors in operation in the writing spaces of war.

War Diaries as emotional practice

Anna Wierzbicka provides some indication of the challenges of studying emotion by making clear that there are "*no* universal" emotion terms and concepts that can be mapped across different languages and cultures.[99] Just as the understanding of emotion and its expression varies across cultures, it is also not universally consistent through time. Differences across time and culture in the social and psychological registers and interpretations of emotion, and the inherent transitory nature of emotion, all pose a series of linguistic and anachronic challenges for researchers. Monique Scheer offers a solution to some of these difficulties by characterising emotion as an embodied practice – "the meaningful cultural activity of ascribing, interpreting, and constructing an event as a trigger."[100] Scheer conceptualises emotions not as spontaneous, natural responses to events, but as active and mindful practices that are situationally and historically contingent. Practices in turn involve actions, which include not only embodied acts such as gestures and facial expressions but also the use of material objects and forms of media to communicate emotion.[101] Understanding emotion as a practice therefore draws attention to "what people are *doing*, and to working out the specific situatedness of these doings," which is exactly the approach this book adopts for the analysis of Unit War Diaries.[102]

Understood as embodied and mindful practices, it becomes apparent that acts of emotion are neither natural nor universal, but are learned, socially situated habitual behaviours cultivated in and shaped by the *habitus* in which they occur.[103] The writing spaces of war can thus be understood as constituting as a specific *habitus* in which the institutional and technological elements outlined in the previous sections are among those factors that condition (but do not necessarily control) emotional engagement and practices. Other important factors conditioning emotion in the writing spaces of war that need to be considered before we proceed with an examination of the Diaries themselves are the broader cultural and social understandings of emotion, which are in turn entangled with how the British Army considered and addressed emotion. Many of the Army's ideas about emotion inevitably reflect what the men who led and designed organisational practices understood about it from their cultural and social backgrounds. Their decisions and regulations created organisational expectations that laid the foundation for specific emotional practices that manifest in the Unit War Diaries.

The army as emotional regime

Alongside the concept of information, the concept of emotion underwent a transformation in the 1800s. Emotion as a "theoretical term" was explicitly identified first in the lectures of Thomas Brown in the mid-Nineteenth Century as a "major psychological category to the academic and literary worlds."[104] Emotion became a subject of scientific enquiry over the remainder of the century. During the Victorian era, scientific studies such as Charles Darwin's *The Expression of the Emotions in Man and Animals* (1872) tended to focus on the physical expression of emotion in animals and people, and to place these in opposition to intellect and reason. Darwin reinforced a developing argument that emotion is generated via its outward physical expression, rather than the other way around, by arguing that giving way to the embodied manifestations of emotion would only intensify feeling: "He who gives way to violent gestures will increase his rage; he who does not control the signs of fear will experience fear in a greater degree."[105] The emphasis on male responses here signals how the lack of emotional restraint became associated with those believed to lack the capacity for reason – animals, children, women, the insane and those races judged as uncivilised. Thomas Dixon therefore connects the "turning away from sentimentalism towards stoicism and emotional restraint" with the rise of imperialism and jingoistic nationalism in the late 1800s.[106] Dixon describes how parenting manuals and education systems (especially public schools) of this period inculcated the notion of the "stiff upper lip" in boys and men as the ideal response to privation, pain or grief.[107]

The officer class (especially the second lieutenants or subalterns, many of whom were responsible for completing the Unit War Diaries) in the British Army were largely drawn from the ranks of the public schools or universities of Britain, which by the turn of the century were advocating self-control and the rigorous limitation of emotion.[108] The cultural emphasis on an ideal of masculinity based on rational self-control folded neatly into a much longer history of the "inculcation of emotional restraint" in soldiers from the classical period through medieval times to the Napoleonic wars and The First World War.[109] Such restraint, most usually achieved through a combination of drills, repetition and simulation, is broadly understood as necessary to "make orderly and rational what is essentially chaotic and instinctive" – to effectively control intense emotional responses, especially fear, amid the discord and pandemonium of the battlefield.[110] The C.2118 form and its accompanying instructions are material iterations of an ideological framework that attempts "to reduce the events of combat to as few and as easily recognisable a set of elements as possible" thereby minimising emotions such as panic and fear.[111] Bureaucratic processes within the military thus attempt to de-emotionalise combat in the belief that this allows soldiers to fight more effectively. The Army's efforts to establish and maintain norms for emotional practices identify it as an "emotional regime" operating within the broader culture. Emotional regimes, according to William Reddy, who coined the term, establish a "normative order for emotions," which operates on a spectrum from looser controls to those more rigorously reinforced.[112] Reddy places military organisations at the end of a spectrum of strict emotional controls, but the ways in which the British Army formulated its emotional regime in both World Wars were perhaps more multi-dimensional than this perspective might suggest.

As Stephen Fineman points out, the work undertaken by organisations to shape their emotional regimes is often hidden.[113] Although much of the British Army's approach to emotion before the First World War operated on principles based on understandings of emotion that were implicit rather than explicit, the training manuals developed and implemented in the wake of the South African Wars provide a glimpse of the qualities the organisation valued, and therefore promoted, within its emotional regime. Most of these were related to the notion of 'character.' Stefan Collini identifies character as a highly adaptable concept used across almost all sections of Victorian society to represent an ideal of both masculine and national identity, but also as a measure of behaviour and as the "favoured explanatory element in the analysis of different human fates."[114] Anxieties regarding the moral state of the nation as a whole, but also specifically the challenges faced by the working class and the poor, were often linked to the supposed failure of character. As Nick Taylor points out, it was exactly these kinds of fears that contributed to the formation, among a range of other organisations aimed at improving the character of the youth (especially boys of the working class), of the Scouting movement, "which sought to instil self-discipline and obedience and improve the moral and physical health of the nation."[115] Possibly close to half the population of young men had signed up to these kinds of organisations by the time the First World War broke out.[116] The popularity of these movements is evidence of the significance of the belief in inculcating the values of "duty, honour and patriotism" in the character of British youth, values that were also, not coincidentally, the "emotional moulds within which British imperial attitudes [were] set."[117] Specific emotional traits were thus linked not only to the notion of character in individuals (specifically men), but also to national identity.

Character was a pervasive "expression of a very deeply ingrained perception of the qualities needed to cope with life" and that included life in the military.[118] Officers, above all, were required to be of "a strong character," according to the Manual for *Training and Manoeuvre Regulations.*[119] For men who were the products of Public-School Education, and of upper and middle-class society in Victorian and Edwardian Britain, possessing moral virtue and practicing self-restraint and willpower were implicit in the notion of good character. But officers were also required by the Army to have "a capacity for overcoming difficulties and for always appearing confident and cheerful."[120] The significance of *appearing* confident and cheerful regardless of what an individual might really be feeling illustrates how emotion can be used as "dramaturgical devices," especially in organisational settings, where the performance of a particular kind of emotion is required to align the individual with the purposes of the organisation.[121] Affecting a casual nonchalance in the face of danger and chaos became a significant and enduring dramaturgical device for British officers, as this chapter and the next will show.

Whereas officers were believed to be already in possession of many of the traits required by the Army by virtue of their character, shaped by both class and education, listed first in the 1914 *Infantry Training Manual*'s "preliminary steps necessary for the efficient training of the soldier" is "the development of a soldierly spirit," followed next by physical training and only afterwards by training in "the use of the rifle, bayonet and spade."[122] The ability "to bear fatigue, privation, and danger cheerfully" and to "use his brains and weapons coolly" regardless of the stress of battle was essential to the development of the spirit of the soldier.[123] These qualities, according to the Manual, are identified as the foundation of the British Army's successes on the battlefield, as well as those of individual regiments.[124] The soldier was to be instructed on "the deeds which have made the British Army and his regiment famous" as well as in "simple lessons" in military history "as his intelligence develops" and the "great[ness]" of the British Empire.[125] Regimental history and identity, connected in the manual to the superiority of the British Empire, were deliberate methods of instilling and sustaining another set of emotions within the soldierly spirit – pride and love for the regiment. The regiment was not only representative of British Imperial Identity and power, it constituted a "military family," worthy of the same kind of loyalty and love that men extended to their own families.[126] Learning about the regiment's past which, as David French points out, generally involved learning about only regimental triumphs, was one way of instilling emotional commitment, but the other was through an emphasis on maintaining a regiment's unique traditions, uniforms and badges.[127] For the British Army, these emotional connections to individual regiments were regarded as essential for how soldiers performed on the battlefield. Cheerfulness, stoic resistance to privation, along with coolness under pressure, were core emotional qualities singled out as essential in the British Army, but the organisation was less clear on how to inculcate the requisite soldierly spirit and its associated emotional qualities in practice through training.

Training in the years leading up to the First World War was hampered, among other issues, by a lack of uniformity, investment and equipment.[128] Following Lord Kitchener's decision to recruit 500,000 civilian volunteers in August 1914, the Army was faced with the considerable challenge of housing, feeding, clothing and arming the almost 2.5 million volunteers who eventually signed up by the end of 1915.[129] The Army additionally had to transform this large mass of civilians into soldiers, while still struggling with shortages of equipment and weapons. Donald Murry, who joined the King's Own Yorkshire Light Infantry, describes training with "pieces of wood for rifles, shaped like a rifle."[130] The training regime consisted initially of basic training involving fitness drills, marching, and later, more specialised exercises such as movements in the field, weapons and marksmanship. Training was intended to promote fitness, discipline and group cohesion, which were all believed to be enough to prepare men for combat. If warfare in the Industrial era was becoming increasingly organised by the higher echelons along the same lines as commercial and manufacturing enterprises, at the other end of the social scale, the experience of labour in other industries helped to translate the experience of soldiering for those soldiers drawn from the working class.[131]

Although the situation may have been very different from the civilian world, John Bourne argues that privation, adapting to authority, hard work and even existential struggles for life and death would have been familiar territory for many in the working class.[132] Similarly, Ian Beckett et al. identify a "predisposition in British working-class popular culture that made light of hardship" and which equipped soldiers with survival strategies.[133] Although soldiering may have been regarded as another form of industrial labour, it differed in one key area. It required training men to kill. One veteran describes how

> fixing bayonets, was part of your rifle drill. On the command 'Fix!' you'd all fix, but then you'd get your old dummy, your sacks o' straw – 'Grrrr…!' – make all the noise you could, and that was part of the training […] We used to do it and enjoy it really – make a lot o' noise about sticking it in, but we used to say 'Wonder what the hell we shall feel like if we have to do it to a Jerry?'[134]

While training involved an enjoyable performance of aggression – yelling 'Grrrr!' – the reality of the emotional experience of combat was less clear to soldiers. The complex range of emotions that could surface during combat was left largely unaddressed by the Army.

The traits most valued in the Army's emotional regime – coolness under pressure, resilience, and cheerfulness – acquired weight and meaning in broader society because they were identified as uniquely British and placed in opposition to the supposed viciousness and aggression of the Germans. A two-page spread featured in *The War Illustrated*, a popular picture magazine published by William Berry devoted to the First World War, quite literally illustrates how different emotional qualities were connected to national identity. On the left side of the page is the "Dauntless Courage of a Highland Laddie" – a pictorial representation of a member of the Gordons playing a mouth organ while advancing with his companions into battle. On the right is an illustration of the "Brutal Cowardice of a Baffled Hun Officer," showing a German officer whipping an already injured British soldier for information while others look on laughing. The illustration of the Gordon is described as one of the "many precious incidents of unique courage, of a gay contempt of death" that characterise British forces, deliberately contrasted with "the other extreme of human character," the cowardly brutality of German forces as reported by a Private Joseph Graves about his capture in Bruges.[135] These two contrasting illustrations are themselves observable traces of emotional practice. They simultaneously represent and reinforce particular expressions of emotion as inherent to national identity. Cheerful courage in the face of death is positioned as uniquely British, and cowardice is associated with the enemy.

Neither the Army's emotional regime nor that of broader British culture paid much attention to one of the most extreme and challenging emotions to surface when men were faced with the reality of killing or being killed on the battlefield. Both the Army and British society appeared to have held to the belief that the inherent 'character' of the officer, and the 'spirit' of the ordinary soldier, should have been enough to inure them against fear. If it was acknowledged at all, fear was addressed in the same way most emotions were understood in both emotional regimes – as something that could and should be subject to rational self-control. Elsewhere in *The War Illustrated*, a rare article addressing the topic acknowledged that soldiers were not "devoid of fear" but argued that through "self-knowledge" and "self-control," fear could be conquered.[136] In reality, fear was manifesting on the battlefield in ways that defied such understanding, and the emotional experience of war was far more complex than such articles imagined. Those emotional experiences, including the experience of fear, played out in the context of a set of integrated norms created by the emotional regimes of both the British Army and contemporary culture that linked emotion to ideas of class, masculinity and national identity.

While the C.2118 form and the indelible pencil are material objects in the writing spaces of the First World War, the immaterial factors that shaped their use are just as significant. I have already investigated the entanglements between the Army's culture of information and bureaucratic organisation and these technologies, but the Army's emotional regime is an equally critical feature of the writing spaces of conflict. My approach, like Scheer's, is not so much concerned with the interior truth or essence of emotion (which is almost impossible to identify with any certainty), as with the "traces of observable action" that remain in the aftermath of mediated emotion-as-practice.[137] First-person accounts, such as memoirs and poetry, are often privileged as yielding special insight into the emotional truth of individuals.[138] But Scheer points out that conceiving emotion as a practice enables the identification of observable traces in texts not usually associated with emotional expression, such as third-person accounts,[139] and as I argue here, official documents like the Unit War Diaries. There are three key areas in which traces of emotional practice can be observed in the First World War Unit War Diaries – emotives, punctuation, and embellished narration. These three are of course intertwined, but for the sake of clarity, I have separated them into separate areas for analysis.

Emotives

William Reddy identifies overt references to emotion in language as "emotives."[140] Using words is a significant way in which emotions are expressed, but language also regulates the experience of emotion in that what we are feeling may be indeterminate or uncertain until we identify it linguistically. Language might also be used to obscure or hide what we are feeling. It is therefore important to note that as instances of emotional practice, emotives are the *performance* of emotion through language, and should not be confused with what the individual might actually be feeling at the time. Emotives are "instruments for directly changing, building, hiding, intensifying emotions."[141] An important caveat for this analysis is therefore that there is a slipperiness in identifying emotives, and subjectivity plays an inevitable role. With that in mind, we identified and manually tagged instances of emotive language in the War Diaries.[142] By instances or occurrences I mean moments of emotional practice that may include single words or clusters of words that name emotions, or that have emotional resonance. Linguistic software (Antconc) allowed us to locate tagged emotives within the corpus and to identify those that were most common. Tracking emotives in this way is an important indicator that, contrary to the widespread perception of official documentation produced by the military as "flat and unidimensional,"[143] Unit War Diaries are channels through which some individuals attempted to process profound emotional experiences, many beyond anything they had ever encountered before, in and through the practices and expressions of the cultural and military emotional regimes in operation during the First World War.

In a corpus constituting 31 files and 58,137 words, there were 150 occurrences of emotives (bearing in mind that these instances may contain clusters of words). The relative scarcity of emotives across this corpus is testament to the power of the bureaucratic structures and controls imposed by the *FSR*, the framework of the C.2118 form and the culture of the Army itself. The majority of reports conform to the limits of official language, as in this example taken from the 5th Bn Notts and Derby's Diary for 28 April 1917:

> Artillery duel from 4.30am–5.30am. Trench mortars & snipers gave considerable trouble. Work on Defence Line continued.
> Enemy fired between 40 or 50 gas shells on Left Company Front. Captain A. Stone, 2nd Lieut J.H. Jones & 2nd Lieut H.C.H. Martin and 50 Other Ranks of "C" Coy attempted to raid enemy trenches and houses about M.24.d.30.25. They were discovered in the wire & were subjected to heavy Machine Gun, Rifle and Trench mortar fire and bombs & were compelled to withdraw. We suffered the following casualties: Captain Stone, 'missing'; 2nd Lieut.Jones, severely wounded; 2 Other Ranks 'missing'; 7 Other Ranks, wounded. Patrols went out immediately party had withdrawn to search for Captain Stone & the other missing men but met with no success.[144]

This report condenses what must have been a distressing and visceral moment of combat into a terse, dispassionate account. But the very scarcity of emotives makes them significant in identifying moments in which individual emotional responses to the experiences of conflict push through the intersections of official structures and cultural norms. Not only are emotives relatively rare, they are also unevenly spread throughout the corpus, with the vast majority appearing in the diaries of the 1st Bn South Staffs from 1915 (35 instances).[145] The next highest majority (20 occurrences) is in those of the 1st Bn Welsh Guards from 1916.[146] These concentrations are at least in part attributable to the style and approaches of individual writers, who regularly push against the restrictions of operational reporting with emotives and literary flourishes to shape reports that may not fit the standard demanded by the Army, and which may be discounted as too subjective for historical records, but which are indicative of individual struggles to accommodate the stresses and challenges of warfare. Emotives in the Unit War Diaries alert us to the presence of the human being amidst the technologies and forces in operation in the spaces of war and examining them uncovers the emotional history of these reports. Two loose groups of emotives emerged – those that were more positive in nature, and those that were negative.

Reflecting the aspiration of at least appearing to maintain the all-important 'stiff upper lip,' there are relatively few mentions of men struggling to deal with combat, even though this war was the first in which the impact of industrial weaponry in warfare was recognised (although not fully understood) as potentially damaging not just for men's bodies, but for their psyches. While the commanders and Army doctors of most combatant countries in the First World War recognised the emotional cost of combat, and treated some cases sympathetically,[147] there was widespread intolerance for expressions of terror on the battlefield as a form of cowardice. Expressing fear on or off the battlefield was regarded as unacceptable or incompatible with contemporary values and ideas, which, as explained in the previous section, broadly held that men should be able to control their fear by exerting their rational willpower. The relative lack of references to fear in relation to the conflict in public discourse and in the British Army made it an "outlaw emotion" in the emotional regimes of both.[148] There is also regimental pride to consider in the acknowledgement of fear in the Unit War Diaries, because, as Joanna Bourke notes, "To protect the reputation of a regiment, evidence of serious forms of shirking or malingering had to be suppressed."[149] The association between fear and 'malingering' was pervasive during the First World War, and as Chapter 2 will demonstrate, it persisted into the Second. Writers of the diaries selected for this corpus consequently very rarely acknowledge fear on the battlefield, and when they do, it tends to be obliquely. There are only two references to men being "shaken." The 1st Bn Cheshires' Diary for 3rd September 1916 describes how an individual, Lt G.W. Richardson, was "very shaken by shell and sent down to Transport," and in the 1st Bn Welsh Guards, coincidentally also in September 1916, men are described in the entry for the 10th, as "being by now a good deal shaken, having fought continuously soon after midnight of the night previous."[150] There are five mentions that refer specifically to shell shock, but all of these occur in lists of casualties. There are only three mentions of sadness and regret, twice in reference to the deaths of individual officers and once as part of an account of an official response to high casualties. The severe emotional toll that combat can exact is thus all but written out of these accounts, and the erasure of fear in particular, as Chapter 2 will argue, would have consequences for how the Army approached its management in the next great conflict.

In keeping with the broader cultural emphasis on understatement, and the official constraints of operational reporting, the majority of emotives relating to the dangers and extremities of war are mostly applied to terrain and conditions. Words such as "miserable" and "awful," for example, are only ever used to describe weather conditions, while iterations of "bad" or "badly," "strain" or "strained" and "horrid" are also generally applied to weather conditions, marches, the state of trenches, or levels of gunfire or shelling. The most common emotive used to describe difficulties or challenges in the conflict is "trying" –

but the way in which it is used occasionally nudges against the restraints of understatement and control. There are ten instances of the use of this word, spread not across the corpus, but predominantly in the Diaries of the 2nd Bn Worcestershires, where it appears six times.[151] Detailing the loss of the village of Gheluvelt, critical in the Ypres Salient, the entries through late October, while concise, manage largely through the repetition of "trying" to convey the desperation and frustration caused by brutal and chaotic conditions. Although Column 2 of C.2118 calls for a "Summary of Events and Information," and the guidelines of the *FSR* encourage the bare minimum of facts about events, the entries for the events on the 22 October 1914 are increasingly subjective and emotive, describing how the "furious bombardment" and "continuous" rifle fire created "a very trying ordeal." The phrase "most trying" is used in quick succession in the next entry, and repeated twice to describe the day and night of the 23rd October.[152]

Repetition in poetry and prose is a stylistic device with a range of different purposes, but it should not be overlooked in writing like this, because it goes beyond the basic requirements of reporting to introduce a level of subjectivity – a distinctly human response to the extremes of mechanised warfare. Although "trying" in this context could be considered an understatement, and therefore characteristic of how responses to difficulties are described according to the norms operating in the Army's emotional regime, the repetition of the word three times in two entries nudges at those norms and signals an individual affective response to the situation. The writer goes further to emphasise the challenges of this situation by underlining "very trying" twice in the entry for the 22nd of October. The act of underlining this phrase is an observable trace of emotion that counteracts the understatement of the phrase itself and the controls imposed by the formal structures of reporting and cultural convention. These pencil marks etched into the page are an intimate indication of the physical hand at work in creating them. They imply that the words are simply not enough on their own to convey the severity of situation and, together with the repetition of the phrase, convey a sense of the writer's emotional state.

In addition to contending with the emotional challenge of overcoming fear and terrible conditions, units were faced with situations that often exceeded not only the control of soldiers, but also of Headquarters. Even before the advent of fully industrialised warfare, with its large-scale ballistic weapons and their chaos-inducing rapid rates of fire and extended range, writers had recognised what some began to call the 'fog of war.' Carl Von Clausewitz called war, amongst other things, "the realm of uncertainty; three quarters of the factors on which action in war is based are wrapped in a fog of greater or lesser uncertainty."[153] There are 67 instances in the corpus in which the Unit War Diaries describe events that are uncertain, messy or chaotic, but without explicit reference to such terms. These include instances of breakdowns in communications, such as that between Brigade and the front-line in the War Diary of the 1st Bn Welsh Guards from September 1915, which details how

50   *Unit War Diaries in the First World War*

orders fell through, or were even destroyed, potentially after the fact, resulting in confusion.[154] They also include instances of friendly fire, such as that described in the War Diary of the 2nd Bn Notts and Derby Regiment for the 1st July 1917, when, due to a communication breakdown, one company was caught in an artillery barrage because it had not received notice of an alteration to the time of attack.[155] But throughout the corpus, there are only eight actual mentions of confusion, and half of these occur in the War Diary of the 10th Bn Worcestershires during the first weeks of the Battle of the Somme. Two of the entries in July 1916 refer to confusion during troop movements either into or out of trenches, and a third to the Bn losing their way while being shelled by tear gas.[156] But one also mentions, with a hint of weary resignation, the "inevitable confusion" that follows the cancelling of an order to attack the German lines.[157] The concentration of explicit references to confusion in these reports is an indication of the actual conditions on the ground, but the relative scarcity of this word in the corpus makes its use here an instance of resistance against the norm. Conditioned by the regulations of the *FSR*, as well as by the neat structures of the C.2118 form and the emphasis on rational structures in the emotional regimes of the Army and in broader society, it is unsurprising that the norm was to downplay or avoid acknowledgement of the fog of war. The use of confusion in the Unit War Diaries of the Worcestershire Regiment works both as an understatement, in that the reports will only go so far in admitting that at times war was chaotic, but its very rarity in the corpus makes it an instance of pushing back against the structures of reporting because it is the closest writers come to overtly acknowledging any loss of control.

While there are scant traces of emotives that provide a sense of the difficulties and challenges of warfare, most emotives emphasise the stoicism and propensity for cheeriness so valued in the broader culture and the Army's emotional regime. Men and individuals are frequently described as being cheery or cheerful. Iterations of this emotive occur seven times, as in the entry for the 25 September 1915 in the War Diary of the 1st Bn Welsh Guards, which describes the state of the men after a long (and mostly pointless) march: "It was a long tiring day, men were very cheery. Good news kept coming from the Front, probably much of it untrue."[158] The use of this emotive illustrates that the stiff upper lip and resolute cheeriness in the face of difficulties were qualities valued enough to be recorded in official documents despite their insistence on brevity, and considered more appropriate than mentioning the outlaw emotions of demoralisation, shock or terror. There is, however, a hint of sardonic humour evident in the observation that the "good news" from the Front was in all likelihood untrue, itself a trace of an emotive practice involving wry observation.

Similarly, while fear is rare and cowardice is never mentioned, pluck and bravery are. Iterations of pluck occur four times, and there are four variations of bravery, all in the reports of the 1st Bn South Staffs from September 1915. The concentration of these emotives in this Unit War Diary marks it as an exception, and an instance of resistance to the structures of operational reporting. These are signed by Lt Colonel Ovens, and although it is impossible to say with any certainty if he wrote them himself, the repetition of emotives and the consistency of the overall style suggest that the same writer is behind all instances of these emotives. Two officers, in the entry for the 30th of September, 1915, are singled out for their actions:

> Lieut PARKES did excellent work during these trying five days & showed grit & pluck. 2nd Lieut BROCKLESBY also, for the six days he was in this battle, did very good work & was plucky & self-possessed.[159]

These entries depart from the concise language required by the C.2118 forms, and they are an example of the kind of embellished narratives that I will discuss in more detail in the next section of this chapter. The use of emotives emphasising cheeriness, pluck and bravery constitutes a performance of these emotions in official documents. This is not to imply that the men were not cheery or brave, or that war does not elicit such responses, but that the emphasis on positive emotions is an indication of how the emotional regime of the broader culture drove individual decision-making about what aspects of the emotional experience of conflict to include in the reports.

The way in which emotives as a form of emotional practice function as a "meaningful cultural activity" becomes particularly evident in the use of the concept of gallantry.[160] Gallantry (and variations such as gallant, gallantly) is the emotive most often used as a description of behaviour or of an individual quality. It occurs in various forms 15 times, most frequently (six times) in the same Diaries of the 1st Bn South Staffs from 1915.[161] Gallantry is a concept that began as an "accepted code of behaviour for men," often in respect to their interactions with women, which stood in contrast to the "barbaric practices" of others.[162] But from the mid-Nineteenth Century onwards, following its integration into a range of state Honours loosely grouped as "gallantry awards," gallantry evolved, increasingly taking on martial overtones as "a heroic trait closely associated with service to Crown, state, nation and society."[163] Gallantry is acknowledged in the Unit War Diaries in citations for medals and decorations, however, its use in the reports of the 1st Bn South Staffs from the Battle of Loos and the Somme offensive is much closer to its function in contemporary military writing, where it was deployed to "dignify mortal risk, self-sacrifice and death."[164]

Despite claiming that "of the gallantry and undying devotion to duty displayed by officers, N.C.Os and men it is impossible to write fully in these pages," the writer of the entry for the actions of the 1st Bn South Staffs on the 25 September 1915 in the Battle of Loos does his utmost to do just that, and there are five uses of the word in this entry alone, as in these examples:

> Lieut COOPER led his men on with the utmost gallantry & was killed on the German wire, had he lived he would have been recommended for the

D.S.O. He was a most gallant officer & much loved and respected by all ranks.

To make a long story short, the gallant 1ˢᵗ Battn SOUTH STAFFORDSHIRE REGT rose to their feet at 6.25am on the 25 September 1915. On the order to "advance" being given, they advanced in extended order at about 3 paces interval between men, & moved steadily forward against this almost impregnable position.[165]

Both the Battle of Loos, which was the largest British offensive at that point of the conflict, and the Battle of the Somme, which superseded Loos in scope and casualties, feature in many war memoirs. Robert Graves' *Goodbye to all That* (1929) is among the more well-known and includes both the Battle of Loos and the Battle of the Somme.[166] Graves gives some sense of the challenges of writing about these events in recounting a moment in the Battle of Loos: "What happened in the next few minutes is difficult for me now to sort out. It was more difficult still at the time."[167] While most memoirists had the luxury of time in which to process their experiences, the writers of Unit War Diaries had neither significant temporal nor spatial distance between them and the events they wrote about. Instead, as in the reports above, familiar emotional practices help to channel the extraordinary experiences of these battles into recognisable and manageable shapes. By calling up the concept of gallantry, the writer gives meaning to battles that even in the wider scope of the First World War were particularly brutal and attritional. The charges of the men and the deaths of the individual officers are reframed through the concept of gallantry as noble endeavours and sacrifices in service of Crown, country and regiment. The concentration and repetition of gallantry as an emotive in these accounts exceeds the requirements of the *FSR* to "avoid literary form."[168] Instead, the writer of this Diary draws on conventions of literary form, especially, as will be made clear in the next section, those of regimental histories, to transform unprecedented events into comprehensible and recognisable narratives.

In addition to the emphasis on gallantry, the Unit War Diary of the 1ˢᵗ Bn South Staffs is the only one throughout the entire corpus to include the emotive 'glorious,' in reference to the Bn's actions at Loos.[169] 'Glorious' is an emotive that disrupts the intended objective tone of scientific rationalism of operational reporting, and which cannot be described as necessary for the effective operation of the Army, or as accurate information for future histories. It is also an emotive that many soldiers abhorred. Wilfred Owen's "Dulce et Decorum Est" is perhaps one of the most well-known repudiations of the desire for "desperate glory," but private letters also contain similar sentiments, such as Roland Leighton's letter to his fiancé, Vera Brittain, written just before the Battle of Loos:

> Let him who thinks that War is a glorious thing, who loves to roll forth stirring words of exhortation [.] let him but look at a little pile of sodden

grey rages that cover half a skull and a shin bone and what might have been Its ribs [.] and let him realise how grand & glorious a thing it is to have distilled all Youth and Joy and Life into a foetid heap of hideous putrescence.[170]

In official reports, individuals did not have the luxury of giving vent to such emotions. Instead, the use of emotives such as gallant and glorious invoke older, almost archaic, notions of warfare in ways that suggest a writer who is attempting to come to terms with appalling loss – the Battalion lost over half of those who attacked the German lines. The use of emotives in the reports of the 1st Bn South Staffs for Loos and the Somme offensive thus pushes against the constraints of the *FSR* and the structure of the C.2118 form. They are instances in which horrific events are transformed via established and familiar emotional practices of both the Army and of the broader cultural emotional regime. The reports emphasising positive emotives are ultimately as effective as those that deploy few emotives in smoothing over the brutality and horror of the conflict.

Ian Isherwood distinguishes between the historians of the First World War, who "could describe the great events of a campaign," and the soldiers writing their memoirs, who "recorded the emotional history of eyewitnesses,"[171] but the presence of emotives in the Unit War Diaries demonstrates that these reports fall somewhere in between official document, historical account and eyewitness testimony. The very presence of emotives in these documents contravenes the instructions for their completion, but tracing the use of emotives in this corpus provides a sense of the contours of historical emotional practices that attempted to smooth over the horrors and trauma of war. War, according to Downes, Lynch and O'Loughlin, "inculcates a new *habitus* of emotional practice – and disrupts former practices,"[172] but the use of emotives in this corpus reveals how individuals both drew on and reinforced, rather than disrupted, established practices in the emotional regimes of broader British culture, and that of the British Army. Emotives punctuate Unit War Diaries with trace marks of individual expression, but punctuation, specifically exclamation marks, are also observable traces of emotion.

Punctuation!

Punctuation is often overlooked (Scheer does not consider it, for example) in textual analysis and the performance of emotion. But punctuation goes beyond words to leverage space for other forms of emotional expression. Jennifer DeVere Brody argues that punctuation disrupts the flow of information and that it is "a means of inscribing bodily affect and presence imagined to be lost in translation" into the text.[173] Of all punctuation marks, the exclamation mark cannot be considered "neutral" and its use is a clear observable trace of an emotional practice.[174] The exclamation mark, or point, is part of what grammarian Lynne Truss calls "expressive, attention-seeking punctuation."[175]

In an age that valued reason over emotion, the expressive exclamation mark was treated with some suspicion. It needed to be used with care, as Fowler's Dictionary of Modern English Usage explains: "Excessive use of exclamation marks is [...] one of the things that betray the uneducated or unpractised writer."[176] Historical attitudes to the exclamation mark are evident in the various names given to it. According to one linguist, by the end of the Nineteenth Century, "it had become the staple of lurid novels and the sensational yellow press, whose printers called it a screamer, a shriek or a bang."[177] A "screamer, a shriek or a bang" was deemed inappropriate for serious literature and certainly unsuitable for any form of official documentation. The terms "screamer," "shriek" or "bang" provide some sense of how the exclamation mark works as a trace mark, stamped into the page, of an affective response. The exclamation mark therefore draws attention to embodied responses of the individual inscribing the mark into the official form, or what DeVere Brody more succinctly refers to as the "human 'being'."[178] The use of the exclamation mark is therefore an emotional practice that introduces affective responses to the scientific, rational discourse demanded by the C.2118 form and its frameworks.

Given its association with overt emotional expression, it should come as no surprise that exclamation marks in the sampled corpus of the First World War Diaries are rare. Their very scarcity makes them worthy of attention. They only occur three times, and all in diaries of the North Staffordshire Regiment. The first instance is oddly apt, given that the exclamation point was sometimes referred to as a "bang." It occurs in an account of the 1st Bn North Staffs of an inter-platoon rifle match "won by a Team of Drummers!"[179] The second is in an entry in the 8th Bn North Staffs for 1 July 1916 noting the weight, "69 lbs at the very least!" required by the "Light Fighting Order" carried by soldiers.[180] These exclamation marks are unnecessary in terms of conveying information, but they are a vivid indication of the response, whether of astonishment or surprise or whatever it might have been, of the individual writer.

Perhaps the most poignant use of the exclamation mark, however, is in the Diary entry for the 1st Bn North Staffs for Christmas Day of 1914. The Bn entered the trenches on the 11th December, and the entries up until the 25th are succinct, detailing sniping and shelling from both sides, and very wet conditions in the trenches, so wet, in fact, that the entry for the 14th remarks that "Rain has washed up lots of the dead we buried the last time we were here."[181] These terse entries downplay what must have been truly horrific conditions in the "knee-deep" mud and water that was causing collapses in part of the trench network. From the evening of the 22nd, however, things quieten down, and the entry for Christmas Eve notes that the Germans requested an armistice, and each side took turns singing songs. The Germans, according to this entry, "win" at this. The 25th has, characteristically for this writer, only a few lines describing the now-famous Christmas truce in which no shots were exchanged, and the Germans buried their dead, with the help of

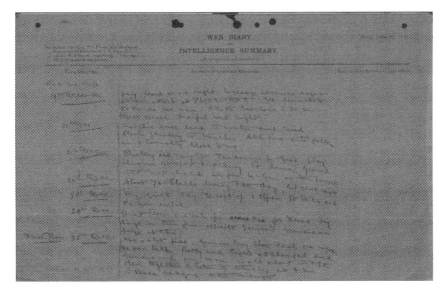

Figure 1.2 1 Battalion North Staffordshire Regiment, 25 December 1914, WO 95-1613-3, TNA, Kew

the men of the North Staffs. What prompted the inclusion of not just one, but two exclamation marks, however, is the observation that after exchanging tobacco and cigars, "Germans and our men walk about in the open together!!"[182] In this handwritten report (see Figure 1.2), the writer gives these marks the same space and weight as he would a word, so that they stand out on the page.

We can only speculate as to the actual emotion behind these double exclamation points – astonishment, disbelief, wonder – but their inclusion here, and in this way, punctures the steady stream of information almost as graphically as the Christmas truce interrupted fighting, and similarly, they are a reminder of the embodied human experiences behind the facts, figures and statistics of this conflict.

Embellished narration

Those entries that go beyond facts, figures and statistics to construct detailed narratives also serve as reminders of what being human in the writing spaces of war entailed. The accounts of the actions of the "glorious" and "gallant" 1st Bn South Staffs in 1915 mentioned earlier are examples of breaks in reporting protocols but these accounts additionally exceed the instructions of the *FSR* and the structure of the C.2118 forms to weave information into narratives embellished with Victorian ideals of war as a noble endeavour, designed to appeal to regimental pride. The entries ranging from the 25th of September

1915 to the 30th describe five heavy days of fighting for the Bn and were in all likelihood written after the events had occurred. Although the accounts contain the type of details requested by the *FSR* such as troop movements, deployment of weapons, casualty figures and weather conditions, this information is embellished with observations that are extraneous to the Army's requirements. The accounts develop into a narrative form that is far closer to a regimental history than an operational report about the Bn's involvement in the Battle of Loos.

I have already discussed how emotives such as bravery, pluck, glorious and gallant are concentrated in this particular War Diary, but it also constructs a narrative that provides insight into the performance of emotion on the battlefield, as in this description of an officer's last moments:

> 'A' Company came on splendidly ably led by Captain Henry de TRAFFORD, who behaved with the greatest coolness and daring, & would have been recommended for the D.S.O. had he not been killed. He fell on the German wire & his last words were 'Don't mind me push ahead.' Truly he & Lieut COOPER & other brave officers & N.C.Os & men, who fell on this fateful day, deserve the undying gratitude & respect of their country & their Regiment.[183]

The account is simultaneously a performance of emotion in its construction of a narrative about the cool nonchalance in the face of death so prized by the Army and the broader emotional regime, as well as a description of emotional practice on the battlefield, in which an individual performs exactly the kind of behaviour most prized by the Army. This passage exceeds the Army's requirements for information, and indicates the role played by emotion in the subjective selections made by individuals in deciding what events to include in the operational reports, and how to describe them. It is not only officers who are credited in this account with behaviour that aligns with cultural and military expectations about emotional behaviour on the battlefield. At various points in the fighting, the "magnificent old regiment" either moved "steadily forward" and "stormed" their objectives or held the line against "every description of fire." Despite heavy casualties, the "immortal old 38th Regiment, the 'Fighting Staffords'," emerged victorious, according to the narrative.[184] The Diaries of the 1st Bn Welsh Guards, also at Loos in the same period, provide a useful contrast. The entry for the 27$^{th\ of}$ September 1915 provides an extended account of the Bn's attack on Hill 70. Despite communication breakdowns and some confusion, the Bn achieves its objective before reluctantly following orders to withdraw from the line. There is no sense here, however, of forward momentum towards glory. The writer of this narrative keeps the account as factual as possible, with only one reference to "gallant acts" – "no less than 7" performed by one man, Pte. Grant.[185]

The Diary of the 1st Bn South Staffs does not conform to these kinds of standards. The sense that this account is self-consciously composing the future history of the regiment is especially evident in the few final notes in the entry from the 25th of September 1915:

> Suffice it to say that they have added a most glorious & ever memorable page to the History of their grand old regiment, & when we who, by the mercy of providence, are still alive, look on the colours of the 1st Battn (38th) South Staffordshire Regt. thickly crowded with the names of great victories won in the past two hundred years, we can feel that the most memorable & glorious incident of our lives has been the fact that we were permitted to fight side by side with our comrades in this 1st Bn South Staffordshire Regiment, a regiment of immortal fame, & with an unsurpassed record of glorious achievement.[186]

As David French points out, regimental histories generally emphasise regimental achievements, and downplay or rewrite defeats by emphasising "acts of individual and collective heroism."[187] The writer of this Diary stitches the events of the Battle of Loos into the "great victories" of the regiment's past while simultaneously looking forward to the future by suggesting that the events of the present will be considered in the same way by those who come after. These are emotional practices common to the writing of regimental histories, which were designed to "bolster pride in the regiment amongst its members, to encourage the present generation to enlist, and then to emulate the heroic deeds of their predecessors."[188] The construction of narrative in this entry deviates from the standards of scientific rigour established by the authority of the British Army's regulations governing the completion of War Diaries, but it also reveals an emotional practice that aligns it with regimental needs. The insistence on reformulating these events into a narrative that emphasises victory and bravery rather than failure and loss leverages space for a distinctly individual response within the bureaucratic confines of operational reporting, and reveals the relationship between individuals and regiment, and how this relationship works in the broader context of the Army as a whole.

The kind of embellished narrative contained in the diaries of the 1st Bn South Staffs stands out because it is rare. But the very process of eliminating emotion from narratives in the reports is a kind of emotional practice. For the war memoirs that were published after the First World War, the challenge was

> to make sense of events that seemed chaotic, traumatic, and often difficult to recall with any degree of clarity. With remembering and narrating came an intellectual process of creating linear stories from disjointed memories, attempts to make sense of a world war that destroyed as much a person's ability to think clearly as it did anything else.[189]

For the writers of the Unit War Diaries, the process was sometimes much the same, even if they did not have the luxury of a significant temporal distance between them and the events they either witnessed or experienced or were called upon to report. The process of crafting a linear narrative from chaotic events in some reports imposes order on the past and enables the writers to make sense of them and to try to identify what went wrong. The Diary of the 1st Bn Cheshires, for example, detailing the events on 3rd September 1916, when the Bn was involved in the attack on Falfemont Farm during the Battle of the Somme, recounts a series of failed attempts to advance and take the German position, hampered by a lack of clear information and miscommunications. Only one line, "Casualties very heavy," gives some sense of the cost of these failures.[190] The entries in this diary are not filled with emotives, and they do not attempt to convert failures into victories, but the organisation of the events into a linear narrative imposes a retrospective sequence of cause and effect on moments that were turbulent and entangled. The rational restructuring of events in narratives like these in the Unit War Diaries are as much a process of rendering moments into something understandable, and integrating them into existing frameworks of meaning, as the more emotional narrative of the 1st Bn South Staffs.

The personal diaries maintained in the trenches by individual soldiers were "spaces in which men could record those reactions to war experiences in which they displayed fear and weakness."[191] Unit War Diaries, as official reports, served a different purpose, but they must also be acknowledged as spaces in which men recorded their reactions to war experiences, even if through the filters and structures of institutional regulations and forms. Although they were not spaces in which fear and weakness were made manifest, they were not without emotion. On the contrary, Unit War Diaries reveal the emotional practices at work in the writing spaces of the First World War. The stoicism and cheerfulness so valued in the broader culture is deliberately emphasised by some writers, while difficulties and trauma are downplayed through understatement, or, as in the case of some of the entries, through emotives that elide the brutality of warfare as much as the sparse accounts that adhere to those restrictions. Elsewhere, instances of repetition and the use of punctuation manage to push at the boundaries imposed by both military and cultural emotional regimes to introduce traces of embodied affective responses, and hint at some of the real strain and trauma of the experiences of industrial warfare. This is not to suggest that any of these reports self-consciously set out to challenge the structures imposed by the Army's instructions for completion of C.2118, but they all provide examples of how individual responses to warfare collide with the formal constraints of bureaucratic processes to generate not just data or information, but accounts that bear the material, mediated traces of the emotions of the writers. They reveal the C.2118 form not as a neutral space for data or information, but as a site of contestation between individuality, bureaucratic systems of containment and control, and the chaos of war. While individual war memoirs may be far more overtly emotional, Unit War Diaries should not be regarded as dispassionate, neutral sets of information. Tracking emotion in Unit War Diaries has revealed that they occupy a unique position somewhere between official document and individual memoir.

Unit War Diaries, as the *FSR* intended, were significant to the subsequent writing of the Official Histories of the First World War. But the sheer bulk of the records posed some unexpected challenges in terms of gathering information for historiography, while the Army's restraints on their content proved to be less than ideal for historians. A question arises, therefore, about whether these documents did, in fact, fulfil their primary purpose of furnishing an "accurate record" for historiography.[192]

War Diaries and the official histories

In 1906, in the wake of the South African and Russo-Japanese Wars, Lord Esher proposed establishing a section within the Committee of Imperial Defence that would co-ordinate the collection of material across the different branches of the military, to ensure that the "lessons of these conflicts" could be organised and made available to military strategists.[193] The idea of 'lessons learned' lay at the heart of the Historical Section's subsequent activities, including the massive undertaking of producing the Official Histories of The First World War. Given that the primary purposes of the Unit War Diaries as outlined in the *FSR* was to provide information for the histories of the war and to allow the Army to wage war more effectively, these documents were important for the writing of the Official Histories, and also featured prominently in the Army's organisational strategies (discussed in more detail in Chapter 2) for moving forward after the First World War.

Even before the end of the First World War, military historians at Historical Section were discovering that gathering, managing and identifying information from Unit War Diaries and other official documents posed its own problems. The gathering of the reports began as early as 1915, when Captain C.T. Atkinson was dispatched to collect Unit War Diaries from the Western Front. Even at that early stage in the war, in a letter on the progress of Historical Section Atkinson noted that "the quantity of the material available is very large and naturally tends to increase."[194] Yet simultaneously, despite the proliferation of paperwork, many records had been lost, and in other cases, units had simply been unable to produce them due to the intensity of the fighting or other difficulties. In terms of the content of the records, the Army's insistence on brevity, while perhaps good for military purposes, was not so useful for historians. "Such an entry as 'August 26. Battle of Ligny: heavy fighting all day' does not assist the historian much," wrote Atkinson in the same report. Embellished narration, which the *FSR* had discouraged, rather than concise statements of fact, turned out to be of more value for historiography, and Atkinson went on to express gratitude "to those diary-writers who have managed in such adverse circumstances to put together [...] very full and precise accounts." Ultimately, Atkinson noted that "while the Diaries will enable one to put together a fairly complete account of what happened, with, in many cases, a fair amount of evidence as to how things happened, they will not allow one to say why things happened."[195] The de-narrativised information so valued by the Army – dates, times, places, weather and casualty figures – was of limited use in explaining the reasons behind events. Atkinson therefore advocated consulting a range of documents in conjunction with the Unit War Diaries to develop a more complete picture of events. The fact that Historical Section did not consider Sir John Fortescue's interim history (which was intended to be a shorter, more accessible version published for the public) sufficiently comprehensive because it was based solely on Unit War Diaries is further suggestive of their sense of the limits of these documents.

The First World War Unit War Diaries constituted at once too little information, but also too much, as the sheer volume of this material posed serious problems of organisation for the Historical Section. By the start of 1917, Atkinson, with very little clerical assistance, had managed to extract and compile 160 "Diary Units" (the complete diaries of one Division for a month), but around 1,000 from the Western Front and the Mediterranean still needed organising.[196] Two years later, after Atkinson had been replaced by Sir James Edmonds, a report from Historical Section estimated that it would "take two officers at least a year to get the War Diaries into order."[197] In the end, Historical Section was faced with managing a corpus of over 25 million pages, including Unit War Diaries, which Edmonds estimated would take his staff nine years just to sort into a system.[198] In addition to ordering and managing documentation, Edmonds notes that the Branch had to support a wide range of requests for information from Staff Colleges, divisional historians, the Imperial War Graves Commission and others. The challenge was such that Edmonds compared it to having "to work at what amounts nearly to war pressure."[199]

While Atkinson mourned the lack of detail in Unit War Diaries, Edmonds cast doubt on their value as accurate records. According to Andrew Green, Edmonds encouraged his team to concentrate not so much on the Diaries of the higher commands, but on those in the field, which Edmonds felt were more accurate than those of Headquarters.[200] Green recounts how Edmonds had uncovered evidence of a narrative being amended in the War Diaries by Sir Archibald Montgomery-Massingberd to smooth over a resistance to General Haig's orders in the Somme, but the diaries of subordinate formations told a different story.[201] Edmonds' insistence on relying on the diaries of the lower formations is suggestive of a belief that those removed from events could not necessarily be relied upon to produce reliable accounts, not only because they did not have all the information, but also because of the impulse to protect reputations, both personal and regimental. Even David French, who is more critical of Edmonds than Green, credits Edmonds "for his determination not to trust naively to the documents" and for supplementing the information they contained by consulting and interviewing as many surviving participants as he could.[202] Information in the First World War Unit War Diaries, despite the Army's best efforts at containment and control via the instructions in the *FSR* and the official C.2118 forms, was in the end uneven at best, and unreliable and unpredictable at worst.

Given the volume of documentation, as well as issues with underfunding and understaffing, it is perhaps unsurprising that the Historical Section took 33 years to produce the 28 volumes on military operations in the First World War.[203] A complex and sometimes contentious undertaking, the Official Histories navigated a difficult path between appealing to a public readership in some volumes while in others providing military personnel with information that would allow them to learn from the conflict.[204] Like the official documents they are drawn from, there is a perception of the Histories as dry and dispassionate accounts of the conflict. John Keegan, for example, credits the compilers for having "achieved the remarkable feat of writing an exhaustive account of one of the world's greatest tragedies without the display of any emotion at all."[205] Andrew Green's comprehensive investigation into the writing of the Official Histories challenges the notion of them as "bland and sterile," as well as perspectives of the Histories as a "deliberately partial, misleading and self-justificatory account written in defence of the military establishment."[206] My interest lies not with their ideological or political agenda, but with the resonances between the Official Histories and the emotional tenor of the Unit War Diaries. As in the Unit War Diaries, it is not so much that the Official Histories are emotionless, but that specific emotions are emphasised over others.

Like the Unit War Diaries of the 1st Bn South Staffs discussed in the previous section, the accounts of Loos in September 1915, and of the Somme in 1918, both draw on the concept of gallantry as an emotive used to dignify sacrifice.[207] In the account of the Somme especially, gallantry surfaces almost always in reference to situations in which battalions and companies were eventually overwhelmed. While all are poignant, one of the most moving is the account of the "very gallant defence" of the Englien Redoubt in March 1918 by the 2/4 Oxfordshire and Bucks Light Infantry, which waited in vain for permission to withdraw until eventually being overwhelmed.[208] Gallantry is mentioned only twice in reference to actions of other Allied forces – once for the French Army and once for the actions of a South African division in a footnote[209] – which suggests it is associated with British national identity. As in the Unit War Diaries, there is little mention of fear in either of these particularly brutal battles. On the contrary, Edmonds takes great care to emphasise that the spirit of the British Army was unbroken in both. Of Loos, he writes that "Notwithstanding the stalemate and the heavy losses, the battle of Loos was far from shaking the faith of the officers and men of the B.E.F. in their power to break through the German line: indeed, their confidence was only increased thereby."[210] He prefaces the account of the Somme by asserting that "the splendid young manhood which filled the ranks was never beaten, never demoralised by retreat, and it may be left to the imagination how it would have fought had it been fully trained."[211] As in the Unit War Diaries, stoicism and courage prevail. Fear barely registers.

There is, however, some acknowledgement of the chaotic nature of both the battlefields of Loos and those of the Somme. Edmonds describes these in sometimes evocative terms, as in this account of the disarray within the Third and Fifth Armies in the German offensive of March 1918:

> No words also could convey any picture of the confusion of the night of the 23rd/24th March: troops wandering about to find their brigades and battalions, in an area without landmarks, devastated a year before by the enemy; dumps burning and exploding; gaps in the line; the Germans attacking almost behind the V. Corps front; the atmosphere charged with uncertainty, and full of the wildest reports and rumours.[212]

But Edmonds always emphasises that order is restored, as it is in this instance. Far from being traumatised, the vast number of "stragglers," separated from their units and wandering through this nightmarish landscape, require only "a little rest," after which they are happy to answer "the call of any officer to follow him back into action."[213] Control is reasserted over traffic on the roads, supply chains and the clearing of casualties.[214] Even the fact that the BEF was forced to abandon caches of food is turned to an advantage, because the account argues that the discovery of luxury provisions by the Germans would have confounded German propaganda that British forces were starving.[215]

The Official Histories thus echo the emphasis on order and control that is evident in the First World War Unit War Diaries examined in this chapter. Like the First World War Unit War Diaries examined here, the Official Histories smooth over the emotional impact and chaos of the conflict, and therefore ultimately delimit the kinds of lessons that can be learned about these dimensions of modern warfare. The outlines of the foundations of two of the central myths that emerge from this war are traceable in the corpus of Unit War Diaries examined in this chapter and in the Official Histories: the idea of noble but doomed sacrifice, and of "daring stoicism in the face of adversity."[216] These parallels between Unit War Diaries and the Official Histories reveal the recursive relationship between written records and historiography. Despite Historical Section's identification of Unit War Diaries as just one source (and not necessarily the best) among many, they both echo and perpetuate older ideologies associated with the purpose and nature of warfare. In the Official Histories, as in the First World War corpus, rational systems of organisation hold firm against the chaos of war, and fear is almost entirely smoothed over in narratives of fortitude and pluck, which are identified as implicitly British traits.

Conclusion

This chapter demonstrated how the organisation of the British Army and its approach to war along bureaucratic principles at the turn of the Twentieth Century created a framework designed to delimit and manage conflict according to rational and scientific practices. In response to challenges posed by new technologies and cultural shifts during the industrial era, the Army established processes for operational reporting intended to produce information that would allow the organisation to measure efficiencies and calculate gains and losses along much the same lines as if war were a form of industrial labour. At a time when "trustworthy knowledge" had come to be understood only as that established "by methods that neutralised the values and emotions of individual scientists,"[217] the application of bureaucratic and rationalist principles to operational reporting reduced war to numbers, times, conditions, events. The practices of operational reporting instituted prior to the First World War and deployed for the first time in this conflict provide the foundations of a long-standing methodological approach that emphasises coherence, clarity and precision above all else in constructing information about warfare that is of use to the Army and to historians. I will continue to interrogate this methodology in Chapter 2, but the extent to which these practices have become normalised can be gauged by the tendency not only in the Official Histories but also in much military history and training to attempt to establish logical lines of cause-and-effect and to identify patterns on the battlefield, despite the fact that imposing order in this way "can lead to blending, smoothing, and rationalising which, intentionally or not, may produce distortion."[218]

While the emphasis on order and rationality is part of military strategies for transforming warmaking into an activity as organised as any other form of labour, it also results in the marginalisation of complexity and chaos, which, as Roger Beaumont observes, become "treated more like a frieze, or as background noise or static" rather than as essential dimensions of combat.[219] These are not neutral practices, and whether deliberate or not, the strategies involved in the transformation of war into work activated an ideology that smoothed over chaos, horror, trauma and the immense destructive power of industrial warfare. Because authority lies with the procedures, rules and formal qualities of operational reporting, rather than with the individual, the system attempts to subsume individuality within a discursive network of "pristine administrative valves and conduits that channel and unleash the flow of death and destruction."[220] The bulk of the corpus of the First World War Unit War Diaries bears testament to the power of this network, with much of the reporting conforming to the standards of storyless information and providing sparse, dry accounts of conflict.

It is thus all too easy to conflate War Diaries with information, and to ignore their material structure, precisely because the Army's own discursive and organisational systems identify them as accurate records containing facts, figures and details important for history and for the Army's operational effectiveness. Ignoring the history of Unit War Diaries as material, mediated artefacts has led to the "cultural and social privileging" not only of technologies such as the steam train and the telegraph,[221] which occupy many of the discussions on command, control and communications as well as on Information Management, but also of the rationalist perspectives and ideologies inherent in the very structures of operational reporting. The principles governing the completion of C.2118 acknowledge the importance of individual assessment

64 *Unit War Diaries in the First World War*

and choices in reporting, but implicit in concessions to individual judgement is the assumption that decisions will be made according to rational principles, which by the end of the Nineteenth Century were considered "objective and universal."[222]

However, the combination of material and close analysis undertaken by this chapter has countered these tendencies and revealed that the system is not quite as pristine as the Army might hope. The indelible pencil, an industrial technology designed to maximise efficiencies in the production of paperwork, allowed soldiers to inscribe their individual presence into the rote structure of the official form. The handwritten diaries are material traces of the physical presence of the otherwise largely anonymous clerks, subalterns and junior officers in the writing spaces of war. Illegibility, gaps in the record, hasty scrawls and errors are all indications of operational reporting in the First World War as an embodied practice, and they disrupt the smooth production of information. Furthermore, the very act of recording observations is not passive but an active process involving "selection and interpretation."[223] This process, as three decades of research into cognition and emotion has demonstrated, is powerfully shaped by the emotions of the observer.[224] While it is impossible for us to determine with any certainty what emotions guided the choices made by the writers of the War Diaries, investigating operational reporting as an emotional practice involved tracking observable traces of emotion in Unit War Diaries – emotives, punctuation and embellished narrative – to reveal how individual soldiers negotiated the acute disjuncture between the experiences of conflict and the bureaucratic controls imposed on how those experiences should be recorded. Instances of emotional practice in Unit War Diaries not only disrupt the flow of information, they also transform the nature of what is reported and push against the channels created by the valves and circuits of operational reporting systems. Tracking observable traces of emotion in Unit War Diaries provided a vivid reminder of the human beings interpolated in the technologies and forces at work in the writing spaces of war and revealed that operational reporting is as much a product of emotional embodied practices as personal memoirs or war poetry.

The next chapter (Chapter 2) investigates how the introduction of the typewriter in the late 1800s revolutionised communications not only by speeding up the creation of documents, but also by unifying their production, and how this machine for writing became an essential tool of warfare in the Second World War. It investigates the significance of the typewriter to the British military and interrogates the notion of standardisation in operational reporting in the context of a conflict which exceeded even the 'War to End all Wars' in terms of complexity and unpredictability.

Notes

1 Ernst Jünger, *Feuer und Blut* (Magdeburg, 1925) 18 quoted in Eric J. Leed, *No Man's Land: Combat and Identity in World War I* (Cambridge: Cambridge

University Press, 1979), 11. The English translation of Jünger's book does not appear to have this quotation.
2 James Beniger, *The Control Revolution: Technological and Economic Origins of the Information Society* (Cambridge MA: Harvard University Press, 1986), 220.
3 For a more detailed discussion of the developing interconnections between science and industry during The First World War, see Anthony Giddens, *The Nation State and Violence* (Cambridge University Press, Cambridge, 1985): 232–233.
4 For examinations of the impact of such technologies on warfare, see Jonathan Bailey, "The First World War and the Birth of the Modern Style of Warfare," in *The Dynamics of Military Revolution 1300–2050*, eds. MacGregor Knox and Williamson Murray (Cambridge: Cambridge University Press, 2001): 132–53; and Albert Palazzo, *Seeking Victory on the Western Front: The British Army and Chemical Warfare in World War I* (Lincoln, NE: University of Nebraska Press, 2000).
5 For a full discussion of how the railways transformed warfare, see Geoffrey L. Herrera, "Inventing the Railroad and Rifle Revolution: Information, Military Innovation and the Rise of Germany," *Journal of Strategic Studies* 27, no. 2 (2004): 243–271.
6 For an excellent study on communications by the BEF, see Brian Hall, *Communication and British Operations on the Western Front* (Cambridge: Cambridge University Press, 2017).
7 General Staff, *Field Service Regulations, Part II: Organisation and Administration*, 1909 (London: HMSO, Reprinted, with Amendments, 1913), 175.
8 General Staff, *FSR II*, 174–175.
9 Paddy Griffith, *Battle Tactics of the Western Front: The British Army's Art of Attack, 1916–18* (Yale: Yale University Press, 1994), 187.
10 Dennis E. Showalter, "Information Capabilities and Military Revolutions: The Nineteenth-Century Experience," *Journal of Strategic Studies* 27, no. 2 (2004): 234.
11 Hall, *Communication*, 306.
12 Palazzo, *Seeking Victory*, 9
13 Jennifer Slack, David Miller and Jeffrey Doak, "The Technical Communicator as Author: Meaning, Power, Authority," *Journal of Business and Technical Communication* 7, no. 1 (January 1993): 33.
14 See for example Christopher Dandeker, *Surveillance, Power and Modernity: Bureaucracy and Discipline from 1700 to the Present Day* (Cambridge: Polity Press, 1990) and Brian Hall, "The British Army, Information Management and the First World War: Revolution in Military Affairs," *Journal of Strategic Studies* 41, no. 7 (2018): 1001–1030.
15 The National Archives, "How to Look for Records of British Army War Diaries 1914–1922," https://www.nationalarchives.gov.uk/help-with-your-research/research-guides/british-army-war-diaries-1914-1922.
16 Hall, *Communication*, 19.
17 Stephanie Downes, Andrew Lynch and Katrina O'Loughlin, "Introduction – War as Emotion: Cultural Fields of Conflict and Feeling," in *Emotions and War: Medieval to Romantic Literature*, eds. Stephanie Downes, Andrew Lynch and Katrina O'Loughlin (New York: Palgrave Macmillan, 2015), 10.
18 Monique Scheer, "Are Emotions a Kind of Practice (and is That What Makes Them Have a History?)? A Bourdieuian Approach to Understanding Emotion," *History and Theory* 51, no. 2 (2012): 193–220.
19 Max Weber, *Sociological Writings*, ed. Wolf Hydebrand (New York: Continuum, 2006), 77.
20 See Christopher Dandeker *Surveillance, Power* for a detailed examination of these intersections.
21 Dandeker, *Surveillance, Power*, 9.
22 Weber, *Sociological Writings*, 77.

66 Unit War Diaries in the First World War

23 Weber, *Sociological Writings*, 78.
24 Ronald Day, *The Modern Invention of Information: Discourse, History and Power* (Southern Illinois University Press, 2001), 8.
25 Michel De Certeau, *The Practice of Everyday Life*, trans. Steven Rendell (Berkeley: University of California Press, 1984), 134.
26 Luke Tredinnick, "Rewriting History: The Information Age and the Knowable Past," in *Information History in the Modern World: Histories of the Information Age*, ed. Toni Weller (New York: Palgrave McMillan, 2011), 182.
27 Toni Weller, "Introduction: Information History," in Weller, *Information History*, 5.
28 Weller, "Introduction," 5.
29 Neil Postman, *Building a Bridge to the 18th Century: How the Past can Improve our Future* (New York: Vintage Books, 1999), 75.
30 Daniel Headrick, *When Information Came of Age: Technologies of Knowledge in the Age of Reason and Revolution, 1700–1850* (Oxford: Oxford University Press, 2000), 6, emphasis in original.
31 Postman, *Building a Bridge*, 76.
32 Weber, *Sociological Writings*, 79.
33 For an explanation of the gradual separation of reason and emotion, see Alison Jaggar, "Love and Knowledge: Emotion in Feminist Epistemology," *Inquiry* 32, no. 2 (1989): 151–176.
34 David Dery, "'Papereality' and Learning in Bureaucratic Organizations," *Administration and Society*, 29, no. 6 (1998): 678.
35 Lisa Gitelman, *Paper Knowledge: Toward a Media History of Documents* (Durham and London: Duke University Press, 2014); Dery, "Papereality."
36 A British Officer, "The Literature of the South African War, 1899–1902," *The American Historical Review* 12, no. 2 (January 1907): 300.
37 Antoine Bousquet, *The Scientific Way of Warfare: Order and Chaos on the Battlefields of Modernity* (London: Hurst Publishers, 2009), 3–4.
38 G. F.R. Henderson, *The Science of War: A Collection of Essays and Lectures, 1891–1903* (London: Longmans Green, 1912), 399.
39 Henderson, *The Science of War*, 399.
40 For good explanations of the historical aversion to doctrine in the British Army, see Aimée Fox, *Learning to Fight: Military Innovation and Change in the British Army, 1914–1918* (Cambridge: Cambridge University Press, 2017) and Palazzo, *Seeking Victory*, 8–9.
41 General Staff, *Field Service Regulations, Part I: Operations*, 1909 (London: HMSO, Reprinted, with Amendments, 1913), 2.
42 General Staff, *FSRII*, 2.
43 Fox, *Learning to Fight*, 32.
44 General Staff, *FSRI*, 14.
45 Fox, *Learning to Fight*, 34.
46 General Staff, *FSRI*, 22.
47 General Staff, *FSRI*, 22.
48 General Staff, *FSRI*, 22.
49 General Staff, *FSRI*, 22.
50 General Staff, *FSRI*, 22.
51 General Staff, *FSRII*, 162–163.
52 General Staff, *FSRII*, 162.
53 For a good overview of the varying histories of the South African Wars and the variations in their quality and authority, see Peter Donaldson, *Remembering the South African War: Britain and the Memory of the Anglo-Boer War, from 1899 to the Present* (Liverpool: Liverpool University Press, 2013), 132–151.
54 General Staff, *FSRII*, 174.
55 Day, *The Modern Invention*, 38.

56 General Staff, *FSRII*, 175.
57 Margaret, Dale, "Learning Organisations," in *Managing Learning*, eds. Christopher Mabey and Paul Iles (London: Thomson Learning, 1994), 29.
58 Hall, "The British Army," 1022.
59 General Staff, *FSRII*, 177.
60 General Staff, *FSRII*, 177.
61 General Staff, *FSRII*, 176.
62 General Staff, *FSRII*, 176, note to point v.
63 Fox, *Learning to Fight*, 64.
64 G.S.O., foreword to *G.H.Q. (Montreuil-Sur-Mer)* (London: Philip Allan & Co., 1920).
65 Paul Stiff, Paul Dobraszczyk and Mike Esbester, "Designing and Gathering Information: Perspectives on Nineteenth-Century Forms," in Weller, *Information History*, 83.
66 Branches and Services: Director of Printing and Stationery Service, WO 95-81-4, The National Archives (hereafter TNA), Kew.
67 Gitelman, *Paper Knowledge*, 32.
68 Director of Printing and Stationery Service, WO 95-81-4 (31 December 1917).
69 Director of Printing and Stationery Service, WO 95-81-4 (31 December 1917).
70 Gitelman, *Paper Knowledge*, 23.
71 Jay David Bolter, *Writing Space: Computers, Hypertext, and the Remediation of Print*, 2nd Ed. (Mahwah NJ: Lawrence Erlbaum Associates, 2000), 21.
72 Gitelman *Paper Knowledge*, 49.
73 Slack, Miller and Doak, "The Technical Communicator."
74 Michel Foucault, *Society Must be Defended: Lectures at the Collége de France, 1975–76*, English Series ed. Arnold I. Davidson, trans. David Macey (New York: Picador, 2003), 124.
75 John Terraine, ed., *General Jack's Diary: War on the Western Front 1914–1918* (London: Cassell, 2001) 57–58.
76 Director of Printing and Stationery Service, WO 95-81-49 (9 January 1915).
77 Director of Printing and Stationery Service, WO 95-81-49.
78 Director of Printing and Stationery Service, WO 95 81-1 (24 July 1915).
79 Director of Printing and Stationery Service, WO 95 81-1 (11 February 1918).
80 Bolter, *Writing Space*, 34.
81 Henri-Jean Martin, *The History and Power of Writing*, trans. Lydia G. Cochrane (Chicago: University Press of Chicago, 1994); Tamara Plakins Thornton, *Handwriting in America: A Cultural History* (New Haven CT and London: Yale University Press, 1996).
82 Bolter, *Writing Space*, 37.
83 Susan Zieger, *The Mediated Mind: Affect, Ephemera and Consumerism in the Nineteenth Century* (New York: Fordham University Press, 2018), 99.
84 Nigel Hall, "The Materiality of Letter Writing: A Nineteenth Century Perspective," in *Letter Writing as a Social Practice*, eds. David Barton and Nigel Hall (Amsterdam and Philadelphia CA: John Benjamins Publishing Company, 2000), 96.
85 Waterman's Pen Advert, *Daily Mail*, 9 November, 1917.
86 Onoto Pen Advert, *Illustrated London News*, 16 December 1916.
87 Swan Pen advert, 1915.
88 Plakins Thornton, *Handwriting*, xiii.
89 Charles Bazerman, "Introduction," in *Handbook of Research on Writing: History, Society, School, Individual, Text*, ed. Charles Bazerman (New York: Routledge, 2013), 1.
90 Henry Petroski, *The Pencil: A History of Design and Circumstance* (London: Faber, 1990), 188.
91 The National Archives, "How to Look for Records."

92 1 Battalion Cheshire Regiment, August 1914–February 1917, WO 95-1571-1; 1/5th Battalion Sherwood Foresters (Nottinghamshire and Derbyshire Regiment), March 1915–May 1919, WO 95-2695-1; 1 Battalion Welsh Guards, August 1915–February 1916, WO 95-1224-1, TNA, Kew.
93 1 Battalion Welsh Guards, WO 95-1224-1-3.
94 Terraine, *General Jack's Diary*, 116; 142.
95 2 Battalion Sherwood Foresters (Nottingham and Derbyshire Regiment), August–December 1916, WO 95-1624-2, TNA, Kew.
96 1 Battalion North Staffordshire Regiment, November 1915–December 1917, WO 95-2213-1, TNA, Kew.
97 1/5th Battalion Sherwood Foresters (Nottinghamshire and Derbyshire Regiment) WO 95-2695-1, Notes Written by T.F.C. Downman, June 1918.
98 Downes, Lynch and O'Loughlin, "Introduction," 4.
99 Anna Wierzbicka, "Talking about Emotions: Semantics, Culture, and Cognition," *Cognition and Emotion* 6, no. 3–4 (1992): 287, emphasis in original.
100 Scheer, "Are Emotions," 206.
101 Scheer, "Are Emotions," 200.
102 Scheer, "Are Emotions," 217.
103 Scheer here draws on Pierre Bourdieu's notion of *habitus* as social structures in which individuals are positioned, but which individuals, via their own perceptions and actions, also help to shape and maintain. The concept of habitus connects the body to the specific social temporalities it inhabits (Scheer, "Are Emotions," 201).
104 Thomas Dixon, *From Passions to Emotions: The Creation of a Secular Psychological Category* (Cambridge: Cambridge University Press, 2003), 109.
105 Charles Darwin, *The Expression of the Emotions in Man and Animals* (London: John Murray, 1872), 366.
106 Thomas Dixon, *Weeping Britannia: Portrait of a Nation in Tears* (Oxford: Oxford University Press, 2015), 201.
107 Dixon, *Weeping Britannia*, 202.
108 See John Lewis-Stempel (2010) for an investigation of how Britain's public schools came to provide the Army with its officers. As the war progressed, and following heavy casualties among officers, there was more class differentiation as officers were commissioned from other ranks to make up the losses.
109 Downes, Lynch and O'Loughlin, "Introduction," 10.
110 John Keegan, *The Face of Battle: A Study of Agincourt, Waterloo and the Somme* (London: Penguin, 1978), 18.
111 Keegan, *The Face of Battle*, 20.
112 William M. Reddy, *The Navigation of Feeling: A Framework* (Cambridge: Cambridge University Press, 2001), 124–125.
113 Stephen Fineman, "Emotions and Organisational Control," in *Emotions at Work: Theory, Research and Applications for Management*, eds. Roy Payne and Carly Cooper (Chichester: Wiley & Sons, 2001), 234.
114 Stefan Collini, "The Idea of 'Character' in Victorian Political Thought," *Transactions of the Royal Historical Society* 35 (1985): 33.
115 Nick Taylor, "The Return of Character: Parallels Between Late-Victorian and Twenty-First Century Discourses," *Sociological Research Online* 23, no. 2 (2018): 404.
116 Ian Beckett, Timothy Bowman and Mark Connelly, *The British Army and the First World War* (Cambridge: Cambridge University Press, 2017), 5.
117 John Springhall, "The Boy Scouts, Class and Militarism in Relation to British Youth Movements," *International Review of Social History* 16, no. 2 (1971): 127.
118 Collini, "The Idea of 'Character'," 48.
119 General Staff, War Office, *Training and Manoeuvre Regulations* (London: HMSO, 1913), 20.

120 General Staff, *Training*, 20.
121 Fineman, "Emotions," 220.
122 General Staff, War Office, *Infantry Training: 4-Company Organization* (London: HMSO, 1914), 1.
123 General Staff, *Infantry Training*, 2.
124 General Staff, *Infantry Training*, 2.
125 General Staff, *Infantry Training*, 2.
126 David French, *Military Identities: The Regimental System, the British Army, and the British People c.1870–2000* (Oxford: Oxford University Press, 2005), 93.
127 French, *Military Identities*, 94.
128 For a more detailed discussion of training in the British Army in the years leading up to the First World War, see Timothy Bowman, *The Edwardian Army: Recruiting, Training, and Deploying the British Army, 1902–1914* (Oxford: Oxford University Press, 2012), 64–105.
129 For more on this process and its challenges, see Peter Simkins, *Kitchener's Army: The Raising of the New Armies, 1914–16* (Manchester and New York: Manchester University Press, 1988) and Peter Doyle, "'Kitchener's Mob': Myth and Reality in Raising the New Army, 1914–15," in *Redcoats to Tommies: The Experience of the British Soldier from the Eighteenth Century*, eds. Kevin Linch and Matthew Lord (Woodbridge: Boydell & Brewer, 2021), 58–82.
130 Imperial War Museum, "Voices of the First World War: Training for War."
131 John Bourne, "The British Working Man in Arms," In *Facing Armageddon: The First World War Experience*, eds. Hugh Cecil, and Peter Liddle (London: Pen and Sword Paperbacks, 1996), 336–35; Beckett, Bowman and Connelly, *The British Army*.
132 John Bourne, "The British Working Man in Arms," in *Facing Armageddon: The First World War Experience*, eds. Hugh Cecil and Peter Liddle (London: Pen and Sword Select, 1996), 342.
133 Ian Beckett, Timothy Bowman and Mark Connelly, *The British Army and the First World War* (Cambridge: Cambridge University Press, 2017), 146.
134 Harry Smith, Imperial War Museum, "Voices of the First World War: Training for War".
135 *The War Illustrated*, "The Dauntless Courage of a Highland Laddie, Brutal Cowardice of a Baffled Hun Officer," 5 February 1916, 588–599.
136 The War Illustrated, "The Fear of Being Afraid," *The War Illustrated*, The Observation Post, 26 January, 1916, xciv.
137 Scheer, "Are Emotions," 216.
138 Scheer, "Are Emotions," 218.
139 Scheer, "Are Emotions," 218.
140 Reddy, *The Navigation of Feeling*.
141 Reddy, *The Navigation*, 105.
142 I will go into this process in more detail in Chapter 3, but the process of tagging emotives involved myself and the transcriber who worked on the Diaries, Dr Stevie Docherty.
143 Roger Beaumont, *War, Chaos and History* (Westport CT: Praeger, 1994), 22.
144 1/5th Battalion Sherwood Foresters (Nottinghamshire and Derbyshire Regiment), WO 95-2695-1.
145 1 Battalion South Staffordshire Regiment, 1914 August–1915 December, TNA, Kew.
146 1 Battalion Welsh Guards, WO 95-1224-1.
147 David Sharp, "Shocked, Shot and Pardoned," *The Lancet* 368, no. 9540 (16 September 2006).
148 Jaggar, "Love and Knowledge," 166.

149 Joanna Bourke, *Dismembering the Male: Men's Bodies, Britain and the Great War* (London: Reaktion Books, 1996), 97.
150 1 Battalion Cheshire Regiment, WO 95-1571-1; 1 Battalion Welsh Guards, WO 95-1224-1.
151 2 Battalion Worcestershire Regiment, 1 August 1914–31 December 1915, WO 95-1351-1, TNA, Kew.
152 2 Battalion Worcestershire Regiment, WO 95-1351-1.
153 Carl von Clausewitz, *On War*, ed. and trans. Michael Howard and Peter Paret (1832; Princeton NJ: Princeton University Press, 1989), 101.
154 1 Battalion Welsh Guards, 27 September 1915, WO 95-1224-1.
155 71 Infantry Brigade: 2 Battalion Sherwood Foresters (Nottinghamshire and Derbyshire Regiment), 1917, WO 95-1624-3, TNA, Kew.
156 10 Battalion Worcestershire Regiment, 1 July 1915–28 February 1918, WO 95-2086-2, TNA, Kew.
157 10 Battalion Worcestershire Regiment, 22 July 1916, WO 95-2086-2.
158 1 Battalion Welsh Guards, WO 95-1224-1.
159 1 Battalion South Staffordshire Regiment, 1 August 1914–31 December 1915, WO 95-1664-2, TNA, Kew.
160 Scheer, "Are Emotions," 206.
161 1 Battalion South Staffordshire Regiment, WO 95-1664-2.
162 Laura Runge, "Beauty and Gallantry: A Model of Polite Conversation Revisited," *Eighteenth-Century Life* 25, no. 1 (Winter 2001): 43.
163 Matthew Lord, *British Concepts of Heroic 'Gallantry' and the Sixties Transition: The Politics of Medals* (New York: Routledge, 2021), 6.
164 Graham Dawson, *Soldier Heroes: British Adventure, Empire and the Imagining of Masculinities* (London and New York: Routledge, 1994), 130.
165 1 Battalion South Staffordshire Regiment, WO 95-1664-2.
166 Robert Graves, *Goodbye to All That: An Autobiography* (London: Jonathan Cape, 1929). See also the account of Frank Richards, Graves' comrade, who also wrote about Loos in *Old Soldiers Never Die* new ed. (1933; Sussex: Naval and Military Press, 2009) 114–134.
167 Graves, *Goodbye*, 196.
168 General Staff, *FSR1*, 22.
169 1 Battalion South Staffordshire Regiment, WO 95-1664-2.
170 Roland Leighton to Vera Brittain, 11 September 1915 in *Letters from a Lost Generation: First World War Letters of Vera Brittain and Four Friends: Roland Leighton, Edward Brittain, Victor Richardson, Geoffrey Thurlow*, eds. Alan Bishop and Mark Bostridge (London: Abacus, 2004), 165.
171 Ian Isherwood, *Remembering the Great War: Writing and Publishing the Experiences of World War I* (London: I.B. Tauris, 2017), 17.
172 Downes, Lynch and O'Loughlin, "Introduction," 3.
173 Jennifer DeVere Brody, *Punctuation: Art, Politics, and Play* (Durham and London: Duke University Press, 2008), 7.
174 Mary Hiatt, *The Way Women Write* (New York: Teacher's College Press, 1977), 39.
175 Lynne Truss, *Eats, Shoots & Leaves: The Zero Tolerance Approach to Punctuation* (London: Fourth Estate, 2009), 135.
176 H.W. Fowler, *A Dictionary of Modern English Usage* (London: Oxford University Press, 1926), s.v. "Exclamation".
177 Geoff Nunberg, "After Years of Restraint, a Linguist says 'Yes!' to the Exclamation Point," *Npr.org*. 13 June 2017.
178 DeVere Brody, *Punctuation*, 6.
179 1 Battalion North Staffordshire Regiment, 1 November 1915–31 May 1919, WO 95-2213-1, TNA, Kew.

180 8 Battalion North Staffordshire Regiment, July 1915–January 1918, WO 95-2085-2, TNA, Kew.
181 1 Battalion North Staffordshire Regiment, November 1914–October 1915, WO 95-1613-3, TNA, Kew.
182 1 Battalion North Staffordshire Regiment, WO 95-1613-3.
183 1 Battalion South Staffordshire Regiment, WO 95-1664-2.
184 1 Battalion South Staffordshire Regiment, WO 95-1664-2.
185 1 Battalion Welsh Guards, WO 95-1224-1.
186 1 Battalion South Staffordshire Regiment, WO 95-1664-2.
187 French, *Military Identities*, 84.
188 French, *Military Identities*, 84.
189 Isherwood, *Remembering*, 14.
190 1 Battalion Cheshire Regiment, 1 August 1914–30 November 1917, WO 95-1571-1, TNA, Kew.
191 Jessica Meyer, *Men of War: Masculinity and the First World War in Britain* (London: Palgrave Macmillan, 2009), 55.
192 General Staff, *FSRII*, 174.
193 Andrew Green, *Writing the Great War: Sir James Edmonds and the Official Histories, 1915–1948* (London and Portland, OR: Frank Cass, 2003), 5.
194 C.T. Atkinson, Letter from Atkinson, 12 May, 1915, 1st Report on Work of Historical Section, 12 May 1915–22 December 1919, CAB 103, TNA, Kew.
195 Atkinson, Letter, 12 May 1915, CAB 103, underscoring in original.
196 C.T. Atkinson, Memorandum on the Work of the Historical Section of the Committee of Imperial Defence, 27 January 1917, CAB 103.
197 Notes on the State of the Historical Section, Military Branch, 30 June 1919, CAB 103, TNA, Kew.
198 General J.E. Edmonds, Ref 13. Report on the Work of the Branch for the Period 1 January 1924–28 October 1924, CAB 103/2, TNA, Kew.
199 Edmonds, Report, CAB 103/2.
200 Green, *Writing*, 57.
201 Green, *Writing*, 59.
202 David French, "Sir James Edmonds and the Official History: France and Belgium," in *The First World War and British Military History*, ed. Brian Bond (Oxford: Oxford University Press, 1991), 86.
203 There are also five volumes on naval operations, six on air operations and a medical history of the war.
204 Green, *Writing*, 3. Green provides an extensive examination of the challenges writing the Official Histories of military operations, including the formation and history of the Historical Section.
205 Keegan, *Face of Battle*, 29; also in Green, *Writing*, 44.
206 Green, *Writing*, 44.
207 Brigadier-General Sir James E. Edmonds, *History of the Great War: Military Operations in France and Belgium 1915*, Vol. ii (London: Macmillan and Co. Limited, 1936); *Military Operations in France and Belgium 1918* (London: Macmillan and Co. Limited, 1935).
208 Edmonds, *Military Operations 1918*, 201. For other mentions of gallant defences in the Somme, see 172, 176, 186, 223, 460 in the same volume. Gallant is only used once to describe the actions of the German Army in a footnote, 310.
209 Edmonds, *Military Operations 1918*, 331 and 417.
210 Edmonds, *Military Operations 1918*, 399.
211 Edmonds, *Military Operations 1918*, vii.
212 Edmonds, *Military Operations 1918*, 381.
213 Edmonds, *Military Operations 1918*, 584.
214 Edmonds, *Military Operations 1918*, 584–586.

215 Edmonds, *Military Operations 1918*, 586.
216 Green, *Writing*, 200.
217 Jaggar, "Love and Knowledge," 152.
218 Beaumont, *War, Chaos*, 23.
219 Beaumont, *War, Chaos*, 24.
220 Beaumont, *War, Chaos*, 28.
221 Day, *The Modern Invention*, 117.
222 Jaggar, "Love and Knowledge," 152.
223 Jaggar, "Love and Knowledge," 160.
224 See, for example, Leonard Martin, David Ward, John Achee and Robert Wyer, "Mood as Input: People have to Interpret the Motivation Implications of their Moods," *Journal of Personality and Social Psychology* 64, no. 3 (1993): 317–326; Rajagopal Raghunathan and Yaacov Trope, "Walking the Tightrope Between Feeling Good and Being Accurate: Mood as a Resource in Processing Persuasive Messages," *Journal of Personality and Social Psychology* 83, no. 3 (2002): 510–525; and Amanda D. Angie, Shane Connelly, Ethan P. Waples and Vykinta Kligyte, "The Influence of Discrete Emotions on Judgement and Decision-Making: A Meta-Analytic Review," *Cognition and Emotion* 25, no. 8 (2011): 1393–1422.

2 The typeset war
Unit war diaries in the Second World War

Introduction: Information, emotion and the war machine

In 1917, while recovering from a shrapnel injury inflicted during the Arras offensive, Alan Herbert began work on his first novel, *The Secret Battle*, drawn from Herbert's own experiences in the First World War. Written from the viewpoint of an unnamed narrator, the novel traces the incremental effect of the war on Harry Penrose, the narrator's close friend, from the first excited days in Malta, where Harry encounters the stories of veterans with the eagerness of "an imaginative, inquisitive child" through Harry's gradual transformation into a man deeply traumatised by conflict.[1] *The Secret Battle* is about the miscarriage of justice that ends in Harry's eventual execution for desertion, and like many novels to emerge from the First World War, it mourns the loss of innocence. But it is also about the failure of official documents to account for the complexities of individual experience in war. Towards the end of the novel, the narrator describes the route taken by the paperwork with the details of Harry's case:

> I can see those papers, wrapped up in the blue form, with all the right information beautifully inscribed in the right spaces, very neat and precise, carefully sealed in the long envelopes, and sent wandering through the rarefied atmosphere of the Higher Formations.[2]

The "right information," however, is not the whole truth of Harry's story, and the result is that men who do not know Harry (and, the narrator suggests, who do not have the same battlefield experience as him) condemn him to death. Although it is a work of fiction, *The Secret Battle* provides a sense of some of the consequences of the gaps and elisions in the official records of war.

Even if they had escaped physical injury and did not suffer mental and emotional trauma, there were few men who returned from the war unchanged. Similarly, there were few on the home front who remained unaffected – by their experiences (especially, but not only, for women) of venturing into different kinds of working environments, or by the strain of separation and the breaking up of families and communities through loss. In the cultural sphere,

DOI: 10.4324/9781003172109-3

novels like Herbert's as well as others such as Erich Maria Remarque's hugely popular *All Quiet on the Western Front* (1929), and the increasing stream of war memoirs that emerged in the late 1920s and early 1930s, along with films and plays, were part of cultural struggles to assimilate the impact and lessons of the First World War. While such accounts were often about individual experience, institutions in the political, economic and martial spheres were similarly attempting to assess the shape of their organisational identities and structures in the wake of the war, and to determine how best to move forward. Contrary to Herbert's account of organised records circulating smoothly through military channels, the war had in fact generated a vast and unwieldy collection of official documents. Working out just what information from the world's first Total War was useful, and from what sources, was part of the challenge faced not just by the British Army, but by other government bodies, including the Public Record Office, as discussed in the next chapter (Chapter 3). However, while information may have been important, the extreme and unanticipated emotional reactions to the war, particularly that of fear, demanded not just acknowledgement, but practical solutions in the present. Far from being secret, the battle to control fear and other emotions was at the forefront of discourse about past and future conflicts, and it posed a series of urgent political and economic problems in the years leading up to the Second World War.

Approaches to processing and managing both information and emotion were central to the British Army's operational practices and decision making in the years leading up to the Second World War and during the conflict itself. Paperwork in general, and Unit War Diaries in particular, remain a core component of the Army's organisational practices and structures in the Second World War. The stresses and strains that shaped the evolution of doctrine in the *FSR* during the interwar period have been widely examined,[3] however, there were also shifts in the British Army's bureaucratic practices and in the production of reports. These should not be overlooked, as they provide insight into how the British Army understood and approached conflict after the First World War. The main aim behind systems of organisation in the Army, according to the 1930 *Field Service Regulations* (*FSR*) Vol. I, was to create "a machine so co-ordinated down to its smallest units and so controlled by its various subordinate commanders and their staffs" that it could be handed to the Commander-in Chief and deployed in any challenges Britain might face either across its Empire or in Europe.[4] War may have been thought of as a form of industrial labour in the First World War, but in the interwar years four subsequent iterations of the *FSR* (published from 1920 to 1935) attempted to establish controls that would enable the Army itself to function as smoothly and efficiently as an industrial machine. These kinds of metaphors matter. Metaphors, as Donald Schön argues, are ways of structuring perspectives on the world – "how we think about things, make sense of reality, and set the problems we later try to solve."[5] The way metaphors are framed in the Army's own discourse on warfare reveals the conceptual thinking underpinning the organisation's approach to everything from recruitment to training and waging war. This chapter begins by investigating the *FSR* as an expression of the persistent belief in the British Army that the unpredictability and the emotional impact of conflict could be minimised or controlled via systems based on "commonsense" principles of organisation.[6]

The challenges posed by actual machines and new technologies to the understanding of warfare were the source of much debate in the Army in the interwar years.[7] Both then and now, the tank, the fighter plane and various other machines of war quite rightly formed the focus of much analysis on their impact on warfare.[8] But another machine had quietly become essential to the operational effectiveness of military forces around the world. Although the typewriter, as explained in the previous chapter, was available during the First World War, by the Second World War it had become essential to waging war. For the American Office of War Information (OWI), the typewriter was a technology that could tame the "chaos" of mechanised conflict and transform it into information essential to combat operations.[9] This chapter moves on to investigating the industrial and ideological intersections between the typewriter and warfare to reveal that the typewriter is a machine of war as much as it is of writing. The typewriter was the perfect instrument for ensuring that information was produced with machine-like efficiency. As a writing machine imbued with "vested institutional authority,"[10] the typewriter played a crucial role in the writing spaces of Second World War, intervening not only between the individual and the text, but also between institutional structures and the chaos of modern warfare.

Yet despite the emphasis on shaping the organisation into an efficient and unfeeling industrial machine through tools like the *FSR* and technologies like the typewriter, emotions were core to the British Army's operational management during the Second World War. While emotions such as fear were considered a problem, others were identified as useful for the Army's operations and cultural values. This chapter next explores the contours of the British Army's emotional regime by investigating three practices of "emotional engineering." "Emotional engineering" is a concept adopted from Stephen Fineman.[11] At its most basic level, engineering involves the use of scientific principles in the construction and maintenance of machines, structures and systems. Emotional engineering is therefore useful in revealing the 'scientific' principles through which the Army attempted to manage, martial, and capitalise on emotions in individuals in the service of the martial machine. Fear was the emotion that posed the most significant threat to the Army's operational capacity, and it was therefore the one that the required the most management. This chapter investigates the "Report of the War Office Committee of Enquiry into 'Shell-Shock'" as a barometer of contemporary attitudes to fear on the battlefield and pivotal to the Army's consequent struggles to recognise and manage fear on the battlefield.[12] But while most of the focus on emotion in the Second World War has been on the experience and manifestation of fear and trauma,[13] this chapter reveals how the Army began to formally recognise the significance of emotional qualities for its organisation in other

76 *Unit War Diaries in the Second World War*

areas, specifically in training and in recruitment. This chapter investigates blood and hate training as part of the Army's attempts to (quite literally) martial emotion. The third and final practice of emotional engineering that this chapter explores is the development of a lexicon for emotional traits in selection processes. The idea of the martial machine shaped practices in the Army that identified emotion in the individual as the grease that either clogged or lubricated operations in the machine of war.

The rational framework of the *FSR*, the technology of typewriter, and the influence of Army's emotional regime all coalesce in the Unit War Diaries of the Second World War. Their convergence in the writing spaces of the Second World War raises the following questions:

> In what ways were the records of the Second World War shaped by the ideological framework of the *FSR* and by the widespread use of the typewriter?
> How, if at all, have traces of emotion evolved or shifted in these records in comparison to those of the First World War?
> What, if any, moments of resistance emerge in the Second World War records, or have these been eliminated?

We cannot fully understand the operational principles of the Army in the Second World War, including the production of Unit War Diaries, without accounting for the role emotion played in their construction. To answer these questions, therefore, the chapter concludes with the linguistic and close analysis of a selection of the Second World War Diaries and their Appendices. It investigates errors and corrections as traces of individuality in the typed text and tracks the usage of punctuation and emotives as part of emotional practices in the records of the Second World War, before turning to examine how the crafting of stories about events in war carve out space for personal expression in the official reports and facilitate the performance of a range of emotional responses, some of which push back against the official controls of information.

Field Service Regulations: Principles for the 'right' information

In contrast to Germany and France, which each developed two sets of doctrinal publications in the interwar years, the British General Staff produced four editions of the *Field Service Regulations* during the same period, which David French considers "proof that the British Army was trying hard to understand the lessons of the First World War."[14] The revisions of the *Field Service Regulations* were part of the Army's efforts to reframe the principles through which it wished to approach future wars but also to re-articulate its organisational structures and practices in the years after the First World War.[15] In terms of the principles for waging war, the *FSR* attempted to strike a balance between the challenges of maintaining one of the largest Colonial Empires in the world, while simultaneously preparing for the possibility of facing an enemy that matched, if not exceeded, Britain's military capacity in another European or global conflict. One of the central challenges that the General Staff faced in developing the *FSR*, therefore, was in formulating one set of principles, or a unified doctrine that could cover both circumstances. In contrast to the *FSR* adopted for the First World War, which had not outlined principles of warfare, the four inter-war versions of the *FSR Vol. II, Operations* published in the 1920s and '30s, attempted to articulate these, with slight variations in order and significance in each iteration.

The evolution of doctrine in the British Army in the interwar years has been the topic of much debate and attention.[16] It falls mostly outside the remit of this chapter, but it is worth noting that the tension between individualism and organisational control that Aimée Fox identified in the *FSR* used in the First World War survives and appears once more, albeit in a slightly different configuration, in the interwar *FSR*.[17] Section 14, Chapter II of the 1935 *FSRII* (the version implemented in the Second World War), advises that orders should be composed in such a way so "as not to interfere with the initiative of subordinate commanders, who should be left freedom of action in all matters which they can or should arrange for themselves."[18] In theory then, the *FSR* encouraged individual initiative. However, subsequent debates around the extent to which doctrine facilitated latitude and the devolution of command to subordinate officers in the field are themselves evidence that during the British Army's engagements in the Second World War (especially in the early years of the conflict), these boundaries were unclear.[19] What is more widely agreed upon, however, is that although the *FSR* emphasised the significance of individual responsibility and decision-making in principle, in practice the Army's training regime did not do enough to equip junior and mid-level officers with the knowledge and skill required to adapt doctrinal principles for varying circumstances in the field of war.[20] It was these kinds of issues, as well as widespread variations in the interpretation and application of doctrine, that new approaches to training implemented in the years after the British Expeditionary Force's (BEF) withdrawal from France attempted to rectify; a topic discussed in more detail later in this chapter.

While the *FSR Vol. II* might have been unclear in terms of how doctrinal principles could be interpreted and applied in the field, there was less ambiguity in the organisational principles outlined in the *FSR Vol. I*, the volume dedicated to Organization and Administration. The notion that modern warfare could be understood through scientific principles and managed through rational systems of organisation that had emerged in the Nineteenth Century was not significantly disrupted by the First World War in British military thinking. If anything, the belief in organisational control as a measure of countering the unpredictability of warfare had intensified. While the notion of war as a form of industrial labour had been evident in the soldier's experience of the First World War and was implicit in the *FSR* of that period (as discussed in Chapter 1), the interwar *FSR* explicitly subjected war to the same principles of efficiencies and systems of management that operated in commercial industrial factories.

FSRII (1935) compares the commander's planning of an operation in the field with that of "[t]he ordinary citizen who is planning a business transaction."[21] Like the man of business, the commander's role includes making logical decisions based on a "balanced statement of the pros and cons of the various choices before them" with a resolute commitment to action supported by their inherent "character."[22] The *FSR* concedes that in war, unlike in business, the commander faces the additional pressures of time, the difficulties of obtaining the right information, and the "psychological factors of fear and exhaustion."[23] However, everyday "commensense [sic] rules," should be enough to allow the commander to prevail against these factors and "the continual succession of unforeseen incidents and obstacles" that threaten to distract him from his objective.[24] Despite the recognition of the unpredictability of modern warfare, the comparison between operating a business and waging war conceptualises war as a rational and transactional activity that can be governed by careful processes of decision-making made by men of character. The belief in character (especially in men of the upper classes) would have very real consequences for the Army's practices of promotion and training, as will become apparent later in this chapter. The *FSR* then shifts to comparing the commander to a boxer in the ring who must always be on his guard and who must make use of his inherent fighting instincts to surprise the enemy and take offensive action.[25] Sporting metaphors run alongside the comparison of war to industry, but the comparison of war to both activities reveals an understanding of war as a finite activity governed by clear principles and rules.

Historians such as David French have considered the implications for doctrine of "attempting to bring the same regularity and order to the battlefield, through the application of the principles of war, as industrialists to the modern factory."[26] However, there are specific consequences of this approach for the Army's organisational systems that should also be examined as they are indications of an institutional belief in bureaucratic processes and documentation as essential mechanisms in waging war. In the *FSRII* used in the First World War, Office Work was folded into a chapter on Casualties, Invaliding and Despatches.[27] With the instructions on the keeping of War Diaries, it warrants a total of around five pages. But both the 1923 and 1935 iterations of the *FSRI: Organisation and Administration* dedicate an entire chapter to Office Work in the Field. In the 1923 *FSRI* that chapter is 11 pages,[28] and in the 1935 *FSRI* it extends to 13 pages.[29] These dedicated chapters are indicative of the importance accorded to producing and managing paperwork and records in war time. The unique ways in which the staff required for maintaining these processes are acknowledged in the *FSRI* provides further evidence of just how significant bureaucratic management systems had become to the Army.

Of all the different roles in the British Army, clerical work is the only form of labour specifically identified as "arduous and [the] hours long."[30] The *FSRI* consequently stipulates that special care should be taken with working conditions for clerks and orderlies. Although clerical staff numbers should be "kept to a minimum" the *FSRI* acknowledges that at times office staff would be "under heavy strain."[31] To ensure that their work remains efficient and of a high standard, their "accommodation and personal comfort" should be "as good as circumstances allow."[32] In many ways, the singling out of clerical staff as requiring personal comfort and good accommodation is extraordinary. In contrast, there is no acknowledgement of the significance of personal comfort or good accommodation for the infantry, whose role might well be described as the most 'arduous' of all arms (after all, they widely referred to themselves as the 'Poor Bloody Infantry'). Despite being identified as the arm that "is the most adaptable and the most generally useful of all arms," and the one that was ultimately responsible for securing success in war, the infantry warrant only "a very high standard of training and resourcefulness and a mobility which only physical fitness and a light equipment can give."[33] But a decline in clerical efficiency caused by "bad conditions of living" could have "far-reaching" consequences on functioning of the Army as whole.[34] The labour of the clerical services is thus situated in the *FSR* as fundamental to the effective functioning of the war machine.

Despite the significance of bureaucratic processes and the comparisons between commanders and businessmen, the *FSRI* recognised that paperwork was not relished by officers. Both iterations of the *FSRI* emphasise the importance of organisation in an office to allow the officer freedom from it: "The better an office is organized, the less time will it be necessary to spend in it."[35] There is also a concern that a plethora of paperwork could clog the war machine. The *FSRI* encourages commanders to limit the number of unnecessary reports, summaries, and other forms of correspondence to "what addressees really want to know and have time to read," although how they are to determine the needs and time pressures of the addressees is not entirely clear.[36] Whereas *FSRII* 1909 had not provided clear guidance on processes for the destruction or preservation of records, the *FSRI* outlines what is in effect a practice of records management. The process involved sorting documents into three categories: 1) those to be kept for current use, 2) those no longer required but which may be of "historical value on questions likely to arise in the future" and which should therefore be sent back to the War Office, and 3) those that did not fall in either category and that could be destroyed.[37] In contrast to the *FSRII* 1909, which identified documents containing "anything of a nature likely to prove useful when the history of the campaign is written" as worthy of preservation,[38] there is a shift here towards retaining documents that might assist in providing evidence for issues *under question* in future historical accounts. This shift is slight, but it is worth noting, as it foreshadows the increasing emphasis on accountability in the keeping of records that shapes much operational reporting today. But as in the guidelines in the *FSRII* 1909 for the management of these documents, it is ultimately left up to the individual to determine what might be of "historical value" and to identify what questions might arise in future. The shape of future war archives was thus determined by the individual decisions of officers and clerks whose motives and choices in the present might well have been influenced as much by concerns with expediency and space as they were by any vague sense of historical worth.

There was, however, no ambiguity about identifying Unit War Diaries as historically significant. The wording describing the two-fold nature of their purpose is identical in *FSRI* 1923 to that of the *FSR* used in the First World War, namely:

i   To furnish an accurate record of the operations from which the history of the war can subsequently be prepared.
ii To collect information for future reference with a view to effecting improvements in the organisation, education, training, equipment and administration of the Army for war.[39]

But the wording in the 1930 version is shortened and also slightly amended: 'To furnish a historical record of operations and to provide data upon which to base future improvements in army training, equipment, organisation and administration.'[40]

In the final version of the *FSRI*, the Diaries are identified as a "historical record" in their own right. Although it is a subtle change, this wording situates these records not so much as primary source material for historiography, but *as* written history, making them, in effect, the first draft of the historical record of the British Army's experiences of conflict. As Chapter 1 argued, the post-war usages of the First World War Unit War Diaries had already demonstrated that these records did not quite meet their remit as "accurate" historical records, and that they were not necessarily that effective in communicating lessons learned. There is a thus a disconnection evident between the Historical Section's difficulties of managing Unit War Diaries and their recognition of these records as limited historical sources (discussed in Chapter 1), and the Army's persistent identification of War Diaries as authoritative historical documents. Of course, the struggles of the Historical Section were not at the forefront of the minds of the General Staff, but the disconnect between intention in the design of the records and their eventual implementation is an early example, if not the first, that the uses of these records did not always unfold in the way their designers intended and imagined.

"Data" has also replaced "information." There is a widespread slippage between these two terms that persists into the present. Emily Goldman, for example, states that "information refers to data."[41] Yet 'data', which has its etymological origins in the Latin *datum*, meaning 'thing given', is much more aligned with facts or statistics, and by the late 1800s was associated particularly with "numerical facts collected for future reference."[42] The use of 'data' rather than 'information' intensifies the focus on facts and figures in official forms, but simultaneously the significance of more detailed narrative accounts is made more explicit in the interwar *FSR* than it was in the regulations for the First World War. A footnote in *FSRII* 1909 indicated that a more detailed account of events could be included as an appendix to supplement the Diaries.[43] The later *FSR* stipulate that in addition to the C.2118 forms, there should also be a "narrative of or report on operations, drawn up by the unit or formation itself, including any sketches or maps relating thereto, to supplement the account of operations furnished in the text of the diary."[44] These instructions open more space in the Second World War records for narrative accounts that go beyond what is included in the C.2118 forms. Analysis of appendices in conjunction with C.2118 forms later in this chapter will reveal the interplay of official constraints with individual expression, and whether these shifted in reaction to the looser formal qualities of the appendix.

An extract from the *FSRI* containing the instructions for the completion of the Unit War Diaries and the maintenance of records was included in a separate Army Form – C.2119. The inclusion of the C.2119 forms in the files meant that the instructions for completion of the Unit War Diaries were readily to hand for those completing the reports. The C.2119 form emphasised the information that the Army valued in its "detailed account of operations" – "Exact hour of important occurrences, factors affecting operations, topographical and climatic."[45] There is a separate note to remind those completing the Unit War Diaries that events were to be set out "at the time they occur, or come to notice," emphasising the importance of daily records, but these were to be supplemented by longer narratives.[46] The structure and shape of Army Form C.2118, in which the Unit War Diaries were to be completed, would have been familiar to any soldier who had completed them in the First World War, with three central columns for Hour, Date, Place/Summary of Events/Remarks and References to Appendices. The only changes are the addition of fields for Month and Year, Unit and Commanding Officer at the top of the form. The continuity evident in the C.2118 form across the two world wars provides material evidence of the persistence of the belief that systems of organisation could be imposed on modern warfare and bring it under containment and control.

The burden of historical and operational accountability placed on Unit War Diaries, together with the *FSRI*'s configurations of office spaces and personnel, indicate an intensification of the Army's belief in documentation as an essential part of warfighting, and of the written record as historical evidence of events. However, it is not quite accurate to say 'written' records. References to handwriting in *FSRI* (1923) were edited out of the later version, probably in recognition that the typewriter was by this stage ubiquitous in most organisations. The typewriter had also, as Marshall McLuhan points out, become increasingly important for military operations – so important, in fact, that McLuhan claimed in his seminal work *Understanding Media*, that "[a]n army needs more typewriters than medium and light artillery pieces, even in the field, suggesting that the typewriter now fuses the functions of the pen and the sword."[47] The next section examines the significance of the typewriter for the British Army, and its impact as a writing machine. Darren Wershler-Henry argues (drawing on Heidegger to do so), that the typewriter reorganises first language, "then the body of the typist, then of [sic] the world around the typist, in its own image."[48] What impact, then, did the typewriter have on reorganising the records of war?

Typewriter – Writing machine of war

An advertisement in *The Times* in 1895 for the American Yost typewriter promises an end to "the drudgery of the pen" and suggests something of the impact of these new writing machines on various spheres of life. "The YOST is an Educator" assisting in "composition, spelling, and correct punctuation" the ad proclaims. In addition to education, the Yost had apparently been adopted by royalty, governments, businesses, journalists, lawyers and creative writers. The ad quotes Rider Haggard calling the Yost "delightfully simple" and "well adapted for literary work."[49] The Yost advert, despite its promotional aggrandisement, is an indication of how these writing machines spread into, and transformed, structures of power and administration. Although writing machines of various kinds had been in development throughout the 1800s, their potential capacity for efficiency, speed and standardisation dovetailed with the drive towards increased productivity and bureaucratisation towards the end of the century, making the typewriter the perfect technology for adoption in businesses and institutions that placed growing value on exactly those capacities.[50] As "a means to – and symbol of – accurate, efficient, depersonalised law-making and administration," the typewriter was especially suited for use by governments and the military.[51] The typewriter is as much a machine of war as it is a machine of writing, not only because of its industrial intersections with weaponry, but because of ideological and metaphorical connections drawn between this machine of writing and the machines of war. Having briefly examined some of these connections, this section will move on to investigate how the typewriter was deployed in the British Expeditionary Forces during Second World War. Although it had been in use in the First World War, in the Second, the typewriter came into its own as a writing technology of command and control.

Austrian inventor Peter Mitterhofer, one of the early inventors of writing machines, made clear the potential usefulness of a writing machine in war. Wilfred Beeching describes how Mitterhofer's petition to Emperor Franz Joseph for funds to develop such a device in 1870 proposed that it was perfect for use by the military during war because it was easy to transport, could be used in all weather conditions, was good for maintaining secrecy because the lid of the machine was shut while documents were being produced, and would eliminate the problem of illegibility in the handwriting of officials.[52] In the U.S., Christopher Latham Sholes' invention was the first of various mechanical writing machines to be called a "typewriter,"[53] and in 1874 became the first to be mass-produced, by Remington, which also manufactured guns. The association between the typewriter and Remington was part of the reason Friedrich Kittler called the typewriter the "discourse machine gun," imprinting new kinds of meaning onto language through the percussive materiality of the typed text.[54] In turn, the Thompson machine gun, which was used by criminal gangs during prohibition in Chicago, earned the nickname of the 'Chicago Typewriter' because of the rapid clicking sound it made when fired. Also known as the 'Tommy Gun' and later used by both British and American forces in the Second World War, the Thompson was designed, as Darren Wershler-Henry points out, by a former Chief Engineer at Remington, John Taliaferro Thompson.[55] Factories in the U.S. and the U.K. that made typewriters went on to use the same manufacturing methods and production lines to make guns in both World Wars, leading to shortages of the machines during both conflicts.

Typewriters and guns were thus linked at the level of assembly, but they were also connected in the ways they operated and their relationship to the human body. In a discussion on the status of the Air Force in February 1918 in the House of Commons, Noel Billing, then Member of Parliament for Hertford, brought up the need for co-ordination between the firing of guns and aircraft in the skies over London. His proposed solution was a "luminous map" which would make it possible "for one man to be sitting at Whitehall with a finger on every gun in the country and operating those guns like a young girl does a typewriter."[56] The degree to which typing as an occupation had become feminised is evident in Billing's simile, but it is also suggestive of a perceived ease with which both words and missiles could be deployed automatically by mechanical means. A few decades later, the News Bureau for the Office of War Information in the U.S. pushed the comparison between typewriter and weapon further by stating that the typewriter was as integral to war "as gun, bullet or shell."[57] The typewriter, like the gun and other weapons, represents "at once a logic of standardisation and a logic of prosthesis" in its ability to blend human and machine through mechanical actions initiated by the hands and body.[58]

But in its standardised arrangement and spacing of letters on the page, the typewriter was more than a prosthesis. It had the capacity to render the human being invisible in its production of a script that appeared to be the product of the machine, not the individual. Friedrich Kittler saw the typewriter as intervening between "pen and body during textual production."[59] In Kittler's view, in the standardised spacings and block letters of the typewritten text, "paper and body, writing and soul fall apart."[60] Kittler was drawing on Heidegger, who saw the typewriter as "tear[ing] writing from the essential realm of the hand. The word itself turns into something 'typed'."[61] Both Heidegger and Kittler's perspectives on writing tend to naturalise the process of handwriting and minimise the pen as a technology of media, but these kinds of observations were not limited to philosophers and the academy. A typically tongue-in-cheek take on the typewriter in satirical magazine *Punch* in July 1941 is more prosaic in its observation that "the whole point of the typewriter is that it is efficient; I mean, that anything typed on a typewriter looks exactly as if it has been typed."[62]

Kittler's tendency toward technological determinism overstates the power of the machine to overwrite human agency, but the idea that the typewriter disassociates writer from text and erases individuality was powerful enough to dissuade some from using it. Despite glowing endorsements by writers such as Haggard in the Yost advert, and perhaps more famously by Mark Twain, who loved the machine, others resisted its use. For decades after the introduction of the typewriter, it was considered impolite or even callous to use it for personal correspondence or communications associated with emotional subjects, such as bereavement, and a handwritten note today still carries a sense of personal intervention and care.[63] Echoes of the belief in machine-produced writing as somehow impersonal and inhuman continue to this day. Barack Obama, for example, wrote his memoirs with a pen and yellow legal pad: "I still like writing things out in longhand, finding that a computer gives even my roughest drafts too smooth a gloss and lends half-baked thoughts the mask of tidiness."[64] Long before the personal computer, the typewriter provided a gloss of professionalism and mask of tidiness to the written word, transforming it into something impersonal and formal.

Chapter 1 revealed how adverts for fountain pens emphasised individuality and style. In contrast, adverts for typewriters emphasised professionalism and technological efficiency. The Yost advert mentioned at the beginning of this section claimed that "three times as much work" could be done on the Yost typewriter as with the pen. A similar advert for the Empire typewriter claimed it contained "every labour-saving device and convenience of detail that Nineteenth Century skill could conceive and execute."[65] Such claims were common in typewriter ads of the time but should not be dismissed as mere marketing hyperbole. Donald Hoke notes that "in contests between speed writers and speed typists, the typists invariably won by 30 words per minute and more."[66] Speed in all its forms was valued by organisations navigating the pressures of industrial life. A Remington ad in *The Daily Mail* in 1937 proclaimed that a typewritten letter would secure employment over a handwritten one, because "In these days business men have no time to decipher handwriting, however good it is."[67] The typewriter produced at speed documents that were uniformly presentable and that did not vary as handwritten documents invariably did, despite the attempts made by handwriting manuals of the late 1800s to create standard writing styles. The uniformity of the typed text not only made it seem impartial and impersonal, but also lent it an authority lacking in handwriting.

The typewriter appeared to echo the authority of print (as discussed in Chapter 1) and to amplify it. A Pitman manual for typewriting released in 1893 proposed that typewritten text demanded "a higher standard of excellence" because it was "clearer" than print.[68] The difficulty of erasing an error in typed text also seemed to encourage precision and discipline. The manual therefore attributes a kind of "candor" to the machine.[69] The idea of writing 'produced' by the typewriter as somehow impersonal and therefore more official carried momentum in an age that valued objectivity and rationalism as ways of understanding the world. The supposed "candor" of the typewriter goes beyond the clarity of its text. Wershler-Henry traces a long association between the typewritten text and ideas of 'truth.'[70] The authority of the typewriter lay in its ability to overlay the text it produced with a patina of precision and mechanisation. Its capacity for depersonalisation, as much as for speed and precision, was one of the aspects that made it perfect for adoption in bureaucratic organisations, especially governments and the military.

The typewriter had been incorporated into widespread use by the British government by the end of the 1800s. On 11 March 1886, a discussion about the state of the facilities in the House of Commons included requests for the inclusion of typewriters in Committee Rooms for the use of members.[71] By 1907, the typewriter was the focus of a special Committee set up to investigate the suitability of the various machines available for use in government offices. The Oliver came out top.[72] As a "symbol of modernity and technological prowess" and tool of bureaucracy, the typewriter was critical to the administration and implementation of British Colonial rule.[73] An advert for the Empire typewriter in 1943 made its connections to imperialism explicit in its copy. "We shall build a better Empire!," the ad proclaims, using machines that are "precision built" and "reliable and efficient."[74] Jessie Hohmann identifies the typewriter as a machine implicated in the violent application of Colonial power as much as other weapons of war.[75] Its significance to the military had become clear by the end of the First World War. Even though concerns regarding the proliferation of paperwork had led to the restricted use of typewriters in the British Expeditionary Force in the First World War, towards the end of the conflict the War Diaries of the Army Printing and Stationery Services (APSS) acknowledged that the typewriter was "a necessity, not a convenience" for the armed forces.[76]

The exponential growth and significance of the Army Printing and Stationery Services during the First World War did not guarantee its survival after the war. Instead, its duties were split between the GHQ Printing Press, located at Arras and headed by Edward Budd, and the Royal Army Service Corps (RASC). The former took over the printing of orders, leaflets and manuals (and, towards the latter part of the war, a large amount of propaganda as part of psychological warfare). The practicalities of distributing typewriters, along with other supplies, fell to the RASC. However, the demand for typewriter mechanics after the outbreak of the Second World War was such that the Typewriter Mechanics Pool (TMP), under the command of Lieut. G.A. Holliday, was formed on the 13 August 1942.[77] Operating out of Cairo, the TMP's functions included the management of mechanics and the even distribution of their labour across the Army as a whole, as well as control over spare parts and the tools of office machinery in general. The TMP, like all other units in the British Army, produced its own War Diaries, which reveal the enormous challenges it faced in maintaining the supply and repair of the machines.

Unlike in the First World War, where the APSS under Partridge had tried to limit the distribution of machines, the typewriter was now considered "invaluable to all operations," to the extent that "operational orders etc could not be turned out and distributed without it."[78] Yet the TMP's War Diaries detail extensive lack of co-operation from other units as regards transport, rations and accommodation, as well as widespread carelessness with the machines. The TMP also had an almost overwhelming workload, which included, by the end of 1942, repairing all typewriters for American forces in the Middle East.[79] The unit never quite managed to stay on top of the demand for repairs. Ironically, they were hampered by the amount of documentation they were required to produce, and the entry for 2 September 1942 notes that some of this paperwork was "discontinued from this date" to allow the Unit to do its actual work.[80] To provide some sense of the kinds of pressures the TMP faced, as well as the extent of the use of typewriters in the BEF, in their first year, the pool repaired a total of 15,486 typewriters, an average of 1,290 per month, in addition to distributing 6,584 and dealing with "several hundred" new machines.[81]

The importance of typewriters to units in the field was critical enough to be raised at parliamentary level. In April 1941, the Secretary of State for War (then David Margesson), was asked

> whether he is aware of the great dissatisfaction existing in many Army units who, whilst ordered to draw up and send in daily returns, often of considerable number and length, are not provided with a *typewriter*; whether he will have machines supplied or have the returns made fewer or done away with altogether.

Richard Law, Financial Secretary to the War Office, responded that there was a delay in delivery of the machines, due to a shortage of supply, and that the possibility of "reducing the number of returns required from units" was under examination in the Department.[82] The typewriter, as this exchange makes clear, was at once boon and bane to the bureaucratic needs of the military. It facilitated the fast production of paperwork, which created an increased pressure on units to produce even more documentation, which meant that the need for typewriters grew even more urgent. Despite attempts to reduce the amount of paperwork demanded of the Army, by 1943, the need for typewriters in the armed forces and in government had grown so acute that a restriction order was passed by the Board of Trade to control the supply of all sales (except second-hand portable machines) and disposal of typewriters.[83] *The Economist* noted that eight out of ten new typewriters were being acquired for Government use in June 1943, and adverts for machines and machine parts emphasised their vital role in winning the war.[84]

The American Office of War Information was (perhaps characteristically) much more overtly enthusiastic than the British government and Army in its endorsement of the significance of typewriters to the war effort. In a press release in July 1942 the OWI claimed that "you can't win today's kind of war without typewriters." Associations between the typewriter and ideas of order and control are explicit in the OWI's statement. For the OWI "legible, accurate and permanent records" were essential for keeping the "chaos" of mechanised conflict from disrupting essential operations in Second World War. The typewriter is identified as a "tool of command efficiency."[85] The typewriter was conceptualised as a machine capable of intervening not only between individual and text, but also between military organisations and the chaos of modern warfare. As well as eliminating the problems of messy individual handwriting in official documents, it also seemed capable of erasing the messiness of emotion, replacing both with uniformity and institutional authority. It was the perfect tool for transforming events in war into neat, accurate, orderly records. The typed text imposed a mask not just of tidiness and legibility on the records of war, but also of control over the chaos and emotional impact of combat. Its "vested institutional authority" augmented the de-personalised authority of the pre-printed C.2118 form.[86] The typewriter was at once emblem and agent of cool, emotionless, organisational efficiency.

The increased emphasis on documentation and on administrative services in the *FSR*, as well as the recognition of the typewriter as essential to operations, are all aspects of the Army's attempts to order its organisation along logical and rational lines. Thus far this chapter has investigated the processes and tools engineered and deployed in the service of creating a smoothly functioning bureaucratic machine in which uncertainty and unpredictability were, if not completely eliminated, at least minimised. But human beings were also components of the military machine, and the Army attempted to manage them through similar principles of rational thought and organisation. The British Army's management of manpower (and indeed women-power) in the interwar years and throughout the Second World War has been extensively investigated.[87] But the management of people inevitably involves the management of emotion. Drawing on principles from the rising field of psychiatry, the British Army attempted to subject emotion to 'scientific' methods of control designed to manage, martial, or capitalise on emotion. Investigating these measures reveals the contours of the British Army's emotional regime before and during the Second World War. For a deeper understanding of how practices, technologies and documentation mediate between the war experiences of individuals and the operation of the Army as an institution, it is essential to also understand the less tangible, but no less significant, emotional milieu in which all these elements were situated and produced.

Engineering the Army's emotional regime in the Second World War

Even in research into the British Army as an emotional organisation, there is a general perception that in its structures and performance before and during the Second World War, the Army "paid little direct attention to the management of male emotions" beyond controlling those that might undermine operations.[88] Fear, one of the core emotions of shell-shock in the First World War and also evident in what was later termed 'war neurosis' or 'battle exhaustion' in the Second, was one of the most obviously disruptive emotions for the armed forces. The Army's struggles to manage fear, to prevent or contain it, have therefore been at the forefront of much of the research into the BEF's relationship with emotion in the Second World War. The relatively new fields of psychiatry and psychology played a significant role in assisting the Army in these struggles, despite some resistance on the part of the Army to acknowledge or facilitate the efforts of professionals from these fields.[89] The '"Shell-Shock' Report" of 1922 was profoundly influential in shaping approaches to fear not only in the Army, but also in British society as a whole, and this section begins by investigating this document to provide insight into the deeply held contradictory attitudes to this particular emotion. But the British Army's efforts at emotional engineering went beyond the management of fear. The Army's training methods and selection processes reveal a growing understanding in the organisation of the significance of emotion to the waging of war and provide a deeper insight into how emotion was in fact central to the understanding of how the British, as both nation and martial power, should wage war.

During the First World War, as Chapter 1 has demonstrated, fear, and other extreme emotions such as anger or grief, were "outlaw" emotions.[90] But that should not imply that fear went unrecognised during the war itself. The battle against fear was in reality far from secret. The fact that many soldiers manifested a range of baffling symptoms to industrial warfare – from hysterical deafness, muteness and/or blindness to paralysis, amnesia and hysteria – had garnered a great deal of attention not just in medical publications like *The Lancet* and *The British Medical Journal* but also in the British press. As early as May 1915, the medical correspondent for *The Times* identified fear as "one of the strongest of the primitive emotions." Modern warfare, particularly shell fire, according to this writer, inflicted "wounds of consciousness," capable of reducing the soldier to an "emotional organism" subject to the control of their subconscious impulses.[91] The correspondent's use of the concepts of the conscious and subconscious is evidence of the spreading influence of the new discipline of psychiatry, but the understanding of fear as a 'primitive' emotion was common in the established medical profession, which broadly held that mental health disorders precipitated a regression to a lower evolutionary state, and that their origin was primarily biological.

In the broader public sphere, the poetry, novels, memoirs, plays and films of the interwar period helped to normalise the idea that fear on the battlefield was to be expected. The soldier emerges from these narratives very much as a sacrificial victim of conflict, and these representations fed into a softening of public attitudes towards fear as an emotional response to conflict after the First World War. The increasing public pressure to review cases of Courts Martial (like the one described in *The Secret Battle*), which resulted in the execution of soldiers during First World War because of desertion or cowardice, is evidence of this shift. But while there may have been more public awareness and tolerance of fear as a response to war, there was disagreement in political and medical circles on how to deal with those who continued to suffer from its effects in the interwar years. A parliamentary discussion in 1919 addressing the necessity of rebuilding and restarting industry and the economy provides insight into some of the contradictions and complexities in the dominant discourse concerning the emotional state of the Britain in the wake of the war.

Lieutenant Colonel Will Thorne raised the issue of the "terrible strain" caused by the war in the wider population, manifesting, as he saw it, in "the general disposition to grumble and grouse about everything and everybody."[92] Lloyd George, then Prime Minister, responded by saying that some allowances needed to be made because "the world is suffering from shell-shock on a great scale."[93] Lloyd George's use of the term 'shell-shock' to describe the emotional state of the general population demonstrates how much the term had come into popular use. Its blanket application to include those who had not experienced shell-fire or warfare directly suggests something of the fuzziness of its actual meaning. But as Lloyd George made clear, the emotional reaction to the 'shock' of war was also "one of the most important contributory causes to the slackness manifest in the workshops of the world."[94] While the exact nature of the kinds of emotions generated by the shock of war was unspecified, what is clear is that these emotions were considered incompatible with the needs of industry and the economy, and were associated with ideas of malingering and shirking social responsibility. What was required, according to the Prime Minister, was for "all classes to pull themselves together." The nation's recovery could not take place without "conscious effort on the part of the patient himself." Recovery from the shock of war, at the level of government, therefore, was seen as "a matter of will and good will."[95] The subtext to the idea that emotional issues could be overcome simply through willpower is that the failure to do so is the result of intransigence and poor character. This debate is representative of attitudes at this level of British society towards the emotional and psychological impact of war, and the belief that nervous strain or fear could be overcome by the power of the rational mind was not uncommon, even in the medical profession.[96]

While war exhaustion and strain were impacting the wider population's ability to contribute to redevelopment of the nation's industry, the issue of 'neurasthenia' or shell-shock in the military posed a more specific economic problem. It was becoming clear that for a large group of soldiers, somewhat to the surprise of doctors who had anticipated quite the opposite scenario, the emotional and mental impact of the First World War was not in fact dissipating with time, physical therapies, or with the application of rational willpower. Even more troubling, some who had shown no symptoms of emotional strain during the war went on to manifest symptoms in subsequent years. The State clearly had a responsibility to take care of these men. Some needed hospitalisation and ongoing care. Others were claiming pensions. The increasing economic pressure of these pension payments, combined with the social pressure to investigate the executions of soldiers during the conflict, led to the commission of an inquiry into shell-shock in 1920, led by Francis Hopwood, Lord Southborough. Its goal was to investigate the "origin, nature, and remedial treatment" of shell-shock, and to ascertain "whether by military training or education, some scientific method of guarding against its occurrence can be devised."[97] It was, therefore, an attempt not only to try to understand the relationship between the First World War and extreme emotional reactions, especially fear, but also to try to find ways of mitigating and managing fear in future wars through the application of "scientific" methods.

The committee published its findings in 1922. As both Ted Bogacz and Michal Shapira have observed, the "Report of the War Office Committee of Enquiry into 'Shell-Shock'" is a deeply ambivalent document in which older, more traditional views that attribute mental illness to biological causes are confronted by newer psychiatric concepts such as unconscious impulses and instincts.[98] But it is also an official document in which a struggle around emotion manifests as the upper echelons of the British establishment, long dominated by the idea that emotion should be subject to rational willpower, come face to face with the undeniable presence of unruly emotional responses to industrial warfare. The tension between deep-seated cultural beliefs (many of which were sexist, racist and classist) in the mastery of character and rational self-control in upper-class British men, and the irrefutable effects of fear and other extreme emotions in most men during and after the First World War, is ultimately unresolved in the Report. The Report was nonetheless influential in shaping official strategies for dealing with fear not just in the Army in the Second World War, but in British society as a whole, and it therefore warrants examination.

The ambivalence inherent in the Report is evident in its very title. One of the only real points of agreement in the Report, despite its bold claim that there was "practical unanimity both in evidence and opinion" amongst the Committee members and witnesses,[99] was that the term 'shell-shock' was a "grievous misnomer."[100] Yet the Committee decided to keep it in the title in acknowledgement of the term's ubiquity and "dramatic significance" in the public domain.[101] It is used throughout the Report, but always in inverted commas as a signal of its unsuitability. The awkward use of 'shell-shock' in the Report reveals the difficulty of finding the conceptual language to address the bewildering range of physical, mental and emotional symptoms men exhibited in response to industrial warfare. But it is also more than a struggle to find a single, all-encompassing term. The difficulties around nomenclature provide insight into institutional and individual responses towards the phenomenon. Some of the reluctance to give the term institutional sanction was the perception that men had used it as a "handy excuse" to avoid "the terrors of the front" during the war and the concern was that it would be continued to be used in a similar way in the future.[102] As in the Parliamentary discussion mentioned earlier in this section, 'shell-shock' was a term associated with 'malingering' or 'skrimshanking'; the idea that men were faking their symptoms to avoid labour in war or peace and worse still, were capitalising on it by claiming pensions.

There is an entire section in the Report devoted to "Malingering and Shell-Shock," with a range of contradictory accounts about the degree to which war neurosis was faked, either consciously or unconsciously.[103] Notwithstanding contradictory witness testimony as to the frequency and difficulty of identifying cases of fakery, the Report reinforces the idea that shell-shock was both "a handy excuse" to avoid the front line and a "parrot cry" in cases of Courts Martial.[104] The association between malingering and war neurosis continued into the Second World War, when the official label the BEF settled on for the condition was similar to the one adopted in the previous war – 'Not Yet Diagnosed' became 'Not Yet Diagnosed (Nervous)' or NYD(N), again in an effort to prevent soldiers from taking advantage of a handy term to avoid fighting. In August 1944, NYD(N) was dropped as a term, and Medical Officers were instructed to apply the term 'exhaustion' as a "generic diagnosis for all psychiatric conditions."[105] As Copp and McAndrew point out, 'exhaustion' or 'battle exhaustion' implies that the condition is temporary, and that rest is all that is required.[106] On no account was a soldier to be sent home with this generic diagnosis. Only after examination from a psychiatrist could such a decision be made.

The persistent concerns about malingering must also be understood in the context of the prevailing medical views on mental health in Britain in the early decades of the Twentieth Century. Mental illness was believed to be primarily biological in origin, and therefore treatable via medication, or through activities that encouraged the patient out of what was thought to be a pathological inward focus, and into a more productive re-connection with the exterior world.[107] Both medication and physical treatments were believed to assist in restoring rational willpower, which was key to maintaining a healthy mind. Failure to respond to treatment was therefore failure on the part of the patient to activate their will to recover. The belief in biological origins of mental disturbances is evident in the first of three categories of shell-shock that the committee established to guide their inquiry. "Commotional disturbance" referred to physical injuries caused by the concussive power of shellfire and explosions, which were thought to lead to subsequent mental illness. The other two were "emotional disturbance" and "mental disorders."[108] Of all three categories, emotional disturbance, especially fear, was established as the primary contributing factor to shell-shock.

One of the witnesses, William Tyrell, delivered perhaps the most detailed explanation of the power of emotional disturbance in disrupting rational control. Tyrell, an international rugby player and decorated medical officer with extensive and distinguished experience in both the Army and the Royal Air Force, appeared to embody masculine ideals of rugged athleticism and good-natured leadership – the qualities believed essential in an upper-class man of character. Such men were thought to be immune to the effects of the battlefield, yet Tyrell had fallen victim to shell-shock. His testimony demonstrates the very real ways in which both cultural and military emotional regimes inflected the understanding and performance of emotion on the battlefield.

Tyrrell describes how in everyday life, "[a] man instinctively masks his emotions almost as a matter of routine," but that in moments of "great crises … the emotion called forth is abnormal" and masking it requires a great deal of "nervous energy."[109] Of all emotions, according to Tyrrell,

> [c]raven fear is the most extravagant prodigal of nervous energy. Under its stimulus a man squanders nervous energy recklessly in order to suppress his hideous and pent-up emotion, and mask or camouflage that which if revealed will call down ignominy upon his head and disgrace him in the eyes of his fellows.[110]

Tyrrell's testimony indicates just how far the repression of emotion for men was regarded as normal in broader society, and how much the war challenged the male soldier's capacity to control or mask his responses. Yet maintaining control was essential because revealing "hideous" emotions such as fear would result in the loss of respect from his fellow soldiers and himself. The idea of extreme emotional responses as somehow abhorrent and abnormal is clear in Tyrrell's testimony, as are the cultural and institutional pressures on controlling them.

Because of the accounts from Tyrrell and others, the Committee was forced to acknowledge that "under the conditions of modern warfare any individual may ultimately break down on the nervous side."[111] Ted Bogacz identifies the recognition that any man, regardless of class, could break down under the pressures of war as the "rock against which many pre-war values shattered."[112] Yet at the same time, the witness statements did not significantly disrupt the belief that fear, like all emotions, could be controlled with the effort of rational will. The constraints on emotion in a culture that valorised the 'stiff upper lip' could, paradoxically, also bolster self-control and act as "a strong incentive to control the expression of fear," as Tyrrell observed.[113] Tyrrell recovered after six months and returned to active service. The potentially radical recognition of the universality of fear in modern warfare was therefore tempered by the reassertion of the more comforting narrative of rational control, especially in upper-class men of 'character.'

If anyone could break down on the battlefield, and if emotion was the cause of "80 per cent of all the cases," difficulties then arose for the Committee in determining what could be considered 'normal' emotional reactions.[114] How could fear be distinguished from cowardice? How could cases in which soldiers faked or exaggerated their emotional responses be identified? And at what point did fear become pathological and induce psychological problems? The Report's efforts to address these questions reveal just how tortuous it was for the Committee and Witnesses to reconcile deep-seated belief in rational self-control with the realities of battlefield experiences. On the question of cowardice, the Report upheld military judgements as justified, but simultaneously acknowledged that "cowardice might be beyond the individual's control."[115] Despite a marked hesitation among witnesses to say with any certainty how cowardice could be recognised, the Report concluded that medical experts should be consulted to identify future instances. The struggles of the committee and witnesses to distinguish between genuine responses to trauma and outright cowardice had enduring consequences. They foreshadowed a long-running controversy related to the 306 executions of British soldiers for cowardice during the First World War. It would take the British Government almost a hundred years, despite numerous committees and debates in parliament, to issue blanket pardons for these men. The issues surrounding these cases were undoubtedly legally and morally complex, but the length of time it took to grant the pardons is symptomatic of persistent institutional struggles on the part of the government and the military to accommodate fear as a force on the battlefield.[116]

The Report's investigation of the question of the relationship between shell-shock and the development of psychological problems also produced ambivalences. The Report maintained that most cases of war neurosis were the result of pre-existing mental health issues, while simultaneously admitting that neurosis could manifest "even in those of sound nervous constitution."[117] It also stated that the trauma of war did not result in any new kinds of mental illness and ultimately, regardless of whether the causes of mental breakdown were of biological or psychological origin, instances should therefore not be classified as battle casualties and should always be regarded with suspicion.[118] These findings had real repercussions on the payment of pensions, and on the BEF's approach to managing fear in the next Total War.[119]

Given that most of the Committee and the 59 witnesses they consulted (drawn from the medical profession and all arms of the military), were members of the upper to middle-class reaches of British society, who had in all likelihood "been exposed since childhood to the tenets of 'character' and the exercise of the will,"[120] it is unsurprising that the report ultimately reaffirmed the pre-First World War belief that character and good leadership in officers would prevent the ordinary soldier from giving in to fear. A direct line was drawn between good leadership and high morale in the rank and file. Both were regarded as critical to mitigating the effects of fear. A large section of the report is devoted to recommendations regarding selection processes and training to prevent cases before they manifest in the field. The definition of morale in the Shell-Shock Report draws on a sporting metaphor, referring to it as "confidence in one's self and confidence in one's comrades. It is collective confidence, the spirit of a good team at football. Morale can be, and has to be, created. It is the product of continuous and enthusiastic training."[121] Although the Report acknowledges the importance of training men for the stresses of active service, it discounted any attempt to reproduce the physical conditions of battle or to provide any special instructions in how to resist shell-shock, because such an approach might "produce the very result it is designed to prevent."[122] Despite the recognition that all men could be subject to fear on the battlefield, the Report upheld the notion that "the predisposition to mental and nervous disorders of the adult is to a great extent determined before he becomes a soldier."[123] The Report therefore advocated careful screening of recruits at the selection phase in order to attempt to identify not only their physical fitness for service, but also their mental and emotional health (it was less clear on the practicalities involved in gathering and assessing such information).

Even if the Army was willing to make changes to its training regime and its selection processes in the interwar years in response to the Shell-Shock Report and the lessons of the previous war, it was severely hampered by budget cuts, shortages of materiél, and struggles with recruitment. Nevertheless, the persistence of an emotional regime that placed so much value on 'character' in its officers, generally defined through a hearty brand of masculinity and rational self-control, should be recognised as contributing to the failure of the British Army in the period leading up to the Second World War to fully accommodate the lessons of the First, especially those relating to the emotional impact of warfare. The traits that were valorised in military leadership in the inter-war period were very much those associated with a 'hearty' sporting spirit. Participation in riding, hunting and polo was generally more important in the officer class than intellectual pursuits into subjects like military history and strategy.[124] The result was not only the cultivation of a culture broadly resistant to changes to its structure and operations (most notably, perhaps, in its insistence on maintaining cavalry at the expense of motorised units) but also one that reasserted an emotional regime in which a mix of self-control, sporting prowess, confidence and enthusiasm were all regarded as key indicators of leadership skills.[125] These traits were believed to be bulwarks against fear on the battlefield, not only in officers, but also in their ability to inspire confidence in their men.

As the BEF entered the next global war, therefore, it did so with the conviction that psychological casualties would be low, and any cases that did arise should not be classified as battle casualties. NYD(N) cases were to be treated by medical officers as close to battle lines as possible, without any inducement to be removed to hospital or elsewhere.[126] Specialists and dedicated treatment centres were considered unnecessary, and treatment, in line with the Shell-Shock Report, would consist broadly of a "common sense" approach that involved "a brief period of rest, strong moral suasion and energetic persuasive methods."[127] The inadequacies of this approach were exposed by the British Army's first major engagement. The BEF's withdrawal from France and the evacuation from Dunkirk (May-June 1940) produced a flood of psychological casualties that had to be housed in facilities originally intended for civilian cases of trauma, which were expected to be more extensive. An article in *The Lancet* pointed out that these were cases "that had not been previously seen by us, either during the war or in years of previous peace-time experience. These were cases of acute 'shell-shock'." The article goes on to note that men "of normal intelligence, personality and work record," with no previous history of psychological problems were manifesting symptoms. In a vivid illustration that the lessons of the First World War about the emotional and mental impact of warfare had not registered in any real way, the idea that all men, even those of "reasonably sound personality" could break down under the stress of combat, appeared to come as a surprise to doctors and the BEF.[128]

As the war progressed, processes for handling psychological casualties were adapted and streamlined, but the struggle to manage these cases continued in the various theatres, and whenever fighting intensified in different campaigns. The management of psychological casualties in the British Army during the Second World War is a topic too large for detailed examination here, but a high-level overview reveals the general organisational attitude and response to the problem of fear in the Army.[129] Although figures tend to vary, a Memorandum to the Executive Committee of the Army Council in 1945 gives some sense of the scale of the problem. It noted that psychiatric cases accounted for almost 50% of casualties immediately following the landing at Anzio, and for 18% of the casualties in the 21 Army Group in a fifty-day period after D Day in Normandy.[130] Given the numbers of psychiatric casualties, psychiatrists and specially trained Medical Officers were required to deal with them, but the relationship between the Army and psychiatrists was often uneasy. Following the flood of psychological casualties after D-Day in Normandy, the Deputy Director of Medical Services (DDMS) for the 21 Army Group intimated that psychiatrists were to blame for the high figures being sent back to the U.K. "Psychiatry is getting out of hand," he observed in his notes following a visit to the beachhead, and should do more to redress the "serious wastage" of manpower.[131] In the same month, Maj-Gen Neil Cantlie, another DDMS, this time of Eastern Command, stated that the primary responsibilities of the psychiatrist were to identify those "incapable of fitting smoothly as cogs in the military machine" and to "fit men for their job, rather than evacuate them when they break down."[132]

The concern, in other words, lay with the overall operation of the military machine, not with taking care of the needs of individual soldiers. However, despite the official line, there were variations in the degree of sympathy towards cases of battle fatigue in individual medical officers and psychiatrists, especially in those away from the urgent pressures of the front, who tended to be more humane in their treatment.[133] But even towards the end of the war, as Lieutenant-Colonel J.H.A. Sparrow noted during his tour of the 21st Army Group in early 1945, officers still struggled to recognise 'battle exhaustion,' and it was still "often a matter of chance whether a man is sent to a hospital or court-martial centre."[134] The idea of fear as a "failure of will" in the individual remained persistent.[135] The inability to control fear was an individual problem, but it was intertwined with national identity. A citizen army would always be a reflection of the society and culture from which it was recruited, and in the case of the U.K., it was felt that "a democracy, especially one enjoying a comparatively high standard of life, was at a disadvantage with an autocracy."[136]

The relationship between national identity, emotion and the waging of war gained more significance as the war progressed. Led by men of 'character,' the

96 *Unit War Diaries in the Second World War*

British citizen soldier's emotional mettle might not have been clearly defined, but initially, the Army believed it would be enough to carry men through regardless of inexperience, inadequate training and chronic shortages of matériél. But when those beliefs were challenged by the losses Britain suffered – the evacuation of Dunkirk, defeats in Greece, Crete, Malaya among them – concern arose that these setbacks were at least partially due to the lack of emotional commitment on the part of the British soldiers. The stiff upper lip, which was so valued in both broader culture and in the Army during the previous war, now seemed a potential weakness. "Let us admit that in past we have taken too much pride in what our neighbours have called 'British phlegm,' in other words, not expressing our feelings," wrote psychoanalyst Edward Glover in 1940, "Too much phlegm may dull our wits. It may even weaken us."[137] Two years later, in a parliamentary debate in the House of Commons following the fall of Singapore (February 1942), it was observed by one representative that the Russians, Chinese, Germans and Japanese all seemed to be "imbued with a spirit of almost fanatical enthusiasm for their cause."[138] But there was a general agreement that the British were "not a fanatical people," and so the question arose as to how to muster the requisite sense of "ruthless purpose" to meet it in the conflict.[139] Writing about that debate, as well as the national response to the fall of Singapore, Harold Nicolson succinctly summarised the core concern: it was "the dread that we are only half-hearted in fighting the whole hearted."[140]

The problem of how to imbue the British civilian with the requisite fighting spirit had initially been addressed in the Army in the same way that it had always approached training new recruits – by hardening them up through "a ferocious regimen of parade-ground marching and spit-and-polish busywork, justified by appeals to the honour of the regiment."[141] But just as the processes for dealing with battle fatigue were challenged by the first real encounter with the enemy, the Army began questioning its training processes in the aftermath of Dunkirk. Lieutenant-General Alexandar, a veteran of the First World War who was also one of the last officers off the beaches in the retreat from France, identified a need to implement a new training regime for British forces, one that would prepare an essentially civilian army with no experience of war for the experience of battle. New battle schools were implemented across the Army, first for officers and later extended to other ranks, from around 1941 onwards.[142] The main goal was to render the doctrine in training manuals and the *FSR* that officers found so difficult to translate in the field into practices that were manageable and understood by all. But battle schools were also an attempt at emotional engineering. They were designed as "a system of *gradual emotional education*," intended to counter "20 years [of] pacifist propaganda which has exaggerated the horror and danger of war."[143] In terms of emotional education, the training was designed to minimise fear, but also to mobilise hate and aggression – exactly the kind of training that the Shell-Shock Report had warned against.

In addition to conditioning soldiers' bodies for new levels of physical fitness, the training was designed to gradually harden soldiers mentally and emotionally to the sights, sounds and smells of warfare. To that end, assault courses and drills were conducted under live fire and with explosions not only to develop the vital tactical principles of fire and movement, but also to counter "nervousness of battle sounds and battle experiences."[144] Some went further, however, by attempting to 'inoculate' soldiers against the effects industrial warfare could have on the human body. Troops were splattered with animal blood when bayoneting dummies, and some schools (GHQ's Battle school at Barnard Castle was one) arranged visits to abattoirs to attempt to familiarise students with death. To mobilise hate and aggression, soldiers attended lectures on German atrocities, were exposed to German war films and photographs of German brutalities and conducted assault courses while instructors yelled slogans such as "you are suffering now because Hitler raped Europe!" or "Remember Hong Kong!" or just simply screamed "hate! hate!" at them.[145] While these methods might be considered extreme, they were at least in part a response to a very real, and by all accounts relatively widespread, "lack of enthusiasm and interest" in the war that Commanders observed in new recruits, according to a Report from the War Office Committee on morale in 1942. The same Report noted that accounts from training camps indicated

> that it is not uncommon for soldiers to ask lecturers whether Hitler has not done a great deal for the trade unions in Germany, and similar questions which reveal that they have no idea of the kind of enemy they have to face.[146]

Blood and hate training, as these drills came to be known, was intended to counter these kinds of attitudes.

The British press, which was invited to view the drills, initially met them with enthusiasm. The correspondent for *The Aberdeen Journal* observed that the drills were transforming the Army into "a grimly efficient force trained in every aspect of the complexities of modern war."[147] The correspondent for *The Times* noted that it was "something new for the British soldier to drill at the double from dawn to dusk and like it." The same reporter remarked on the "infectious enthusiasm" to the drills, which were intended to make British soldiers "faster and tougher than the Germans."[148] The enthusiastic response to the new training regime by both the participants and the press appear to identify this moment as a turning point in the general emotional mood after the disillusionment and disappointment of the retreat from Dunkirk. There is also the possibility that these articles were meant to be reassuring – there was a real fear that a German invasion was both possible and imminent. The training was widely praised for its "realism," and at least one correspondent thought that the value of the new drill lay not so much in improved levels of fitness and battlefield readiness, but more in "the measure of character it provides."[149]

Blood and hate training was intended to override the emotions considered central to British character, which was supposedly gentle, reserved and peaceful, and to transform British civilians into warriors aggressive enough to meet the Germans, who were by then, as Geoffrey Picot noted in his memoirs, widely perceived as "the most disciplined and ferocious nation in the world."[150] The men of the German army were thought to have spent their time "stalk[ing] through Europe killing, destroying, pillaging" and "perfecting the art of killing."[151] In contrast, the world of the 3.5 million civilians who were called into service in the Army had mostly been made up of gentler pursuits – "radio serials and cinema matinees, dance halls and motorcycles, small families, paid holidays and indoor plumbing."[152] Blood and hate training was designed to take civilians from the emotional regime of their civilian lives, in which many of them, like Geoffrey Picot, had thought of themselves as "unargumentative, unoffending, unquarrelsome, unaggressive, unbrave," into a new emotional regime where they became aggressive enough to battle the supposed disciplined Germans or the fanatical Japanese.[153] The training and the discourse around it reveal how central emotion was to martial and national identities, but it was precisely the intersection between these two regimes that prompted opposition to hate and blood drills.

Following a BBC radio broadcast on the new battle drills in April 1942, blood and hate training became the focus of a very public debate. Much of it centred on the idea of hate training as antithetical to British national identity. James Hutchison Cockburn, Moderator of the Church of Scotland General Assembly, was explicit in connecting the inculcation of hatred with a spiritual descent to the kind of tactics deployed in Nazi Germany. In contrast to the Nazis, "[t]he absence of hate and desire for vengeance on the part of the British people," Cockburn wrote in a letter published in the *Dundee Courier*, "has been the outstanding spiritual mark of the war."[154] Just what exactly was required of the English soldier in terms of emotional temperament on the battlefield in these discussions was unclear. One commentator noted the absurdity of clergymen who were comfortable with condoning killing in a "righteous war" as long as it was done without hate and pointed out that killing with no emotion was "an all but impossible thing."[155] What was clearer was that hate and aggression were qualities associated with the enemy, and not with British national or martial identity.

Despite the public furore, hate and blood training had already met with internal resistance in the Army. Psychiatrists in the Army, including Lt. Col. T. F. Main, the psychiatrist attached to GHQ, opposed these methods from the start.[156] Both Ahrenfeldt and Place point out that Lt-Gen. Montgomery was among those who "condemned it as un-British."[157] The training proceeded despite their protests, however, but was carefully monitored. Psychiatrists observed that the blood training was, in fact, having the opposite effect, just as the Shell-Shock Report had predicted. Exposure to slaughter in abattoirs, according to Main, rather than hardening men, had caused some to vomit and faint.[158] Brigadier John R. Rees, consulting psychiatrist to the British Army at home, noted that some of the "best and keenest students" of the battle school courses had afterwards not only "lost interest" but had also "gone into depression."[159] In contrast, some soldiers reportedly found hate training hilarious.[160] Largely as a result of the intervention of psychiatrists, in May 1942, General Paget called a halt to the training. In a widely publicised letter, Paget condemned the attempt to inculcate hate and blood lust as doomed to failure because "an attitude of hate is foreign to the British temperament."[161] However, other aspects of the battle schools such as the emphasis on physical fitness, exposure to live fire and the practical application of battlefield tactics appeared to improve general morale and confidence, and they continued. The reports of the War Office Committee on Morale throughout 1942 note a positive response to "[t]he increase in the scale and intensity of battle training."[162]

While the attempts at emotional engineering that involved blood lust and hate proved tricky to implement, there were other emotional qualities that the Army began to identify as valuable to the military machine. The reshaping of the Army's selection processes involved not only streamlining the recruitment of the right individuals to the right services and roles, but also the identification of what emotional qualities those roles required. The German and American armies had changed their selection processes in response to the lessons learned from the First World War, but in the British Army there was little change in this area the inter-war years, apart from the application of a few tests for mental aptitude in specific services, such as the Signal Corps.[163] Despite the Shell-Shock Report's emphasis on the significance of thorough selection processes to prevent the selection of unsuitable or unstable men, the British Army went into the Second World War with a simple interview (often conducted by those with little to no training in interview skills) as the primary selection method for the general rank and file. The process of selection for officers was scarcely more refined and relied on methods similar to those adopted in the First World War. The identification of those with POM (Potential Officer Material) by officers or NCOs during training was more often than not based on vague notions of 'character' associated with beliefs in inherent leadership qualities in those of a certain class, or in those who had attended public school, or those with sporting abilities (or a combination of all three). Ahrenfeldt notes rather bitterly in his post-war history of the role of psychiatry in the Second World War,

> If it were characteristic of human nature to learn from the experience of past events, [the findings of the Shell-Shock Report] and the early history of the First World War might have been accepted as ample evidence of the need for an active and comprehensive policy of personnel selection in the British Army.[164]

The deficiencies of the entire selection process in the early years of the war were soon exposed.

The wave of psychiatric casualties after Dunkirk was one of the key factors in forcing the Army to re-evaluate its selection processes. Although it was clear that all men could break down under combat stress, it was also apparent that the selection process was failing to identify those who should never have been placed in that position in the first place. But the recruitment of men unsuited for combat was not the only problem caused by poor selection processes. Natzio speculates that the frustrations caused by the under- or over-utilisation of men and women placed into roles incompatible with their skill-sets was at least as significant in contributing to psychiatric disorders as the stresses caused by active combat.[165] The mismanagement of personnel was not only unproductive for the Army's operations, it was also a key factor in stress and low morale. At the other end of the Army's hierarchical spectrum, the high failure rate of office cadets from Officer Training and the "numerous complaints" about the process of officer selection rendered those processes untenable.[166] The massive wave of recruitment into the Army following Dunkirk presented additional challenges. From June to August in 1940, around 275,000 men were called up, necessitating the formation of 120 new infantry battalions, which also desperately needed officers.[167] The Army, understandably, struggled to sort through this massive intake, and mismatches of skill were unavoidable.

Following his appointment to Adjutant General in June 1941, Lt.-Gen. Sir Ronald F. Adam set up the Directorate of Personnel Selection, as a "hub" for a centralised, "co-ordinated selection scheme" to deal with the challenges.[168] Adam recognised that the Army needed a selection process that did more than weed out men who were, at the time, widely referred to as 'dull' and who were thought to be particularly susceptible to psychological damage from warfare. The Directorate, staffed by officers as well psychologists drawn from industry and academia, had a remit to establish a "rational system for matching capabilities quickly and accurately" in the Army.[169] The process of understanding warfare as a specialised form of industrial labour, begun in the First World War, has practical application in the Second in the porting of 'scientific' methods of selection, job analyses, developing testing procedures, and conducting follow-up investigations from the corporate sector to the military. If men had felt like they were working in an industrial concern in the First World War, in the Second their military lives were even more overtly organised according to practices and principles adapted from industry and commerce.[170] Such organisation also necessitated an extensive support system to process the administration of documentation required to manage the allocation, training, transfers and healthcare of troops. By November 1941 there were thirty-one Record Offices devoted to this task.[171] Bureaucratic organisation of the Army was increasingly requiring more personnel in the 'tail' than in the 'teeth.'[172]

In May 1942, the Army Council agreed to establishing a General Service Corps (GSC), to which everyone, regardless of trade or potential as officers, would be initially recruited. After a period of six weeks of basic training, during which individuals could be assessed for both strengths and weaknesses, recruits would be allocated to specific regiments and roles. The GSC reduced the failure rate in training and improved and evened out the supply of skilled men and officers among the different arms of service even though the fighting needs of the Army meant that not all men would receive the posting they wanted.[173] War Office Selection Boards (known as Wozbees), were established to process those identified as POM. Assessors at Wozbees were drawn from both military and psychology staff, but the President was a senior officer who always had the final say. Wozbees involved further tests, physical and mental, as well as leadership, teamwork and problem solving, and were regarded as a much fairer and less class-based system for officer selection. The GSC and Wozbees remained in place until the end of the war, and both contributed to an improvement in general morale.[174]

The work of job analysis (initially largely ignored by the Army) was begun in order to assist civilian psychologists in the Directorate to understand the Army's requirements, but job analysis received a new urgency following the establishment of the GSC.[175] Industrial psychologists "with experience of personnel selection and other human problems in industry" worked alongside specially selected officers to develop an analysis of Army trades and jobs.[176] The War Diaries of the Directorate reveal that job analysis was an ongoing process, with regular revisions in response to organisational changes in the Army.[177] The data from job analysis in turn fed into the design of selection tests. A streamlined, technical guide to jobs that Personnel Selection Officers could use during selection was developed to ensure standardisation across training camps and regiments. It became clear during this process that the officers across the Army were using different words to describe the "temperamental characteristics" required for each job.[178] Psychiatrists and officers worked together to develop a lexicon of terms that could be used to pin down desirable attributes for different roles. This lexicon organises into official language the emotional qualities that the Army was beginning to recognise and value. Instead of vague notions of 'character,' the lexicon of terms marks a moment when the British Army formulated a net of words through which emotional traits might be identified, captured and put to use.

Twelve key terms for "temperamental characteristics" were developed.[179] Not all of these can be described as emotional attributes – "leadership", "perseverance", "methodicalness" and "obedience" for example, are not emotives, although they may involve the performance of emotion. But the first two stand out as most definitely emotive. The first is "aggressiveness", associated with words such as "fighting spirit", "dash", "daring" and "guts." Aggressiveness is described as "a quality necessary only for fighting troops and to the greatest extent by those which are used in an attacking role."[180] While blood and hate training attempted to *mobilise* aggression, the identification of aggression as a quality desired in all fighting troops in the Army's official nomenclature is a more subtle instance of emotional engineering in which the institution attempts to establish practices to *capitalise* on an existing emotional quality in individuals. Despite the significance of aggressiveness, "Calmness under pressure" is second in the list. The associated terms for calmness under pressure include "cool", "steady", "imperturbable" and "equable temper."[181]

Calmness under pressure is the only term for which there is no description, nor is there any indication of what roles this kind of quality would best fit. The implication seems to be that calmness under pressure is widely understood, and desirable for all roles. There is no indication of how aggressiveness and calmness under pressure might work together, or of how being unexcitable might be reconciled with being dashing and daring. The tension between aggressiveness and calmness under pressure echoes broader cultural impulses that veered between wanting the Army to be belligerent enough to match those qualities of ferocity and hate widely believed to be implicit in the German and Japanese forces, but to still retain the coolness and evenness of temper similarly believed to be intrinsic to British national identity.

One example of how the tension between these two emotions played out for soldiers in the intersection of individual emotions with institutional requirements can be found in Norman Craig's account of his experiences during a course for "junior leaders" at Bournemouth. Craig was no stranger to training designed to 'harden' troops. He had undergone this kind of training at Lochailort and had later taken responsibility for designing a similar course for his company.[182] But the officer's training course he attended at Bournemouth was "more gentlemanly and academic" and involved theoretical exercises known as TEWTs (Tactical Exercises Without Troops).[183] Craig realised that doing well in TEWTs involved making choices that demonstrated "the required spirit of well-bred aggressiveness."[184] Craig's account demonstrates not only how the Army as an organisation wanted to capitalise on individual emotional qualities, but also, perhaps more importantly, how individuals navigated the institution's emotional regime. Aggression in this exercise does not exceed cultural and institutional boundaries, but it is also not something that Craig actually feels. Instead, it is a performance of the required emotions via strategic decision-making and the use of appropriate language, such as "sorting out the Hun."[185] Emotions in this instance become what Fineman refers to as "dramaturgical devices" allowing Craig to perform the emotion expected by the organisation.[186]

Later, on the battlefield, emotion as dramaturgical device became even more significant for Craig. In a passage that recalls the studied nonchalance of the First World War officer described in the War Diaries of the South Staffs in Chapter 1, Craig goes describes the role of the subaltern as "essentially histrionic" because "he had to feign a casual and cheerful optimism to create an illusion of normality and make it seem as if there was nothing in the least strange about the outrageous things one was asked to do."[187] Feigning nonchalance is thus not a 'dispassionate' response to combat, but one involving the deliberate management of emotion in response to situational and organisational requirements and norms. While the official lexicon adopted by the Army officially inserts the emotional quality of aggression into the organisation's practices of selection, regardless of the need for guts and daring, qualities of calmness or nonchalance continued to be valued as important national traits in the Second World War.

Despite the emphasis on systems of rational control expressed in the revised *FSR*, the British Army's attempts to manage fear, to martial hate and aggression and to identify and capitalise on emotional traits in the individual reveal the Army as an organisation taking official steps towards engineering emotion for its own purposes. All of these processes shaped the experience of the Second World War for soldiers – they determined where soldiers went, what roles they took on, how (or even if) they fought, and what happened if they were fearful of fighting. They also shaped how individuals responded to and interacted with the institution, as Craig's experiences indicate. Emotions – the unruly, unpredictable responses and traits in individuals – were subject to the rational and scientific controls and principles that transformed the British Army into "not only an instrument of war but a great factory of warriors."[188] The Second World War Unit War Diaries and their Appendices are the spaces in which all these factors – the rational framework of controls imposed by the *FSR*, the technology of the typewriter, the influence of the Army's emotional regime and the individual soldier – intersect at a granular level. What emerges from these writing spaces? How is the record of the Second World War shaped by and through them?

Individuality and emotional practices in the Second World War Unit War Diaries

Of the Second World War C.2118 forms (which constitute the War Diaries), 37 files, consisting of 115,172 words were analysed.[189] Of these, only six files were handwritten, and all the rest typed. 58 files of the Appendices were analysed, consisting of 110,040 words. All Appendices were typed, and consist not only of after-action reports, but also intelligence reports, orders of the day and special messages from Commanders to their Units. The C.2119 form reminds those completing Unit War Diaries that events were to be set out in the C.2118 forms and ordered according to "the time they occur, or come to notice."[190] The relatively static nature of trench warfare on the Western Front in theory made such reporting possible (although not always in practice, as detailed in Chapter 1), but the supposition that it was possible to maintain hourly, or even daily, reports during fighting was challenged across the many battlefields and fronts of the Second World War. The clerks and junior officers responsible for completing War Diaries adopted different methods of dealing with the challenge of keeping up to date, including relying on additional accounts in the Appendices, but also by retrospectively reconstructing events in the C.2118 forms of the War Diaries, or a combination of both. There is therefore more of a sense in these records of the blurring of lines between day-to-day reporting, and the recording of events after they had occurred. It is worth noting again that the examples examined in more detail in this section are a small selection of the Second World War corpus, and of a much larger body of documents in the records of Second World War. It is not my intention to make this corpus representative of the whole, but to reveal what emerges from the official record when these documents are not evaluated for factual accuracy, but for how they mediate between individual, institution and the war itself.

Chapter 1 has detailed how handwriting preserved traces of individuality in Unit War Diaries. According to Darren Wershler-Henry "[t]he only thing that is always visible in typewriting is the typewriter itself" but there are ways in which individuality manifests in the typed text.[191] This section begins by investigating typographic and other forms of errors as instances in which individual identity surfaces and disrupts the veneer of institutional order and control. This section then moves on to investigating operational reporting, as did Chapter 1, as a form of emotional practice. To briefly recap, as articulated by Monique Scheer, emotional practices are mindful and embodied activities communicated through specific mediums and technologies, and they are cultivated by and situated in the particular contexts, or *habitus*, in which they occur.[192] Emotional practices of the past can be identified in the observable traces they leave in mediated objects or representations. Chapter 1 has noted and analysed three forms of observable traces of emotion in the First World War records – emotives, punctuation and embellished narration. The more explicit instruction in the interwar *FSR* that Unit War Diaries should be supplemented by a more detailed "narrative of or report on operations" contributed to the production of a variety of accounts written after the events had occurred.[193] Unlike in the First World War corpus, therefore, the presence of embellished narratives in the Second World War corpus does not necessarily push against the regulations, given that the instructions explicitly call for more detailed accounts to supplement the daily records in the C.2118 forms, and the boundaries between these two kinds of reports are not always clearly maintained. After-action accounts create space in the record of war for the construction of narratives that occupy an uneasy space between official report, historiography and personal testimony. By analysing the spread of emotives, the emotive use of punctuation, and by delving into close reading of narrative accounts in the Second World War reports, this section investigates the changes or continuities in the observable traces of emotional practices in the records of the Second World War from those from the previous world war.

Disruptions in the typed text: Individuality through errors

Typographic errors (typos) and other kinds of errors such as spelling and grammatical mistakes challenge the apparent authority of machine-produced text, which is why the Pitman Manual of typewriting was at pains to suggest that the typewriter demanded "a higher standard of excellence" than even printed material.[194] Typos and other mistakes disrupt associations between the typewriter and accuracy and efficiency. In the First World War diaries and appendices, the rate of errors or spelling mistakes was very low (there are only eight errors in the entire corpus), but as discussed Chapter 1, the illegibility of the handwriting in some documents is so problematic that it sometimes obscures the meaning of sentences and inadvertently subverts the very purpose of the C.2118 form. The typewriter, to a degree, solved the problem of the illegibility of handwriting. That is not to say there are no instances of illegibility in the reports of the Second World War, but in the typed samples these are due in the main to the fading or blurring of ink, or the tearing or folding of the fragile typed paper. The use of the typewriter, however, paradoxically appears to have promoted spelling and grammatical errors, in addition to typographic mistakes. Neither form of error renders the documents illegible, but similar to handwriting, they constitute trace marks of individuality in the writing spaces of the Second World War.

Most of the errors in the War Diaries and Appendices can be loosely grouped into typographical and orthographical errors, following distinctions drawn by Kyongho Min, William Wilson and Yoo-Jin Moon.[195] Typographical errors are errors of mistyping, for example, hitting two keys at once, hitting the wrong key, or missing a key. Orthographical errors, in contrast, "arise from errors in cognitive processing such as guessing, or phonetic attempts at spelling, or selecting the wrong word."[196] In the latter category, the repeated misspelling of words provides glimpses of individuality. Some words in the English language are commonly misspelled, but there is something uniquely individual about having a blind spot when it comes to one specific word. The writer of the 2nd Bn Cheshire Regiment's Unit War Diaries for March 1943 repeatedly misspells "patrols" as "patrolls", for example, while in the Diaries of the 1st Bn South Staffs for 1944, the writer struggles with "bivouacked" throughout.[197] These kinds of repeated errors disrupt the neat contours of the Unit War Diaries and insist on the presence of the human being behind the text.

High concentrations of errors in Unit War Diaries and Appendices, although they do not obscure meaning, similarly disturb the veneer of order and control in the official reports of war. An account from the Unit War Diary of the 2nd Bn North Staffs during their withdrawal from Belgium to France in May to June of 1940 provides examples of a range of errors, from typographical to grammatical (in bold):

> Bn stood to at 0345 for an hour and **everyting** was unusually quiet until at about 0500 hrs very heavy fire came down and heavy rifle and L.M.G. broke out over the whole Bn front – from reports received it appeared that the enemy had **cross** the river to our left and in the sector held by the Grenadier Guards and having crossed they **swing** South and came in on the left flank of the Bn. Heavy fighting continued for approx. 2 hours but the Bn **stodd it's** ground, "B" and "D" Coys both suffering some casualties.[198]

Almost every entry for that month has similar errors. The person typing these reports may have been unaccustomed to using a typewriter, or may have been typing at speed, or a combination of both, or there may have been other factors in this individual's writing space that distracted them from their work. From the nature of this narrative, it is likely that these accounts were compiled after the events, and not as they were occurring. Scrawled and hasty entries in the War Diaries of the First World War examined in Chapter 1 conveyed something of the difficult conditions under which they were generated. The typewriter does not allow for that kind of embodied reflection, but high error rates are material traces of the labour involved in composing these reports..

Attempts to correct these kinds of errors, such as the correction by hand of "everyting" to "everything" and "cross" amended by hand to "crossed" in the Diary Entry for the 2nd Bn North Staffs mentioned above, further disrupt the orderliness of the typed text.[199] Such corrections raise questions of authenticity because it is impossible to accurately pinpoint when they were made, or to be certain whether they were made by the typist. They draw attention to the errors they are trying to hide, inadvertently highlighting them on the page. In other cases (see Figure 2.1), instead of retyping entire pages, a section of paper with the corrected information is pasted over the section that needed retyping, although it is likely that in these cases the errors lay in the information, rather than in typographical or orthographic mistakes.

Corrections by hand and the pasting of retyped sections disturb the continuity, both temporal and material, of the typed text, but other kinds of corrections, such as the crossing out of words, most often using the X key to cover the error, were more obviously made as the document was being produced.

All forms of corrections break the flow of the typed text and the act of reading, even if only momentarily. They are material traces not only of the various hands in contact with these pages, but also of the record's transformation over time, of its own history, and they trouble the supposed linearity of that history. Regardless of the nature of the correction they all create fissures in the perceived stability of the typed text. According to Marta Werner, corrections

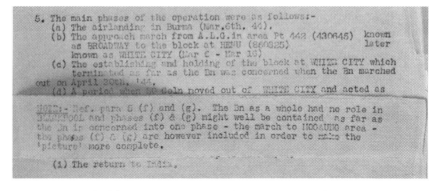

Figure 2.1 1 Staffordshire Regiment, "Introductory Notes to the War Diary 1st Bn The South Staffordshire Regiment for the Period March–July 44," WO 172-4920

(especially cancellations), disrupt "the teleology of composition: in place of a seamless continuity of argument or a chain of evidence, there is deviation."[200] Corrections are trace evidence of moments in which these documents were re-read and reshaped, and instances in which information was re-evaluated and transformed. They disrupt the supposed smooth production of information in the reports of war and are reminders that official records are not inert documents but are open to re-formulation from the moment of their creation. Because they draw attention to the materiality of the record, they additionally draw attention to the mediated nature of the information they contain and serve as essential reminders that these records are re-presentations of events, constructed and re-constructed by individuals using technologies of writing.

Typographic errors, repeated misspellings, grammatical errors and corrections do not produce illegibility in the records of the Second World War. They are, however, as much evidence of embodied human activity in the typed text as handwriting is in written records. Errors introduce elements of unruliness to the records of war, and push back, no matter how inadvertently, against the Army's attempts to eliminate variation and to depersonalise reporting. They disrupt the veneer of order and efficiency created by the typed text and are evidence of moments of discord between individual and writing machine. Attempted corrections to those errors in turn reveal some of the discontinuities in the production of the records and disturb their supposed stability. Traces of individuality can therefore still be identified in typed records, and as the next sections will show, the typewriter did not quite succeed in eradicating emotion from the official reports either.

Emotives

Emotives, as previously established, are a form of emotional practice that allows for the performance of emotion through language. Emotives might not represent what individuals are actually feeling, which is in any case impossible to establish in representations from the past. Emotives can be used to communicate and enact emotions that are considered appropriate to particular contexts. As mentioned earlier in this chapter, Norman Craig's account of deploying specific phrases to demonstrate a spirit of aggression in TEWTs provides a good example of the performative use of emotives. They can also be used to mask emotion, a function important for the performance of a particular version of British masculinity, as William Tyrell's testimony to the Southborough Committee about masking or camouflaging fear made clear. Identifying emotives always involves a certain level of subjectivity and is therefore not an exact science. Part of the very nature of emotional practices is that they do not conform neatly to precise parameters. In the C.2118 forms, or the War Diaries themselves, there were 369 instances of emotives (recall that this does not mean there were 369 emotive words, as this also refers to phrases or clusters of words). In the Appendices, 867 instances of emotives were identified and tagged. While emotives remain a small percentage of the overall wordcount, they are sparser in the C.2118 forms (at around 0.3% of the total) but appear at a higher percentage in the Appendices (0.8% of the total). The higher percentage of emotives in the appendices suggests that these accounts, freed from the structure and regulations of the C.2118 form, allow for a freer kind of emotional practice.

In both the C.2118 forms and the Appendices selected for analysis, positive emotives are accentuated, as they were in the First World War corpus, and those emotives that relate to emotions considered unwanted are minimised or downplayed. Fear remains an outlaw emotion. The diary of the 1st Cheshire Regiment stationed in Egypt early in the war comes perhaps closest of any selected for this corpus to referencing nervousness in the troops. The appearance of what appeared to be signalling activity in lights at night made whole battalion "jumpy," according to the entry for the 21st June 1940, and although a few days later it turned out that these lights were not due to enemy activity, they continued to "make the troops rather 'jittery'", according to the entry for the 24th June.[201] Nervousness is not quite the same as fear, of course, but the 1st Cheshire Regiment's Diary is unusual in acknowledging anxiety in any form in the selected sample of Diaries and Appendices.

Also similar to the First World War reports, there are few references (seven in total) to being shocked or shaken throughout the Second World War corpus. Shell-shock is only mentioned once throughout the entire corpus, in the War Diary of the 2nd Bn Cheshires for 21st March 1943, which describes a direct hit from a 21 cm Heavy Howitzer on one of the platoon's own gun emplacements, destroying the gun and leaving one man "severely shell shocked" and others "severely shaken." The Diary goes on to say that these men would "not be fit for action for some time," and also mentions, with characteristic understatement, that a second gun team, although uninjured, was "also affected" implying that they too, were traumatised by the blast.[202] It might be expected that there are few references to shell-shock, given that the use of the term was discouraged in Army discourse, so its appearance in one of the C.2118 forms is an instance of pushing against the norms of reporting and the army's regulations around language. The use of these emotives therefore provides some sense of how badly men were affected, and it suggests that the writer was himself shaken enough to use a term discouraged by the Army.

However, even the preferred term for psychological casualties after 1944, namely battle exhaustion, or exhaustion, occurs infrequently. It is mentioned three times in entries in the C.2118 forms, only in casualty lists of the Unit War Diaries of the 6th Bn North Staffs, as "exhaustion due to enemy action."[203] The account of the Battle of Calabritto (1943) in the Appendices of the 5th Bn Sherwood Foresters comes closest to using this term to hint at emotional and psychological trauma. It describes how a wounded officer's batman, who had remained with him throughout the day under intense fire, attempted at nightfall to fetch stretcher bearers for him, "but was too exhausted to do so."[204] It may well have been that the man was simply physically drained, but there is something about the use of this term, especially considering the extreme situation, that hints at more than physical exhaustion. The relative lack of emotives relating to fear and/or battle exhaustion is worth noting, as events such as the BEF's retreat from France in 1940 and the Italian campaign, both of which generated large numbers of psychological casualties (as mentioned previously in this chapter) and caused a widespread dip in morale, are covered by the Diaries and Appendices selected for this corpus. Of course, the numbers of psychological casualties would have been noted in the War Diaries of medical units, but the absence of any mention of psychological trauma in the records of those units directly involved in the fight is a measure of how effectively emotives related to emotions regarded as unacceptable in the dominant emotional regimes have been squeezed out of official reports.

Difficulties and challenges and their attendant emotions are similarly minimised in the Second World War reports. Whereas in the First World War corpus the spread and use of 'trying' nudged at the restraints of control, it appears more sparingly in the reports of the Second World War, as if the word were fading out of regular use. Instead, variations of 'unpleasant,' which occur a total of 18 times, appear to have replaced the use of 'trying.' In contrast to the use of 'trying,' which continues in the Second World War records to nudge at the limits of official language, the deployment of 'unpleasant' manifests as an emotional practice that utilises cultural norms of understating drama and trauma to process and re-present sometimes appalling events or circumstances. In North Africa, for example, the War Diary for the 6th Bn Cheshires on the 12th May 1943 describes an attack from a Nebelwerfer, a formidable weapon capable of launching devastating attacks with multiple rockets, which the Cheshires had nicknamed "the mangle," as "quite unpleasant."[205] In addition to understatement being a cultural characteristic, it can be interpreted as a performance on the part of the writers of these reports of imperturbability or coolness, the trait valued so highly in the Army's list of desirable attributes. Tyrrell's testimony to the Southborough Committee noted how the masking of emotions for men was "almost routine" in everyday life, and the paucity of emotives related to fear and other extreme emotional responses to industrial warfare in this corpus suggests that masking difficult emotions had, by the Second World War, become a matter of routine in the Army's records.[206]

Masking, or downplaying chaos, is also a matter of routine in the Second World War corpus. David Holbrook, a tank officer who fought in Normandy, vividly describes the chaos of combat in his largely autobiographical novel, *Flesh Wounds*:

> In the field there was always chaos, confusion, squalor; and each man was lost in the impersonal hell, where metal chased flesh, in one great mêlée. No individual made effective decisions, but reacted for the most part blindly to stimuli, and fought wild.[207]

Those completing the daily reports, or after-action accounts, had to process chaos and confusion on the battlefield into accounts that could be understood and used by the Army (and potentially later by historians), and they did not have the luxury of these kinds of emotive descriptions used by veterans in their memoirs and novels. There is therefore no mention of "chaos" or the kinds of things described by Holbrook anywhere in the Second World War corpus. At worst, situations are described as "confused" or "obscure", even in reports of extremely disorderly and messy events. The BEF's withdrawal from France, for example, which was complicated by German attacks by air and on the ground, mis-information and heavy congestion on the roads, is described in the various Unit War Diaries and Appendices addressing these events using exactly these terms.

The 2nd Bn North Staffordshire Regiment, for example, after having marched for almost twenty-five miles in one day with no food, reports in the entry to their Unit War Diary for 27th May, 1940 that they stalled their advance due to enemy shelling, after which "the situation became obscure," as the Bn pushed on in the darkness and under heavy fire and became separated.[208] One of the Appendices for the 1st Bn Welsh Guards describes the chaotic situation on the roads in Steenvoorde in Northern France in similar terms:

> The confusion which existed in Steenvoorde was inconceivable. There were a number of junior liaison officers from G.H.Q. in their own cars attempting to get Eastwards away from Cassel – there were French Gunners attempting to get South – there were a number of British Motor Ambulances, all empty, quite unable to make up their minds which way they wished to go. Added to this two Companies of the Battalion, with Transport, came piling into the cross roads in the middle of the town.[209]

Mentions of confusion are higher, at 14 instances, in the Appendices than they are in the Unit War Diaries (there are only five explicit mentions of confusion in the C.2118 forms). But although the Appendices detail sometimes random and chaotic events – communication breakdowns, instances of friendly fire, platoons and/or individuals going missing during fighting, operations going awry –a general sense of control is maintained through the narratives themselves, which suggest that these events can be ordered into cohesive accounts in which chaotic events can be explained and rationalised as momentary instances of confusion. The understatement of chaos in the Second World War corpus should not, however, be interpreted as a misrepresentation of events. Writers of these reports are conforming to the Army's demands for clarity and linearity as expressed through institutional regulations, and also to culturally determined impulses to impose rational frameworks on irrational and haphazard events. But in doing so, the reports contribute to "blending, smoothing, and rationalising, which, intentionally or not, may produce distortion."[210] The erasure of chaos and the understatement of confusion in the Second World War corpus continues the trend toward the distortion of war into order, begun in the records of the First.

Other emotives related to extreme emotions, such as hate or aggression, are also rare, despite the botched attempts to inculcate hate in training and the value placed on aggression in the Army's lexicon of desirable traits. Hate is used generally to refer to enemy action, as in the entry in the 1st Bn Cheshire Regiment's Diary for the 16th January, which refers to the heavy shelling at dawn and dusk as "the usual morning and evening 'hate'."[211] The only instance throughout the corpus in which hate is directed at the enemy occurs in a letter dated 11th February 1944, to the Fifth Army from its American commander, Lieutenant General Mark W. Clark. Enemy attacks in Anzio, according to the letter, should be welcomed because they provide "additional opportunities to kill your hated enemy in large numbers. It's open season in the ANZIO bridgehead and there's no limit to the number of Germans you can kill."[212] As an American, Clark was situated in the emotional regimes of a different culture, which to a certain degree might explain the explicit reference to hating the enemy and the implicit bloodlust in the statement, which is aimed at motivating troops. I am not suggesting that no British commander ever expressed hatred for the enemy in official communications, but that in the corpus selected for this book, the kind of emotives used by Clark are unusual enough to stand out as an exception.

However, while overt hatred is rare, aggression manifests in the Second World War corpus through the deployment of derogatory racial epithets, in particular 'Boche' or 'Bosche' in reference to the Germans. The term appears only three times in the C.2118 forms, but in the Appendices it appears 73 times – another indication of how the more open format of the Appendices encouraged the performance of emotion in a different way to the more formal constraints of the C.2118 forms. The etymology of 'Boche' is unclear, but it predates the First World War, when, according to the recorded usage in the Collins Dictionary its usage spiked significantly.[213] Despite the extensive usage of the term during the First World War, it does not appear extensively in that corpus.[214] Collins defines 'Boche' as a derogatory term for Germans, particularly German soldiers. But usages of slurs like 'Boche' have implications that extend far beyond their lexical meaning, as many in the field of the philosophy of language have argued.[215] The "primary function" of racial slurs and pejoratives, according to Christopher Hom, "is to conventionally convey negative, emotional content beyond the truth-conditional content that they are normally taken to encode (if any). This emotional content reflects the derogatory attitudes of their speakers."[216] However, the attitudes of those using the term, as Hom acknowledges, may vary significantly in intensity. Jennifer Hornsby similarly argues that these kinds of terms are "commonly understood to convey hatred or contempt without being in a position to say at all exactly what commitments those who see fit to use it may incur."[217] Ethnic slurs, perhaps even more than any other linguistic form, thus operate as emotives that convey meanings that exceed their semantic dimensions, and which also, to a certain degree, render the emotional intensity or intention of the user immaterial.

112 *Unit War Diaries in the Second World War*

The term is particularly concentrated in the Appendices of the 5th Bn Sherwood Foresters and in those of the 2nd Battalion North Staffordshires. In accounts of three different engagements in Italy by the 5th Bn Sherwood Foresters it occurs a total of 47 times.[218] In the Appendices of the 2nd Battalion North Staffordshires, the term appears 21 times in a single long narrative of the Battalion's experiences in Africa and Italy.[219] The experiences of the Foresters in crossing the Volturno and engaging Germans is indicative of its usage:

> Between 1000 and 1100 hrs Bosche tried to counter-attack the Fosse frontally. This was sp by mortar and gun-fire, but failed owing to the lack of cover and Bren and rifle fire. Five Bosche who reached in 100 yds of our posn gave themselves up and seemed delighted to do so.[220]

Those who deploy such terms, according to Richard Vallée, "know that using them conveys more than the official content, that these words suggest something different from what is said, and that they have a strong impact in linguistic communication."[221] 'Boche' conveys more than 'German,' it "conveys the idea that *Germans are despicable because of it*, namely *because of being German*."[222] The repeated choice of 'Boche' over German, is therefore a performative emotional practice that activates hate and contempt by "cast[ing] a wide net of prejudices," although it is not possible to gauge the depth of those feelings in the writer.[223] However, despite the extensive deployment of the term in these two Appendices, the use of 'Boche' as an emotive does not necessarily push at the boundaries of operational reporting. Like Norman Craig's use of the term 'Hun' in the TEWTS, the use of 'Boche' remains in the confines what Craig describes as the "spirit of well-bred aggressiveness."[224] As Craig's experience demonstrates, the deployment of terms like Hun and Boche was an emotional practice condoned, and at times even expected, in the emotional regime of the British Army.

As in the reports of the First World War, positive emotives are emphasised throughout the Second World War corpus, especially those believed to be associated with British national identity. While enemy action was characterised as a form of hate, the reports of the Second World War corpus emphasise that the British endured and fought with "fortitude and cheerfulness."[225] Cheerfulness and coolness are more widespread than negative emotives such as shock or fear in the Second World War corpus, as they were in the First. There are nine mentions of coolness, the emotional state valued so highly by the Army that it applied to all roles. In the disastrous first attempt at a major night-time glider operation to launch the Allied invasion of Sicily (Operation Ladbroke), during which only 12 of the 147 gliders launched landed roughly where they should have been,[226] the diary entry for the 14th July 1943 of the 2nd Bn South Staffs notes "the discipline and coolness" of those who landed in the sea, observing that there "was no case of panic" despite the fact that many men drowned.[227] Coolness is similarly deployed in the description of Operation Veritable in the Reichswald in the after-action account of the 2nd Bn Welsh

Guards, which notes how the infantry, despite the lack of tanks to support them, "advanced with great coolness and determination" in the face of "extremely heavy and accurate shell fire" in March 1945.[228] But even more than coolness, the value of cheerfulness as a trait in the British soldier is illustrated by its distribution across the corpus, where it is mentioned 17 times, mostly in the Appendices. The idea of cheerfulness as a national trait in the British soldier clearly persisted after the First World War. The men of the 5th Bn Sherwood Foresters 'A' Company, for example, earned the admiration of the writer of the after-action account of the Battle of Calabritto because despite never having "heard a shot fired in anger before [they] cheerfully accepted an almost critical situation" while facing heavy shelling.[229] The deployment of cheeriness and coolness, like all emotives in the records, has a performative dimension, and it should not be taken to mean that British soldiers really were cheery by disposition, or felt calm under pressure.

Veteran accounts of coming under artillery fire in the Second World War suggest a complex range of emotional responses that go far beyond cheerfulness, coolness or even fear. Alex Bowlby describes how he began sobbing while frantically trying to dig himself a fox hole during a mortar attack, but also that in the aftermath of a shell exploding almost in his face he felt an unexpected sense of calm.[230] If subalterns and officers feigned "a casual and cheerful optimism,"[231] there is every chance that ordinary soldiers, at least at times, pretended a cheerfulness or a calmness they did not feel. According to Geoffrey Picot, who describes taking heart from the steadiness of his men only to find out later that they were all frightened, "Nearly all of us played this concealment game. Thus, a man pretending to be brave gave bravery to his comrades; as they, with their pretence, likewise gave bravery to him."[232] It is also possible that the men writing the accounts chose to emphasise cheeriness to bolster regimental reputation. Alternatively, it is conceivable that the writers of war records misinterpreted the men's emotional state completely. Alexander Baron describes just such a moment in his account of the Wessex Regiment, which, although fictional, was based on his own wartime experiences in the Pioneer Corps:

> The battalion was marching back towards the line. As the grumbling of the guns grew louder, the jesting and singing in the ranks died away and the men felt the sickness of fear deep in them; for they had not forgotten.
> But the padre, standing at the road junction as they trudged dustily by, saw only the firm brown faces, the cigarettes perked up at the corners of their mouths, the tousled hair under their steel helmets; and he marvelled that men could be so strong.[233]

In all probability, British soldiers were as likely, if not more, to be "browned off and bloody minded," as Alan Allport refers to them, as they were to feel cheerful or calm.[234] The use of positive emotives in the British Army's records of war do not constitute falsehoods or misrepresentations. They are examples of complicated interactions between the writers of the accounts and the needs and expectations of individual and Regimental pride, the Army and of British culture, which result in the smoothing over of the complexity of individual emotional responses and reactions to warfare.

Gallantry remains an important positive emotive, as it was in the First World War, but it has undergone a slight recalibration in the records of the Second. As in the First World War corpus and in the Official Histories, gallantry is used in most instances in relation to acts of self-sacrifice. It is used only six times in the C.2118 forms and occurs another 24 times in the Appendices. Of the six instances, four occur in the South Staffordshire's Unit War Diaries describing the Glider attack during Operation Ladbroke in Sicily in July 1943. Despite the devastating loss of gliders and men in this Operation due to combination of a lack of adequate preparation, high winds and anti-aircraft fire, the South Staffs succeeded against overwhelming odds in their objective, which was to take and hold the Ponte Grande bridge. The deployment of gallantry in these C.2118 forms is thus relatively unsurprising, given the many acts of bravery and sacrifice, such as the Corporal who drowned while helping men out of one of the 65 gliders that landed in the sea.[235] But its repeated use in this War Diary is unusual enough to stand out as an instance in which emotives push against the boundaries of the C.2118 form and its restrictions.

In almost half of the instances of the use of gallantry, however, it is used to describe acts that *do not* end in disaster or sacrifice. Of these, eight instances refer to events in which men were on the attack, rather than to defensive actions, withdrawals, or rescues. There is a hint in these accounts of a shifting understanding of the concept of gallantry, moving it away from sacrifice in service of monarch and country and bringing it closer to martial ideals of heroic aggression. Melvin Smith's study of the history of the Victoria Cross (VC) illustrates that shift more clearly. The V.C., described as of December 2022 on the U.K. government's web pages for medals, is the "premier Operational Gallantry award" for "bravery, or some daring or pre-eminent act of valour or self sacrifice, or extreme devotion to duty in the presence of the enemy." Yet of the 182 VCs awarded in the Second World War, the clear majority were given for offensive actions, leading Smith to conclude that "A hero does not save the wounded. A hero does not engage in meaningless acts of a symbolic nature. The hero kills the enemy."[236] In the deployment of gallantry in the First World War corpus, there was a sense of an old concept being used to make sense of a new kind of war. The widespread use of gallantry across the Appendices of the Second World War corpus, however, implies an increasing association between the concept and the militaristic value of aggression.

Despite the typewriter's reputation for generating authoritative, official text, it did not remove traces of emotives from operational records. The practice of accentuating positive emotions continues in the Unit War Diaries and the Appendices of the Second World War. The erasure of negative or unwanted emotions in the reports of the Second World War corpus reinforces the perception that war can be understood without accounting for the intensity of horror, terror and trauma and the complexities of its emotional dimension. Similarly, the turbulent, random and unpredictable nature of industrial warfare is downplayed throughout the corpus. Despite the occasional moments in which emotives push against the restraints of the C.2118 forms, and the increased use of emotives in the Appendices, emotives overall in the Second World War corpus are folded into official accounts and are routinised by use. Although some have shifted slightly in comparison to the First World War corpus – trying, for example, is not used as frequently and gallantry is deployed differently – the minimisation of outlaw emotions, the practice of understatement especially in extreme situations, and the accentuation of positive emotives are all emotional practices that conform to, rather than push against, the contours of cultural and institutional emotional regimes. But the neatness of the typed text could be disrupted by another form of emotional practice – the use of the exclamation mark, which continues to push against the structures of the official report.

Disruption in the typed text: Punctuation

As established in Chapter 1, punctuation marks are a vivid reminder of the embodied presence of the human being in the writing spaces of conflict and constitute what Jennifer DeVere Brody calls "an archive of feelings" not evident in words alone.[237] The exclamation mark especially injects emotion into texts, over and above the meaning of words. As mentioned Chapter 1, the exclamation mark had been "banished to the literary margins" by the beginning of the Twentieth Century.[238] As a measure of how rare the exclamation mark was not only in literature but also in official forms of communication, it was not included as a key on the keyboards of most typewriters.[239] Typewriters were associated with efficiency and standardisation, after all, not with supposedly frivolous declarations of emotion. Producing an exclamation mark in typed text consequently involved typing a period, then backspacing and adding an apostrophe above it. Even for a skilled touch-typist these actions constituted a break in typing, a disruption of the production of the typed text. The inclusion of exclamation marks in typed, official forms such as the Second World War Unit War Diaries and Appendices is thus an even more deliberate indication of an affective signifier or response than in written accounts.

"A high frequency of exclamation points," according to Donald Rubin and Kathryn Greene, instead of signalling the excitability of the writer, "can be regarded as a sort of orthographic intensifier signalling, 'I *really* mean this!'."[240] The use of a double exclamation mark occurs only three times in the entire corpus, and all occur in reports of the 6th Bn Cheshires. It is therefore tempting to suggest that the reports were written by the same man, but they are not signed, and it is not possible to say this with any certainty. It occurs once in the Bn's War Diary, in a description of heavy fighting around Tunisia in 1943. The entry for 'C' Company's report on the 7 May is a single line: "It was rumoured that the enemy were thinning out!!"[241] The double exclamation mark stands out on the page, darker than the surrounding text, as if the writer had hit those keys harder than the others.

In all three cases the use of the double exclamation mark intensifies the significance of the words, but I would suggest not quite in the way Rubin and Green describe the use of the exclamation mark as an orthographic intensifier. They draw attention not to something the writer really means, but to something beyond the words – a sense of something ineffable that the writer cannot, or perhaps will not, put into words in the confines of an official communique. They disrupt the flow of information with a performative gesture of emotion that in typed records had to be executed with deliberate care. Even if it is uncertain what emotion prompted their inclusion, the double exclamation marks make clear that emotion was present in the writer. They are a momentary disruption not only of the act of typing, but also of the typed text on the page. They create an affective pause in the reading that connects to the affective pause in the typing and that connects, even if fleetingly, the human beings in very different writing and reading spaces.

There are no other instances of double exclamation marks elsewhere in the Second World War corpus. Single exclamation marks are more prevalent in the Appendices, where they occur 12 times as opposed to two instances in the C.2118 forms. Four of these are concentrated in one record – that of the 2nd Bn Welsh Guards from October 1944.[242] The relatively liberal use of the exclamation mark in this account indicates how far this particular after-action report diverts from the norm. It is a detailed account of an illicit excursion undertaken by the writers in search of alcohol and other diversions, which will be discussed in more detail in the next section. The writer's description of a desperate attempt by the German Forces to destroy the Nijmegen bridge in the fierce fighting to secure the salient provides some sense of the overall tone: "Oh dear! Oh dear! – the Venetian Divers! Those twelve intrepid seal-like figures who swam down stream to lay their devastating charges against the massive piers of the bridge."[243] The exclamation marks are part of the conversational tone adopted throughout this report, which is also accompanied by hand-drawn illustrations. Both the narrative and the illustrations are playful subversions of the formal requirements of operational reporting, and the use of exclamation marks are part of the stylistic elements that set this report apart from the others. The remainder of the exclamation marks nudge more subtly at the boundaries of official reporting by introducing notes of embodied affective responses, as they did in the First World War records. They are emotional notes that resonate beyond the meaning of the sentences, and the effort required to create them is suggestive of heightened emotion that disrupts, even momentarily, the official language of the reports.

Like errors in the typed reports, the deployment of the exclamation mark provides glimpses of the human beings in the writing spaces of Second World War, as do the different approaches to narratives that emerge in the corpus.

War stories

The speed of the typewriter facilitated the production of paperwork, and longer narratives emerge in the records of the Second World War than those found in the First World War corpus. These vary considerably in style and content, from first-person testimonies of individual experiences in specific battles to third-person narratives covering particular engagements or sweeping through entire campaigns. The "'uncertain' nature between literary and historical writing, between fictional and documentary, spontaneous and reflected narrative" of the personal diary has, as Jochen Hellbeck observes, presented a quandary for both literary and historical writers.[244] Although they are not personal diaries, the accounts in the Appendices occupy a similarly indeterminate zone between official record, individual testimony, and historiography. They carve out space for personal expression in the official reports, and facilitate not only the increased use of emotives, but the performance of a range of emotional responses, some unexpected. Like Natalie Zemon Davis, what I am interested in here is not the factual value of these accounts, but in "their forming, shaping, and molding elements: the crafting of a narrative."[245] Assessing these documents only by virtue of their historical 'accuracy,' or dismissing them because of their subjectivity, overlooks the ways in which their writers, very similarly those of the Sixteenth Century pardon tales examined by Davis, "made sense of the unexpected and built coherence into immediate experience" through narrative.[246] Analysing how these stories were told, rather than evaluating the information they contain about events, reveals the ways individuals navigated the interstices between war, private reflection and institutional requirements, and sometimes leveraged space inside them for moments of resistance and unruliness.

That is not to suggest that there are no accounts in the Second World War corpus that do not emphasise data over narrative. The Unit War Diaries of the 1st Bn Sherwood Foresters in action near Tobruk in June 1942, for example, are so sparse that they provide the very bare minimum of data. The entry for the 6th of June 1942, for example, reads

> Two platoons (Anti Tank) in action at dawn. Eleven enemy Tanks accounted for. Lieut. E.J. Woodsend, 2nd Lt J. Dolphin and 45 other ranks reported missing. Seven Guns (6pdr) lost.[247]

But in others, especially in situations in which it was impossible to keep daily accounts, events were recounted in narrative form after they had occurred in both the C.2118 forms and the Appendices accompanying them. The records of the 1st Bn South Staffordshire Regiment, engaged with the Japanese in what was then Burma in 1944, illustrate how narratives of the same action are spread across different reports, and take different shape. An Introductory Note to the War Diary for the Bn explains that

118   *Unit War Diaries in the Second World War*

> due to the nature of operations carried out during the period, it has been impossible for security reasons, to keep a full day to day war diary of the Bn. For this reason, the diary has been compiled from code notes kept during operations and from the files at Rear HQ 77 Ind Inf Bde in whose War Diary appropriate references will be found.[248]

The entry in the War Diary for the 21st March 1944 gives some sense of why it was so difficult for the Bn to maintain records while events unfolded. It describes an attack on the Bn's position by the Japanese, which

> continued throughout the night and was flung in regardless of casualties. Hand-to-hand fighting of the greatest savagery continued for nearly eight hours, during which time, S.D. continued overhead. At mid-night [sic] life-buoys cleared one posn near 38 Coln HQ, but the Japanese succeede d [sic] in occupying the whole of the perimeter side of BARE HILL and 38 Coln HQ Hill, though the crest was still in our hands. The confusion in the pitch blackness was total.[249]

The fighting continued into the following day, when the Japanese finally were forced to retreat, after which things quietened down a little for the Bn. The narrative constructed in this War Diary about these events conforms to the regulations governing reporting in the War Diary by keeping the account as bare of emotion and as factual as possible.

A supplementary account in one of the Appendices to this Diary, however, demonstrates how the more open format of the after-action account facilitated a different style of narration. The Officer composing the account of the fighting was not part of the Bn but was a staff officer of 3 India Division, also operating in the area. His account also describes the fighting as defined by "savagery," but goes further to say that

> it is difficult indeed to envisage it, unless one has seen it. It was, at times, almost 'medieval' – as more than one person phrased it. Hand-to-hand combat was the order of the day – and night, and this went on almost literally, for hours on end, rifle and bayonet against two handed feudal sword, kukri against bayonet, no quarter to the wounded, while hand grenades lobbed over the heads of the combatants incessantly.[250]

In this report, the writer provides the supplemental information that the *FSR* requests, but the events are crafted into a narrative that organises the events in a reassuring ideological framework. The unprecedented savagery of the fighting is largely explained as a response to the fanaticism of the Japanese, who would continue to fight "from the ground and will shoot or stab in the back from where they lie until killed themselves." An attack on the Japanese in the village of Mawlu is part of a decision by the officer in command to "smite them," and the resulting action "smote them in hip and thigh." The use of language generally associated with archaic, and particularly Biblical, texts implies righteous action against an unholy enemy, and it justifies a particularly brutal attack on the Japanese by Gurkha forces. The Gurkhas, who were isolated and suffered losses due to unexpected delays and communication breakdowns in the rest of the attack force, "lost their temper completely" and "inflicted grisly horrors on their enemies" until the Japanese broke and ran.[251] The fighting in this region was amongst the most brutal in the war, with horrors inflicted by all sides. Whereas no explanation for the savagery of the fighting is made in the Unit War Dairy, the after-action account explains the actions of the British forces, which profoundly disrupt notions of the spirit of well-bred British aggression, through a more reassuring ideological narrative of righteous, almost Biblical, vengeance in response to blind fanaticism.

Similar contrasts can be drawn between narrative accounts in the War Diaries and Appendices detailing the BEF's withdrawal from France. The Unit War Diary of the 2nd Bn North Staffordshire for May-June 1940 details their fighting withdrawal from Belgium to Dunkirk, for example, and like the account of the fighting in Burma, was most likely composed after the events. The account in the Diary, although not by any means terse, is as dispassionate as possible and conforms to the rational structures of reporting in the C.2118 forms, but the after-action report in the Appendix, as in the example of the account in Myanmar, infuses the events with meaning. The difference in narrative styles is illustrated by the reports of a counter-attack ordered by the Brigade Commander as the Bn struggled to maintain their defensive lines against the advancing Germans. In the Unit War Diary, this moment is described in detail in the entry for the 21st May 1940, but without emotion: "The Colonel then ordered Major F.G. Matthews who was in command of "'A' Coy to counterattack with 2 Pls in the direction of ESQUELMES (903389) supported by our Carrier pl." Events do not go as planned. The platoons fail to co-ordinate, and after the attack, "no trace could be found of Major Matthews."[252] In the description of the same events in the Appendix, the attack was

> very gallantly lead by Major Matthews and though owing to enemy fire the co-operation of the Carrier Pl was never thoroughly established, the counter attack succeeded in preventing further enemy penetration on the left of the Bn. In this action Major Matthews and his Company covered themselves with glory but they lost heavily and Major Matthews was seen to fall.[253]

In the Appendix, the counter-attack and the loss of Matthews and his men is reassuringly reframed as a glorious moment in a sequence of events that, if not entirely ordered, unfolded comprehensibly. Both forms of report narrativise events, and both are situated as historical records in the Army's discourse on reporting, but this example demonstrates how the Appendices made room for a style of narration that makes sense of difficult, sometimes upsetting events by processing them via reassuringly ordered stories that reframe events through familiar ideologies, in this case the nobility of self-sacrifice.

The accounts of the withdrawal from France, as well as the fighting in Burma, go further than their primary remit of supplementing the accounts in the C.2118 forms. They give meaning to events that were so far beyond the expected, even in warfare, that they challenged the very idea of what fighting should be, and they organise moments of defeat and chaos into orderly narratives that imply that such states can be understood and reversed. But the Appendices also served other purposes, such as communicating lessons learned. Lieutenant Eric Davies's account, which details the steps he took to escape and evade capture following the glider attack in Sicily in July 1943, provides one example.[254] In contrast to the two accounts above, Davies's is a first-person narrative, bringing it closer in style to a memoir rather than an operational report. From the opening description of the glider crashing into the sea through to Davies's capture by Italian Forces and eventual escape, the tone remains light, and the narrative conforms to the cultural norm of understating difficulty. Following one escape attempt, he describes a beating as being "thoroughly pasted" by the guards, and later details being "interrogated in style" which involved "all the usual approaches" including having his life threatened. The crafting of the narrative is itself a performance of coolness in which Davies, who was later awarded a Military Cross for his actions, casually describes events such as resetting the broken bones in a fellow soldier's hand while others held the injured man down, tricking a dentist into drilling several holes in his teeth just so that he could steal a set of forceps, suffering through several instances of Allied bombardments and of almost being shot by pursuing German soldiers. The only hint that he might have suffered emotional strain is in the final sentences, when he warns those who might find themselves in a similar position that they might experience "depression when one doesn't care if one succeeds or not," but he exhorts them to "keep going, it's worth it."[255] The account does more than provide practical advice for those who might face similar trials. It models a way of responding to them based on institutional and cultural ideals of the imperturbable British officer, who remains cool and never gives in, regardless of adversity. The insouciant tone and style blur the lines in this report between the literary and documentary, the personal and the official account. Although it is a highly individualised narrative, it nevertheless conforms to both cultural and institutional norms in representing events in conflict.

One Appendix, that of the 2nd Bn Welsh Guards for October 1944 is a deliberately transgressive take on the very function and form of operational reporting. From late September to early October 1944, the Guards were involved in the operation to secure the Nijmegen Bridge and salient. Towards late October, however, things had settled down for the Battalion, and according to the entry for the 27th of that month, much of their time was spent "checking personal kits, recreational training, and drill," which presumably allowed the writer the time not only to compose this report, but also to undertake some of the events described in it.[256] The Appendix, with characteristic understatement, is titled "The Nijmegen Nuisance." It begins with a tongue-in-cheek description of working with the Americans, including a comment on their "unorthodox" methods of reporting: "'Everything fine and dandy and a smile of everybody's face' was their official report after a somewhat severe enemy counter-attack."[257] The writer's account of the engagements around Nijmegen goes on to be far more unorthodox than the reporting style of the Americans.

It begins with an elaborate metaphor in which the Corps Commander is compared to a "harassed housewife," the First Airborne Division compared to a "beloved son" and the bridge itself to a "newly acquired cook" and a "precious liability which had to be insured and watched with constant apprehension."[258] A sketch reinforces these metaphors (see Figure 2.2).

Despite the unorthodox tone, the report displays an awareness of some of the key issues involved in the engagement around the Nijmegen. It is critical of the decision to evacuate the First Airborne Division "at the end of a record 500 mile breakthrough," suggesting that this boosted German morale and dampened that of the Allied forces.[259] The report displays awareness of the crucial implications facing the Allies in terms of maintaining the initiative and the difficulties of keeping supply lines open after Operation Market Garden had not quite gone as planned: "But gradually it became apparent that one could not go gaily on into Germany with supplies that took nine days to come up a road which at several points during its latter stages passed in two miles of the enemy."

It describes some of the challenges in the engagement, such as the failed supply drops before the bridge was taken, "very little of which reached our troops in Arnhem," as well as the successful glider drop that eventually brought in reinforcements.[260] It notes the continued attacks on the bridge by the Germans after it had been captured, including numerous air attacks by the Luftwaffe and the failed attempt to blow the bridge by German Marine Commandos, the "Venetian Divers" mentioned earlier in the section on punctuation. The attacks, and the measures taken to defend the bridge, are also illustrated.

While there is thus at least some attempt to address military matters in the report, even if they are all couched in an informal and satirical tone, the Appendix departs from military reporting to describe a partridge shoot (also illustrated) conducted by Officers in the Dutch countryside very much as they would a shoot in Cambridgeshire. The remainder of the Appendix is devoted to a mission undertaken by the writer and one fellow soldier in response to a "high level decision" made by the "Ministry of Gastronomic Warfare" to investigate "conditions prevailing in those principle production centres of Gallic sunshine – Rheims, Bordeaux and Cognac." In other words, to go in search of wine and spirits. The trip, taking six days in total, included a visit to the brothels of Montmartre (there is a promise of a more detailed report to be made on the findings of this excursion for "limited distribution" – if there was one, it was not included in the Appendices!), as well as visits to relatives and

Figure 2.2 2 Welsh Guards, "The Nijmegen Nuisance," WO 171-1260, TNA, Kew

stays in various hotels and cafés along the route. The report includes philosophical musings, attempting to find meaning from "these seemingly crazy days" by drawing a comparison between human nature and the process of making wine, in which grapes are "cut off in their prime, crushed in the agony of the press, made to give their all" but go on to create a "spirit which, for purity, vigour and character, stands unrivalled."[261] The piece ends with the pair's reluctant return to their Bn in a car loaded with liquor.

Like most of the Appendices selected in this corpus, the "Nijmegen Nuisance" is difficult to classify. It is neither an historical account of the Bn's experiences (and might well be ignored by military historians), nor an account containing information that would in any way help the Army to wage war more effectively. It is closer to individual memoir than anything else, but its structure as a report complicates that classification, although it simultaneously transgresses all the expectations and regulations of operational reporting. It should not, however, be dismissed or ignored, as it is a moment of resistance, not only against the structures of operational reporting, which it both mimics and mocks, but also against the war itself. Its deliberately careless tone, particularly in recounting the details of the partridge shoot and the illicit excursion into France, is a performance of lightness in the face of awfulness. It represents a reaching back to a different kind of world and life outside of the war, but at the same time, illustrates the complexities of the war experience, which involved not only desperate engagements over strategic bridges, but also unexpected pleasures and even the occasional adventure. "The Nijmegen Nuisance" inserts these experiences into the official record of war. It is an insistent articulation of the self in the midst of the constraints of institutional life and the pressures of combat.

As personal accounts of experiences articulated through an institutional framework, with the needs of the institution in mind as well as a consciousness of future histories, the after-action Appendices are documents that do not fit comfortably any one genre. They are indeterminate spaces that insert individual reflection and the interpretation of events into the official record of war. In the main, these reflections shape narratives that craft coherence from chaos and meaning from trauma and loss, applying institutional and cultural emotional practices and ideological principles in order to do so. But there are instances, such as the account of the events around Nijmegen, that push back against the formalities of reporting, and by doing so, draw attention to their structures. Their subjectivity, and their overt use of emotives, might in some cases undermine their authority as reliable historical sources, but they are important reminders of the multiplicity of experiences and perspectives in war and of the sometimes creative techniques adopted by individuals using institutional structures of reporting to process challenging moments and events.

Conclusion

From Belgium to the jungles of Myanmar, the deserts of North Africa, the rivers and bridges of Holland, and the offices on the home front in Britain, the spaces in which clerks and officers of the British Army composed the reports of the Second World War were many and varied. According to the Army's own conceptualisation of Unit War Diaries, these reports constitute a historical record of operations, making them the first draft of the history of the Second World War. Although the physical spaces in which they were composed varied radically, there were ideological, cultural and technological dimensions shared across the writing spaces of this conflict. The reports of the Second World War took shape in an institutional framework that retained its faith in "commensense [sic] rules which have guided all fighting since the earliest days" and rational, scientific approaches to warfare.[262] The British Army was meant to be an efficiently functioning industrial machine, and its human components were managed through 'scientific' processes of selection and training, which included the engineering of emotions to suit the Army's needs. The typewriter fitted neatly into practices that emphasised efficiency and order. As a tool of command and control, it was considered essential for the fast and efficient production of information and was deployed widely.

The records of the Second World War selected for this book reflect, inevitably, the influence of the British Army's ideological investment in rational systems of order and control. Whereas in the First World War corpus there was a sense of emotives pushing back against these structures, in the Second World War, despite the increased spread of emotives through Appendices, there is more of a sense of the use of emotives as part of practices that conform to the Army's emotional regime. The sampled reports of those units involved on the ground in the fighting do not acknowledge fear. Instead, they emphasise cheerful resistance, coolness under fire and gallant action. Displays of aggression remain inside acceptable cultural boundaries or are explained away as responses to aggressive actions on the part of the enemy. The expression of these kinds of emotives conforms to the emotions associated with British national identity at the time. Emotion is not written out of the first draft of the history of Second World War, but those emotions that are considered manageable, or desirable, are emphasised above any others.

The result is a smothering of what Joanna Bourke referred to as "the underlying glossolalia of combat – that hubbub of sounds, screeches and stutterings that are the language of emotions."[263] There may well be no place for screeches and stutterings in the official records of war, but the erasure of horror, terror, fury, pain and other extreme emotions from the record simplifies the account of warfare. The masking of extreme emotions, which at the very least might impede decision-making, implies that the rational controls and routines implemented by the Army through training or doctrine are generally effective. The absence of clear acknowledgements in official records of how, and when, such controls fail, and individuals are overwhelmed by emotion makes it difficult for the Army as an organisation to learn from such moments and develop efficient responses to them.

The masking of extreme emotion in the Second World War corpus is part of a rhetoric of control that also relies on the eradication of any real acknowledgement of unpredictability and chaos. The *FSR* acknowledged, to a certain degree, the difficulties of uncertainty and unpredictability on the battlefield. "The first and most constant difficulty of the commander in war – apart from the inherent elements of danger and fatigue," according to the 1935 version, "– is the continual succession of unforeseen incidents and obstacles which tend to impede him in accomplishing what he has set out to do."[264] The *FSR* go on to explain how the practiced application of "commonsense" approaches can counter unpredictability. It was not, therefore, that British doctrine did not acknowledge chaos in war after the First World War, but that the Army retained the belief that character, training and organisation were enough to mitigate against it. Like the records of the First World War, the records of the Second sampled for analysis do not fully engage with chaos on the battlefield. They sweep away the fog of war in accounts that work hard, sometimes desperately, to manufacture coherence from confusion, and that therefore adhere to the principles of order that the Army attempted to impose on warfare. To a degree, the crafting of ordered narratives from chaotic events in official reports is understandable, as it was in the records of the First World War. After all, as Roger Beaumont notes, "Descriptions that convey ambiguity or uncertainty are less likely to be accepted than those presented in a self-confident tone."[265] But they convey the idea that unpredictability and disorder are ultimately explicable and manageable, and therefore generate a distorted perception of the nature of modern warfare.

The typewriter appeared to be a machine perfectly suited to expressing the rhetoric of control in the records of war. It increased the legibility of official documents and eradicated the unevenness and unpredictability of individual handwriting. It did not, however, succeed in fully depersonalising official documents. The typewriter, paradoxically, generated more errors than the pen, possibly because it could be used at greater speeds. Typographic and orthographic errors disrupt the mask of tidiness and legibility that the typewriter imposed on the records of war. They also disturb the typed text's "vested institutional authority" by providing a glimpse of the flawed human being producing the document.[266] Although they do not necessarily obscure the meaning of the text, typos and other errors insert individuality into the impersonality of the records of war while simultaneously drawing attention to their mediated, material nature. The use of the exclamation point similarly disrupts the typed text and insists on the presence of emotional responses that lie beyond rational forms of expression. The inclusion of exclamation marks in typed text involved forcing the machine to produce a character that it was not designed to create. Exclamation marks can therefore be considered as a form of resistance, no matter how small, to the technology itself, as well as to the overall structures and norms of institutional forms of communication.

The typewriter also encouraged the production of narratives of greater length and detail. The *FSR* called for supplementary narratives but did not specify exactly what these should entail. Partly because those needs were not necessarily clearly expressed, the supplementary accounts in the Appendices of

126 *Unit War Diaries in the Second World War*

the Second World War corpus are an indeterminate genre, somewhere in-between the official structure of the C.2118 forms and individual narrative. Although these narratives contribute to the mask of coherence and order of official records, they draw on cultural and individual perspectives to generate meanings that move beyond the accounts given of the same events in the C.2118 forms. The inclusion of multiple perspectives of the same events in the records of war allows space for some of the complexity of the experience of warfare to emerge. The breadth of these reports resists neat classification, but this chapter has argued that moving beyond attempting to assess their value as factual information reveals the nature of these narratives as mediated representations intervening between individual, event, institution and history.

This chapter's examination of selected reports of the Second World War revealed a complex set of records that represent much more than data or information about the conflict. They are themselves mediated representations of the past, shaped by the interactions of forces and technologies at work in the writing spaces of this conflict. The next chapter (Chapter 3) moves on to analyse the forces and technologies that in turn shape the understanding of the records of both world wars in the reading spaces of The National Archives.

Notes

1. Alan Herbert, *The Secret Battle* (London: Methuen & Co, 1919), 5.
2. Herbert, *The Secret Battle*, 240–241.
3. See, for example, David French, "Doctrine and Organization in the British Army, 1919–1932," *The Historical Journal* 44, no. 2 (2001): 497–515, David French, *Raising Churchill's Army: The British Army and the War against Germany 1919–1945* (Oxford: Oxford University Press, 2001); Martin Samuels, "Doctrine for Orders and Decentralization in the British and German Armies, 1885–1935," *War in History* 22, no. 4 (2015): 448–477, Geoffrey Sloan, "Military Doctrine, Command Philosophy and the Generation of Fighting Power: Genesis and Theory," *International Affairs (Royal Institute of International Affairs 1944–)* 88, no. 2 (2012): 243–263.
4. General Staff, *Field Service Regulations Vol. I: Organization and Administration* (London: HMSO, 1930, Reprinted with Amendments, 1939), 3.
5. Donald Schön, "Generative Metaphor: A Perspective on Problem-Setting in Social Policy," in *Metaphor and Thought*, ed. Andrew Ortony (Cambridge: Cambridge University Press), 137.
6. General Staff, *Field Service Regulations Vol. II: Operations – General* (London: HMSO, 1935), 23.
7. See, for example, Colonel J.F.C. Fuller, *The Foundations of the Science of War* (London: Hutchinson and Co., 1926), and Basil Liddell Hart, *The British Way in Warfare* (London: Penguin, 1932). Fuller and Hart were among the most vocal advocates for the mechanisation and modernisation of the British Army in the interwar years.
8. For an overview of the impact of some of these technologies, see W. Murray and A. Millett, eds., *Military Innovation in the Interwar Period* (Cambridge: Cambridge University Press, 1996).
9. Office of War Information (henceforth OWI), Advance Release for Tuesday Morning Papers, July 28 1942, X1232, OWI 152.

10 Lisa Gitelman, *Scripts, Grooves and Writing Machines: Representing Technology in the Edison Era* (Stanford CA: Stanford University Press, 1999), 189.
11 Stephen Fineman, "Emotions and Organisational Control," in *Emotions at Work: Theory, Research and Applications for Management*, eds. Roy Payne and Carly Cooper (Chichester: Wiley & Sons, 2001), 224.
12 The Right Honourable Lord Southborough et al., *Report of the War Office Committee of Enquiry into 'Shell-Shock'* (London: HMSO, 1922).
13 See for example Amy Bell, "Landscapes of Fear: Wartime London, 1939–1945," *Journal of British Studies* 48, no. 1 (2009): 153–175; Richard Overy, *The Bombing War: Europe 1939–1945* (London: Allen Lane, 2013); Jason Crouth and Peter Leese, eds., *Traumatic Memories of the Second World War and After* (Basingstoke: Palgrave Macmillan, 2016).
14 French, *Raising Churchill's Army*, 14.
15 See French, *Raising Churchill's Army* for a more detailed examination of the various committees established to sift through the lessons of the First World War, such as the Army Reorganisation Committee 1919 led by Sir William Bird, the Committee on Staff Organization (6 March 1919) led by Sir Walter Braithwaite as well as the Lessons of the Great War Committee led by General Sir Walter Kirke (1932). The Kirke Committee was set in motion by Sir George Milne, Chief of the Imperial General Staff, after he read the account of the Somme in the Official Histories compiled by Sir James Edmonds, in order to ensure that the lessons of the First World War were being carried forward into the Army's training and doctrine.
16 French covers this at some length in *Raising Churchill's Army*, 13–47, but see also Samuels, "Doctrine for Orders"; Sloan, "Military Doctrine," and Jonathan Fennell, *Fighting the People's War: The British and Commonwealth Armies and the Second World War* (Cambridge: Cambridge University Press, 2019), 23–51.
17 Aimée Fox, *Learning to Fight: Military Innovation and Change in the British Army, 1914–1918* (Cambridge: Cambridge University Press, 2017).
18 General Staff, *FSRII* (1935), 27–28.
19 See, for example, French, *Raising Churchill's Army*, Sloan, "Military Doctrine," and Fennell, *Fighting*.
20 Although Fennell and French have different perspectives of the level to which the *FSR* encouraged British officers to exercise their initiative, both agree on the issue of the lack of adequate training to allow Commanders to operate effectively in this framework. Fennell, *Fighting*, 36–37; French *Raising Churchill's Army*, 56–62.
21 General Staff, *FSRII* (1935), 22.
22 General Staff, *FSRII* (1935), 22.
23 General Staff, *FSRII* (1935), 22–23.
24 General Staff, *FSRII* (1935), 23.
25 General Staff, FSRII (1935) 23–24.
26 French, *Raising Churchill's Army*, 20.
27 General Staff, *Field Service Regulations, Part II: Organisation and Administration*, 1909 (London: HMSO, Reprinted, with Amendments, 1913), Chapter XVI.
28 General Staff, *Field Service Regulations, Vol. I: Organization and Administration*, 1923 (London: HMSO), Chapter XV, 139–150.
29 General Staff, *Field Service Regulations, Vol. I: Organization and Administration*, 1930 (London: HMSO, reprinted with amendments 1939), Chapter XVIII, 270–283.
30 General Staff, *FSRI* (1923), 145.
31 General Staff, *FSRI* (1930), 273.
32 General Staff, *FSRI* (1930), 273–274.
33 General Staff, *FSRII* (1935), 7–8.
34 General Staff, *FSRI* (1930), 274.
35 General Staff, *FSRI* (1923), 139–140; (1930), 270.

128 *Unit War Diaries in the Second World War*

36 General Staff, *FSRI*(1930), 270.
37 General Staff, *FSRI*(1930), 277.
38 General Staff, *FSRII* (1909), 162.
39 General Staff, *FSRI*(1923), 146–147.
40 General Staff, *FSRI*(1930), 280.
41 Emily Goldman, "Introduction: Information Resources and Military Performance," *Journal of Strategic Studies* 27, no. 2 (2004): 196.
42 Online Etymology Dictionary, s.v. "data" (n.), https://www.etymonline.com/search?q=data.
43 General Staff, *FSRII* (1909), 176.
44 General Staff, *FSRI*(1930), 282.
45 Army Form C.2119, iv.
46 Army Form C.2119, Para. 4. Note.
47 Marshall McLuhan, *Understanding Media: The Extensions of Man* (Cambridge MA: MIT Press, 1994), 259.
48 Darren Wershler-Henry, *The Iron Whim: A Fragmented History of Typewriting* (Toronto: McClelland and Stewart, 2005), 136.
49 The Yost, Typewriter Advert, *The Times* (10 December 1895).
50 Martyn Lyons, *The Typewriter Century: A Cultural History of Writing Practices* (Toronto; Buffalo; London: University of Toronto Press, 2021), 26.
51 Jessie Hohmann, "The Treaty 8 Typewriter: Tracing the Roles of Material Things in Imagining, Realising, and Resisting Colonial Worlds," *London Review of International Law* 5, no. 3 (2017): 382.
52 Wilfred A Beeching, *The Century of the Typewriter* (Bournemouth: British Typewriter Museum Publishing, 1974), 20.
53 Chas Weller, *The Early History of the Typewriter* (La Porte, Indiana: Chase & Shepherd, Printers, 1918), 20.
54 Friedrich Kittler, *Gramophone, Film, Typewriter*, trans. Geoffrey Winthrop-Young and Michael Wutz (1986; Stanford CA: Stanford University Press, 1999), 14.
55 Wershler-Henry, *The Iron Whim*, 246–247.
56 103 Parl. Deb. H.C. (5th ser.) (1909–81), col. 1211.
57 OWI, Advance Release.
58 Mark Seltzer, *Bodies and Machines* (London: Routledge, 1992), 10.
59 Kittler, *Gramaphone*, 14.
60 Kittler, *Gramaphone*, 14.
61 Heidegger, Martin, *Parmenides*, trans. Andre Schuwer and Richard Rojcewicz (1942–43; Bloomington IN: Indiana University Press, 1992), 81.
62 *Punch*, "The Typewriter," *Punch* 201, no. 5237 (July 1941): 74, Punch Historical Archive, emphasis in original.
63 Beeching, *Century of*, 35–36; Gitelman, *Scripts*, 213; Lyons, *Typewriter*, 90.
64 Barack Obama, *A Promised Land* (New York: Random House, 2020), xiii.
65 Empire, Typewriter advert, *The Economist* (18 December 1897).
66 Donald Hoke, "The Woman and the Typewriter: A Case Study in Technological Innovation and Social Change," *Business and Economic History* 8 (1979), 78.
67 Remington, typewriter advert, *The Daily Mail* (1 January 1937).
68 Pitman & Sons, *A Manual of the Typewriter: A Practical Guide to Commercial, Literary, Legal, Dramatic and all Classes of Typewriting Work* (London, 1893) 8.
69 Pitman & Sons, *Manual*, 8.
70 Wershler-Henry, *The Iron Whim*, 34–51.
71 303, Parl. Deb. H.C. (3rd ser.) (1830–91), col. 512.
72 Stationary Office, Report of Committee on Typewriters, 6 May 1907, STAT 12/5/8, The National Archives, Kew.
73 Hohmann, "The Treaty 8," 382.
74 Empire, typewriter advert, *The Times* (1 April 1943).

75 Hohmann, "The Treaty 8," 386.
76 Branches and Services: Director of Printing and Stationery Service, January 1918–December 1918, WO 95-81-5, The National Archives (hereafter TNA), Kew.
77 Royal Army Service Corps, Appendix B, "Printing and Stationery Services, Standing Orders for Typewriter Mechanic's Pool, M.E.F.," 1 August 1942–31 December 1942, WO 169/5768, TNA, Kew.
78 Royal Army Service Corps, WO 169/5768 (18 August 1942).
79 Royal Army Service Corps, WO 169/5768 (19 December, 1942).
80 Royal Army Service Corps, WO 169/5768.
81 Royal Army Service Corps, Appendix A, January–December 1943, WO 169/11516, TNA, Kew.
82 370, Parl. Deb. H.C. (5th ser.) (1909–81).
83 390, Parl. Deb. H.C. (5th ser.) (1909–81), col. 2.
84 *The Economist*, "Typewriters," 12 June 1943.
85 OWI Advance Release.
86 Gitelman, "Scripts," 189.
87 See, for example, Georgina Natzio, "British Army Servicemen and Women 1939–45: Their Selection, Care and Management," *The RUSI Journal* 138, no. 1 (1993): 40; Douglas Delaney, Mark Frost, and Andrew L. Brown, ed., *Manpower and the Armies of the British Empire in the Two World Wars* (Ithaca NY: Cornell University Press, 2021).
88 Lucy Noakes, "Communities of Feeling: Fear, Death, and Grief in the Writing of British Servicemen in the Second World War," in *Total War: An Emotional History*, eds. Lucy Noakes, Claire Langhamer and Claudia Siebrecht (Oxford: British Academy, 2020. British Academy Scholarship Online, 2020), 123.
89 For an overview of the relationship between the British Army and psychiatry from the First World War onwards, see Ben Shephard, *A War of Nerves: Soldiers and Psychiatrists, 1914–1994* (London: Pimlico, 2002); Edgar Jones and Simon Wessely, *Shell Shock to PTSD: Military Psychiatry from 1900 to the Gulf War* (Hove, New York: Psychology Press, 2005). For accounts more contemporary to the Second World War, and from the perspective of some in the psychiatric field, see Brigadier John R. Rees, *The Shaping of Psychiatry by War*. (London: Chapman and Hall, 1945); Stephen MacKeith, "Lasting Lessons of Overseas Military Psychiatry," *Journal of Mental Science* 92, no. 388 (July, 1946): 542–550; Robert H. Ahrenfeldt, *Psychiatry in the British Army in the Second World War* (New York: Routledge, 1958). For representative examples of research into the relationship between psychiatry and the military in the Second World War see Ben Shephard, "'Pitiless Psychology': The Role of Prevention in British Military Psychiatry in the Second World War," *History of Psychiatry* 10 (1999): 491–524; Edgar Jones, "War and the Practice of Psychotherapy: The U.K. Experience 1939–1960," *Medical History* 48 (2004): 493–510; Michal Shapira, *The War Inside: Psychoanalysis, Total War, and the Making of the Democratic Self in Postwar Britain* (Cambridge: Cambridge University Press, 2013).
90 Alison Jaggar, "Love and Knowledge: Emotion in Feminist Epistemology," *Inquiry* 32, no. 2 (1989): 166.
91 Medical Correspondent, "Battle Shock," *The Times* (25 May 1915).
92 119, Parl. Deb. H.C. (5th ser.) (1909–81), col. 1989.
93 119, Parl. Deb. H.C. (5th ser.) (1909–81), col. 1990.
94 119, Parl. Deb. H.C. (5th ser.) (1909–81), col. 1990
95 119, Parl. Deb. H.C. (5th ser.) (1909–81), col. 1993.
96 For a good explanation of the British medical profession's approach to mental health, and its resistance to psychiatry see Michael J. Clark, "The Rejection of Psychological Approaches to Mental Disorder in Late Nineteenth-Century

British Psychiatry," in *Madhouses, Mad-Doctors, and Madmen*, ed. Andrew Scull (Philadelphia: University of Pennsylvania Press, 1981): 271–312.
97 Southborough et al., *Report*, 3.
98 Ted Bogacz, "War Neurosis and Cultural Change in England, 1914–22: The Work of the Committee of Enquiry into 'Shell-Shock'," *Journal of Contemporary History* 24, no. 2 (1989): 227–256; Shapira, *War Inside*.
99 Southborough et al., *Report*, 194
100 Southborough et al., *Report*, 4.
101 Southborough et al., *Report*, 5.
102 Southborough et al., *Report*, 141.
103 Southborough et al., *Report*, 140–144.
104 Southborough et al., *Report*, 141.
105 D.D.M.S. 21 Army Gp. Medical Administrative Instructions, Serial 2, TNA WO177/316, TNA, Kew. The struggles around finding the right language for addressing the psychological and emotional damage caused by armed conflict continue to this day. They are not only suggestive of the difficulty of acknowledging trauma in language, but also about the way particular diagnoses, and the application of specific labels (e.g. the choice of Post Traumatic Stress Disorder, rather than anxiety or depression) might activate pathways of institutional responsibility and care. For a comprehensive overview on the evolution of the understanding of these issues, see Jones and Wessely, *Shell Shock*. Stress has increasingly become a catch-all phrase for all difficult, or unwanted emotions in the Army. Lauren McAllister, Jane Callaghan and Lisa Fellin, "Masculinites and Emotional Expression in U.K. Servicemen: 'Big Boys Don't Cry?'," *Journal of Gender Studies* 28, no. 3 (2019): 262.
106 Terry Copp and Bill McAndrew, *Battle Exhaustion: Soldiers and Psychiatrists in the Canadian Army, 1939–1945* (Montreal: McGill-Queen's University Press, 1990), 43.
107 Clark, "The Rejection," 275–276.
108 Southborough et al., *Report*, 4.
109 Southborough et al., *Report*, 30.
110 Southborough et al., *Report*, 31.
111 Southborough et al., *Report*, 97.
112 Bogacz, "War Neurosis," 247.
113 Southborough et al., *Report*, 34.
114 Southborough et al., *Report*, 94.
115 Southborough et al., *Report*, 140.
116 Blanket pardons had been resisted up until 2006, precisely because of the difficulty of distinguishing between deliberate desertion, cowardice and cases of trauma. In 2006, however, Defence Secretary, Des Browne was prepared to acknowledge that all the men had been "victims of the First World War."

Pardons were also issued for those executed under the 1911 Indian Army act for similar reasons. Although these pardons were issued in a very different emotional climate to that of the war itself and of the time of the Shell-Shock committee, there are nonetheless faint echoes from the first decades of the 1900s still reverberating in Browne's decisions. Browne upheld the authority of the commanders in the field, and the pardons relate only to the executions. Although pardons for the executions were given, the convictions still stood and no right to compensation was granted. Richard Norton-Taylor, "Pardons for Executed Soldiers Become Law" *The Guardian*, 9 November 2006.
117 Southborough et al., *Report*, 97.
118 Southborough et al., *Report*, 112; 119; 121.
119 A 1939 investigation into war neurasthenia, psychosis and pensions, headed by Frances Prideaux, adopted most of the harder-edged findings of the Shell-Shock Report, especially those relating to the idea of self-control. The Pensions Report

drew directly on the Shell-Shock report in adopting the position that the trauma of war did not produce new kinds of neurosis, and that those with long-term issues had pre-existing conditions which war exacerbated but ultimately did not cause. The result was a decision, as the country stood poised on the brink of another war, to withhold all pensions during conflict, and to pay them only to those cases deemed deserving afterwards. Dr Frances Prideaux et al., "Neurosis in War Time," (3 July 1939), PIN 15/2401, TNA, Kew.
120 Bogacz, "War Neurosis," 238.
121 Southborough et al., *Report*, 208.
122 Southborough et al., *Report*, 155.
123 Southborough et al., *Report*, 148.
124 Brian Bond, *British Military Policy Between the Two World Wars* (Oxford: Clarendon Press, 1980), 70.
125 This is not to suggest that there were no attempts in sections of the army's leadership to address the issues of mechanisation, or to attempt reform, including overturning the previously restrictive system of promotion and making changes to training. J.F.C. Fuller and B.H. Liddell Hart were among the most vocal advocates of reform. These issues fall outside my remit, but Murray and Millett, *Military Innovation*, French, "Doctrine and Organisation" and more recently Fennell, *Fighting*, are amongst those who explore the Army's struggles to embrace new technologies, and to develop a progressive combined-arms doctrine in the interwar period.
126 Copp and McAndrew, *Battle Exhaustion*, 22.
127 Southborough et al., *Report*, 133.
128 William Sargant and Eliot Slater, "The Acute War Neuroses," *The Lancet*, July 1940.
129 For more details of the different approaches undertaken in various theatres and armies throughout the conflict, see Copp and McAndrew, *Battle Exhaustion*.
130 Psychiatric Service in Operational Theatres 1945, "Memorandum by A.G. for consideration by the Executive Committee of the Army Council at their 220th meeting to be held on Friday, 29th June, 1945," TNA WO 32/1150, TNA, Kew.
131 D.D.M.S. Army Group, "Notes by Colonel R.F. Walker, 21 Army Group, 4 July 1944," TNA WO 177/316, TNA, Kew.
132 Psychiatric Service in Operational Theatres 1945, "Report of Conference on Psychiatry in Forward Areas, Calcutta, 8–10 July, 1944," TNA WO 32/1150.
133 Jones, "War and the Practice," 498.
134 War Office Morale Committee: Reports, Lieutenant-Colonel J.H.A. Sparrow, Report on Visit to 21 Army Group and Tour of Second Army, 30 March–5 May, WO 32/15772, TNA, Kew.
135 War Office: Historical Monographs, *Morale of the Army 1939–1945*, compiled by Lieutenant-Colonel J.H.A. Sparrow, WO 277/16, TNA, Kew.
136 War Office Meetings, "Minutes of the Fourteenth Meeting of the Army Council, 11 August, 1942," WO 163-51, TNA, Kew.
137 Edward Glover, *The Psychology of Fear and Courage* (Harmondsworth, Middlesex: Penguin, 1940), 12.
138 378, Parl. Deb. H.C. (5th ser.) (1909–81), col. 144.
139 378, Parl. Deb. H.C. (5th ser.) (1909–81), col. 90.
140 Nigel Nicolson, ed., *The Diaries and Letters of Harold Nicolson, Vol. II, The War Years, 1939–1945* (New York: Atheneum, 1967), 214.
141 Alan Allport, *Browned Off and Bloody-minded: The British Soldier Goes to War 1939–1945* (New Haven CT: Yale University Press, 2015), xxiii.
142 For a detailed explanation of exactly how Battle Drills evolved and spread through various Divisions, see Timothy Place, *Military Training in the British Army, 1940–1944 – from Dunkirk to D-Day* (London: Frank Cass, 2000), 49–61.

143 Psychological Experiments, "Object of Battle Inoculation," WO 199/799, TNA, Kew, undated, my emphasis.
144 War Office, *Instructors' Handbook on Fieldcraft and Battle Drill*, 1942, 2.
145 Special Correspondent with the Army, "Realistic Army Training," *The Times*, 7 April 1942, 2; Special Correspondent with the Army, "The New Battle Drill," *The Times*, 25 November 1941, 5.
146 War Office Morale Committee: Reports, Report for the Second Quarterly Period, May–July 1942, WO 32/15772.
147 John D'arcy Dawson, "Getting Ready for the Day," *Aberdeen Journal*, 20 October 1942, 2.
148 Special Correspondent, "The New Battle Drill," 5.
149 Special Correspondent, "Realistic Army Training," 2.
150 Geoffrey Picot, *Accidental Warrior: In the Front Line from Normandy till Victory* (Lewes: Book Build, 1993), chap.1, Kindle.
151 Harry Ashbrook, "Men Learn to Kill without 'Hate'," *Sunday Mirror*, Sunday Pictorial, 24 May 1942, 7.
152 Allport, *Browned Off*, xxi.
153 Picot, *Accidental Warrior*, chap.1, Kindle.
154 James Cockburn, "Teaching Soldiers to Hate: Moderator's Protest," *Aberdeen Journal*, 5 May 1942, 2.
155 Dundee Courier, "'Viewyness' in War-Time," *Dundee Courier and Advertiser*, 7 May 1942, 2.
156 Committee on the Work of Psychologists and Psychiatrists in the Services, "The Work of Army Psychiatrists in Relation to Morale, Appendix C, 1944", CAB 21/914, TNA, Kew.
157 Ahrenfeldt, *Psychiatry*, 200; Place, *Military Training*, 57.
158 Ahrenfeldt, *Psychiatry*, 199.
159 Rees, *The Shaping of Psychiatry*, 80.
160 Daily Express, "War 'Hate' Training Attacked," *Daily Express*, 22 May 1942, 3.
161 Paget qtd in Our Own Reporter, "Army Training in Hate and Blood to Cease," *Aberdeen Journal*, 25 May 1942, 2.
162 War Office Morale Committee: Reports, Report for the Second Quarterly Period, WO 32/1577.
163 War Office: Historical Monographs, *Army Personnel Selection: The Second World War 1939–1945*, compiled by Colonel B. Ungerson, 2, WO 277/19, TNA, Kew.
164 Ahrenfeldt, *Psychiatry*, 30.
165 Natzio, "British Army Servicemen and Women 1939–45," 40.
166 *Army Personnel Selection*, 55. See Ahrenfeldt *Psychiatry*, 52 for details of failure rates.
167 War Office: Historical Monographs, *Manpower Problems: The Second World War 1939–1945*, Compiled by Major-General A.J.K. Pigott, 16, WO 277/19. A Report from Lt.-Gen Sir Ronald Adam to the Army Council in November 1941 puts this number closer to 324,000. War Office and Ministry of Defence and Predecessors, "Use of Manpower in the Army," 62, WO 163/50, TNA, Kew.
168 *Army Personnel Selection*, 13.
169 *Army Personnel Selection*, 13.
170 This was, in fact, a two-way process. After the war several methods Adam instituted in Officer selection were adapted for use by companies like Unilever and Philips Electrical in appointing high level managers and executives. Roger Broad, *The Radical General: Sir Ronald Adam and Britain's New Model Army* (Stroud: Spellmount, 2013), 120.
171 *Use of Manpower in the Army*, Appendix C.
172 Tooth-to-tail ratio generally refers to the numbers of support or logistic troops required to support those units directly involved in combat.

173 *Use of Manpower in the Army*, 48.
174 *Morale*, 19–18.
175 *Army Personnel Selection*, 34.
176 *Army Personnel Selection*, 33.
177 Directorate of Personnel, WO 165/101, June 1941–December 1942, TNA, Kew.
178 *Army Personnel Selection*, 34.
179 *Army Personnel Selection*, Appendix IV: 110.
180 *Army Personnel Selection*, Appendix IV: 1, 110.
181 *Army Personnel Selection*, Appendix IV: 2, 110.
182 Norman Craig, *The Broken Plume: A Platoon Commander's Story, 1940–45* (London: Imperial War Museum, 1982), 30–31.
183 Craig, *The Broken Plume*, 32.
184 Craig, *The Broken Plume*, 33.
185 Craig, *The Broken Plume*, 33.
186 Fineman, "Emotions," 220.
187 Craig, *The Broken Plume*, 75.
188 David Fraser, *And We Shall Shock Them: The British Army in the Second World War* (London: Cassell & Co, 1983), 93.
189 These 37 files were selected from the overall total of 58 pieces.
190 Army Form C.2119, para. 4, note.
191 Wershler-Henry, *The Iron Whim*, 77.
192 Monique Scheer, "Are Emotions a Kind of Practice (and is That What Makes Them Have a History)? A Bourdieuian Approach to Understanding Emotion," *History and Theory* 51, no. 2 (2012): 193–220.
193 General Staff, *FSRI*(1930), 282.
194 Pitman & Sons, *Manual*, 8.
195 Kyongho Min, William H. Wilson and Yoo-Jin Moon. "Typographical and Orthographical Spelling Error Correction" (paper presented at Second International Conference on Language Resources and Evaluation (LREC '00), Athens, Greece, 2000).
196 Min, Wilson and Moon, "Typographical."
197 2 Cheshire Regiment, 1943, WO 169-10190; 1 South Staffordshire Regiment, 1944, WO 172-4920, TNA, Kew.
198 2 North Staffordshire Regiment, 1 September 1939–30 June 1940, WO 167-830, TNA, Kew.
199 2 North Staffordshire Regiment, WO 167-830.
200 Marta Werner, "Writing's Other Scene: Crossing and Crossing Out in Emily Dickinson's Manuscripts," *Text* 17 (2005): 202.
201 1 Cheshire Regiment, 1 February 1940–31 December 1940, WO 169-349, TNA, Kew.
202 2 Cheshire Regiment, 1943, WO 169-10190, TNA, Kew.
203 6 North Staffordshire Regiment, 1 January 1944–31 August 1944, WO 171-1374, TNA, Kew.
204 5 Sherwood Foresters, Nottingham and Derbyshire Regiment, "Battle of Calabritto," WO 169-10296, TNA, Kew.
205 2 Cheshire Regiment, TNA WO 169-10191.
206 Southborough et al., Report, 30.
207 David Holbrook, *Flesh Wounds* (1966, Gloucestershire: Spellmount Limited, 2017), 219.
208 2 North Staffordshire Regiment, 1 September 1939–30 June 1940, WO 167-830, TNA, Kew.
209 1 Welsh Guards, "Account of Movements and Actions Fought by the 1st Bn Welsh Guards in France and Flanders from 17th May to 1st June 1940," WO 167-696, TNA, Kew.

210 Roger Beaumont, *War, Chaos and History* (Westport CT: Praeger, 1994), 23.
211 1 Cheshire Regiment, January 1941, WO 169-1710, TNA, Kew.
212 6 Cheshire Regiment, Letter to the Officers and Men of the Fifth Army, WO 170-1375, TNA, Kew.
213 *Collins English Dictionary*, s.v., "Boche," https://www.collinsdictionary.com/dictionary/english/boche.
214 It only appears five times, all in the records of the 1 Battalion Welsh Guards, August 1915–February 1916, WO 95-1224-1, TNA, Kew.
215 Jennifer Hornsby, "Meaning and Uselessness: How to Think about Derogatory Words," *Midwest Studies in Philosophy* 25, no. 1 (2001): 128–141.; Christopher Hom, "Perjoratives," *Philosophy Compass* 5, no. 2 (2010): 164–185Joseph Hedger, "Meaning and Racial Slurs: Derogatory Epithets and the Semantics/Pragmatics Interface," *Language & Communication* 33, no. 3 (2013): 205–213.; Luvell Anderson and Ernie Lepore, "Slurring Words," *Noûs* 47, no. 1 (2013): 25–48.
216 Hom, "Perjoratives," 164.
217 Hornsby, "Meaning and Uselessness," 137.
218 5 Sherwood Foresters (Nottinghamshire and Derbyshire Regiment), "Action on River Volturno by 5 Foresters 12/13 Oct 1943" and "Battle of Calabritto", TNA WO 169-10296; "5th Battalion the Sherwood Foresters at the Rio Cosina, 1945," WO 170-5068, TNA, Kew.
219 2 North Staffordshire Regiment, "From Medjez to Grande," WO 169-20091, TNA, Kew.
220 5 Sherwood Foresters (Nottinghamshire and Derbyshire Regiment), "Action on River Volturno by 5 Foresters 12/13 Oct 19431; Morning Attack," WO 169-10296.
221 Richard Vallée, "Slurring and Common Knowledge of Ordinary Language," *Journal of Pragmatics* 61 (2014): 89.
222 Vallée, "Slurring," 82, emphasis in original.
223 Vallée, "Slurring," 89.
224 Craig, *The Broken Plume*, 33.
225 5 Sherwood Foresters (Nottinghamshire and Derbyshire Regiment), "Battle of Calabritto," WO 169-10296.
226 Samuel Mitcham Jr. and Friedrich von Stauffenberg, *The Battle of Sicily: How the Allies Lost their Chance for Total Victory* (Mechanicsburg PA: Stackpole Books, 2007), 74.
227 2 South Staffordshire Regiment, 1 June 1943–31 December 1943, WO 169-10299, TNA, Kew.
228 2 Welsh Guards, 1945, WO 171-5152, TNA, Kew.
229 5 Sherwood Foresters (Nottinghamshire and Derbyshire Regiment), "Battle of Calabritto," WO 169-10296.
230 Alex Bowlby, *Recollections of Rifleman Bowlby, Italy, 1944* (London: Leo Cooper, 1969), 29.
231 Craig, *The Broken Plume*, 75.
232 Picot, *Accidental Warrior*, chap.1, Kindle.
233 Alexander Baron, *From the City, From the Plough* (London: Jonathan Cape, 1948), 162.
234 Allport, "Browned Off."
235 2 South Staffordshire Regiment, WO 169-10299.
236 Melvin Smith, *Awarded for Valour: A History of the Victoria Cross and the Evolution of British Heroism* (Basingstoke and New York: Palgrave Macmillan, 2008), 189.
237 Jennifer DeVere Brody, *Punctuation: Art, Politics, and Play* (Durham NC and London: Duke University Press, 2008), 2.
238 Geoff Nunberg, "After Years of Restraint, a Linguist says 'Yes!' to the Exclamation Point," *Npr.org*. 13 June 2017.

239 The exclamation mark was still excluded from typewriter keyboards as late as the 1970s. Lynne Truss notes that the "standard keyboard of a manual typewriter in the 1970s – on which I did my first typing – did not offer an exclamation mark." Lynne Truss, *Eats, Shoots & Leaves: The Zero Tolerance Approach to Punctuation* (London: Fourth Estate, 2009), 135.
240 Donald Rubin and Kathryn Greene, "Gender-typical Style in Written Language," *Research in the Teaching of English* 26, no. 1 (1992): 27, emphasis in original.
241 2 Cheshire Regiment, WO 169-10191.
242 2 Welsh Guards, "The Nijmegen Nuisance," WO 171-1260, TNA, Kew.
243 2 Welsh Guards, "The Nijmegen Nuisance," WO 171-1260.
244 Jochen Hellbeck, "The Diary between Literature and History: A Historian's Critical Response," *The Russian Review* 63, no. 4 (2004), 611.
245 Natalie Zemon Davis, *Fiction in the Archives: Pardon Tales and Their Tellers in Sixteenth-Century France* (Stanford CA: Stanford University Press, 1987), 3.
246 Zemon Davis, *Fiction*, 4.
247 1 Sherwood Foresters (Nottinghamshire and Derbyshire Regiment), 1 January 1942–31 August 1942, WO 169-5062, TNA, Kew.
248 1 Staffordshire Regiment, "Introductory Notes to the War Diary 1st Bn The South Staffordshire Regiment for the Period March–July 44," WO 172-4920.
249 1 Staffordshire Regiment, "Introductory Notes," WO 172-4920. S.D. in this context refers to supply drops. Life-bouys were flamethrowers.
250 1 Staffordshire Regiment, Appendix J2, WO 172-4920.
251 1 Staffordshire Regiment, Appendix J2, WO 172-4920.
252 2 North Staffordshire Regiment, WO 167-830.
253 2 North Staffordshire Regiment, "An Account of the Actions in which 2 Bn The North Staffordshire Regiment was Engaged over the Period 10 May–1 June 1940," WO 167-830.
254 2 South Staffordshire Regiment, "Statement of No. 207782 Lieut. E. Davies, 2nd Bn The South Staffordshire Regiment – Escaped Prisoner of War," WO 169-10299.
255 2 South Staffordshire Regiment, "Statement of No. 207782," WO 169-10299.
256 2 Welsh Guards, WO 171-1260.
257 2 Welsh Guards, "The Nijmegen Nuisance," WO 171-1260.
258 2 Welsh Guards, "The Nijmegen Nuisance," WO 171-1260.
259 2 Welsh Guards, "The Nijmegen Nuisance," WO 171-1260.
260 2 Welsh Guards, "The Nijmegen Nuisance," WO 171-1260.
261 2 Welsh Guards, "The Nijmegen Nuisance," WO 171-1260.
262 General Staff, *FSRII*, 1935, 23.
263 Joanna Bourke, "The Emotions in War: Fear and the British and American Military, 1914–45," *Historical Research* 74, no. 185 (2001): 314.
264 General Staff, *FSRII*, 1935, 23.
265 Beaumont, *War, Chaos*, 48.
266 Gitelman, "Scripts," 189.

3 The matter of materials and archives

Introduction: Knowing and showing in The National Archives

Documents, as Lisa Gitelman argues, "are epistemic objects; they are the recognizable sites and subjects of interpretation across the disciplines and beyond." But archives too are epistemic, and deeply involved in what Gitelman refers to as the "know-show function" which involves "the kind of knowing that is all wrapped up with showing, and showing wrapped with knowing."[1] Understanding documentation and its preservation as epistemic practices of knowing and showing emphasises the dynamic nature of both. Neither the meaning nor the matter of records is fixed, but both are open to ongoing and entwined reinterpretations and remediations. Similarly, a large body of work recognises that archives are not neutral storage facilities but are actively involved in shaping the historical record.[2] Archives play a key role in determining what is important enough to be preserved and how it is made accessible. The experience of being in an archive is often described as having "near magical qualities."[3] Affective sensory responses to material traces of the past – the crinkling sound of yellowed pages, the sight of the traces of ink on paper or parchment, the smell that rises from files and boxes – combine to create a feeling of authentic interaction with a time otherwise lost, as though a portal to the past had been opened. Yet before any of that is possible, the visitor must navigate the archive itself – its physical architecture and its processes-all of which add layers of mediation onto the material artifacts it stores. If archives are portals to the past, they are already mediated, and they modulate our interpretations of what we see through them. To fully account for how Britain's past conflicts are represented, or how they come to be known, through Unit War Diaries, we must investigate how these documents are re-presented and re-interpreted by the institution responsible for curating them, before moving on to analysing the materials and technologies through which they are accessed.

Once Unit War Diaries enter the public domain, they can be accessed via The National Archives (TNA). TNA occupies both physical and virtual spaces. TNA's physical location is in Kew, a district of the London Borough of Richmond-Upon-Thames. It consists of two large, interconnected buildings,

DOI: 10.4324/9781003172109-4

known as 'Q1' and 'Q2,' approached by a concrete pathway running between two large water features replete with resident swans and other birdlife. Q1, opened in 1977, was designed by architect John Cecil Clavering in the brutalist style of architecture. Brutalism, with its spare, heavy design, was particularly suited to government buildings where cost did not allow for a great deal of embellishment. Like many buildings in the brutalist style, Q1 is an imposing building – low, blocky and geometric, with narrow slitted windows slashed into heavy slabs of concrete cladding. Q2, added in the 1990s, is a sprawling building with more glass than concrete. Q1 is TNA's public-facing building, and Q2 is used for administrative functions. A Tweet from TNA's official account describes Q1 as "A fine example of brutalist architecture. That's it. That's the tweet" (@UkNatArchives, 22 April 2021). A follow-up tweet adds "Love it or hate it, there's no denying it's iconic. It definitely adds to the experience of visiting Kew for the first time." The building housing the official records of the U.K. is unapologetic in its assertion of institutional power. What Q1 adds to the experience of visiting the archives is a sense of the imposing and intimidating magnitude of official authority. It is not just Q1 that is considered iconic. TNA's website describes the records it holds as "iconic national documents."

Most of TNA's users will encounter TNA via its website (www.nationalarchives.gov.uk), making the online space as crucial, if not more, as the physical location at Kew as a site of interaction between users and the institution. TNA's official report for 2018–19 gives some indication of the difference between onsite and offsite activities. During this period, TNA delivered 518,593 records to onsite users, and 274,332,549 online.[4] It is therefore is no longer the case, as Ed Folsom once argued, that "archives are all about physicality."[5] In contrast to the unapologetic authority of Q1's imposing bulk, TNA's online spaces are designed with "warm, rich" hues and clear, bold fonts to make the site as appealing and accessible as possible.[6] Tensions between institutional authority and accessibility in TNA's organisational identity are manifest in and through its physical and virtual spaces, and they inflect the historical record with meaning before a single box or file has been opened. TNA, like all archives, is thus not a neutral repository or reading space for historical records. It is part of an ecosystem of interrelated institutions, structures and technologies that inflect the meaning, understanding and uses of the material traces of the past.

Chapters 1 and 2 investigated how the confluence of individuals, institutions, technology and conflict in the writing spaces on the battlefields of the First and Second World Wars shaped the creation of Unit War Diaries. But examining the writing spaces of these documents is only one part of their story. This chapter investigates how Unit War Diaries are re-presented through TNA's practices of knowing and showing within its actual and virtual reading spaces. Reading Unit War Diaries in and through TNA's reading spaces, both physical and virtual, involves sometimes affective interactions with an institution that imprints these experiences with aspects of its institutional identity. Interrogating the reading spaces of TNA must therefore begin by examining the evolution of TNA as an institution. Knowing and showing, as Gitelman points out, implies responsibility.[7] Responsibility in turn mobilises relational vectors between archives and the cultural, political and social contexts in which they evolve. This chapter begins by briefly tracing some of those vectors. It identifies how the state archive's history is intertwined with many of the same forces that shaped the record of war – the rise of bureaucracy, the reconceptualisation of information, and the increasing significance of paperwork as a way of understanding not just the transactions and activities of corporations and institutions, but of events in war. It also reveals the critical influence of war on the evolution of the state archive, from its early incarnation as the Public Records Office (PRO) to the re-shaping of its identity as The National Archives in the Twenty-first Century. War played a large role in shaping the state archive's physical and operational structures, but this chapter will argue that the archive's institutional identity, or its "archival grain," to use the concept developed by Ann Stoler, in turn plays a key role in mediating the experiences of accessing and interacting with the records of war.[8]

This chapter foregrounds how interactions with TNA as institution, as physical and virtual space, as well as with the practices of archival description, generate meanings that inflect the reading and understanding of the records. This book's investigation of the writing spaces of war included engaging with the traces of the human beings within them. This chapter reinstates "the missing researcher" in archival research.[9] In this chapter, I use my own interactions with TNA and the forces and technologies at work in its reading spaces to continue the analysis of the messiness of interactions between individuals and the institutional systems of control exerted over the records of war. A book that interrogates the mediation of textual traces of the past, and questions the ways in which mediated materials are interpreted and used in historiography, by necessity demands a self-reflexive examination of its own uses of materials and technologies. This chapter ends by detailing and anatomising the interactions of all who worked on Unit War Diaries for this book with the documents and the technologies used to present them, including the transcription of the records, with the aim of finding out what might have been lost, or gained, as the records cycled through material and digital formats.

Reading the archive: From Public Record Office to The National Archives

Just as it was necessary to investigate the factors shaping the evolution of the British Army as in institution to understand its approach to record keeping, it is equally crucial to trace the history of the state archive to understand how this institution manages the records that cycle into its care. In the early 2000s, as TNA's website describes, four government bodies, the Public Record Office (PRO), the Royal Commission on Historical Manuscripts, Her Majesty's Stationary Office and the Office of Public Sector Information were

The Matter of Materials and Archives 139

brought together to form one organisation – The National Archives. The history of the Public Record Office provides a crucial context for the configuration of TNA's current organisational identity. The early years of the PRO's development, along with those of other archives in the world, are sometimes described as the "custodial era," during which archives dealt with a manageable "mass of records," relatively simple technologies of "records creation, storage, and retrieval" and "assumed a passive role in shaping the documentary record."[10] The PRO's history, however, reveals a much more complex picture. The archive developed its identity and authority while engaged in a constant battle against a burgeoning tide of paperwork that threatened at times to overwhelm it. It was formed at a time that coincides with the rise of bureaucracy and documentation and was shaped by many of the same forces that influenced the British Army's practices of record keeping. War, as will become clear, played a key role in shaping the State Archive's physical and operational structures, which in turn go on to shape the way the records of war are re-presented to the public.

"Archival grain" is useful in revealing how interactions, both historical and contemporary, between an archive and the institutions whose interests it serves, as well as between the archive and its holdings and users, generate and reflect a shifting set of presumptions, ideologies and values that in turn inflect the ways archival records are accessed and understood. Explaining Ann Stoler's concept, Blouin and Rosenberg consider archival grain as "the 'text,' as it were, of archival processes that has to be read as carefully as the documents themselves."[11] While archival processes of selection, cataloguing and preservation are important to understanding archival grain, the ways in which archives define and present themselves as institutions are equally critical to how they mediate access to the record, yet these aspects of archival grain are often overlooked. An archive shapes the "context for interpretation and retrieval" of information from its records,[12] and its institutional identity and archival grain are core to that context. Investigating TNA's history will show how the institution's archival grain has been shaped primarily by a tension between a sense of institutional authority and its responsibility to make records publicly available, and that the relationship between the state archive and ideas of history and national identity is core to TNA's sense of what it knows about itself. Reading TNA's archival grain will reveal how and why TNA came to think of itself and the records it holds as 'iconic' and creates a vital context for interrogating how the archive's practices of knowing and showing inflect the ways Unit War Diaries are accessed and read.

The Public Record Office (PRO)

It is not my intention to include a comprehensive history of the PRO here. That ground has already been meticulously and extensively covered elsewhere, although the influence of war on the archive is generally understated.[13] Instead, I want to examine those moments in the PRO's development that fed into the formation of key aspects of its institutional identity – its authority, relationship to history, and the tension between its custodial responsibilities and the remit to make records public. 'Reading' the PRO's archival grain through its history makes clear that these properties are subject to ongoing realignments and recalibrations. This is an approach like the one taken by Ann Stoler, who

> treat[s] archives not as repositories of state power but as unquiet movements in a field of force, as restless realignments and readjustments of people and the beliefs to which they were tethered, as spaces in which the senses and the affective course through the seeming abstractions of political rationalities.[14]

Reading TNA's archival grain requires an understanding of the shifting pressures, challenges and opportunities in which it was forged, in order to understand why and how it shapes affective and intellectual engagements with the records of war today.

In August 1838, following a series of commissions and enquiries into the state of record keeping, the British Government passed the Public Records Act. The Act was intended to bring control of official records, which were at that point "in the keeping of several Persons" in "unfit buildings," under one central office, the Public Record Office, and one authority, the Master of the Rolls. 'Records' are defined by the Act as "Rolls, Records, Writs, Books, Proceedings, Decrees, Bills, Warrants, Accounts, Papers, and Documents," but referred primarily to legal documents. The Act also made the Master of the Rolls responsible for managing "the Admission of such Persons as ought to be admitted to the Use of the Records, Calendars, Catalogues, and Indexes in his Custody."[15] At its inception, the PRO was thus primarily concerned with the preservation and ratification of legal records, and with making those records accessible presumably mainly to searchers from the legal profession, but in principle, also to a wider public. The PRO's custodianship of legal records, as well as its ability to ratify any copies of those records, lent the Office a measure of authority from the moment of its foundation.

Chapter 1 touched on the rise of bureaucracy and its influence on the British Army over the course of the 1800s, but bureaucracy also shaped the nature and purpose of the state archive as an institution over the same period. The proliferation of paperwork produced by bureaucratic state processes necessitated systems for storing and managing it. Only two years after the Public Records Act was passed, the PRO began accepting the papers and documents from government departments, which initiated a series of conflicting priorities and demands upon the PRO that were to persist for almost the next hundred years of its history, and which would exert a profound influence on the shaping of the archive as an institution. Departmental records remained under the auspices of the departments that produced them. The PRO had no real influence over how government departments produced or managed their records, but its responsibility for holding them on behalf of departments created a series of stresses and strains between the archive, its curatorial responsibilities, its relationship with government departments and the public.

No formal legislation was in place to regulate the transference of records from departments, and decisions about how and when they became public were not uniformly applied. Permits from some departments, including the War Office, were required for the public to access their records. Record Officers at the PRO were responsible for checking these permits. This was not a simple task because permits were inconsistently implemented, subject to shifting restrictions, and occasional fees.[16] The PRO also had to respond to periodic calls from departments to "withdraw certain volumes from the public view and knowledge, or to seal up certain papers apart from the other contents of a volume" when records had a bearing on sensitive current affairs.[17] By 1880, the Deputy Keeper's Report noted that the PRO's work for government departments had become intensive – the "searches for, and references to, the Documents wanted, often occupy many days; and long copies of Documents are frequently required, and made, for those Departments."[18] The incorporation of departmental records additionally changed the nature of the archive itself and shaped its relationship to history.

The inclusion of government records into the official archive of national records, a space reserved for documents related to legal and social processes regarded as having significance for state activities, confers a similar weight and meaning on the documentation that was the product of bureaucratic procedures and transactions.[19] The PRO, like other state archives of the time, became "increasingly regarded as an integrated, systematic, and authoritative set of sources for processing the past of the nation-state."[20] Archives like the PRO were an essential part of authenticating and authorising the prodigious documentation generated by bureaucratic governmental organisations as legitimate expressions of processes of power. As the official repository of texts thought significant to the state, the PRO reinforced the authority of textual material, and by the start of the Twentieth Century, both history and archiving "converged on a conception of the authentic document as source and evidence" about the past.[21] The "establishment of historical truth," according to a letter to the Master of the Rolls in 1851, was only possible through a painstaking process of sifting through the "evidence of Public Documents," which were themselves regarded as "the only sure foundation of historical truth."[22] The letter was signed by a number of "historical writers" and members of literary societies, and it provides an insight into how the documentary record had become history's raw material from which the historian could extract and recreate an 'accurate' narrative about the past. By the time Unit War Diaries were implemented by the British Army, documentation had become considered as essential evidence for past events. History had established itself as a 'scientific' profession through the perceived ontological stability of documentation as evidence of "an empirically knowable past" and archives were central to its development.[23]

But not all documentary evidence was made available to the public, complicating the notion of the PRO's holdings as a foundation for historical 'truth.' In addition to checking the permits required for searchers wishing to access the records of some departments, the staff of the PRO were required to check any notes or copies made by readers of departmental records for content that might be considered contentious. There were some guidelines issued for what might constitute objectionable material – the names of secret service agents, personal details of individuals and references to individual criminal convictions fell under this category, for example. But staff were also required to be alert to "references to scalping and other atrocities in war" and the rather more nebulous "passages likely to give offence abroad."[24] The role played by Record Officers in monitoring access to departmental documents and in checking the notes made by readers thus demanded an ability to identify connections between the past actions of the British State and its contemporary affairs, and to make active judgements regarding information that might be considered harmful to State interests, either past or present. Even if operating under instructions from State Departments, the PRO's regulation of information at this stage of its history is a manifestation of active control over the version of the past that emerges from archival records, and it complicates any ideas of the institution as a neutral repository.

As a national archive, the PRO was responsible for a collection of documents considered by various dominant actors and agencies to be representations of significant moments in the nation's history, or records of important activities and transactions conducted by the state and government. The kinds of historical narratives that could be constructed from these records, therefore, were "driven 'naturally' by the archives to an emphasis on politics and the nation."[25] But while the PRO's practices and its holdings shaped the nature of the history produced within the archive, there is more to be considered here in terms of the relationship between the PRO and notions of history. The records were not only regarded as a source of 'truth' and evidence, but they were also considered as a kind of monument to a past that was a source of national pride. Charles Dickens described the records as constituting "the most complete and valuable" archives in existence.[26] Antiquarian Samuel Robert Scargill-Bird was later quoted in an article in the illustrated newspaper *The Graphic* as forming "a magnificent monument of the past, mutilated here and there, it is true, by the ravages of time and neglect, but still speaking in an authoritative voice to the centuries to come."[27] As the Public Office of the nation's records, the PRO validated the authority of documentation, but the PRO also *gained* authority and status through its custodianship of records understood to be not only a source of truth, but also a monument to a great national past. The official authority of the PRO and authenticity of the public record discouraged interrogation by historians of how the records came to be, or indeed, of what parts of the past they might obscure, not only as history established itself as a profession, but also for some time afterwards. The withholding of information regarding the activities of Empire in particular, or the erasure or omission of that information, had consequences that lasted long after the PRO had transformed into TNA. As Caroline Elkins points out, "[t]he power of the archive shaped the ways in which the future understood the British imperial past for decades; indeed, the 'official mind' reflected that which the archives beckoned us not only to remember, but also to forget."[28] There are traces of the idea of the records as a monument to the past still evident in TNA's description of them as "iconic."

But even as the PRO was steadily involved in authorising the documentary record of state activities as an iconic 'monument' to the national past, it was also struggling to manage the prodigious amount of paperwork that bureaucratic processes produced. While there is no doubt that digital records pose challenges of scope and scale on a new level for archives, there is perhaps a tendency to overlook or forget the fact that the paperwork generated through the activities and transactions of the bureaucratic nation state posed continual problems of organisation, space, and management for archives of the 1800s and the 1900s. The provisions of the 1838 Records Act were not set up to address the unexpectedly prodigious increase in documentation that characterised organisational activities over the course of the 1800s. Subsequent Acts, such as the Public Record Office Act of 1877, made some provision for the disposal of records by departments (subject to inspection by members of the PRO and of the relevant departments), but the proliferation of paperwork outpaced any attempts at destruction. The challenge of managing the flood of documentation was particularly acute during times of war.

Even as early as the Crimean War, the War Office had begun to transfer "a great quantity of papers" to the PRO, albeit somewhat haphazardly, creating extra pressure on space in the archives.[29] The First World War vastly accelerated the production of paperwork. The number of papers registered daily in the War Office increased from around 600 in 1913 to 10,000 in 1916, at least in part due to the "vast commercial enterprises" generated by the war, providing material evidence of the complex relationship between modern warfare and industry.[30] By 1919, the number of records held by the War Office and other departments outside of the PRO, and which would at some point come into their custody, was estimated to exceed all the PRO's existing holdings.[31] In addition to the issue of bulk, the First World War also changed the configuration of government departments, with some disappearing and others – such as the Historical Section of the Committee of Imperial Defence mentioned in Chapter 1 – emerging with new needs in terms of documentation. The 1919 Royal Commission on Public Records advocated "weeding operations of a drastic nature," and although it suggested that the PRO should be assisted in this process by the formation of an ad hoc set of advisors and clerical staff, not much changed in the wake of its report.[32] The deluge of documentation showed no signs of abating, and efforts to contain or control were proving inadequate.

The Second World War brought a new set of problems, including the very real danger that the buildings in which records were kept would be destroyed.

Hilary Jenkinson, author of the hugely influential *Manual of Archival Administration* (1922) and who later became a controversial Deputy Keeper in the PRO, described some of the measures undertaken by the Office to protect their records. The PRO made structural alterations to buildings and set about identifying and removing specific records from urban areas.[33] The latter were selected through a process that focussed on those records that had not been printed, and which were part of a group regarded as "of primary importance."[34] Jenkinson also reluctantly acknowledged that "some concession was made also to the predilections of historians and other students, and to popular or spectacular values."[35] The decisions around what to preserve reveal some of the attitudes towards which records were identified as of national and historical importance. For Jenkinson, the "predilections" of users of archives were low on the list of priorities. Preserving the records, especially those that predated modern history, came first. Eventually around "ninety thousand carefully numbered and indexed packages" were removed to various sites, including "a castle, private mansions, a prison, and a casual ward."[36] The Service Records of the First World War, housed at the War Office Records Store in London, were not included in the records removed to safer locales. Almost two thirds of the Service Records were destroyed by an incendiary bomb in September 1940, and the remaining third, now referred to as the 'Burnt Records,' were severely damaged. While these records did not meet Jenkinson's criteria of being old enough or perhaps even spectacular enough to be protected, their destruction has subsequently proved to be a significant loss for researchers of the First World War. Their handling provides an extreme example of how institutional attitudes in the archive might come to influence what remains of the records of conflict.

By the end of the Second World War, the accumulation of documentation had become so acute that in June 1952, a Committee headed by Sir James Grigg was established to investigate the problem. The Grigg Committee's Report gives some sense of how much the production of paperwork had accelerated by noting that the records then in custody of government departments exceeded "by three times to one, the amount of preserved material already in the Public Record Office, though this latter covers a period of very nearly a thousand years."[37] The Report also noted the role played by technologies like the typewriter in contributing to the increase in paperwork.[38] The generation of paperwork via bureaucratic administrative processes and technologies thus proved to be a substantial bureaucratic administrative problem in and of itself. The Grigg Report set about addressing that problem directly. It redefined the concept of records to include "documents accumulated by the central Government, irrespective of whether there is any general right of access to them."[39] It then set out a system of appraisal for the identification and destruction of records thought to be of little value, and for the selection of those intended for preservation. The goal was to reduce the "frightening mass of paper" through a series of staged reviews, designed to decrease the volume of documentation that would eventually be closely evaluated for selection based on a notion of historical worth.[40] Crucially, the Grigg Report recommended that the PRO be involved in the later stages of the review process with departments, and that departments would have to obtain the agreement of the PRO for their reviewing procedures.[41] In addition, the Report recommended that records should be transferred from departments to the PRO 30 years after their creation, and that they should be made public after a period of 50 years. The 1958 Public Records Act formally implemented these measures and timescales, superseding the 1838 Act and shaping the PRO's operations and identity throughout the rest of its history. The PRO thus became actively involved in designing and managing procedures for the destruction or preservation of records in government departments.

Even within the rigorous system of appraisal suggested by the Grigg Committee, which above all emphasised the destruction of records, the Report identified Unit War Diaries (which at the time of the report occupied 9,000 feet of shelving in the Cabinet Office) as "a valuable source of study for the Fighting Services" as well as "original source material for the historian," and it advised against their destruction.[42] Unit War Diaries were thus singled out as worthy of preservation for the same reasons they had originally been implemented by the British Army. The historical worth of Unit War Diaries was thus taken as implicit by the Grigg Report, which also endorses their worth, but other records of war had to be evaluated. Despite the basic practice of records management outlined in the *Field Service Regulations I* mentioned in the Chapter 2, the war had still produced an overwhelming amount of paperwork. By 1968, the PRO reported that despite "steady progress" on the selection process, there were "approximately 100,000 feet of records" from the Second World War still awaiting review.[43]

In the same year, an amendment to the Records Act reduced the access period from 50 to 30 years, thereby allowing the records of the First World War to become publicly available. The release of the records of the war generated a great deal of public interest, and the PRO reported a 21% spike in daily attendances from 53,300 in 1967 to 64,600 in 1968.[44] In 1975, all departments agreed to opening the records of the Second World War. The release of the records of the two World Wars was part of a gradual shift in the public identity of the PRO as an institution primarily concerned with the preservation and provision of the legal records of early history, into one that provided access to the records of the Twentieth Century.[45] Partially due to the increase in visitor numbers, which the PRO's offices at Chancery Lane could not accommodate, but also due to the pressures of storage space, the site at Kew was commissioned and opened in 1977. The records of the two World Wars thus posed a challenge of storage and organisation for the archive, but they also contributed to the reshaping of its organisational identity through the Grigg Report, to its growth and to increased public awareness of its operations, which in turn led to increased visitor numbers.

While preservation and conservation remained at the top of the PRO's priorities (it was still listed first in the Keeper's Report for 1989), the PRO operated within a growing tension between its responsibility to preserve and protect the documents in its care, which it generally prioritised, and its duty to allow the public access to the records. The 1838 Public Records Act encouraged general public access to the records, but visitors to the PRO soon proved more diverse than anticipated. As early as 1843, the Deputy Keeper's annual report noted a "great and increasing use of the Records by the public."[46] The Office had around 3,000 visitors that year, and the Keeper notes that these were not only "persons practising in the different branches of the law," but included those conducting searches for historical purposes, as well as "common workmen" interested in matters related to manufacturing. The Report makes a point of remarking on how "many of the unprofessional persons so making searches have acquired the habit of prosecuting them with great patience, intelligence, and perseverance."[47]

While some of the 'unprofessional' searchers may have been diligent, they created extra pressure for the Assistant Keepers, who were expected to support them in their activities. An Assistant Keeper was "required to give all applicants for searches and inspections of Records, every assistance and information in his power, not merely from Calendars and Indexes, but also from his own knowledge of Records."[48] While this was beneficial for applicants, it created demands that were sometimes seen as unwelcome for the staff. Some Deputy Keepers demonstrated a tendency towards judging the perceived worthiness (or lack thereof) of applicants and the nature of their queries and were at times either dismissive of those who did not appear to meet expected intellectual standards or expressed uneasiness at demanding nominal fees from applicants with cultural or social status.[49]

This is not to suggest that all searchers at the PRO were met with hostility. In October 1900, a newspaper article on the "historical treasures" and "social life" of The Public Record Office in *The Graphic* included this quote by Walter Rye (a widely-published antiquarian):

> Nowadays it would be difficult to find a place where study and search can be carried on more easily and pleasantly than at the Public Record Office, and certainly at no place are the officials from the highest to the lowest more courteous or more willing to help. The beginner, stumbling along and only half conscious as to what he is looking for, is well treated and listened to as patiently as the *habitué*: [...] all searchers, however different their objects, are made welcome.[50]

Thirty years later, an article in *The Times* in January 1926 was similarly appreciative of the support offered by PRO staff, describing the "superintendent" in attendance in the reading rooms as "a man of vast knowledge, with a happy gift of divining the knowledge peculiar to each searcher."[51] While individually, PRO staff no doubt provided a great deal of help to applicants in the various reading rooms, the point is that its institutional focus for much of its history was more firmly directed towards the records in its charge.

The ways in which the PRO understood its priorities are reflected in the structure of the annual reports of the Deputy Keepers through the Nineteenth Century. Most of the emphasis in the reports is given to the accruing, arrangements, repairs and preservation of documents at each site operated by the PRO, and then to the production and publication of finding aids such as calendars and indexes. Much less space is devoted to the nature and purpose of visitors to the Office, and some reports devote almost no attention to applicants at all.[52] Even in those that do, the tendency to provide the numbers of documents requested rather than individual visitor numbers demonstrates where the PRO's focus as an institution lay. Jenkinson's work on archiving made clear how archives should manage the tension between their responsibilities. The archivist's primary concern lay firstly with "the safeguarding of his Archives and for their custody," secondly with the archivists' responsibility to produce and publish calendars, indexes and other finding aids, thirdly with providing for the needs of visitors, and this last only if they had time to spare.[53]

To a certain degree, the focus on the acquiring and care of records in the early years of the PRO rather than on its visitors was at least in part because visitor numbers were relatively low. While exact figures are hard to come by, Cantwell estimates that in 1942, for example, "they could rarely have exceeded 20 or so persons a day."[54] The physical provisions for searchers were low on the list of priorities. One reader complained in a letter to *The Times* in 1862 that the "beggarly dimensions" of the reading rooms were unsuited for "studying this most magnificent collection of historical materials."[55] Even in the design of the new, expanded quarters for the PRO in Chancery Lane (construction started in 1851 and continued in phases through to 1895), concerns about keeping the building fireproof included eschewing central heating at the expense of the comfort of visitors.[56] The original provision in the plans for this building was to provide space for no more than 30 searchers.[57] But by the 1860s, extensions were necessary, brought about in part by the increased pressure on the PRO by the documentation produced by the War Office and Admiralty during the Crimean War. Under John Romilly, then Master of the Rolls, the extensions included improved provisions in the form of an attractive glass-domed reading room, the Round Room, for literary searchers, and a separate room, known as the Long Room, for legal searchers.

Although the PRO's reports do not give the actual number of visitors, the numbers of papers requested in the Chancery reading rooms continued to increase, suggesting a concomitant rise in users. In 1892, for example, the total number of papers and files produced in the reading rooms came to 42,950.[58] In 1896, that figure was 46,862.[59] By 1900, it had reached 47,568.[60] Numbers continued to rise into the Twentieth Century, fuelled by the heightened interest in the archives following the release of the records of the two World Wars and contributing to the opening of Kew. The needs of users were considered in the design of the building at Kew, with two reading rooms each seating "250 readers in comfort in a high level of natural illumination without glare, with air conditioning and special measures to reduce noise."[61]

The gradual but continual increase in visitor numbers inevitably exerted pressure on the PRO's hierarchy of priorities, and the increase in readers naturally also meant increased wear on the records. The Thirty-First Annual Report at the end of the following decade provides some indication of the PRO's struggles to manage the effects of the steady increase in visitors on the records. The Report identifies the "risks to documents from careless handling, misplacing and, in some cases, wilful damage or theft" as one of the PRO's primary concerns for that year, exacerbated by a lack of staff to properly invigilate the reading rooms.[62] As a result, new rules for conduct in the reading rooms were introduced, and visitors were required to sign an undertaking that they had read and would observe those rules when their reader's tickets were issued. This report makes clear that managing and preserving records was still very much the PRO's primary purpose in terms of its priorities, but in the next decade, the tension between taking care of the records and making them publicly accessible underwent a realignment.

In 1992, the PRO became an Executive Agency as part of broader reforms undertaken by the British government aimed at improving management structures and service delivery throughout the civil service. Executive Agencies are administratively distinct from central government, giving them in principle greater latitude in terms of the organisation of their frontline operations. They are "'business-like' organisations whose budgets come from government and whose staff remain public sector employees."[63] As an Executive Agency, the PRO had more operational autonomy, but it was organised along lines that came closer to those of private corporations, with the Keeper becoming a Chief Executive. The Keeper's annual reports from this period onwards reflect an emphasis on business-like activities such as marketing, demonstrating operational efficiencies and strategising. The Fortieth Annual Report, for example, includes the PRO's "user charter" and describes the setting of a target for user ratings of staff knowledge (which the PRO did not meet).[64] It also details measures for attracting new visitors, and its aim to reach existing users not only through finding aids, but also, "through our shop."[65]

From one perspective, it is more than possible to see the PRO in the 1990s being swept up in the general valorisation of market mechanisms and logics that characterised the rise of neoliberalism during Margaret Thatcher's Britain and beyond. Visitors are 'users' whose satisfaction is measured through performance metrics, and there is more than a hint of commodification in the promotion of both the archive as an institution and of the records themselves. But to read the PRO in this way at this stage of its history provides only a partial picture. There was also through the 1980s and into the 1990s an argument developing among archivists that called for a realignment of the priorities of archival institutions. Archives were entering what some identified as a "post-custodial era" prompted in part by the rise of what was then termed electronic forms of communication and information storage.[66] As digital technologies changed the nature of records and processes of record keeping, archivists began to question the nature and purpose of archiving as a practice. Terry Cook, for example, argued that archives needed to move from "archives to archiving" by becoming actively involved in the creation, management and use of records.[67] As an organisation not only responsible for holding national records, but also for shaping the national record through its work in records management with government departments after the 1958 Records Act, the PRO was already on a trajectory from archives to archiving.

The gradual shift in emphasis onto users and accessibility in the PRO can be read as part of processes of commodification, but there was a wider recognition in the profession that archiving was not only about preservation. Timothy Ericson, for example, pointed out that ultimately, for archives "[t]he *goal* is *use*. We need to continually remind ourselves of this fact … if, after we brilliantly and meticulously appraise, arrange, describe and conserve our records, nobody comes to use them, then we have wasted our time."[68] Barbara Craig in turn went so far as to argue that the very classification of visitors to archives as users was misleading. Craig suggests instead that those who make use of archives should be regarded as "participants in the archival mission."[69] Although preservation remained at the top of its list of priorities, by the end of the Twentieth Century the PRO was pushed into increasingly acknowledging the significance of public accessibility by the steady increase in visitor numbers, by its transformation into an Executive Agency and by the recognition among archivists that archives as institutions needed to do more to facilitate the use of their records.

The PRO was shaped by its holdings and by the long-running battle to accommodate their rapid growth, but also through an enduring tension between the shifting demands of the institutions it worked with and for, the requirements of preservation, and the pressure of facilitating public access. A measure of authority, a multi-faceted institutional identity created through multiple responsibilities, and an intricate relationship with concepts of national history were core properties of the PRO's archival grain by the end of the final decade of the Twentieth Century. When the PRO began its transformation into The National Archives in 2003, these properties became part of the grain of the new organisation's identity. The continual growth of user numbers of the PRO and the challenges posed by digital technologies on all aspects of record keeping, together with an intensified awareness of the power of information in an age more saturated with it than ever before, led to an increased public and political focus on archives at just the time the PRO was reconstituted as The National Archives. In addition, the Freedom of Information Act (November 2000), which requires most public bodies to publish information about their activities upon request from the public, resulted in an intensified focus on the significance of records not only for historical purposes, but as evidence that could be used to hold state and corporate bodies to account for their actions. The Act therefore drew attention to the state archives as playing a role in democratic and civic processes.

The National Archives (TNA)

As a result of the factors mentioned above, during the first decade of the Twenty-first Century, archives in general in Britain became the focus of attention from government, culminating in 2009 with the publication of a new government policy document on archives, *Archives for the 21st Century*. The policy identifies state archives as essential to democratic process, both in terms of contributing to "evidence-based policy making," as well as in empowering individuals to play a role in civic processes.[70] The policy's focus on access and service made clear that any lingering tendency in national archives towards being more inward facing needed to be dispelled. TNA's own published material reveals how the institution is attempting to realign aspects of its past identity in response to the challenges of the present, including those posed by the Government's policy paper. The strategies and reports made public by TNA are intended to champion the cause of archives in general, promote the institution in particular, and demonstrate how it is fulfilling, or perhaps even exceeding, the targets set for it by government. The language used in this material is that of corporate enterprises, but these documents are also expressions of TNA's organisational identity. They should therefore not be dismissed as mere marketing rhetoric, but should be considered, as Barbara Craig argues of similar documentation, as ways in which archives like TNA articulate "their role in a changing record environment."[71]

TNA expresses its authority by using dynamic action verbs and high impact phrases in its "business priorities," which in its strategy for 2018–19, include providing "expert advice and scrutiny to government," "inspiring" the public, "leading" the archival sector and "advancing" knowledge.[72] TNA claims authority through its curatorship of records that it identifies as "unique."[73] The records themselves are positioned as central to democratic and legal processes of holding government, individuals and institutions to account by ensuring transparency.[74] In addition to aiding democratic processes, TNA's records are situated in much of this discourse at the intersection of local and national identity, with the power to explain the nature of both.[75] According to this perspective, archives like TNA therefore have the capacity not only to hold political and corporate entities to account, but also to "change people's lives" by revealing aspects of their past.[76] While these strategy documents and reports are intended to promote the institution's importance in a challenging funding environment, they place authority at the forefront of TNA's current archival grain.

But the dynamism of the language in TNA's strategic goals and priorities rubs up against persistent metaphors of storage and neutrality. TNA is "the evidence store for our histories," in one report, and the "window on more than 1,000 years of the nation's history" in another.[77] The idea of a 'store' for history draws on the familiar notion of the archive as a storage facility, if not a kind of 'one-stop-shop' for evidence, while the metaphor of the window implies both easy access and transparency. Both these metaphors additionally imply that the archival record *is* history in and of itself, and not what has survived of selected and already mediated, traces of the past. The 'nation's history' is portrayed as essentially inert, awaiting discovery, or, through the deployment of another metaphor, 'unlocking': "Until they are unlocked, archive records are just papers, images or sequences of bytes. Once revealed, they can tell us our stories, bringing alive the people, events and decisions that got us here today."[78] It is not entirely clear how the archival record is 'unlocked' – presumably simply by ensuring public access – but there is a confluence of older and more recent suppositions about history at work in the description of the records as 'just' papers, or other kinds of media that have stories 'locked' inside them.

The idea that there is a narrative about the past simply waiting to be unlocked in archival records echoes early conceptualisations of the archival record as the primary source of historical truth, as expressed in the letter from historical writers to the PRO. But while there was a sense then that the narrative of history had to be carefully composed and compiled by sifting through the records by the researcher in the reading rooms of the PRO, there is much more of a sense now that the narrative is already there in the record and is only waiting to be unlocked. By describing its purpose as "connect[ing] people with the millions of stories contained in our collection," TNA contributes to a perception that the archival record easily yields coherent historical narratives that in turn provide insight into individual and national identity.[79] The emphasis on individual history and its connection to community throughout TNA's strategy documents and reports of the last two decades is due to the increase in users pursuing personal rather than academic interests, and to the boom in family history. The rise of family history and genealogists is a global phenomenon, in Britain fuelled particularly by the television programme *Who Do You Think You Are?* (BBC, 2004–), but also by websites such as ancestry. com and others.[80] Family historians are now TNA's largest user group, and its efforts to address the needs of this group and its other users in its decision-making processes move it closer to Barbara Craig's vision of users not as visitors or customers, but as "participants in the archival mission,"[81] and further the reorientation that started in the PRO in the late 1990s towards the user end of the spectrum of archival priorities.[82]

TNA's latest strategy goes further to refract its entire operation through the lens of inclusivity, which demands scrutiny of all its practices and of the archive's identity. *Archives for Everyone*, a strategy published online on TNA's website, aims to set a trajectory for the institution that will "transform The National Archives more profoundly than at any point since the founding of the Public Record Office in 1838." The strategy acknowledges the "historic mission" of the national archive – "to collect and preserve the record, to use our expertise and knowledge to connect people with their history through our unrivalled collections, and to lead, partner and support archives at home and worldwide." It reaffirms the institution's authority as a leader in the sector, and its significance for government, the academy and other users. The strategy conceptualises the record not only as source of authority for the archive, but also as an institutional resource which can be exploited to "realise value." But it goes further than previous strategies have by aiming to transform TNA into an institution that "builds trust and tears down barriers to access, participation and understanding." The strategy outlines a firmer reorientation of the archive towards its users, in light of a broadening understanding of the nature and needs of the social, political and cultural context in which it operates.[83]

Despite its claims for radical disruption in *Archives for Everyone*, the core elements of the PRO's archival grain – authority, a relationship to national history, and a tension between the demands of curatorial responsibilities and the needs of public access – can still be identified in its institutional discourse. They are, however, enhanced or overlaid by the contours of an evolving organisational structure and shifting priorities. Older ideas of authority are fading (or are being smoothed over) and being replaced with the idea of authority as expertise, especially in areas of information management and archiving practices. Whereas once the archive shaped the kinds of histories that emerged from it into narratives of nation and of politics, there is now much more of a sense of attempting to parse national history through the 'stories' of individuals. Records are broadly conceptualised in much of this material as history in and of itself, waiting only to be 'unlocked,' an approach that disregards the mediated nature of the records. TNA has become even more multi-faceted as an organisation to meet the needs of its many priorities, but it is increasingly turning towards the needs of its users, while continuing to emphasise its traditional responsibilities for preservation and curation in the digital age. *Archives for Everyone* was, like much else at the start of the 2020s, disrupted by a global pandemic, and the strategy has not yet been fully realised, leaving the organisation in a state of transition.

The ways in which records are read and understood are filtered through interactions with TNA, whether in its virtual or physical spaces. Traces of TNA's archival grain, currently in a process of redefinition through its latest strategy, infuse its reading spaces and inflect the ways in which records are interpreted and understood. The idea of easily discoverable narratives helps to attract users with little to no experience with archives, but these marketing strategies have created complications for how the institution operates in reality, suggesting an ease of access that is not necessarily the case in practice either in TNA's digital or its physical spaces. Chapters 1 and 2 have also demonstrated that this book's chosen set of records, Unit War Diaries, are not the records of individuals, and they do not necessarily yield neat narratives, which complicates TNA's ideas of easily 'unlocking' the past through the record. The archival experiences involved in accessing Unit War Diaries, as well as other records, are not as simple as TNA's discourse suggest. As the next section will demonstrate, they involve complex interactions between the institution's archival grain, and the technologies and materials present in its reading spaces.

Reading Unit War Diaries in TNA's reading spaces

Chapters 1 and 2 examined the mingling of individuals, technologies of writing, cultural and institutional influences and ideologies, as well as the force of war itself at work in the writing spaces of the two World Wars, but these spaces and times are inaccessible to the researcher. This chapter, however, is about the spaces in which those material traces of the past are selected, organised, read, copied and used. I cannot ignore my own presence as the researcher within the reading spaces of the archive, just as I cannot ignore the presence of the archive itself, which regulates and informs my interactions with the record. I am therefore speaking for myself in much of this section and locating myself within the process of researching Unit War Diaries. This section additionally details interactions with the technologies at work in the reading spaces of the archive, and traces what might be lost, or gained, as the Unit War Diaries cycle through them.

In an article in *The Times* in 1926, the writer describes how a huddled group of "dryasdusters" wait outside the PRO in Chancery Lane, eager for the doors to open and the day's research to begin.[84] The idea of archival research as a dusty endeavour was picked up much later by Steedman who, in *Dust*, examines both the literal and figurative residue of the past in archival materials. The 'allure' of the archive, as Arlette Farge referred to it in the title of her book, is in no small part due to the particular appeals of interacting physically with the material traces of the past.[85] The archival experience, as Sally Swartz describes, and as Steedman and Farge explore at length in thoughtful detail, is a peculiar mix of "delight, disappointments, obsessions, boredom and moments of exhilaration."[86] It is, in most accounts, above all, a physical experience of interacting with the records. TNA's reading spaces, however, involve a confluence of technologies, both digital and otherwise, and therefore a convergence of experiences, some of which do not involve physical interactions with the records. Furthermore, the archive itself as institution and place remains mostly in the background in accounts of working with material records. Although Steedman mentions that the PRO is "by far the most likely site" for contracting the various fevers and diseases that might still linger in the dust on the records,[87] and Farge includes short imaginary descriptions of what it is like to enter the archive for a male and female reader, for the most part, the physical spaces of the PRO and other archives in these discussions are oddly immaterial and under-examined.[88] The archive is described variously as a site of "longing and appropriation" and a "place of dreams" for Steedman,[89] while Swartz draws a comparison between the archival record and the unconscious realm.[90]

The descriptions of archives as the place of dreams and the unconscious are at odds with the bulky, immutable presence of Q1 at TNA's site at Kew, which discourages flights of fancy by its very physicality. TNA is approached by a concrete pathway, running between two large water features replete with resident swans and other birdlife. The garden setting is perhaps designed to soften the impact of Q1, but brutalism resists softening. It is not only through the discourse TNA produces that its archival identity is expressed and can be read. Physical architecture, as Blouin and Rosenberg observe, especially in the case of state archives, often reflects the essential qualities of archival grain.[91] Authority, an element core to TNA's institutional identity, is indelibly stamped into the brutalist structure of its physical site at Kew. The national records housed by the PRO were once described by Scargill-Bird as a "magnificent monument to the past," which in turn lent the PRO status as curator of that monument.[92] Today the monumental nature of Q1, like that of other state archives such as those in the U.S. and in Russia, "valorises the importance of its holdings."[93] Q1 is a substantial material representation of older aspects of institutional identity and authority that remind the visitor of the weight and worth of the records it holds.

Pushing through the revolving doors takes the visitor into a lobby that would not be out of place in any corporate office building – a space where sound bounces off the polished floors and echoes under the domed glass ceiling. While I was not expecting the "gloomy, dimly-lighted, mouldy-smelling alleys" described by Charles Dickens in a visit to one of the sites operated by the PRO, the bland corporate neutrality of the entrance is both surprising and confusing.[94] The glass, steel and highly polished floors of TNA's entrance foyer reinforce the sense of the archive as an official and authoritative institution, but the foyer does not convey the sense of what the institution does, or even what it is. There are staff at hand to explain to the first-time visitor where to go, and what to do. Unlike a museum or library, where the visitor can (within reason), wander at will, and make their own way through the exhibitions or browse the shelves, TNA by necessity must direct and explain the nature of its operations, and how visitors might make use of them. The interaction between visitor and institution is therefore of a different register to those in other heritage sites.

Directed by staff to turn left into its public-facing spaces in Q1, the visitor is greeted first by a gift shop and coffee shop to the right and left respectively. These spaces have recently been redesigned by architectural firm AOC, who have attempted, since 2017, to re-energise them with a contemporary interpretation of the original brutalist design – stripping the suspended ceiling to reveal the original concrete, changing the lighting and introducing softer fabrics and colours to break up the space. The goal of the redesign is to transform the archives into a "cultural destination" much like a museum or library and to make the archive a more welcoming space.[95] Specialists are on hand to offer advice – not necessarily on how to conduct archival research, but on how to access the records. In another indication of how the State Archive is changing, in the early 1990s the enquiry desk was 6ft high and set on a raised platform, making approaching it daunting. Today, the enquiry desk is more welcoming, although as of this writing, still shielded by a transparent screen in the wake of the Covid-19 pandemic. There are also staff on hand to greet visitors arriving on the 1st floor, and to direct them as necessary.

These efforts at redesign, which extend to the 1st Floor of the archives, as well as its efforts to humanise the space with welcoming and helpful staff, are physical manifestations of attempts to overlay qualities of older archival grain with newer institutional strategies. They are material representations of moments of transition and contestation between the archive as authoritative institution in control of material important for the state, and a cultural destination open and welcoming to all. But order, control and authority remain embedded in TNA's material architecture. These elements are not easily reconciled with inclusivity. In addition to augmenting the significance of its holdings, the sense of order, control and authority in TNA's physical spaces implies that the national record is an equally ordered, controlled and authoritative body of texts, simply awaiting discovery or unlocking to reveal their narratives of the past. The process of navigating TNA's spaces and procedures is marked by a sense of the institution's mastery and control, and they make unlocking the record a trickier undertaking than much of TNA's discourse implies.

I was directed through the process of obtaining a reader's card, given some guidance on how to navigate the website to order a record, instructed on how to obtain my records, and where and how to read them, either by staff, or by the signage in the building. These granular encounters with aspects of the archive as institution were sometimes affective – generating confusion about where to go or what to do, mild embarrassment at not reading the signage properly and inadvertently breaking a rule, and feelings of inadequacy generated by failing to understand instructions and having to ask again. Emotion in the archive is generally associated with responses to the records,[96] but encounters with aspects of archival grain are the source of affective responses *before* any interaction with the record has occurred. Farge, for example, describes how her imaginary male reader, faced with having to navigate several unknown doors in the majestic spaces of the judicial archive, pauses, "slightly intimidated, before affecting an air of false certainty" and following another, more confident, visitor.[97] The physical architecture of TNA's spaces and its orderly processes are as resonant of meaning and as much a source of emotional response as the records the archive holds. Some emotions – intimidation, inadequacy, frustration, for example – need to be overcome for the research process to continue, and they are part of the experience of navigating TNA's reading spaces. Of course, not all visitors will experience these kinds of emotions, and most will simply work through them as I did, but they should be acknowledged, not only because they are part of the research process for many, but also because for some visitors at least, especially those with no experience of any kind of research at all, they might prove powerful enough to discourage further visits.[98] While these encounters were for me (mostly) friendly, they were infused by aspects of archival grain, as through them TNA's authority and control of the records and the space was made clear.

The experience of navigating TNA's spaces is not only about physical interactions with the institution and the records, but also about encounters with its digital spaces, which can be equally fraught. Although the old catalogues still exist and can be consulted, records must be ordered digitally via Discovery, TNA's online catalogue, which is hosted on its website. As TNA's website explains, Discovery is designed to be a one-stop-shop that is not only the online catalogue for TNA, but also a node connecting to the holdings of over 2,500 other archives across the U.K. Discovery links to all records held by TNA, whether they have been digitised or not, and adheres to the logic of archival description. To help users navigate the complexities of archival cataloguing and description, the website additionally provides research guides. There are over 350 of these finding aids grouped by subjects or available via an index.[99] Just as TNA's physical site can be intimidating and confusing for a first-time visitor, its website can be a daunting and bewildering space, where despite the design team's best efforts, the distinction between searching the website and searching the catalogue is not always clear, largely because there is only one search box for both.[100] Just as it is not uncommon for visitors to the site to expect to see materials laid out for them to browse at will, it is also not uncommon for users of Discovery to expect a link to take them directly to the record they are searching for, rather than to a description about that record in one of the Guides, as TNA's own research into their website shows.[101] There is also the possibility of accidently slipping through the links onto another website, either that of a different archive, or one of TNA's commercial partners (some of which require payment for records), without the user being aware of the transition. Just as first-time visitors to TNA's physical site might arrive with expectations from other heritage sites such as museums or libraries, users of TNA's website have expectations that it will operate like Google or Amazon.

Discovery, however, does not operate along the same lines as commercial search engines. It cannot be searched in the same ways by using key phrases or terms. Discovery functions according to the logic of archival description, which is primarily organised according to the principles of *respects des fonds*. *Respects des fonds* is an archival precept that organises records according to their originating body and maintains their original order. *Respects des fonds* thus emphasises the provenance of the record, organising the record by its origins – the individual, office or organisation that created the record – rather than by subject or chronology or any other kind of category related to the content. Original order refers to the way in which the originating body arranged or filed the records, which is retained and preserved by archival description. According to Blouin and Rosenberg, the authority of state archival records is thus located by archival description not in their content, but in the "bureaucratic process responsible for their generation" and in the legitimacy of the originating organisations.[102] As a process, *respects des fonds* assumes an inherent stability in the records themselves, and it limits the context of their production to the office or individual responsible for their creation.[103] By respecting provenance and limiting decisions regarding the order of documentation and other records, the archivist is supposedly at a remove from power structures and uninvolved in making meaning. These principles of arrangement and order are meant to allow the records to "speak for themselves," in the words of Andrew Janes, TNA's Head of Archival Practice and Data Curation.[104]

The supposed neutrality of the process of archival description based on *respects des fonds* is a subject of much debate within archival discourse.[105] Much of the complexity of that debate, which includes the merits or otherwise of different description systems, as well as discussions regarding what constitutes the boundaries of digital records and their contexts, falls outside the parameters of this book, but there is one strand of it that is relevant, and that concerns the nature of archival description itself. Archival description, like archival records, is a "mediation of reality."[106] As a representation of reality via a particular medium, archival description inevitably privileges certain perspectives over others because choices must be made as to what aspects of reality are represented. The choices made in archival description of all kinds, according to Duff and Harris, always involve working with context – "continually locating it, constructing it, figuring and refiguring it."[107] By identifying and shaping the context of records, archival description is effectively a form of storytelling about the record. Some archivists argue that the story constructed about the records in archival description is designed to be unobtrusive to support the integrity of the record's contents, but like Tom Nesmith and Duff and Harris, I consider archival description as a narrative pathway that configures particular understandings and ways of reading the record.[108]

The narrative pathway to the Unit War Diaries for the First World War begins with WO 95. WO is the department code for the records created or inherited by the War Office, Armed Forces and other related bodies, including the records "from commands, headquarters, regiments and corps," according to TNA's description of the code on Discovery. WO is the department, 95 indicates the series. A series is a "sequence of records with a relationship resulting from a shared history of creation, storage or use."[109] In this case, the series contains the War Diaries for units in the British and Colonial forces serving in theatres of operations between 1914 and 1922, and those of the Armies of Occupation between 1919 and 1922. The series is then broken down into a hierarchy of sequential layers represented by numerical codes: operational theatre → General Headquarters → Army → Corps → division→ unit. The Second World War Unit War Diaries are not contained in one series, like WO 95, but are organised according to different theatres of operations. WO 166, for example, refers to the Home Forces, WO 167 the British Expeditionary Force in France, WO 168 the British North-West Expeditionary Force and so on consecutively up until WO 179, the records of the Dominion Forces. The War Diaries of one regiment from the Second World War might therefore be spread across various series, depending on the theatres that regiment was engaged in over the course of the conflict. The series vary in size, from the smallest at 49 pieces for WO 174 (British Forces in Madagascar) to the largest at 24,939 pieces for WO 169 (British Forces in the Middle East).[110] Each 'piece' is a box of files, or a file, of varying size. Whereas the records of the First World War are thus positioned by archival description as an integrated whole, the records of the Second are fragmented according to the logic of organisational structures connected to each theatre.

Archival grain manifests in archival description. TNA's responsibility to uphold the integrity of the processes of record keeping within government departments is an intrinsic element of the narrative that emerges within the pathway that overlays Unit War Diaries. Through the selection of which aspects of context to include, and which to ignore, archivists effectively "help author records by the very act of determining what authoring them means and involves, or what the provenance of the records is."[111] Archival description in the case of Unit War Diaries privileges the Army as organisation over the individual as author and contributes to the erasure of the individual from the bureaucratic process discussed in previous chapters. The context for the creation of Unit War Diaries discussed at length in Chapters 1 and 2 – the individuals who composed the records, the cultural and social forces at work in the spaces in which they were written, along with the affordances and limitations of the technologies they used, as well as the extraordinary circumstances of two global conflicts – is not the context that is important for archival description. Instead, hierarchical institutional structures are selected by archival description as the most significant contextual information for the records of war. The story of the creation of Unit War Diaries according to archival description is thus one of a linear process following an orderly trajectory from particular theatres of war through the structures of the Army to the governing body it answers to. Archival description continues the work of the official documents used by the Army and other military bodies designed to collect information about conflict. It subsumes the trauma and chaos of warfare into neat, linear narratives that tell the story of conflict as managed by institutions, not as experienced by individuals.

As with the processes of operational reporting in war, control and systemisation might seem appropriate approaches to the management of records. After all, we don't want chaotic archives in which nothing can be found. But as with operational reporting, archival processes naturalise the privileging of institutions over individuals, of rational frameworks as ways of apprehending and describing events, and of textual traces as evidence of those events. Because these practices today seem logical and natural, they discourage close examination and interrogation, yet archives themselves are implicated in their naturalisation. TNA's practices and approach to 'managing' its records are meant to be as transparent as possible, to allow the records to "speak for themselves."[112] But loaded with authority, and with a sense of a special relationship to national history and identity, TNA's spaces and practices overlay the records with a mask of rational order and coherence – a metaphor I deploy deliberately here to counter the 'naturalness' inherent in the association between archives and dream or memory, or the inert qualities of the store or the one-stop-shop. Far from allowing the records to speak for themselves, before a single digital file or box has been opened, the archive informs me that the records have the weight of iconic national documents, are the product of orderly processes and will yield ordered narratives about the past.

Finally, after navigating TNA's physical spaces, and working through the difficulties of identifying the required records in Discovery, orders for the actual records can be placed. There are a range of technologies, both digital and otherwise, through which Unit War Diaries can be accessed, and each brings its own layer of meaning to the material traces of the past.

Technologies and transformations

Most of the First World War Unit War Diaries have been digitised by TNA and, due to custodial concerns for preservation, the paper copies have been removed from public access (they can still be viewed, but only after a case is made by the requester that justifies the need to see the paper version). The First World War Unit War Diaries are downloaded from Discovery via the Portable Document Format (PDF). PDF is particularly suited to TNA's digitisation of archival records because it is free to view and use, and compatible with most hardware and software. The format is now so ubiquitous that it has achieved a transparency almost on a par with technologies like the pen or typewriter. This section begins with an examination of the PDF, to reveal that like the pen and the typewriter, its history is intertwined with the rise of documentation, and like all media technologies, it is neither neutral nor transparent, but shapes interactions with the content it represents. The Second World War Unit War Diaries, however, are only available in paper format, and they are accessed in boxes and files brought to the physical spaces of TNA's reading rooms. Of all the practices and materialities in the reading spaces of the archive, the cardboard box and file are among the most invisible, but containers of records, both literal and figurative, have been the focus of much of this book, and the humble cardboard box and file deserve attention too. This section tracks the transformations of Unit War Diaries as they cycle through these old and new technologies of containment and re-presentation in the reading spaces of the archive.

In 2011, TNA began a large project to digitise WO 95, the Unit War Diaries of the First World War, by scanning them and converting them to PDF. In digital form, the First World War Unit Diaries are no longer confined to the spaces of TNA and are available in PDF (for a small fee, to enable TNA to recoup the costs of digitisation) for users around the world to download. PDF has outpaced other formats to become the most prevalent file format for the exchange of documents not only in the corporate sector, but across a range of others, including academia and the heritage sector, where the PDF/A has become particularly significant (if controversial).[113] Developed by John Warnock of Adobe Systems in the early 1990s, the PDF was designed to provide a solution to the difficulties of sharing and printing documents of various kinds across different computer hardware and operating systems and via different applications. The format evolved during what Adobe calls on its website the "paper-to-digital revolution" – a time in which the vision of a paperless office was gaining traction as digital technologies transformed working practices and other areas of life. Digital technology appeared at this stage to hold the solution to many of the problems of paperwork discussed throughout this book – issues of bulk, storage and transmission, for example.[114] Warnock believed that the PDF could ultimately replace paper, but at the same time, it replicated one of the key affordances of paper in that it was designed to ensure that documents in this format would always look the same, no matter how they were accessed. It replicated, via a digital interchange format, practices of photocopying or sharing paper documents via post. PDF thus represents the tendency in digital media identified by Jay David Bolter and Richard Grusin to "refashion the older medium or media entirely, while still marking the presence of the older media."[115] It remediates paper and refashions documents of all file formats into electronic images that are viewed via an interface that preserves the original appearance of the text and/or graphics.

Precisely because the PDF was designed to maintain what David Parmenter, director of Data & Engineering at Adobe Document Cloud, refers to as "author intent," it appears to the be perfect format for the conversion of Unit War Diaries to digital form.[116] The "author intent" that PDF was originally designed to preserve was not that of individuals, as Gitelman points out, but that of "corporate authorship," where standardisation and the control of documentation is essential.[117] Gitelman additionally points out that the PDF has a long association with grey literature, which generally refers to material that is not produced or disseminated by traditional publishers, but which contains information significant to specific sectors or organisations.[118] The PDF is thus especially suited to the C.2118 form, which emphasises institutional authorship, as its interface is specifically designed to reproduce the formal qualities of official documentation. The Army's authority and ownership of these records is reiterated through the formal regularity that the PDF interface emphasises, over and above the individuals who completed the forms. The emphasis on reproduction limits the format's capacity for allowing the documents to be modified, which additionally increases its suitability for archival purposes.

Scrolling through the First World War Unit War Diary Portable Document files (PDfs), the regularity of the C.2118 form is a repeated and constant frame around the irregular handwriting of those who completed it, broken intermittently by the scraps of notes, letters and orders that are also included in the files, but all are made uniform within neat black frames. In their conversion to PDfs, the traces of the older technology of paper in Unit War Diaries retains a kind of ghostly materiality, evident in the ragged edges of some of the paper pages. Evidence of the dismantling of the files for scanning purposes is in the holes remaining where documents were originally bound into their files.

I interact with the ghostly materiality of the PDf War Diary via a similarly ghostly replica of a small white hand, but I cannot feel the fragile pages. The hand shaped curser is, according to Gitelman, "a reader's hand, in effect, not an author or editor's hand."[119] The ghostly extension of my hand hovers over the images of the pages with no material effect, unlike the material traces left by the numerous 'hands' at work in the completed forms. The qualities of each page – some ragged, some in good shape – and the variety of documents in the files are flattened out in TNA's digitisation process, turning them all into one large document, some over a hundred pages long. The experience of reading them is perhaps easier, as I can skim them and scroll down quicker than I could were I looking at paper, which would require careful handling.

But if reading the documents is easier in PDF, the "subliminal context that comes with the finding, filing, handling and searching through the physical file" is lost.[120] "[S]ifting through the archives" to gather up documents of a certain type facilitates an awareness of the broader context that surrounds the documents you have chosen to focus on.[121] The affordances of paper files lend themselves to browsing and to the occasional accidental discovery as pages are turned and something unexpected is revealed or falls out of the file. In digital format, and particularly when there is a cost involved in downloading PDfs, researchers are much more likely to target specific files, rather than browse through a selection, and the chances of accidental discoveries leading the researcher in a different direction are minimised. Handling documents was for so long central to the experience of archives, but here, the act of "combing through archives" becomes scrolling through pages on a screen, without the "slowness of hands and thought" so valued by researchers as a potential "source of creativity."[122]

The loss of material interaction with Unit War Diaries involves a loss of context and changes the process of research, but there are trade-offs involved in the conversion to digital formats that must also be acknowledged. PDF allows historical records to be appropriated, circulated and used in ways that could never have been anticipated by their originators. This includes TNA's own use of the First World War Unit War Diaries. There were impulses other than curatorial at work in TNA's selection of one of its most popular sets of records for digitisation. The interest generated by the digitisation of the First World War Unit Diaries during the groundswell of publicity for the centenary of First World War allowed TNA to enhance its profile on an international stage through a project known as Operation War Diary. Developed in partnership with the Imperial War Museum and a crowd sourcing web portal known as Zooniverse, Operation War Diary allowed TNA to open the digitised war diaries to volunteers or 'citizen historians.' The website for Operation War Diary stated that the volunteers were needed to "reveal" the "story of the British Army on the Western Front" but the project itself was less concerned with building a narrative and more concerned with the conversion of the diaries into usable data sets. Volunteers did not work on complete diaries (and whole narratives), as this would allow access to the material at no charge, and there would consequently be no way for TNA to recoup the considerable costs involved in digitising the diaries. Instead, pages of the diaries were presented out of context and in random order. The hope was that curiosity about the fragments of events mentioned on random pages might prompt volunteers and visitors to the online project to seek out the complete diaries on TNA's website – an example of how TNA maximises the value of its holdings to attract more users.

In terms of the data itself, TNA initially established a set of key tags for citizen historians, while still allowing users to create tags for other information that they considered significant. These initial tags – specifically individual names, place names, dates and times – were selected by TNA because they are significant search terms for family historians, but they echo some of the parameters that the Army set for these records in the *Field Service Regulations* and are evidence that the Army's emphasis on the measurable and countable dimensions of conflict persists as a way of understanding war. Operation War Diary ran for about five years, and the data gathered from the tags on the 900,000 documents is still being processed in various ways.[123] TNA's use and re-presentation of Unit War Diaries reveals the archive as an active site in which records are not simply stored, but also undergo an ongoing process of reconfiguration and reinterpretation, one which in this case, involved the transformation of Unit War Diaries into data sets. Data sets might be useful for some approaches and shed light on some aspects of the experience of the war, but there is also a loss in the transformation of the diaries to data. While they might provide evidence of larger trends and conditions in the conflict, the granular experiences of individuals that emerge through the Unit War Diaries is lost, which is at least in part why this book adopted an approach that merges both data analysis and close textual analysis.

While archival documents could always be copied, either laboriously by hand, or later via photocopy or by photography (a process described in more detail later in this section), TNA's conversion of the First World War Unit War Diaries to PDF enables the download of entire files in a relatively short space of time. These files can then be kept and examined by the user outside of the spaces and times of the archive, potentially facilitating a deeper interaction with the content of the files. Like the paper files they mimic, the PDfs of Unit War Diaries cannot be searched by mechanical means. They are image files, not text files, and they do not lend themselves easily to Optical Character Recognition (OCR), due to the variations in handwriting and quality, hence the need for citizen historians to conduct manual searches in Operation War Diary, and the need for the purposes of this book to transcribe the records from PDF to plain text format. Later in this chapter, Stevie Docherty, who was responsible for most of the transcription for this book, describes the particular physicality of interacting with Unit War Diaries in PDF rather than in paper format, such as the ability to zoom in on specific words, and the format's ability to engender an unexpected intimacy with the record. While there may be a loss of broader context in the transformation of records to digital forms, and the loss of the tactile interaction with records that has for so long defined the understanding of the archive, Stevie's description of her interactions with the documents in PDF is a valuable reminder that physical interactions with records are not entirely lost in the digital world, but transformed in ways that have the power to bring researchers into different relationships with the mediated traces of the past. Stevie's experiences are also a reminder that while TNA's process of digitisation smooths out the surface irregularities of paper files and emphasises institutional authority, at a deeper level, the First World War Unit War Diaries continue to push against these kinds of structures through the irregularity of individual handwriting and the occasional unruliness of their content.

In the case of the First World War Unit War Diaries, the physical process of transforming paper records to digital files is largely hidden. In the case of the

Second World War records, which have not been digitised, this labour shifts to the researcher. Ordered via Discovery, the Second World War Records are delivered, three pieces at a time, to a numbered locker corresponding to the same desk number in the reading room allocated to me via TNA's online ordering system. The entrance to the reading rooms and the spaces themselves are monitored by TNA staff and by security cameras, and the visitor is restricted in terms of what can or cannot be brought into these spaces. Bags need to be left in locker rooms on the ground floor, but digital devices are permitted, and the user can request a desk with a mount for a digital camera to take their own images of the records. Just as the PDfs of the First World War Diaries merge older technologies of writing with digital technology, the physical spaces of TNA's reading rooms involve a confluence of older and newer technologies in tangible forms. Alongside my laptop and digital camera, the cardboard boxes of the Second World War Unit War Diaries, some of which have lost their structural integrity with age and use, appear anachronistic.

The moment of opening a box or bundle of records has been romanticised in much of the literature around archives. Blouin and Rosenberg describe how the "near magical qualities" of encountering boxes with their "fragile and faded remnants of long ago events and transactions" can fire "even the most resistant imaginations."[124] Steedman talks about the anticipation and "supreme satisfaction" of unfastening the "bundles that have been waiting" for the historian.[125] There is something close to reverence evident in Farge's account of "gently [...] undoing the cloth ribbon that corsets [the bundle] around the waist, revealing a pale line where the cloth had rested for so long."[126] But the boxes, files and other containers themselves are often overlooked in these accounts, as researchers rush to examine their contents. They are placed to one side on the desks of reading rooms and ignored in favour of the records they contain. But like all the other forms of organisation and containment discussed throughout this book, the material objects of storage are also the products and expressions of the cultures in which they evolve. "The package is also the message," writes Cheryce Von Xylander, paraphrasing Marshall McLuhan, and the cardboard boxes and files in which the Second World War Unit War Diaries are packaged have their own subtle inflections of meaning.[127]

Both the cardboard box and the file are examples of what Craig Robertson calls "the material history of efficiency" and they emerged within the rise of capitalist corporate practices over the course of the last two centuries.[128] Developed in the late 1800s, the cardboard box – light, disposable, yet strong enough to protect its contents – introduced a quiet revolution in the circulation of goods and contributed to the rise of the consumer society. It is a "symbol of industrialisation and commercialisation" and yet it is so ubiquitous it is generally unnoticed.[129] Most of the ways the cardboard box is used in the commercial world lead to its disposal or recycling, but in the archive, it has a more permanent status. Cardboard boxes are not just essential for the transactions and transitions of everyday life, they are also "epistemic tools in ordering, containing, and classifying the worldly mess."[130] Developed to handle "the logistics of exchange" in the commercial world, the cardboard box assists in a different kind of exchange in the archive.[131] It enables the storage of files, but more perhaps even more importantly, their tracking and transport from stacks to reading desk and back again. The cardboard box is transitory, permanent, but nevertheless replaceable, unlike the files it contains. Also, unlike the paper it contains, the box has no "claim to cultural authority" and yet it imposes order over its contents.[132]

The cardboard boxes containing the Unit War Diaries of the Second World War are physical manifestations of archival description. The careful identification of pieces, or boxes, in each series of the Second World War Unit War Diaries implies a sense of control over their contents and creates divisions between the records — these boxes belong to this theatre, this context of time and space. Even the term, 'piece,' conveys the way in which the record of the Second World War has been divided and segmented, broken down into supposedly manageable chunks. Each individual box separates its contents from other records and creates a relationship between them — these records fit together in this context, in this box. The cardboard box hypostasises archival order and control. In terms of logistical exchange, it not only enables the showing of its contents to the user, but it also conveys a way of knowing the records it re-presents.

The contents of the boxes are most usually contained in cardboard files. Some pieces are not boxes at all, but large files containing smaller ones. Like the cardboard box, files are associated with commercial enterprises. As bureaucratic enterprises increased their reliance on paper records, and the technologies discussed in Chapters 1 and 2 such as the fountain pen, indelible pencil, typewriter and carbon paper facilitated the production of more paperwork, the need arose to organise and store it all. Until as late as the mid-1800s, according to Craig Robertson, paper was stored in everything from bound collections, to piles in pigeonholes or spikes on desks and shelves, most of which risked damage and loss.[133] Files and filing systems addressed these issues, as Robertson details. But like the cardboard box, the development of the file was more than simply functional. The file emerged at the same time as information became understood as a commodity, something separate from knowledge.[134] Robertson therefore argues that filing paperwork was part of a shift towards systems through which information could be classified, split into discrete units and grouped together — systems which have been discussed throughout this book in relation to the recording of information about war.[135]

In the production of the Unit War Diaries, the file is one of the first steps in the process of classifying and arranging the documents, but in the archives, it is the last one encountered before the records themselves. The files separate records by Unit and date, generally by year, although in some cases they may contain the records for more, or less, than one year. The boundaries created by the files between the records are thus both hierarchical and temporal. Both the file and the box divide the records of conflict and re-present them as discrete, manageable sections, ordered by the Army's hierarchical structures, and specific times and places. While most of the writing about archives focuses on the *opening* of the box or file, both are implicated in what Schlünder eloquently argues is the *closure* of knowledge into distinctly Western epistemological systems of order and containment.[136] Like the official forms they contain, the box and the file are part of rational systems that attempt to reduce conflict to specific co-ordinates and data points, and that separate information about war into discrete units. But they are also material artefacts, and as such, they are the source of responses that exceed their intended purposes.

The rules of the reading room limit my engagement with the record of war to three 'pieces' at a time, regardless of the size of the box of files, or file. The sheer physical bulk of some of the pieces is daunting, in a way that the PDfs of the First World War Diaries were not, even when they extended to hundreds of pages. I place the boxes with a slight thump on my allocated desk, where they sit incongruously besides the digital technologies I've brought with me. I find I am not immune to the affective impact of the material traces of the past, although I am not sure that I would describe the experience as 'alluring,' like others have. While much is made of the tactile experience of holding or handling the records, something Farge refers to as the "privilege of 'touching the real,'" for example, it is the *sight* of the colours of the cardboard boxes and files that provokes the first response in me.[137] They are a distinctive faded brown, a colour I recognise immediately and associate with military administrative files, seen on the desks of offices in the air force base where I spent my early childhood. Although the First World War Diaries as PDfs include images of the files, the colour did not register in the same way it did when I was confronted by them in actuality. As I open the box, a scent drifts up that I register with an involuntary and affective shock of recognition. The scent, even more than the sight of the distinctive shade of faded cardboard, transports me back to the linoleum-floored corridors of the air force base I have not visited in many years. But these records are not material traces from *my* past. They are not records of the air force, and they predate my childhood. I am aware that these responses will be uniquely mine, but I am the researcher in this reading space with these records, and I bring with me the influences – cultural, social, political – that have shaped me. Instead of thinking about the Second World War as I open the first box, the scent takes me back an air force base in Apartheid-era South Africa in the 1970s.

The ways in which these affective responses might have influenced my subsequent research are difficult to pinpoint through the formal conventions demanded by academic writing. The inchoate emotions prompted by these sensory interactions are part of the messiness of what Farge refers to as the "excess of meaning" generated by archives.[138] They fall outside of "scientific examination" and on their own "would do little to satisfy historians" or others in many academic fields.[139] But I note them here because they are part of my memory of encountering the materiality of the Second World War Unit War Diaries in the reading rooms of TNA, and they are a source of meaning over and above that which I went on to find in the records themselves.

I want to make them visible because much emotion is invisible in the reading spaces of archives, as it was in the writing spaces of the battlefield. They are evidence that the physicality of material traces of the past, including those of the containers of the records, can provoke sometimes unexpected reactions that are not connected in any way to content and are difficult to quantify or even explain through the traditions of academic writing. In much the same way, the physicality of the material spaces of the two World Wars must also have prompted responses that did not always make their way into the records of war. The sights and scents of the records prompted an unanticipated re-connection with a space and time very different from either the reading room or the writing spaces in which the records were produced. They suggested unlooked-for continuities between very different spheres of military life – the British Army and the South African Air Force – and implied the endurance of some organisational structures across time and space. Such unpredictable affective responses, and the unknown ways in which they might direct research, are lost in the transformation of material records to digital formats, even if others might be gained.

The process of sifting through the material files by hand was much slower than scanning through PDfs, largely because of the care needed to avoid damaging the paper record. Generally filed in cardboard folders with string binders, the pages of the Second World War Unit War Diaries needed to be lifted carefully before being turned to avoid tearing them at the point where holes had been punched in them to allow them to be filed. In paper form, the variety of the pages contained in these files was much more apparent than in the PDfs of the First World War Diaries. Much of the paper in the files of the Second World War Unit War Diaries is brittle and fragile, and some pages are almost transparent. Some pages curl up at their edges, making them difficult to read. Even the C.2118 forms lose their regularity, as conditions vary across each page, and as Stevie notes, in some cases the forms were not used at all, making it difficult to distinguish between after-action account and War Diary. The blurring of the lines between these two kinds of reports, discussed in Chapter 2, thus has a material reality in the choice of paper used to record them. There is more of a sense of general context in examining box after box, and I make accidental discoveries, such as the illustrations of the "Nijmegen Nuisance" in the records of the Welsh Guards described in Chapter 2, which stand out against the formal structures and containers of administrative procedures.

The containers of the record insist on the relationships between them but discovering exceptions like the "Nijmegen Nuisance" brings home the fact that some of these things are not like the others, and they resist easy classification. Not only did someone produce material that breaks all the rules of operational reporting, but someone also included it, perhaps deliberately, perhaps accidently, in official files, which then made their way through the hierarchical structures of the Army to the archive, subtly undermining their authority. I hold the illustrations and wonder at the steps that brought these sheets of paper from Holland in 1944 to this file, this box, this reading room, to my hand. These are not questions that came to mind when scanning through the PDfs of First World War Unit War Diaries. They emerge from my tactile interaction with the material, that sense of "touching traces of the past" with my actual hand, rather than hovering over the digital image with a ghostly digital facsimile of a hand.[140] That sense of direct contact with the past in handling archival records must be acknowledged as powerful and persuasive, but it reinforces the conceptualisation of records as unmediated gateways to history, reiterated in TNA's own descriptions of the record as inert, and waiting to be unlocked, and obscures the fact that these are carefully constructed, mediated representations of selected moments from the past. Affective response to the records as material artefacts punctuate the process of archival research, but they are part of the experience, and not the whole of it, despite what the metaphors about archives as treasure chests or stores waiting to be unlocked might imply.

After those initial sensory interactions with the boxes and files, and despite the occasional accidental discovery and tactile response, much of my interactions with the records became routine, although they were far more physical than the term 'reading room' implies. TNA would not permit the use of a digital scanner on the Unit War Diaries for fear of damage to the record, and each page therefore had to be individually photographed. Although TNA provides stands for digital cameras, which to a certain extent makes the process of photographing pages of documents easier, the variations in size and quality of the Unit War Diaries, as well as the awkward bulkiness of the files, meant that each image needed to be checked before the photograph could be taken, and the camera or page repositioned every time. Farge describes the "slow and unrewarding artisanal task of recopying texts" by hand as part of attempting to find a way to hold on to the archival record.[141] The process of imaging the War Diaries feels similarly slow and unrewarding in that it is monotonous and laborious, resulting in aching eyes, shoulders and neck at the end of every day. It also feels endless, extending over days, weeks and months as I chip individual images out of some of the 88,244 pieces that make up the vast record of the Second World War Diaries. Farge notes how recopying the record by hand, as opposed to taking notes, felt in some way like "an exclusive and privileged way of entering into the world of the document, as both accomplice and outsider."[142] The idea of a privileged connection created from hand to hand through the act of copying is something Stevie also mentions in her description of transcription later in this chapter. Translating documents into images, however, seems to do exactly the opposite. Standing and capturing the image of page after page, I lose connection with the textual content of the diaries and become more concerned with the formal composition of their images on the screen of my camera. Rather than entering the 'world' of the record, I am pulling pieces of that world out of the writing spaces of the Second World War and the reading spaces of TNA and into the digital network of images and texts that constitutes my own archive.

Images on most digital cameras are stored using the JPEG (Joint Photographic Experts Group) compression standard. JPEG is an algorithm that compresses images and allows them to be uploaded quickly and easily to be viewed on screens of digital devices of all kinds. Like the PDF, and indeed like many of the other technologies discussed in this book, JPEG is so pervasive that it is often overlooked. But unlike pens, paper and even PDF, as an algorithm or set of protocols JPEG really is invisible, unless, as Paul Caplan points out, you are a programmer and can find it in software.[143] Compression enables more files to be stored on memory cards, which in turn enables me to take many more photographs than I would have been able to take with a camera using film. Paul Caplan therefore argues that the excess of images supported by digital technologies therefore makes for a practice "arguably different than 'photography' with its connotations of professionalism, scarcity, art and deliberation." From Caplan's perspective, the practice I am engaged with is consequently better referred to as "imaging."[144] JPEG not only facilitates profligate image-taking, but its protocols are also designed to support the saving and organisation of those images, and their further distribution and use. Once I have transferred the individual images of the Second World War records to my laptop, they must be re-combined into files and converted to PDF. The transition of the Second World War Diaries through JPEG protocols is therefore transient, and it might seem immaterial in both sense of that word, but the fragmentation of the record into individual images before that transition introduces a different perspective of the Diaries.

The images I take lack the neat uniformity of TNA's digital versions of the First World War Records. The borders of the pages are not always neatly aligned, and the edges of the files themselves are sometimes visible. At times, the curled pages could not be smoothed back, and they obscure parts of the text. At other times, my fingers appear in shot, holding down the curled edges, or attempting to secure a page. The image of my hand interacting with the paper record is similar to the handwriting or typographic errors in the Diaries themselves – it is a reminder of the presence of the human being in the reading spaces of the archive. While the professional images and PDFs of the First World War Unit War Diaries produced by TNA smooth out irregularities and insist on clarity, the JPEG images I take are inadvertent reminders of the messiness of the paper files and their location in boxes and files. The digital images paradoxically draw attention to the material qualities of the records as pieces of paper, even as it renders them immaterial and more malleable than they are in paper form. The process of imaging the Diaries insists on an interaction with their material form and draws attention to it in ways that simply handling or reading them, or copying out their contents by hand, or requesting digital versions from TNA would not. Even when recombined into PDFs, the messiness of the images is a reminder not only of the process of research, but also of the materiality of the paper form.

These digital formats – JPEG and PDF – enabled the Unit War Diaries selected for this book to be removed from the reading spaces of the archive.

But the pathways and the technologies involved in accessing Unit War Diaries matter. Reading Unit War Diaries in and through TNA's reading spaces, both physical and virtual, involves sometimes affective interactions with an institution that, despite the shift towards inclusivity and user-friendliness, retains traces of authority and power in its archival grain. It is above all an institution that emphasises order and control. "One cannot help but marvel," Caroline Elkins writes about TNA, "at its benign efficiency, or the rigor with which its rules are enforced."[145] Elkins notes the sharp disparity between TNA's quiet and neat spaces and the disorder of Britain's Colonial records, and a similar contrast can be drawn between the ordered systems of the archive and the records of war. TNA's discourse, spaces, practices and the technologies it uses to re-present the records are all designed to bring order to vast collections of documents, including those generated by the two World Wars.

By emphasising the idea that the past can be accessed through carefully managed records that contain clear narratives, TNA's practices smooth over the disorder and chaos of events such as global wars, and places them, both literally and figuratively, in boxes. On a more subtle level, the authority of the institution, as well as the valorisation of its records in descriptions of them as iconic national documents discourages critique of either the archive or its holdings. These are dimensions of archival grain that must be resisted and deserve interrogation. In practice, the size of the records generated by the two World Wars far exceeds the capacity for neat narrative framing, and at the level of the individual record, is neither as organised nor as neat as archival systems might suggest, as Chapters 1 and 2 have detailed. Similarly, the idea that records are "just papers, images or sequences of bytes" until they are unlocked overlooks the vital role played by technologies and formats in shaping the understanding and uses of the records.[146] The technologies and formats, from cardboard box to digital files, through which the Unit War Diaries cycle in the reading spaces of the archive, inflect them with meaning, prompt sometimes unpredictable affective responses, and enable them to be used in unexpected ways, as this section has demonstrated.

Like most researchers, however, I am one of the "hostages to the archive" in that despite interrogating the shape and form of archival influence over the record, I am entangled in its processes.[147] By necessity and convention, some of the organisational features created by TNA and imposed on the records must be retained, even if the sample of Unit War Diaries selected for this book was eventually removed from the spaces of the archive. The files need to be arranged via the archive's alpha-numeric codes, which retain the logic of archival description, in order that they can be correctly cited as part of the standards of professional academic writing to demonstrate mastery over archival material. The War Diaries, and other archival material, are 'primary' sources, a term that, as Tredinnick argues, implies a hierarchy among textual references and positions the archival record like much of the discourse around TNA does – as the 'raw material' of history, rather than mediated representations deliberately designed to meet the needs and purposes of the organisations

170 *The Matter of Materials and Archives*

that deploy them.[148] In appropriating a section of the vast bulk of Unit War Diaries for my research, I am participating in the creation of a "complex documentary record of textual makings and remakings, in which [my] own scholarly investments directly participate."[149] This process is inevitably embedded within the very systems of rational order and coherence that this book has interrogated.

Both the First World War PDfs downloaded from TNA and the Second World War Unit War Diaries that I collected through the process outlined above, are organised into my personal archive. They are saved in folders with icons that resemble neat and uniform cardboard tabbed files; a sharp contrast to the tattered and tired cardboard folders that enclose the paper War Diaries. My laptop 'desktop' itself is based on a metaphor in that it is designed to resemble and replicate older analogue systems of desk and paper files. The remediation of the tools and symbols of the office into digital devices was deliberately designed to make computer interfaces familiar and comfortable for those who worked in offices.[150] The practices of corporations and institutions shaped by bureaucratic systems that relied on the production and control of documentation, over a century later continue to influence the technologies that I use to organise digital copies of some of the files produced as a result of similar organisational practices in the Army. These convergences and synchronicities demonstrate how deeply bureaucratic approaches and rational systems of organisation and control are embedded in almost every aspect of our everyday practices, and why they are so difficult to unpick.

My systems of organisation replace TNA's, and like the archive itself, I attempt to exert control over the records through coherent and ordered processes of naming and filing, applying a mask of orderliness of my own over the records of war. While these systems and processes are necessary, we should nevertheless be alert to their limitations. The idea of mastery and control is an illusion, or as Sally Swartz puts it, the "lie" buried in the narratives we construct out of archival research.[151] Far from containing neat narratives, the archival record of the two World Wars is so large and so varied that it exceeds any attempt at control. It can never be known, or mastered, despite the veneer of control exerted through academic practices. "Western epistemology," according to Schlünder, "hides its rules, its limits and exclusions in its infrastructures of thinking."[152] This chapter has thus far been concerned with exposing the rules and infrastructures that shape and limit the understanding and use of archival primary sources. The transcription of records from one textual form to another is also a practice often hidden in archival research, although it frequently takes place outside of the reading spaces of the archive.

Unit War Diaries outside of TNA's reading spaces: Transcription

I therefore want to end this chapter by including an account of how the process of transcription involved a different kind of engagement with Unit War

Diaries outside of the spaces of TNA, through the archive I constructed and its associated network of texts and formats. Because they are image files, the PDFs of both the First and Second World War Diaries cannot be scanned or searched. The files therefore had to be transcribed to plain text format to allow their contents to be searched using Antconc, the linguistic software programme I selected and used to identify emotives in the War Diaries. Plain text format erases all differences between Unit War Diaries and renders them down to a textual form that is essentially data, or information that can be mined. On one level, plain text realises the original intention of the Diaries in that it transforms them into uniform, organised sets of information, stripped of all idiosyncratic formal qualities.

Transcription, like all the other processes described to this point, is not a neutral process. While most discussions of the transcription process refer to the transformation of oral discourse to text,[153] Susan Tilley's observation that a transcriber leaves "interpretive/analytical/theoretical prints" on a transcribed text is equally valid for the transcription of written and printed text to other textual forms.[154] Transcription in the case of this book involved the rearrangement of textual material to transform it into useable sets of data, and the interpretation of the content to identify and tag emotives and variations in the material, such as typographic errors. Because it is often not carried out by the researcher, transcription is regarded as an activity adjacent to core research practices, but it is a practice that can provide different insights into the material.[155] As a transcriber who was not a researcher on this project, Stevie's experiences of working with the Unit War Diaries were different to mine but are as crucial to the way the material subsequently came to be understood and analysed. Transcription is another form of remediation of the Unit War Diaries, and it involves not only technologies, but Stevie herself. As Stevie details in her account of the process, transcription mobilises a different set of engagements and relationships between Unit War Diaries, technologies, the researcher and the transcriber. The writing spaces of transcription are also reading spaces, and Stevie details how the elements at work in them shaped her interpretation and analysis, and the prints she left on the data as a result.

Box 3.1 "War Diaries transcription notes" by Stevie Docherty

I first began working on the diary transcription in the spring of 2015 and continued to work on it intermittently for the rest of the year, although I can't remember exactly when this first phase ended (it's a bit surprising to realise how hazy my own recall is about this aspect of the work, in light of the fact that the project was centred on records of events). I combined the diary transcription with my work as a full-time research student, working on the diaries for an hour or two in the evenings several days a week. I also went to the university library to work at weekends. Occasionally I worked in transit, if I was travelling by train and the journey was long enough. In the library I always used one of the university desktop computers rather than my own laptop. At the time I had an ASUS EeeBook, which was very light and portable but had a small screen and limited memory. The bigger screens on the library desktops made it much easier for me to read and navigate within the PDFs and allowed me to work more easily across two windows at once, via split-screening. To avoid overloading my EeeBook I usually saved any in-progress .txt files on to a USB drive and uploaded both the in-progress and finished versions to the shared cloud space set up for the project.

I began working on the Second World War Diaries in March 2021 and stopped at the end of April. The time I spent with these files was therefore much shorter and more concentrated than my time working with the First World War diaries. I had finished my own research but was by then working full-time in a different field, so again the transcription was something I did in the evenings and at weekends. Circumstances had also changed drastically as a result of the pandemic. The country was still in lockdown when I started work on the Second World War diaries and I therefore completed the second phase of the transcription at my parents' house, where I had moved during the first lockdown in 2020. I could have gone back to using the university library as restrictions began to ease, but I didn't want to be in a public space with lots of other people unless it was absolutely necessary.

At the technical level, my EeeBook became less and less usable over the course of the transcription of the Second World War Diaries. Despite repeated clean-ups, it had accumulated so much system clutter over the years that the little bar indicating how much disk space was left was constantly in the red. Running more than two programmes at once or having more than three or four browser tabs open frequently led to low memory warnings or crashes. The machine held out until later in the summer, when the keyboard began to fail. Eventually a letter key that was part of my Windows password stopped responding. Though the laptop still worked, after a fashion, I was locked out of it. I'm writing these notes on its replacement – a Dell Inspiron. This is a better computer for work with a more generous screen. However, it's far less robust. I dropped my EeeBook multiple times over the course of our working relationship, with no visible damage. Recently I managed to crack the LCD display on the Inspiron simply by applying too much pressure with my thumb when trying to close the lid. The external surface of the screen was fine, but the underlying display was fractured beyond use and required a full replacement.

In his tracing of the history of word processing, Matthew Kirschenbaum asks why (or if) it matters whether we know what kind of writing technologies or software authors use – the kind of table Jane Austen wrote at, for instance, or the fact that George R.R. Martin writes his books on something called WordStar. "We don't know exactly why it is important to know these things," he suggests, "but we know we would rather know them than not."[156] So does it matter what kind of computer I used, or what kind of screen it had? I think it does, because these were essential components in both the practical work of the transcription and my personal experience of that work and of the diary PDfs themselves. The transcription could *only* be done with/on screens – a combination of desktop and laptop screens, in public and private settings. Together these were crucial in forming the space of reading and of writing in which I was working at any given time.

In the medieval tradition, the scriptorium is a room dedicated to writing, often in a monastic setting – a fixed place in which the scribes spend strictly defined hours doing a specific type of labour. Yet as Jenneka Janzen notes, this vision is "easily complicated…The physical scriptorium, meaning a space designated for manuscript making, is a hazier matter."[157] While there are historical references to scribes and scriptoria, she points out that there is less evidence for the physical existence of the latter in any monasteries during the early Middle Ages. By the later Middle Ages, Jenneka writes, the "physical environment of scribes grows clearer," suggesting that spaces such as the cloister or the chapter house may have been used for copying work. Such spaces may have been social in the sense that more than one scribe worked there at once, but the individual cell may also have served as a workspace for the "lone scribe."[158] Elsewhere Erik Kwakkel describes the difficulty of finding contemporary images of medieval scriptoria that can give us an idea of what these spaces actually looked like, or that show multiple scribes working together.[159] One of the images he did find, from a Gospel Book produced at Eternach Abbey in Luxembourg circa 1020, shows a monk and a lay individual jointly working on a manuscript. The monk is copying out the text while the layman is providing the decoration. This "peculiar blend of two worlds" was not unusual, with the services of artists or other professionals from outside the monastery sometimes being brought in – literally "hired hands."[160]

The idea of the scriptorium resonates with me partly because it situates the transcription of the diaries within a much older evolving tradition, as well as with a media ecological approach. Leaving aside the question of what older scriptoria looked like or whether they ever really existed as we might imagine them, the scriptorium is more than a room: it is a reading/writing ecosystem, comprising constellations of bodies, techniques, and tools, among many other things, much like the reading/writing spaces described elsewhere in this book. The screens and the software I used were part of my scriptorium, along with the physical locations and the times of day or night I worked. It links in too with the idea of the interface, which I'll come back to shortly.

In addition to being necessary for me to carry out my work, the screens I used rendered the transcription safe(r). Firstly, they put me at a distance from the material I was transcribing. Though the content of the diaries was often upsetting (war, death, injury, destruction), the screen afforded detachment. Over a 100 years after the end of the First World War and over 80 years since the start of the Second, we are used to scrolling through and past all sorts of violent and disturbing content on a plethora of screens. It feels normal, for want of a better word, whereas an off-screen experience of the diaries might have removed this safety glass. Secondly, it was safer for the diaries themselves. In ensuring there was no need for me to touch or shuffle through the original papers, risking accidental loss or damage, the screens I used (together with the keyboard, the mouse, and the trackpad) were preservational, prosthetic. I'm borrowing the idea of prosthetics from McLuhan's theory of media as extensions of the body, but I'm also put in mind of how archives or libraries will give you gloves to wear for accessing or handling special or fragile books or papers. Preservation is often about intermediation.[161]

No touching, then, in the immediate sense – I never 'handled' the diaries, except at many removes. Yet the process also involved a great deal of 'doing by hand.' What does it mean to speak about touch in this context? What forms of tactility were involved in working with these digitised files (and why do these matter for the understanding of the historical record, if they do)? Anna Chen makes an important point about digitisation opening up new ways of experiencing hand-written historical documents (e.g., through interactive screen displays in museums) – you may not be able to touch the original, but you can swipe and tap and play the digital version. On the other hand, this may lead to the digital version over-writing the original. As Chen suggests, drawing on Jay David Bolter and Richard Grusin's work on remediation:

> The digital representation of the manuscript is made to seem more transparent to the user than the original manuscript itself by imposing upon the document yet another mediating layer – the computer screen – which the user nevertheless perceives as granting unmediated access to its contents.[162]

This resonates with my own personal experiences of the transcription of the Diaries of both World Wars. For example, if I came across an illegible word in the PDfs, I could try zooming in or out on it to see if this helped me to recognise it. Sometimes this kind of repetitive hand-eye adjustment was revelatory and the word became clear, but it was often frustrating, even if it worked. Zooming in, for instance, meant that I 'lost sight' of part of the rest of the page in a way that I wouldn't have if I were looking at the actual piece of paper. Similarly, there were whole pages of entries from the First World War that were impossible to see at once because the handwriting was too small to read unless I increased the zoom. Increasing the zoom, however, might mean that I lost the first two columns of the page, which in turn meant having to continually scroll sideways back and forth to keep checking I hadn't crossed into a new date entry.

The key point here is that reading the diaries in PDF – although I couldn't 'touch' the documents – was a very manual, physical kind of reading. It required me to make constant small adjustments by dragging and clicking, peering at the screen, shifting posture, adjusting the contrast. The by-hand effort required to read and transcribe the images of the manuscripts in PDF is something which derived very specifically from the digitised format of the diaries. It introduced its own form not necessarily of transparency but of *closeness* to the record. The difficulty of reading the handwriting or typewriting in the PDfs testifies to the materiality not just of the original documents but of the material bodies who created them: the work of many different hands. The tactile (in terms of the transcription work) was not about actually physically touching the documents themselves, but was primarily about indirect contact through different, subtler forms of embodiment, or movement – the physical act of re-iterating and re-writing the same words already written by someone else, and in the case of re-typing typewritten text, involving potentially similar or approximate movements of the hand and of the eye. Sometimes I felt that the stiffness in my neck and shoulders (the result of my poor posture at the keyboard) or the (mild) strain in my wrists after prolonged bouts of typing forged a connection between my body and hands and the other bodies and hands who had produced the diaries – *some* of the writers must have tended to slouch or hunch over their work, placing stress on similar muscle groups. These slight discomforts which I experienced while transcribing made me perhaps more susceptible to noticing descriptions of other kinds of discomfort: repeated references to rain, mud, heat, cold, damp, exhaustion.

The transcription process turned me into a medium or conduit – part of an interface through which these descriptions had to pass in order to become 'readable' for the purposes of the book. The goal in undertaking the transcription was to render the contents of the diaries – the words inscribed within them – into text that could be analysed using software. AntConc, a concordance and corpus analysis toolkit, was chosen for the latter purpose. The original ink on paper was obviously *un*-readable in AntConc: we might think of it as too-hard-ware. But the PDF versions were not suitable either, for various reasons. One of the selling points of the PDF is that the content of the file is meant to look the same no matter where it comes from, where it is opened or printed. A technology of dissemination, then – but crucially, of apparent reproduction as well: the faithful reproduction of the appearance of the document. PDfs have become ubiquitous partly for these reasons. As Lisa Gitelman notes in her exploration of documents as a genre of media, the PDF is today "being promoted as an archival standard."[163] This is important, because as Gitelman also points out, documents that have been digitised (to a greater extent than documents with no previous non-digital incarnations) "appear as pictures of themselves."[164] From this perspective, the content of the diary files is not text at all, but the apparition of it.

AntConc could not 'read' the original handwritten diaries, but neither could it 'read' these digitised PDfs. In a sense, the PDfs could not even 'read' themselves. All PDfs have to be opened in a PDF reader programme

(I used Adobe's own Acrobat Reader). In doing so, however, the PDF reader did not 'see' any text. Instead, it treated the scanned diaries as image files, which is what they in fact were: they consisted of photographs that had been taken of the pages of the diaries in the National Archives. As a result, it wasn't possible to use the 'find' function in Acrobat Reader, or the text highlighting tool, although it was still possible to add comments. In Acrobat, these take the form of skeuomorphic little post-it notes, which Debra used to indicate the start and end of sections to be transcribed, and which I occasionally used to mark my place.

The transcriptions themselves were typed into Notepad++, an open-source source-code and text editor, and then saved as .txt files. Notepad++ was written by Don Ho in the C++ programming language in 2003 and is a richer alternative to Microsoft's basic built-in Notepad app. According to one interview, Ho was motivated by his frustration with the source code editor he was using in his work as a software engineer.[165] Notepad++ has many affordances and features I never had call to use, since I was using it for basic purposes, but I found its tabbed editing and auto-complete functions invaluable. The former meant that I could have multiple files open in different tabs within a single window, while the latter saved me from having to re-type common or recurring words every single time. I wish I had kept a note of the versions of Notepad++ that I used over the course of transcribing the Diaries, but it didn't occur to me at the time. I do remember being prompted to download updated versions of the programme when they became available, so it's safe to assume that I did this more than once. Software underpinned and enabled our work of exploring the two World Wars, but it was not embedded within the unfolding of these conflicts as they happened. While researching these notes in the summer of 2022, I discovered that several new Notepad++ releases have been accompanied by explicit political messages (both in the version titles and descriptions) relating to incidents of terrorism, state oppression, human rights, or war – a part of the programme I'd been completely unaware of. In late February 2022, for instance, a few days after Russia launched its invasion of Ukraine, Notepad++ Version 8.3.2 was released with the title "Make Variables Not War."[166] For me, this was a reminder that software is subjective; there are hands behind it too. More than that, though, it was a lesson in software's totally quotidian and diffuse implication in present-day war.

What this could mean for future archival research is a topic for a whole other book, so instead here's a note on the type. The default font in Notepad++ is Courier New (10 pt.), `so all of the transcriptions look like this`. Although it's possible to go into the settings and change the font, I only discovered this after I had finished. This introduced an incidental, glancing resemblance between the typed transcribed text and the typescript in the PDFs. Courier was originally designed as a typeface for IBM typewriters, albeit not until 1955, before being converted for use with computers, according to Typedia's pages on the font. Courier New, one of its successors, has been described as "perhaps the most recognizable typeface of the 20th century – a visual symbol of typewritten bureaucratic anonymity, the widespread dissemination of information (and a classification of documents), stark factuality, and streamlined efficiency."[167]

The Courier family of fonts are monospace, which means that each character takes up the same amount of horizontal space – as opposed to variable-width fonts, where different characters might take up varying amounts of space across a line. Partly for this reason, it is a common and established system and programming font. Large blocks of code can be easier to read in monospaced than variable-width fonts, for example. Similar characters can also be easier to distinguish from each other (e.g., 1/l/I), and it is easy to keep lines or columns of text or characters in alignment.[168] These aspects certainly made the transcription easier in some respects and the transcribed text looks very regimented. However, the wider Notepad++ setting did make it difficult to replicate the *layout* of information on the pages in the PDFs: where special titles or headings had been written or typed in the centre of a page, for example, or where there was unusual spacing between paragraphs. But to go back to seeing and reading, this sort of spacing was – as far as I'm aware – not registered by Notepad++ or the concordance software as anything but absence (blank space, a lack of information), whereas to our eyes it was part of a potentially meaningful organisational structure. The same goes for things like the use of block capitals – the latter being something we could easily replicate, but which were also perhaps not being seen by the software as we saw them.

Transcription of the War Diaries was a sensitive and complicated process that spanned the translation of the diaries into images of themselves, and the re-translation of these images into .txt. As mentioned above, the process of transcribing the PDFs also turned *me* into a medium or conduit – part of an interface through which the words had to pass to become 'readable' for the purposes of the project. In Lori Emerson's formulation in relation to digital reading and writing,

> interface is a technology – whether it is a fascicle, a typewriter, a command line, or a GUI – that mediates between reader and the surface-level, human-authored writing, as well as, in the case of digital devices, the machine-based writing taking place before the gloss of the surface.[169]

More widely, an interface can also be understood as "a liminal or threshold condition that both delimits the space for a kind of inhabitation and opens up otherwise unavailable phenomena, conditions, situations, and territories for exploration, use, participation, and exploitation."[170] This I think links back powerfully to the idea of the scriptorium I touched on earlier – a space, but not just a physical one; a "form of relation" as well as a system; a collection of given and chosen elements that opened up ways for me to come into contact with the diaries, and the diaries with me.[171]

Things come into relation with each other at the interface and are reconstituted in the process. But the word 'conduit' above feels fitting too because I often *did* feel that the words were simply passing through me, the way a current passes through a wire. I wasn't always focused on reading the diaries *as* diaries, or as historical records. Instead, I was often focused much more on *reading to re-write them* – making sure I was typing everything up correctly and accurately, with the right words in the right sequence. It was very easy to get into a state of flow or auto-pilot for stretches at a time, though this was certainly interspersed with times when I switched in to paying closer attention to the other layers of meaning of what I was reading *while* I was typing (e.g., when tagging emotive content), or when I read ahead, or doubled back to re-read something I had just re-written (I'd say this was distinct from the kind of bodily closeness I sometimes felt to the diaries, discussed previously).

Distraction can be understood as "a partial loss of touch with the here-and-now" which involves "simultaneous temporalities" – it "requires vigilance while it also allows for and even promotes automations and 'spacing out.'"[172] If we think of the diary transcription as an experience of (intermittent) distraction, autopilot, zoning out, etcetera, then this can also be understood as something that derives somewhat from its nature as screen-based work – a kind of "glaze."[173] Importantly, though, I think it also derives from the fact that working with the digital files involved *experiencing more than one time at the same time*. These temporalities included:

1 The structural timeline of the diaries, which was enforced by the linear sequence of the entries on the page and the order of the pages themselves within the PDF files. This was sometimes only *apparently* linear, with files turning out to be chaotic on closer reading: they were complicated by the inclusion of appendices (which might cover the same or different points in time covered in the entries themselves), gaps (i.e., where a diary jumped from one date to another without any entries for the dates in between – what happened on those days?), and occasional bits of paper appearing in the wrong order in the photographed files (so I had to click forward or back a few pages to figure out what the 'right' sequence was).
2 The timelines *in* the diaries – the dates and time stamps attached to entries, for example. Again, these were often quite chaotic and not always easy to follow. Then there were long entries or appendices that could not possibly have been written in the midst of the events they were describing, and/or were clearly stated as being 'recollections' or 'reports' written at a later time – thus imposing a kind of narrative timeline and order on the messiness of warfare.
3 The fuzzy temporal surround of 'the war' (whether the First or Second) – a general sense of what else might be going on and where at a given point in the 'history' of the fighting, or an awareness that the

timeline of the diaries might be about to converge with some major event or date.
4   Hardware time – having to speed up to finish a section because my laptop battery was about to die, for example, the seconds it took for documents to load or save, or for OneDrive to log me in.
5   The temporal rhythms of everyday life going on around me while I was working.

Overall, I was constantly moving through time(s) during the course of the transcription – not all of which were unique to the digital, but some of which were. This movement through and within different temporalities probably did contribute to the fluctuations of attention and distraction I experienced. I don't recall there being a particular pattern, however – and I don't remember there being a specific common prompt for moments when I was more or less engaged or attentive. More than memories of distinct moments that moved me or how, what stands out the most now is a diffuse sense of having *been* moved.

Of course, every time I sat down to do some work, I was in a different emotional and/or physical state informed by various external or internal factors – I was never the same scribe twice. This inevitably shaped how I felt about what I was typing. Above, I mentioned how we are quite used to experiencing traumatic events and crises as scrollable content. A great deal of this is audio-visual. I do wonder if experiencing the diaries as the complete opposite – no interspersals of sound, photos, or videos – contributed to the way I responded to them emotionally. On top of this, there was a huge disruption in wider everyday life between working with the First and the Second World War Diaries, in the form of the Covid-19 pandemic. While the diaries were being written (with the exception perhaps of entries dating from later in 1918 and 1945), I imagine that it must have been very difficult for the diarists to have had much sense of an ending – when the war would end, or how. It's only occurred to me in retrospect that the transcription of the Second World War diaries was carried out in a similar space of uncertainty. In 2020, we also didn't know if or when the pandemic would end, or how life could go back to 'normal.'

I always found the work soothing, on some level – the defined nature of it and the slow accumulation of completed files was immensely satisfying. But the diaries themselves could be disruptive. It was notable that the files of the Second World War were much messier and more sprawling than those of the First. While it was usually easy to distinguish between diary entries proper and supplementary material in the First World War files, this line was far blurrier in the Second World War files. The Army diary forms I had been used to seeing in the files of the First World War often weren't used in the Second, so whole months of diary entries might be typed onto blank paper – which I was used to associating with appendices. It took me longer to work out exactly what kind of record I was transcribing in each section, and therefore how to transcribe it (what kind of file naming convention and numbering system to use, for instance). To orient myself, I often had to refer back to the network of texts that had been created by Debra *around* the diary files: there was a huge spreadsheet in which Debra had catalogued the files and sections she had photographed, with notes about how many words they contained, the date ranges they spanned, the events they described, where the unit was located at the time (and/or where they moved to), and the type of section it was (e.g., diary entry, report, letter, an account by an individual participant in a specific action or event, intelligence update, and so on). If I wasn't sure if something was a diary entry or not, I could always check the spreadsheet. I also used it to log my progress, updating it to mark when a section had been transcribed and uploaded to the cloud. While the spreadsheet was very useful, it could also be overwhelming. Each time I updated a section as complete I felt a sense of achievement – clear, measurable progress! – but there were so many other lines and lines in the sheet that I still had to mark off. From very early on it became clear we wouldn't be able to transcribe everything, but seeing the whole corpus laid out in the spreadsheet was a reminder of a) how much more there still was to do and b) how much we wouldn't get to do or might miss.

Tangential to the idea of things missing is the idea of correction and/or mistakes. Some of the diary files contained more corrections than others, and there were lots of different types of corrections (e.g., scorings-out and insertions of text by hand, versus typewriter strikethroughs and over-writing). What does it mean to make a mistake in the recording of these events, and then to correct the record in one way or another? The hand corrections could have been made at any point whereas it seems more likely that typed corrections would have been made *at the time* in order to allow the typist to move on, without having to reinsert the sheet or paper into the machine later. The type of correction made might also relate to the timing of *when* mistakes were noticed. Also, I wonder to what extent the typewriter makes it easier to make mistakes in the first place, and/or to overlook or miss them. Both the machinery of the keyboard and the act of interfacing with the machine introduce the potential for mechanical/manual errors that don't exist with handwriting – such as hitting the wrong key, hitting two keys at once, not hitting a key hard enough resulting in a blank, and so on.

To try and track corrections in the transcription of the Second World War diaries, I initially tried using the tag <hc> for "hand correction" and <tp> for "typed correction," but this quickly proved too time-consuming because of the high frequency of both. It also wasn't mapping back onto the original text very closely. If there was a typed correction, for example, the original 'mistake' might have been obliterated by being typed over such that I couldn't read whatever was underneath. Only the 'new' word next to it was legible. If there was a handwritten correction, or the error had just been scored through, I might be able to see the previous word underneath, but this is also not taking into account mistakes of omission, where words had to be inserted instead of replaced. I was never quite sure whether I should be including the 'original' word or phrase (if I could see it), or just the replacement, but I also couldn't figure out how to accurately and usefully represent this in the .txt format.

The <hp> and <tp> tags therefore only really functioned to indicate "someone changed or corrected something here with a pen and ink," or "someone retyped something here." In the end, I stopped using the tags altogether. Instead, I thought that if corrections were of particular interest it would probably be easier to go directly to the source files themselves for examination of examples of over-writing or amendments to the record, if required. This is a good example of where the strictures of the .txt format mitigated against a (potentially) richer translation of the original diaries, forcing a kind of cutting back. This was different for spelling mistakes where there had been no attempt to correct them: I transcribed any mis-spelled words as they appeared but tagged them with <sp> to indicate the mistake was in the original and was not a typo or a transcription error.

As part of our e-mail correspondence about the Second World War diaries, Debra noted that correcting mistakes in typed sheets might have been more difficult or onerous for the original typist – and that there must have been instances where mistakes were made that are now invisible to us because the typist simply discarded the first sheet and started a new one. As Debra also noted, the corrections and mistakes in both the typed and handwritten diaries draw attention to the "human behind the machine" – "an assertion of individuality, or the evidence of humans literally being human in the interaction with these bureaucratic tools." By contrast, when *I* made a mistake while transcribing I could simply back-space or click to where the error was and fix it quickly without leaving a trace, either as I went or during a final skim-read of the finished .txt file.

And I very frequently *did* make mistakes, including but not limited to:

- Typos/spelling mistakes (a drawback of speed-typing/touch-typing, but also a luxury of word-processing software – type fast, check later).
- Forgetting to add tags after words or phrases (attention/distraction again).
- Skipping over whole entries, paragraphs, lines, paragraphs, or words. In short, "eye-skip" – a common error that "occurs when a scribe inadvertently omits a portion of a text during the process of transcription due to the fact that the beginnings of two lines in the source text are similar."[174]
- Accidentally repeating chunks of diary text and typing them out twice (dittography).
- Incorrectly numbering entries in the .txt files or copying and pasting dates for convenience and then forgetting to change them (these being metadata entry errors, as opposed to errors in copying out the diary entries).

182   *The Matter of Materials and Archives*

> Succumbing to errors like eye-skip and dittography knits my work with the Diaries further into the historical tradition of transcription, as does their erasure from the finished files. In the Institutions of Divine and Secular Knowledge, the Fifth-Century scholar Cassiodorus sets out a series of detailed instructions for scribes including on the matter of corrections: he writes that "[t]he books should be corrected to prevent scribal errors from being fixed."[175]
>
> Although the transcribed .txt files have been corrected many times – both manually and automatically (such as whenever I used the Find/Replace All function in Notepad++ to fix metadata entry errors) – *none* of these corrections are apparent in the finished transcriptions. Which, finally, raises the question of apparitionality. PDF transforms the diaries into images of themselves (the appearance of text, but *not* text in the way the project needed it to be). A human could read the words in the 'right' way, but the concordance software could not. The transcription of the PDfs into .txt files transformed the apparition of the diaries back into (another form of) text. This form of text has a completely different appearance. Instead of the traces of the people behind the original diaries and the media apparatuses they used to make these records – the different types of handwriting, the better or worse typewriter keys, the waning ink ribbons, the discoloured or torn paper – there are no apparent similar traces in the .txt files (or are there just traces that aren't immediately visible – that don't *appear* on the surface of the screen? And does it matter if there are traces in the transcription output, or if there aren't?).

Stevie ends by questioning whether the invisibility of aspects of the transcription process matters, yet she did leave imprints on the transcribed material – the organisation of the material that mimicked the Diaries in PDF and which therefore allowed me to find and connect text across PDF and plain text easily, but perhaps even more importantly, the tags indicating instances of emotives or errors. These tags are insertions of interpretation, separated from the uniformity of the remainder of the text by chevrons: <emotive>, <sp>. They stand out not only for the purposes of searches using Antconc (which can be instructed to regard them as separate from the body of the text) but also because they are traces of moments of Stevie's interpretation and analysis. At times, I would find instances that I might not have identified as emotives, but which Stevie did, or vice versa. These moments underscored the slipperiness of the process, which I consequently highlighted as an element in the research process. It additionally enabled me to identify blind spots or assumptions that I was making in my analysis and challenged me to think more clearly about what constituted emotive expression. My discussions with her throughout the process of transcription also clarified my understanding of the materiality of the documents – as in the e-mail exchange she mentions in her account in which I became aware of the physicality of typing as an embodied act and realised why it mattered. Such interactions and interventions in the process of transcription are frequently overlooked, especially in the transition of textual forms (rather than oral discourse) to text, but this process is rich with meaning, and like all the other forms of mediation discussed throughout this book, it shapes the interpretation and use of its content.

Conclusion

"When we emerge from an archive," writes Ed Folsom, "we are physically and mentally altered. We emerge with notes – photocopies if we're allowed – but never with the archive, which remains behind, isolated from us."[176] The archive might remain behind us, but its regulations, systems of description and technologies it provides for access, are part of what we take with us when we leave its reading spaces, whether virtual or actual, and they shape not only the parameters of archival records, but also our access to them and the way we interpret them. I am tempted here to claim that the steps involved in navigating the reading spaces of the archive each leave their own traces of meaning over the record, like a coating of dust, some of which can be blown away, and some of which persists. The simile is appealing, if only because dust features in so many of the discussions about the material dimensions of archives.[177] But like other metaphors that accrue around archiving (comparing it to memory, dreams, the unconscious), the comparison hides as much as it appears to reveal. Dust, even if it is filled with toxins from industrial processes, is in part a product of natural processes of entropy, but there is nothing natural about state archives.

The evolution of The National Archive was inexorably entangled with the spread of bureaucratic processes in state institutions in the Nineteenth Century. During this period, as information became a concept distinct from knowledge, detachable from individuals and rhetorical discourse, it also became increasingly conflated with documentation. The documentation produced by the transactions and activities of state institutions was therefore a resource to be managed and organised, but also, crucially, preserved. The PRO and later TNA, and the processes of archiving developed within them, both reflect and reify bureaucratic systems of organisation as well as broader mechanisms through which information itself is defined and delimited. The archive claims authority from its records of state activities and is consistently identified as the custodian of the 'nation's history,' which in turn authorises the records as official versions of the past. Most historians, archivists and other researchers will be aware that the past as read through state records should be questioned and interrogated, but TNA's institutional identity, its physical and digital structures, all need to be navigated in order to do so. TNA's spaces, systems and technologies combine to create a mask of order and control over the records of the two World Wars, and they reiterate and reinforce the notion embedded in the Army's practices of reporting conflict that war can be apprehended, both literally and figuratively, through rational systems of carefully organised paper records.

But as Chapters 1 and 2 have shown, emerging from behind the mask of coherence and order is a sometimes riotous record of individual experience and an array of what Steedman refers to as the "mad fragmentations that no one intended to preserve."[178] The range of different handwriting, the individual approaches to completing the forms, the narratives that went beyond what was required, or the sparse accounts that provide little to no explanation of events, complicate the notion of coherent 'stories' about the past that are simply waiting to be uncovered in the archival record of conflict. The "networks of rationality," to borrow a phrase from De Certeau, in which Unit War Diaries are embedded, from paper to PDF to .txt, exert their own pressures on the interpretation of these records, and are part of the conventions that encourage the rejection of those that do not conform to expected standards of order and coherence.[179] In her interrogation of the records of Colonial rule, Stoler argues that those that push against convention should not be considered as outside either the official structures in which they are produced or the archive, but as "subjacent coordinates of, and counterpoints within, them."[180] Moments that deviate from the standard controls of the production of records do more than push at the boundaries of structures of official documentation and the systems designed to contain and preserve it, they throw the nature and purpose of those boundaries and systems into sharp relief. By engaging with the illegible, the incoherent, the emotional and the descriptive record, this book has interrogated and questioned the role and value of bureaucratic practices and rational systems, from battlefield to archive, in understanding warfare.

Notes

1 Lisa Gitelman, *Paper Knowledge: Toward a Media History of Documents* (Durham NC and London: Duke University Press, 2014), 1.
2 For a concise summary of that body of work, see Ann Stoler, *Along the Archival Grain: Epistemic Anxieties and Colonial Common Sense* (Princeton NJ: Princeton University Press, 2008), 44–46, or for a fuller history, see Francis X. Blouin and William G. Rosenberg, *Processing the Past: Contesting Authorities in History and the Archives* (Online Edition, Oxford Academic Online, 2011).
3 Blouin and Rosenberg, *Processing the Past*, 25.
4 The National Archives, *Annual Report and Accounts of The National Archives 2018–19*, HC 2401, 26.
5 Ed Folsom, "Database as Genre: The Epic Transformation of Archives," *PMLA: Publications of the Modern Language Association of America* 122, no. 5 (October 2007): 1577.
6 Emma Allen, "Our Website: A Design Journey," (blog) TNA, 16 September 2013.
7 Gitelman, *Paper Knowledge*, 5.
8 Stoler, *Along the Archival Grain*.
9 Christine Sylvester, "War Experiences/War Practices/War Theory," *Millennium: Journal of International Studies* 40, no. 3 (2012): 93.
10 Gerald Ham, "Archival Strategies for the Post-Custodial Era," *The American Archivist* 44, no. 3 (Summer, 1981): 207.

11 Blouin and Rosenberg, *Processing the Past*, 120.
12 Virginia Dressler, "Archive as Medium," *Preservation, Digital Technology & Culture* 47, no. 2 (2018): 46.
13 See for example Philippa Levine, *The Amateur and the Professional: Antiquarians, Historians, and Archaeologists in Victorian England, 1838–1886* (Cambridge, New York: Cambridge University Press, 1986); John Cantwell, *The Public Record Office, 1838–1958* (London: HMSO, 1991); and Aidan Lawes, *Chancery Lane: The Strong Box of the Empire* (London: PRO Publications, 1996).
14 Stoler, *Along the Archival Grain*, 32–33.
15 Public Records Act, 1838, 1 & 2 Victoria c. 94, https://statutes.org.uk/site/the-statutes/nineteenth-century/1838-1-2-victoria-c-94-public-records-act.
16 First Report of the Royal Commission on Public Records, Appendices, vol. 1, part II, 1912–13, Cd 6395, at 59.
17 First Report of the Royal Commission, Appendices, at 58.
18 Forty-First Annual Report of the Deputy Keeper of the Public Records, vol. 38, 1880, C.2658 at vii.
19 Blouin and Rosenberg, *Processing the Past*, 23.
20 Blouin and Rosenberg, *Processing the Past*, 23.
21 Blouin and Rosenberg, *Processing the Past*, 23.
22 Thirteenth Report of the Deputy Keeper of the Public Records, Appendix, vol. 21, no. 1498, 1852, Literary Inquiries.
23 Luke Tredinnick, "Rewriting History: The Information Age and the Knowable Past," in *Information History in the Modern World: Histories of the Information Age*, ed. Toni Weller (New York: Palgrave Macmillan, 2011), 181.
24 First Report of the Royal Commission on Public Records, Appendices, at 61.
25 Blouin and Rosenberg, *Processing the Past*, 27
26 Charles Dickens, "The Adventures of the Public Records," *Household Words* 1, no. 17 (July 1850): 396.
27 The Graphic, "The Public Record Office," *The Graphic*, 27 October 1900. British Library Newspapers, gale.com/apps/doc/BA3201474910/BNCN?u=xeter&sid=bookmark-BNCN&xid=911e228b.
28 Caroline Elkins, "Looking Beyond Mau Mau: Archiving Violence in the Era of Decolonization," *The American Historical Review* 120, no. 3 (2015): 854.
29 First Report of the Royal Commission, Appendices, at, 17.
30 Third Report of the Royal Commission on Public Records, Appendix V, vol. III, part II. 1919, Cmd. 368, at 121.
31 Third Report of the Royal Commission on Public Records, Appendix V, at 123.
32 Third Report of the Royal Commission on Public Records, Appendix V, at 123.
33 Hilary Jenkinson, "British Archives and the War," *The American Archivist* VII, no. 1 (January 1944): 9–10.
34 Jenkinson, "British Archives," 10.
35 Jenkinson, "British Archives," 10.
36 Jenkinson, "British Archives," 10.
37 Sir James Grigg, Committee on Departmental Records Report, vol. 11, 1953–54, Cmd. 9163, 5.
38 Grigg, Departmental Records Report, 5.
39 Grigg, Departmental Records Report, 9.
40 Alfred Mabbs, "The Public Record Office and the Second Review," *Archives* 8, no. 40 (1968), 180.
41 Grigg, Departmental Records Report, 50.
42 Grigg, Departmental Records Report, 56–57.
43 Tenth Annual Report of the Keeper of Public Records on the Work of the Public Record Office, vol. 45, 1968–68, 370, at 5.
44 Tenth Annual Report of the Keeper of Public Records, at 1.

45 Jeffery Ede, "The Public Record Office and its Users," *Archives* 8, no. 40 (1968): 186.
46 Fourth Report of the Deputy Keeper of Public Records, vol. 47, 28 February 1843, 474, at 21.
47 Fourth Report of the Deputy Keeper, at 21.
48 Second Report of the Deputy Keeper of Public Records, vol. 32, 1841, at 4.
49 Levine, *The Amateur*, 106.
50 The Graphic, "The Public Record Office," 623.
51 The Times, "In Chancery Lane," *The Times*, 21 January 1926, 17. www.gale.com/apps/doc/CS286988853/TTDA?u=exeter&sid=bookmark-TTDA&xid=e0071cd5.
52 See, for example, The Fifth Report of the Deputy Keeper of the Public Records, vol. 41, 1844, 553; The Thirtieth Report of the Deputy Keeper of the Public Records, vol. 26, 1868–69, 4165; The Thirty-Sixth Annual Report of the Deputy Keeper of the Public Records, vol. 65, 1875, C. 1301.
53 Hillary Jenkinson, *A Manual of Archive Administration*, revised ed. (London: Percy Lund, 1937), 15.
54 Cantwell, *The Public Record Office*, 84.
55 A Reader in the Public Record Office, letter to the editor, *The Times*, 11 March 1862, 12, The Times Digital Archive, gale.com/apps/doc/CS202152555/TTDA?u=exeter&sid=bookmark-TTDA&xid=5620a9b3.
56 Cantwell, *The Public Record Office*, 183. Despite the passing of the 1838 Act, it took the Treasury and Parliament until the 1850s to recognise the PRO's pressing need for a dedicated repository.
57 Cantwell, *The Public Record Office*, 183.
58 Fifty-Fourth Annual Report of the Deputy Keeper of the Public Records, vol. 48, 1893, C. 7079, at 3.
59 Fifty-Eighth Annual Report of the Deputy Keeper of the Public Records, vol. 48, 1897, C. 8543, at 3.
60 Sixty-Second Annual Report of the Deputy Keeper of the Public Records, vol. 33, 1901, Cd. 617, at 4.
61 Philip Howard, "Records Held in Most Efficient Repository," *The Times*, 14 October 1977, 17.
62 The Thirty-First Annual Report of the Keeper of Public Records, 20th Century House of Commons Sessional Papers, 1989, HC 635, at 4.
63 Christine Cooper, Jonathan Tweedie, Jane Andrew and Max Baker, "From 'Business-Like' to Businesses: Agencification, Corporatization, and Civil Service Reform under the Thatcher Administration," *Public Administration* 100 (2022), 195.
64 The Fortieth Annual Report of the Keeper of Public Records, 20th Century House of Commons Sessional Papers, 1998, HC 615, at 8–9.
65 The Fortieth Annual Report of the Keeper, at 13–14.
66 Gerald Ham, "Archival Strategies for the Post-Custodial Era," *The American Archivist* 44, no. 3 (Summer 1981): 207–216.
67 Terry Cook, "Electronic Records, Paper Minds: The Revolution in Information Management and Archives in the Post-Custodial and Post-Modernist Era," *Archives and Manuscripts* 22, no. 1 (1994): 302.
68 Timothy Ericson, "'Preoccupied with Our own Gardens': Outreach and Archivists," *Archivaria* 31 (1990): 117, emphasis in original.
69 Barbara Craig, "What are the Clients? Who are the Products? The Future of Archival Public Services in Perspective," *Archivaria* 31 (1990): 141.
70 Ministry of Justice, Department for Digital, Culture, Media and Sport, *Archives for the 21st Century*, 2009, Cm. 7744, at 2.
71 Craig, "What are the Clients?," 139.
72 TNA, *Archives Inspire: The National Archives Plans and Priorities 2015–19*, 8–11.

73 TNA, *Archives for the 21st Century in Action: Refreshed, 2012–2015,* "Introduction."
74 TNA, *Archives for the 21st Century in Action: Refreshed,* "Introduction"; "Archives Unlocked: Releasing the Potential Brochure 2017," 7; *Archives Inspire 2015–19,* 3.
75 TNA, *Archives for the 21st Century in Action: Refreshed,* "Introduction."
76 TNA, "Archives Unlocked 2017," 2.
77 TNA, "Archives Unlocked 2017," 2; TNA, *Archives Inspire 2015–19,* 4.
78 TNA, "Archives Unlocked 2017," 2.
79 TNA, *Archives Inspire 2015–19,* 2.
80 To give some sense of the impact of *Who Do You Think You Are?*, there was an 18% increase in first-time visitors to TNA's website following the broadcast of the first series in 2004. Amy Holdsworth, *Television, Memory and Nostalgia* (Basingstoke: Palgrave Macmillan, 2011), 95. In the U.S., *Roots* (ABC, 1977) had a similar impact, increasing interest in genealogy in general, and bringing more African Americans into archives. Jessie Kratz, "The 'Roots' of Genealogy at the National Archives," (blog) U.S. National Archives, 22 February, 2019. https://prologue.blogs.archives.gov/2019/02/22/the-roots-of-genealogy-at-the-national-archives.
81 Craig, "What are the Clients?," 141.
82 User Advisory Groups contributed to the development of the PRO's online catalogue, and continue to advise on matters of social inclusion, how to improve services, and to inform TNA's strategy.
83 TNA, *Archives for Everyone 2019–2023.*
84 The Times, "In Chancery Lane," 17.
85 Arlette Farge, *The Allure of the Archives,* trans. Thomas Scott-Railton (New Haven CT: Yale University Press, 2013).
86 Sally Swartz, "Asylum Case Records: Fact and Fiction," *Rethinking History* 22, no. 3 (2018): 294.
87 Carolyn Steedman, *Dust* (Manchester: Manchester University Press, 2001), 28.
88 Farge, *Allure,* 19–23 and 47–53 respectively.
89 Steedman, *Dust,* 81 and 150 respectively
90 Swartz "Asylum Case Records," 294.
91 Blouin and Rosenberg, *Processing the Past,* 125.
92 In The Graphic, "The Public Record Office," 623.
93 Blouin and Rosenberg, *Processing the Past,* 126.
94 Dickens, "The Adventures," 397.
95 Ellie Duffy, "National Archives in London, UK by AOC," *Architectural Review,* 17 March 2022. https://www.architectural-review.com/awards/w-awards/national-archives-in-london-uk-by-aoc.
96 Again, Arlette Farge and Carolyn Steedman discuss this at length, but see also Erika Larsson's account of the significance of emotion in opening perspectives on the past in "Feeling the Past: an Emotional Reflection on an Archive," *Journal of Aesthetics and Culture,* 12 (2020).
97 Farge, *Allure,* 20.
98 For a discussion of frustration, confusion and disorientation in researchers, see Wendy Duff and Catherine Johnson, "Accidentally Found on Purpose: Information-Seeking Behavior of Historians in Archives," *Information, Community, Policy* 72, no. 4 (2002): 472–96. For a detailed breakdown of how uncertainty manifests in archives, see Joseph Pugh, *Information Journeys in Digital Archives* (EngD Thesis, University of York, 2017), 149–168.
99 Mihai Diaconita, "New Feedback Form for Our Research Guides" (blog), TNA: Behind the Scenes, Technology and Innovation, 11 January 2019. https://blog.nationalarchives.gov.uk/feedback-form-research-guides.

100 In previous work, I have detailed the challenges faced by TNA in designing and maintaining this interface, using it to explore what digital change means for archives. Debra Ramsay, "Tensions in the Interface: The Archive and the Digital," in *Digital Memory Studies: Media Pasts in Transition*, Andrew Hoskins, ed (New York: Routledge, 2017): 280–302.

101 Matt McGrattan, "Technical Discovery: Project Alpha," (blog), TNA, 19 December 2019. https://blog.nationalarchives.gov.uk/technical-discovery-project-alpha.

102 Blouin and Rosenberg, *Processing the Past*, 20.

103 Wendy Duff and Verne Harris, "Stories and Names: Archival Description as Narrating Records and Constructing Meaning," *Archival Science*, 2 (2002): 264.

104 Andrew Janes, "A Series of Unfortunate Events," (blog) TNA, 6 February 2014.

105 Cook's overview of archival theories and positions includes aspects of this debate. Terry Cook, "What is Past is Prologue: A History of Archival Ideas Since 1898, and the Future Paradigm Shift," *Archivaria* 43 (February 1997), 17–63. For more detailed summary of the various approaches as well as a discussion of the different forms of description, see Duff and Harris, "Accidently Found."

106 Tom Nesmith, "Seeing Archives: Postmodernism and the Changing Intellectual Place of Archives," *The American Archivist* 65, no. 1 (Spring-Summer, 2002): 30.

107 Duff and Harris, " Stories and Names," 276.

108 In addressing this topic, Andrew Janes, for example, while making clear that he is condensing a complex argument, emphasises that although archival description might construct narratives about "the histories of how [the records] were created and of the people or organisations that made them," it should always be in such a form that it "allow[s] the records to speak for themselves." Janes, "A Series".

109 Janes, "A Series".

110 Michael McGrady, "Abbreviation and Identification: Cataloguing War Diaries 1939-46," (blog), TNA, 25 November, 2021. https://blog.nationalarchives.gov.uk/abbreviation-and-identification-cataloguing-war-diaries-1939-46.

111 Nesmith, "Seeing Archives," 35.

112 Janes, "A Series."

113 For some of the issues involved in the use of this format for archival purposes, see Marco Klindt, "PDF/A Considered Harmful for Digital Preservation," in *Proceedings of iPres – 14th International Conference on Digital Preservation*, Kyoto, Japan, 25–29 September 2017. https://ipres2017.jp/wp-content/uploads/15.pdf; Tim Evans and Ray Moore, "The Use of PDF/A in Digital Archives: A Case Study from Archaeology," *International Journal of Digital Curation* 9, no. 2 (2014): 132–138.

114 The paperless office never materialised. For a full discussion of why it proved to be a 'myth' see Abigail Sellen and Richard Harper, *The Myth of the Paperless Office* (Cambridge MA: MIT Press, 2003).

115 Jay David Bolter and Richard Grusin, *Remediation: Understanding New Media* (Cambridge MA: MIT Press, 1999), 47.

116 Quoted in Rob Walker, "The Inside Story of How the Lowly PDF Played the Longest Game in Tech," *Marker*. Everyday Design Icons. 14 January, 2021.

117 Gitelman, *Paper Knowledge*, 130.

118 Gitelman, *Paper Knowledge*, 115.

119 Gitleman, *Paper Knowledge*, 129.

120 Andrew Hoskins, "Digital Records Take Something Precious from Military History," *The Conversation*, 4 February 2015. https://theconversation.com/digital-records-take-something-precious-from-military-history-36328.

121 Farge, *Allure*, 65.

122 Farge *Allure*, 56.

123 For an example of an academic usage of the data, see Richard Grayson, "Life in the Trenches? The Use of Operation War Diary and Crowdsourcing Methods to Provide an Understanding of the British Army's Day-to-Day Life on the Western Front," *British Journal for Military History* 2, no. 2 (2016): 160–185. ISSN 2057-0422. For some examples of data visualisation projects see Andrea Kocsis, *The Challenges of Working on the Operation War Diary Records* (blog), TNA, 6 April 2022. https://blog.nationalarchives.gov.uk/the-challenges-of-working-on-the-operation-war-diary-records. TNA did not have a clear plan for managing the data gathered from Operation War Diary. There was an intention to incorporate the tags into Discovery, the online catalogue, but there were concerns regarding overloading the system's capacity. The lack of contextual information on individual pages also caused issues with tagging. In some diaries, for example, the year might be provided only on the first page, but not on following pages, making it impossible to date the pages out of context.
124 Blouin and Rosenberg, *Processing the Past*, 26.
125 Steedman, *Dust*, 74.
126 Farge, *Allure*, 3.
127 Cheryce Von Xylander, "Cardboard. Thinking the Box," in *Research Objects in their Technical Setting*, eds. Alfred Nordmann, Bernadette Bensuade Vincent, Sacha Loeve and Astrid Schwartz (London: Routledge, 2017): 176.
128 Craig Robertson, *The Filing Cabinet: A Vertical History of Information* (University of Minnesota Press, 2021), 4.
129 Maria Rentetzi, "The Epistemology of the Familiar: A Hymn to Pandora," in *Boxes: A Field Guide*, eds. Susanne Bauer, Martina Schlünder and Maria Rentezi (Manchester: Manchester Mattering Press, 2020), 447.
130 Martina Schlünder, "The Generative Possibilities of the Wrong Box," in Bauer, Schlünder and Rentezi, *Boxes*, 29.
131 Von Xylander, "Cardboard," 167.
132 Von Xylander, "Cardboard," 176.
133 Robertson, *The Filing Cabinet*, 72.
134 Robertson, *The Filing Cabinet*, 4.
135 Robertson, *The Filing Cabinet*, 18.
136 Schlünder, "The Generative Possibilities," 30.
137 Farge, *Allure*, 12.
138 Farge, *Allure*, 32.
139 Farge, *Allure*, 32.
140 Farge, *Allure*, 16.
141 Farge, *Allure*, 18.
142 Farge, *Allure*, 17.
143 Paul Caplan, "What is a JPEG? The Invisible Object You See Every Day," *The Atlantic*, 24 September 2013. https://www.theatlantic.com/technology/archive/2013/09/what-is-a-jpeg-the-invisible-object-you-see-every-day/279954.
144 Paul Caplan, "London 2012: Distributed Imag(in)ings and Exploiting Protocol," *Journal of Media and Communication* 2, no. 2 (September 2010): 26.
145 Elkins, "Looking Beyond," 85.
146 TNA, "Archives Unlocked 2017," 2.
147 Barbara Brookes and James Dunk, "Introduction: Bureaucracy, Archive Files, and the Making of Knowledge," *Rethinking History* 22, no. 3 (2018): 285.
148 Tredinnick, "Rewriting History," 188.
149 Jerome McGann, "Database, Interface, and Archive Fever," Special issue, PMLA 122, no. 5 (October 2007): 1592.
150 For a full discussion of the development of the desktop interface, see Steven Johnson, Interface Culture: How New Technology Transforms the Way we Create and Communicate (New York: Basic Books, 1997), 42–75.

190 The Matter of Materials and Archives

151 Swartz, "Asylum Case Records," 295.
152 Schlünder, "The Generative Possibilities," 31.
153 Transcription as a process of translating oral discourse to written text is not as overlooked. See, for example, Jane Edwards and Martin Lampert, eds. *Talking data: Transcription and Coding in Discourse Research* (Hillsdale NJ: Lawrence Erlbaum, 1993) and Judith Lapadat and Anne Lindsay, "Transcription in Research and Practice: From Standardization of Technique to Interpretive Positionings," *Qualitative Inquiry* 5, no. 1 (1999): 64–86.
154 Susan Tilley, "'Challenging' Research Practices: Turning a Critical Lens on the Work of Transcription," *Qualitative Inquiry* 9, no. 5 (2003): 752.
155 Tilley, "'Challenging' Research Practices," 767; Cindy Bird, "How I Stopped Dreading and Learned to Love Transcription," *Qualitative Inquiry* 11, no. 2 (2005): 232.
156 Matthew Kirschenbaum, *Track Changes: A Literary History of Word Processing* (Cambridge MA: Harvard University Press, 2016), 7.
157 Jenneka Janzen, "Pondering the Physical Scriptorium," (blog) *medievalfragments*, 25 January 2013.
158 Janzen, "Pondering." https://medievalfragments.wordpress.com/2013/01/25/pondering-the-physical-scriptorium.
159 Erik Kwakkel, "Where are the Scriptoria?," (blog) *medievalfragments*, 5 November 2013.
160 Kwakkel, "Where are the Scriptoria?"
161 Marshall McLuhan, *Understanding Media: The Extensions of Man* (London and New York: Routledge, 2001).
162 Anna Chen, "In One's Own Hand: Seeing Manuscripts in a Digital Age," *DHQ: Digital Humanities Quarterly* 6, no. 2 (2012): paragraph 20.
163 Gitelman, *Paper Knowledge*, 125.
164 Gitelman, *Paper Knowledge*, 125.
165 Andy Orin, "Behind the App: The Story of Notepad++," *Lifehacker*, 17 June 2015. https://lifehacker.com/behind-the-app-the-story-of-notepad-1711936108.
166 From the release notes for V8.3.2: "'Oh no, not another political message from a Notepad++ release again!' you might say. Yes, it is certainly political – but everything nowadays is political. It makes no sense to pretend otherwise. And here, we just want to speak out on the injustice we feel from deep inside our heart. The invasion must be condemned […]" (Notepad++ 2022). The titles and notes of subsequent versions continued to encourage solidarity with Ukraine and with all Russians opposed to the invasion.
167 Tom Vanderbilt, "Courier, Dispatched," *Slate*, 20 February 2004. https://slate.com/human-interest/2004/02/goodbye-to-the-courier-font.html.
168 Maggie Lin, "Between the lines: The story of Courier," *Medium*, 25 February 2019. https://medium.com/@plin14/between-the-lines-the-story-of-courier-760e5311cf6d.
169 Lori Emerson, *Reading Writing Interfaces: From the Digital to the Bookbound* (Minneapolis: University of Minnesota Press, 2014), xi.
170 Branden Hookway, *Interface* (Cambridge MA: MIT Press, 2014), 5–6.
171 Hookway, *Interface*, 4.
172 Margaret Morse, *Virtualities: Television, Media Art, and Cyberculture* (Bloomington IN University Press, 1998), 100; 110.
173 Chris Chesher, "Neither Gaze nor Glance, but Glaze: Relating to Console Game Screens," *Scan Journal* 4, no. 2 (2007).
174 Harvard's Geoffrey Chaucer Website, METRO Glossary, "eyeskip," https://chaucer.fas.harvard.edu/metro-glossary#elision.
175 Cassiodorus, *Institutiones*, trans. James W. Halpern and Barbara Halpern. Undated.
176 Folsom, "Database," 1577.

177 Steedman, *Dust*; Folsom, "Database"; McGann, "Database, Interface".
178 Steedman, *Dust*, 68.
179 Michel De Certeau, *The Practice of Everyday Life*, trans. Steven Rendell (Berkeley: University of California Press, 1984), 144.
180 Stoler, *Along the Archival Grain*, 24.

Conclusion

From the age of information to information overload

This book began with the first few decades of the Twentieth Century and the writing spaces of the battlefields of the First World War, and it ended in the reading rooms of The National Archives (TNA) in Kew in the first few decades of the Twenty-first Century. Just as industrial technologies radically altered the battlefields of the two World Wars, digital technologies are among the forces that have changed the character of the battlefield, if not the nature of armed conflict itself.[1] The practice of operational reporting started with indelible pencils and paper forms in the First World War. Since the war in Iraq in 2003, operational reporting has been primarily digital and extends across a range of formats and technologies, including e-mails, images, videos and audio. The reports are no longer called Unit War Diaries but Operational Records (OR). Reflecting the changing character of warfare, which in recent conflicts associated with the so-called "War on Terror" has become more difficult to pin down in terms of the beginning or end of hostilities, reporting now starts six months prior to a unit's deployment and ends when that deployment is completed. Known today as Operational Record Keeping (ORK), the process and the technologies through which OR are produced may have changed, but there are elements that have endured since the process of record keeping was first described in the *Field Service Regulations* of the early Nineteenth Century.

I want to finish this book by looking at some of the new practices of ORK and by tracing the trajectory of the older ones through them. This book's investigations into the records of the two World Wars was intended as an investigation of the origins of the practices of keeping Unit War Diaries in the British Army, and it therefore concludes by considering what questions still need to be asked about Operational Record Keeping, past and present, in the U.K. and elsewhere. Finally, and perhaps most importantly, this book ends by revealing some of the implications of the smoothing over of complex emotions, especially fear, and the distorting of war into order through the structures and practices of operational reporting, for the British Army today.

DOI: 10.4324/9781003172109-5

Conclusion 193

Operational Record Keeping: The presence of past practices

The Land Forces Standing Order 1120 (*LFSO*) of 2009 revised the parameters for record keeping in the British Army. Maintaining a record of activities while deployed on operations either at home or abroad is not just a matter of institutional policy in the Army but is now a legal requirement. According to the *LFSO* 1120, these records are important for the Ministry of Defence (MoD) because they support a "a wide range" of activities "from the validation of war pension claims, to the compilation of official histories."[2] While the records are still considered important to help the Army make operational improvements and for historiography, they are more significant as "evidence of actions and decisions" which may later come under scrutiny either in reviews in the Army or through legal challenges to its actions and demands for compensation.[3] OR is therefore regarded as essential in providing "protection to Units and Commanders against litigation."[4] Protection against potential litigation is an issue of some urgency for the British Army as it has faced a range of allegations of potential criminal offences in the operations in Iraq and Afghanistan and elsewhere. These include, but are not limited to, the Baha Mousa Inquiry (2008–2011), the series of allegations of abuse and torture by British soldiers in Iraq investigated by the Iraq Historic Allegations Team (2010–2017), and a smaller set of similar allegations in Afghanistan investigated by Operation Northmoor (2014–2019).

The increasing emphasis on ORK as a means of countering litigation in the Army is an example of what Terry Cook identified as early as 1994 as an "accountability framework" driving record keeping practices.[5] Cook recognised that an increasing awareness of the need for accountability in corporations and governments had become significant in facilitating cooperation between organisations and archivists and in enhancing the authority of the archivist, but he warned against the danger of "**only** identifying as archival those records necessary for corporate accountability."[6] Cook's concern was primarily with the *selection* of records for archiving, but the shift towards accountability also shapes the *production* of records. As the "most important source of information available to the Army" in responding to legal charges, OR is required to be as detailed as possible:

> [W]here comprehensive OR have been kept these have often been found sufficient to dismiss claims made against the Army. Inadequate OR have had the opposite effect, leaving the Army effectively unable to defend itself. The inclusion of all information which will – or could – have a bearing on any future legal case is, therefore, considered essential.[7]

As I argued in Chapter 1, the *Field Service Regulations* formalised writing practices and leveraged the practice of keeping records into the space of the battlefield as part of an initial strategy to provide empirical source material for the historiography of warfare. In the *LFSO* 1120, the practice of record keeping is

194 Conclusion

leveraged into battle spaces to ensure that the British Army can protect itself in legal challenges. Although these records are no longer in paper format, the reliance on documented interpretations of events as a form of "papereality" not only persists, but has intensified in the British Army.[8] Just as soldiers were once expected to identify any information that might have historical significance, they are now required by the *LFSO* 1120 to identify information that could be essential for legal purposes. The first two chapters of this book demonstrated that the decisions made around what might be considered of historical value, and of how to craft narratives in response to that imperative, varied considerably among individuals. Although the cultural and political contexts of the Twenty-first Century are radically different from that of the two World Wars, it is not unreasonable to suppose that soldiers of more recent conflicts, most of whom are unlikely to have legal expertise, might also have varying understandings of what constitutes information of legal value, which raises questions around the nature of ORK as a practice that produces accurate information.

Knowing that the records might be used in cases of litigation may affect the way they are maintained. As Sir James Edmonds identified in the First World War Unit War Diaries, reports can be susceptible to falsification for various reasons. It should not be a surprise, therefore, that in one of the cases brought against the Special Forces for operations in Afghanistan as part of Operation Northmoor, there was the suggestion that some reports, specifically Operational Summaries, had been falsified to provide cover stories that justified the actions of the squad that produced them. Reports made repeated, and remarkably similar, references to attacks on the squad, despite different patrols, situations and locations, all of which ended with the squad killing the alleged attackers.[9] Although these reports were included in ensuing investigations, there was ultimately insufficient evidence for prosecution. Yet the events the reports described were improbable enough to arouse the suspicion of some in the Army and questions remain about their authenticity.[10] Official reports can thus be used by both individuals and the institution to protect and enhance reputations, providing a structure that mediates between event, individual, Army and the law.

The structure and principles underlying OR continue to attempt to manage the unpredictability and chaos of modern warfare through the control mechanisms of bureaucratic organisation. The *LFSO* 1120 describes an extensive network of texts, organized in "Annexes" labelled A-Z through Army Form C.2119, which provides a frontsheet for the record. The typewriter's contribution to the proliferation of paperwork fades into insignificance compared to the profusion of documents facilitated by digital technologies. The *LFSO* points out that the annex list can be expanded and "units are encouraged to do so to cater for their specific circumstances."[11] The C.2119 provides a framework intended to manage the proliferation of documents and materials generated via digital technologies, and to bring them under control. As in the two World Wars, the entire OR is required to be produced in duplicate. One copy is to be sent monthly to Historical Branch (Army), the unit responsible for managing these records, and the other to be kept by the unit or formation. The *LFSO* provides detailed guidance on how to complete each of the documents intended for the Annexes.

First on the list is the "chronological overview." The chronological overview is completed using a template that is only a slightly revised of the original C.2118 form used in the First World War. Despite the differences between the battlefields of the First and Second World Wars and those of current conflicts, the C.2118 form has remained relatively consistent despite slight modifications. It is a point of continuity, a reassuring framework that serves as a material reminder of stability and order in the Army's internal processes regardless of the challenges and changes the organisation might face. The endurance of the C.2118 form is evidence of the resilience of bureaucratic processes and of deep institutional faith in bureaucracy as both practice and ideology. However, whereas in the First World War the information in the C.2118 forms constituted the primary record supplemented by Appendices, the chronological overview has now become the "document which glues the OR together."[12] It is the principal reference grid for all other documents contained in the annexes, working as a kind of hypertext connecting and anchoring all the documents in the OR as a whole. Like its antecedent, the First World War Unit War Diary, it is intended to contain only concise information – a "short summary of each day's fighting/operations" that might include changes in command, location, equipment and organisation, as well as information received, decisions made, orders given, weather, factors impacting decision-making.[13] Brief statements of opinions and recommendations regarding tactics, organisation and morale can be included. The *LFSO* stresses that entries should be made daily to ensure that there are no "gaps in the chronology," ordering events in a linear narrative structure.[14] The *LFSO* instructs those responsible for completing the record to ensure that the contents are "accurate, honest and objective" and notes that "Authors should avoid the temptation to exclude unpalatable facts."[15] These instructions echo the 1909 *Field Service Regulations'* rules for the Unit War Diaries, which were to provide "a concise and accurate record" of events in war and are evidence of the persistent belief in documentation as a process and medium that produces accurate, linear representations of events.[16]

If the Army once believed in brevity, the profusion of material that now accompanies the C.2118 forms is an indication that the approach has shifted to encouraging the production of as much information as possible to accompany the concise entries in the chronological overview. The Annexes include a summary of operations (Annex B), which is intended to provide an "analytical overview of operations."[17] It was these documents that proved contentious for the Special Forces teams investigated in Operation Northmoor. There are also Annexes for watchkeeper's logs, radio logs, Situation Reports, Action and Incident Reports (including Combat Reports), Orders of Battle, intelligence reports and summaries, standing orders, maps and other geographic images, a separate Annex for any other information relevant to potential legal matters (including information on Prisoners of War) as well as welfare, deaths and injuries, lessons learned, environmental incidents, and any top secret information. The extensive annexes of texts and materials that make up the OR from recent conflicts constitute a hypertextual network designed to filter war through rational, routinised and standardised principles that have their roots in the early organisation of records at the start of the Twentieth Century. They reiterate modern warfare as a phenomenon that can be represented, analysed and contained through rational structures of documentation and Information Management. The importance of accuracy and objectivity in these documents has an increased weight now that these documents are considered as legal evidence of events, which makes it even more critical to understand the factors involved in shaping their contents.

This book's examination of the history of Unit War Diaries in the two World Wars provides a model for understanding how official records represent conflict. It revealed how cultural and technological shifts shape the records of war, and how individuals and institutions have influenced how war is understood and waged. Chapter 1 and 2 demonstrated how the cultures and technologies involved in the production, storage and circulation of Unit War Diaries contributed to the shaping of a "reassuring grammar of war," to use David Holbrook's evocative phrase, that eliminated unpredictability, chaos and fear.[18] The C.2118 form, as an official pre-printed blank document, was designed to facilitate and shape information-gathering for the British Army and to dehumanise the record of war through its very structure. The indelible pencil was associated with standards of productivity and reliability in producing paperwork easily, without the fuss of ink, and which could be duplicated without much effort. The typewriter in turn, was an emblem of efficiency and precision, capable of removing the human from its mechanised text. But by considering the official document as a component within a writing space, this book revealed the C.2118 form as a complex interface between cultural influences, the authority and needs of the British Army, and the individual expression of experiences in war through technologies of media like the pencil and typewriter.

By considering the C.2118 forms not as information *about* war, but as representations *of* war, this book brought to light individual affective responses to conflict. Despite the attempts to dehumanise the reports of war, and to filter them through bureaucratic technologies and controls, moments of resistance and unruliness emerged in the analysis of both corpuses selected for this book. The indelible pencil facilitated individuality through handwriting, which unexpectedly at times confounded the accessibility of the information because of its illegibility. The typewriter, despite its reputation for impersonal efficiency, disrupted the neat mask of order in the records by engendering spelling and typing errors. The use of exclamation marks, a form of punctuation associated more closely with pulp novels and the yellow press,[19] was investigated in this book as an injection of ineffable expression into the official record of war that serves as a reminder of humans *being* in the spaces of conflict. The typewriter facilitated the production of lengthier narratives, as well as contributing to the general increase in the scale of documentation. This book additionally investigated how expanded narratives can sometimes work as an articulation of the self in the constraints of institutional structures through the parsing of sometimes appalling events via established cultural understandings, or with humour to counter the horror of conflict.

Yet despite these moments of resistance and unruliness, the Unit War Diaries are embedded in, and circulated through, broader structures that augment the idea that war can be subdued and controlled through rational systems. In The National Archives, the Unit War Diaries are positioned along with other records as the raw material of history, capable of 'speaking for itself.' Although historians and archivists will be aware of significance of the nature of the record as mediated representations of the past shaped by historically situated technologies and institutional cultures and needs, much of the discourse produced by TNA itself obscures these material qualities. I have argued that just as operational records are intended to tame the chaos of warfare, archival description brings order to the records of war, organizing them in linear structures that privilege organisational management over individual experience. Records are boxed or transformed into digital files that classify and order them, reinforcing the relationships of institutional provenance and purposes, and segmenting the vast body of the records of war into manageable 'pieces.'

Chapter 3 demonstrated how, in the digital realm, paper records break loose from the archive, and can be transformed by technologies into formats that enable them to be analysed as data sets. In the process, physical interactions with the record that bring attention to its materiality are lost, along with the sense of the larger context to which a document might belong. I highlighted the danger, in the transformation of Unit War Diaries to data, of sustaining the mindset that evolved along with the industrial battlefield that assumes that the primary way of understanding war is through the things that can be counted or measured. In contrast, this book has focused on the things individuals created that escaped, or pushed against, the "networks of rationality" spread over the incoherence and complexity of modern warfare by institutions, bureaucratic and archival practices.[20] At the start of this book, I pointed out that concentrating on a sample of the records is intended to allow for detailed analysis. More research into larger samples of the records of the two World Wars, from varying theatres and units, is needed to discover whether diverse shades of emotional resonances, different kinds of resistance to bureaucratic structures, or disparate uses of the technologies emerge.

Similar questions posed about Unit War Diaries need to be asked of today's records of war, and with some urgency given the status of these documents as legal evidence. More than a century after its implementation, the regulations and structures governing Operational Record Keeping are designed to maintain the same controlled and reassuring nets of rationality. Keeping records in the British Army has been a mediated practice from its inception, but in the digital world, it involves even more kinds of media technologies, from pcs to digital cameras to surveillance drones, all of which produce prodigious amounts of material.

Questioning the future record of the past

I have argued throughout this book that the mediated nature of written records is neither transparent nor neutral, and that media technologies are part of a series of factors influencing what is represented of war, and how. In records of current conflicts, it is equally important to understand how the suite of media technologies deployed in their creation affect how operations are represented. Questions need to be raised about how each of these media technologies represents conflict, and how they shape the resulting record of war.

Images, video and audio files are all part of the records of current conflicts, for example, and each of these media refract events in war through their own unique affordances. Historically, TNA has not stored much multi-media material. Photographs are kept if they are already part of a file to preserve the integrity of the record, but large sets of images, films or video and audio files are held instead by the Imperial War Museum, which has the technology needed for the specialist storage of this material, and for making it publicly accessible. But to maintain the integrity of the OR, TNA will need to find ways of preserving and making accessible images, video and audio footage. The geographic images that belong in Annex Q, for example, might include thousands of photographs taken by patrols of wadis and compounds and other topographical features, with no accompanying information as to why the individuals who took them thought they might be important. These are untethered fragments of information from the operation that need to be kept as part of the record according to archival principles of record integrity, but without context it is difficult to see which of these images might be meaningful or why, raising questions about the value of their preservation. But the OR might also include combat footage, or other kinds of visual evidence of events or people, in turn raising questions about their inclusion in public records that go beyond security to ethical issues around privacy. Sorting these images, which might run into millions, and combat footage, which might run to thousands of hours, to filter out that which has no historical significance, or that which presents a security risk, or which poses ethical quandaries, presents a daunting task for those responsible for managing and curating the OR.

The authority of state archives has, for a large part of their history, rested on the authority of the text – "of words that can be quoted and analyzed with other words" – but the development of digital visual technologies has transformed practices of documentation and evidence.[21] Susan Brayne, Karen Levy and Bryce Newell point to an "increasing reliance on video as a check on power, as well as a source of ostensible authority when accounts are in conflict" in courts of law.[22] Video or audio footage produced during combat might reveal emotional responses and enable a representation of the chaos of combat that the written text does not. But such footage needs to be treated with care as evidence, because digital video and imagery is as prone to subjectivity, inaccuracy and omissions as written representations of conflict can be. The digital visual media produced as part of the official OR is located, like official documentation, at the intersection between individuals, institution and conflict. In an argument that aligns with the one made in this book about official documents, Brayne et al. maintain that "the process of transforming lived experience into digital, visual evidence can engender accountability, facilitate resistance to power, and reshape relations between the individual and the state."[23]

The awareness of the significance of video footage as evidence has shaped behaviours in the field, but the presence of digital cameras also introduces a level of uncontrollability into official accounts of warfare. In 2013, Sergeant Alexander Blackman, a Royal Marine, was convicted of killing a wounded Afghan fighter in Helmand Province during Operation Herrick in September 2011. Blackman and men from his patrol, finding the fighter wounded but alive after an attack from an Apache helicopter, dragged the Afghan man out of sight of the Persistent Ground Surveillance System (cameras tethered to balloons) where Blackman shot him in the chest. The events were, however, captured by the helmet camera of one of the other marines. While the event was not recorded by an official camera, the footage from the helmet camera contributed to Blackman's arrest and sentencing. In 2017, however, following an appeal, Blackman was released on grounds of diminished responsibility. The court found that, due to a range of factors, Blackman was suffering from adjustment disorder, which, according to the judges, led to an inability to control his emotions and "substantially impaired his ability to form a rational judgment."[24] Blackman's case thus illustrates both the role of digital technology and the continuing significance of emotion on the contemporary battlefield. Similarly, the video of Donald Payne used in the Baha Mousa inquiry was taken from a personal digital camera carried by one of his fellow soldiers.[25] In both cases, official visual records did not cover the incidents, but the ubiquity and use of personal recording devices, however, demonstrates how these technologies have ruptured the control of official imagery from combat zones. Issues of containment in the digital world are not only related to the production of material outside of the OR, however.

Although the *LFSO* 1120 stipulates that extraneous material such as "games, joke emails and 'chuff' charts" should be excluded from the OR, separating this kind of material from a digital data set can be time intensive and tricky.[26] Many units on deployment have neither the time nor the inclination to delete this material or remove it from the official record. Do digital media therefore make for a much more unruly record of warfare, one that pushes back so radically at the structures of rationality that they destabilize it? Does the sheer scope of digital records make more room for the representation of the chaos of warfare, and for its emotional dimension? Or has the smooth universality of digital text and formats squeezed out individuality entirely and finally succeeded in dehumanizing conflict? After all, as Andrew Hoskins observes, the handwritten or typed document is

> more likely to preserve a stream of consciousness and the thoughts of the writer in the field at the time. The word-processed account militates against the survival of these original thoughts and hides edits made along the way by the author and by others.[27]

Video or audio footage produced during combat might reveal more of the emotional and chaotic dimensions of combat than the written text, but at the same time, affective responses are easier to erase in digital text, disappearing with the press of the backspace or delete key. Research into the records of contemporary conflicts is needed to answer these questions, but such research might well be hampered by the very nature of the digital record.

The OR of recent conflicts thus constitutes a range of material, from images to e-mail to instant messages, generally combined into one hard drive and sent to the Army's Historical Branch. Historical Branch (Army) is responsible not only for curating these records, but also for the formidable task of searching them for relevant information in the case of queries or litigation. The complexity and scale of the material, in addition to shaping the record of war, presents a considerable challenge of records management for both the Historical Branch and The National Archives (TNA). Both organisations are required to sort through these data dumps to determine which records should remain confidential for security reasons, which should be destroyed (such as the 'chaff' e-mails) and which should be made publicly available. Government records in the U.K., according to the 2010 Constitutional Reform and Governance Act, are now made public after 20 years. In 2023, the records generated during the 2003 Iraq War are due to cycle into TNA. As of this writing, therefore, it remains to be seen how the massive multimedia data records of current wars might be shaped by institutional selection processes, and how they will subsequently influence the future histories and understanding of warfare.

"What kind of history," asks Andrew Hoskins, "is likely be distilled from what could potentially be millions of documents compared with the writings of wars of the previous century?".[28] While digital files are searchable in ways that paper files are not, effective searches require an existing knowledge of relevant terms and acronyms. Acronyms are widespread in the British Army, but it is also common for Units to adopt their own unique shorthand and terminology. Without the knowledge of general army acronyms and of the ones adopted by individual units, researchers might well be unable to effectively search for information buried in vast data files. Searching thousands, potentially millions, of images or audio files also poses a problem, as these are not machine searchable in the same way as text. The sheer bulk of OR from recent conflicts, exponentially distended by digital technologies and shaped by their affordances, far exceeds a "factual summary of events,"[29] to the extent that it might present significant challenges to the very process of summarizing facts into a coherent historical narrative. The practice of keeping records was organised and implemented during the start of the age of information, but it has ended in information overload, and the question of what that means for the understanding of these wars in the future is yet to be answered.

While investigation into the records of Iraq and Afghanistan is crucial, the reports of other conflicts and operations should not be overlooked and should be subject to the same kinds of questions in future research. Between the end of the Second World War and the recent conflicts in Iraq and Afghanistan, the British Army was involved in conflicts and engagements of all kinds, from the Korean War (1950–53), the 'troubles' in Northern Ireland (where the British Army was deployed from 1969–2007, making it the longest single deployment in its history), the Falklands War (1982) and peacekeeping operations in Bosnia (1992). Research into the roles played by technologies, institutions and individuals in shaping the records of these operations is essential to revealing how they are represented and mediated in the official record, and how that in turn has inflected the understanding, memory and history of each of these engagements. Comparative analysis is especially needed to reveal what has happened to the record of war as it transitions from analogue to digital technologies.

Record keeping in other armies, past and present

Comparisons between the reporting practices of the armies of other nations would be valuable in providing insight into how varying cultures and technologies shaped representations of the same wars. In the First World War, for example, the German Army's process of reporting began with the practice of developing after-action reports in training, but it was only during the battle of the Somme that practices of information-sharing were systematically implemented.[30] Similarly, the American Expeditionary Forces only consolidated their systems of reporting towards the end of hostilities, with four pages in the General Orders detailing instructions for a range of different reports, including War Diaries.[31] In contrast to the British Army Unit War Diaries, for the American Forces the War Diary was intended to support the facts given in Situation Reports. Much more emphasis was placed on narrative rather than information in the American approach:

> the mere giving of such facts constitutes the least part of the keeping of the war diary. What is of most importance is that there should be a narrative of the operations from which the history of the unit can be gathered and also professional and especially tactical instruction.[32]

Reporting practices in the German and American Forces have been the focus of discussions of Information Management and the development of doctrine,[33] but the question of how records were formulated through institutional needs and regulations, as well as by the technologies and different emotional regimes at work in the writing spaces of the First World War, remains open to investigation. How have these representations shaped the understanding of the First World War, and of warfare in general, in these different nations? What contrasts might emerge between them?

In terms of investigating record keeping in the militaries of other nations in subsequent conflicts, practices in the U.S. Army constitute a potential case study of some magnitude and urgency. Record keeping in the U.S. military since the Vietnam conflict has been in disarray, with serious and wide-ranging consequences. According to the Christopher Lawrence, Executive Director and President of The Dupuy Institute, which has generated six reports on record keeping in the U.S. Army from 1998 to 2000, the U.S. Army records of Red Cloud's War (1866–1868) are in a more complete state than those of the Vietnam War.[34] In the 1991 Gulf War, the practice of operational record keeping effectively collapsed, and only around 13% of battalion daily records were preserved.[35] As a result, when soldiers in the U.S. Army began succumbing to Gulf War Syndrome, almost no records were available to validate their claims. The issues have persisted in the conflicts associated with the War on Terror, despite periodic attempts to address the problems. An official investigation into the management and production of records by the U.S. Army during Operation Enduring Freedom in Iraq, found that the "volume, location, size and format" of records from the operation was "unknown," resulting in a failure to capture significant historical and operational information.[36] In Afghanistan, a combination of issues, including a "lack of command interest and a continued failure to provide for a more systematic records collection and retirement system" resulted in a "virtual vacuum of operational records from 2004–2007," with little improvement in the U.S. Army's practices after that.[37] Soldiers suffering from Post-Traumatic Stress Disorder as a result of these conflicts have been unable to process claims for support, but the U.S. Army faces a different kind of challenge in attempting to accommodate lessons learned from these engagements. Historians, meanwhile, fear that they may never be able to "know clearly what happened in Iraq and Afghanistan because we don't have the records."[38]

Investigating the range of issues involved in the failures of operational reporting in the U.S. Army, such as the collapse of a SharePoint portal in 2008 which caused the loss of some records from Iraq, could shed light on the role played by digital technology in shaping the records of current wars. Similarly, investigations into the U.S. Army's approach to the significance of records management could illuminate key differences in the understanding and use of information. For example, the White Paper produced for the Department of Defence (DoD) on Records Management is far more open than the British Army's guidelines on record keeping about the use of information collected by the Army: "The reason why the military stores information and collects the knowledge which is produced is not to reflect reality, but to manipulate it."[39] Investigating record keeping practices across different militaries is therefore needed to provide a picture of the different ways in which armed conflict and war is represented within military organisations, but it is even more critical because manipulation of information has become key to military doctrine in contemporary conflicts. "Failure to properly manage information can lead to the failure of the mission," according to the DoD's White Paper.[40] The British Army's response to what it identifies as "an era of constant competition and confrontation in which our adversaries exploit the grey area short of combat operations to seek advantage" is to adopt the position that "it is the triumph of the narrative that is decisive, not necessarily the facts on the ground."[41] While information has always been significant in any armed conflict, it is a critical element of the suite of weapons and tools deployed in contemporary conflicts, lending research into how information is shaped and produced in different militaries even more significance and weight.

It is crucial to understand how information about war is formulated in official records not only for legal reasons and for historiography, but because that information contributes to the ways wars are conceptualised and waged. Jon Lindsay points out that "If a military is unable to connect its internal representations to external realities, then it cannot know where to aim, it cannot hit the things it aims at, and it receives poor feedback about what it hits and misses."[42] But in addition to that, if a military's internal representations do not fully represent the realities of conflict, then that military will struggle to accommodate warfighting in all its dimensions, and will learn its lessons slowly, if at all.

Emotion, chaos and common sense

The British Army entered the First World War with the belief that war could be managed via scientific and bureaucratic systems. The Unit War Diaries of the First World War selected for analysis for this book process the war through the principles associated with those systems, creating a representation of the conflict which, despite occasional deviations, emphasises the things valued in scientific methodologies and bureaucratic assessments of performance. The reports therefore struggled to accommodate the dimensions of armed combat that could not be easily counted, calculated, or measured. The preeminence of reason as the ultimate mode and measure of behaviour in British men in social, cultural and military spheres, positioned emotion as irrational and unwanted. Unit War Diaries accordingly pushed fear, together with other intense emotional responses, out of the official reports of the First World War.

Regardless of whether the dreadful chaos of combat or the fear of war was represented and acknowledged elsewhere, and regardless of attempts by individuals to translate the lessons they had learned about mechanised warfare into doctrine in the interwar years, the British Army went into the Second World War with its beliefs in the power of rational systems of organisation as a counter to chaos, and reason as a powerful antidote to emotion, intact. There are complex reasons for the British Army's struggles in the first few years of the

Second World War, including inadequate training, resourcing and selection processes. However, the organisation's failure to develop effective measures to account for unpredictability in conflict, and its profound misunderstanding of emotion on the battlefield, must also be acknowledged as playing a part. Although the Army adapted as the war continued, the records of the Second World War selected for the corpus for this book represent conflict through a similar rational framework as that evident in the First World War, and they continue to marginalise unwanted emotion and to minimise the chaotic and unpredictable.

The legacy of these structures and approaches can be identified in some of the British Army's subsequent organisational practices and in the slow evolution of its culture after the Second World War. Very little research into the psychological consequences of combat was conducted in the U.K. in the years after the Second World War until the start of the Twenty-first Century, despite the British Army's involvement in significant operations around the world during that period.[43] It is almost as if the subject of emotional trauma and psychological damage as a result of armed conflict faded into the background, not only in the Army, but also in academic and political spheres in the U.K. The Army's understanding of the psychological consequences of combat in that time did not move very far past those articulated in the Shell Shock Report. Long-term mental health issues after combat were attributed to pre-existing psychological problems, but it remained an agreed fact that anyone could break down in war.[44] The approach to treating those who did break down up until the 1980s followed the principles of Forward Psychiatry developed during the Second World War. Treatment was administered in the field and as close to the time of the breakdown as possible, without the individual being removed from the operational zone, and with the intention of sending the soldier back to duty.[45]

Forward Psychiatry continued, despite the changes in operations that meant that war zones were not as easily defined and front lines dissolved. In the 1980s, the recognition of Post-Traumatic Stress Disorder (PTSD) as an official diagnostic category by the American Psychiatric Association, partly because of work done with veterans of the Vietnam War, disrupted some of these ideas, but the dearth of research in the U.K. into the topic continued up to the beginning of the new century. However, in the early 2000s, over 2,000 British military personnel brought a class action against the Ministry of Defence. The claimants, who had served in operations in Northern Ireland, the Falklands, Bosnia and the first Gulf War, alleged that the MoD had failed to prepare or protect them from the psychological consequences of exposure to combat. They lost their case, as the judge ruled that the MoD could not be expected to have a higher duty of care to its employees than any other organisation, despite the increased risk of injury or death to those in its employ.

Although the claimants lost, the case reveals the persistence of some attitudes towards unwanted emotion in British military culture in general, and in the Army in particular. The questions raised in this case echo those raised in the

Shell Shock Report of 1922: "Exactly what type of psychiatric disorder could be caused by war? Were these only short-term illnesses, or could they become prolonged? Alternatively, could their onset be delayed?".[46] The repetition of these kinds of questions reflects some of the difficulties in precisely defining and measuring a variable and volatile condition. The MoD argued that it had remained abreast of psychiatric research into the topic, and that its measures to manage the condition throughout the Twentieth Century were backed by accepted wisdom in psychiatry; an argument upheld by Justice Owen. But claimants argued that the MoD had failed to train personnel to deal with fear in combat. The arguments around fear reveal that it remained an unwanted emotion, and a thorny issue for the military. The MoD countered the claimants' argument by pointing out that there was no evidence to show that training in fear helped to reduce psychological damage in combat but that informal briefings on fear were conducted by officers at their own discretion. Justice Owen agreed that the MoD had not been negligent and that there was no evidence to support the efficacy of formalised fear training.[47] Both sides of the case acknowledged fear as something all soldiers will face, but the case reveals that in engagements in the latter half of the last century, the British Army continued to address it indirectly, through "time-honoured methods such as morale, leadership, and above all, combat training."[48] The interwar beliefs in morale, leadership and individual responsibility as effective counters to fear thus survived the Second World War to shape the Army's approach to subsequent conflicts.

Admitting to fear or other unwanted emotions was, according to the claimants, made difficult by a "macho culture in the forces, particularly in the Army, in which psychological problems were seen as a sign of weakness and personnel were reluctant to report them for fear of damaging their careers."[49] While agreeing that psychological issues were seen as a sign of weakness in the military, Justice Owen stated that this was no different to attitudes in society in general and that "a culture of toughness" would always be necessary in the armed forces due to the nature and purpose of military operations.[50] Although the claimants argued that military culture was "antipathetic to psychiatric problems," the MoD countered by saying that attempting to change the organisation was difficult, in part because the military needed to maintain that 'culture of toughness,' but also because it reflected attitudes in broader society, and because the organisation is "large, complex, and inherently conservative."[51] The reasons for the Army's institutional intransigence when it comes to acknowledging and dealing with the trauma and unwanted emotions are varied and complex. But this book has demonstrated from only a sample of the records of the two World Wars that the organisation's reports, which were intended to allow the Army to learn the lessons it needs to wage war more effectively, render intense emotions all but invisible, which inevitably creates difficulties in the Army's ability to account for the impact of emotion both on the battlefield and off it in the years after these wars. More research is needed into the records of the operations and conflicts after the two World Wars to reveal whether they continue the trend of masking emotion in rational structures, but the Army has only recently begun what might be a slow sea change in its emotional regime.

Only a few years after this case, in 2005, Malcolm New, a Staff Sergeant in the Royal Welch Fusiliers who alleged the MoD had failed to support him in treatment for combat stress after five tours in Northern Ireland, was awarded £620,000 in damages, one of the first to win a claim of this kind against the MoD.[52] Claims for PTSD have subsequently continued, although the Armed Forces Compensation Scheme, which provides compensation for injury or illness caused by service on or after April 2005, including mental health issues, now deals with most.[53] The financial pressure of these claims may have played a part in more recent measures undertaken by the Army to address the questions of unwanted emotions, and of attempting to mitigate through training the psychological and emotional damage that some soldiers suffer as a result of combat. The 2000s also saw a general increased awareness in the significance of mental health and wellbeing across political, social and corporate sectors. A report conducted in 2017 at the request of Theresa May, then Prime Minister, found that the cost of poor mental health for the government was between £24 to £27 billion, making it a topic of political urgency.[54] Within this context, the Army began implementing measures to address the mental and emotional health of those in its service, although there is some evidence to suggest that the 'culture of toughness' remains a core part of its emotional regime.

Among these measures is the Trauma Risk Management Programme (TRiM), initially introduced by the Royal Marines in 1996, and formally adopted by the British Army in 2007. TRiM is a peer-to-peer support system designed to take advantage of existing relationships in organisations, rather than involving a health professional who might be a stranger, to provide support in the aftermath of a traumatic event. TRiM practitioners are trained to carry out risk assessments, to provide support to those who require it and to identify the signs in those who might need specialist help to recover. TRiM is believed to contribute to an increased probability that those negatively impacted by trauma will look for help thereby reducing future issues (and possible future claims for compensation).[55] The "Don't Bottle it Up" campaign, launched by the MoD in October 2011, marks the first attempt in the British Army to address the stigma attached to mental health issues in the organisation by endeavouring to highlight and break down the cost of emotional reticence and the stiff upper lip, still so much a part of the Army's emotional regime almost a century after the First World War. The extent and power of the stigma still attached to conditions such as Post Traumatic Stress Disorder have been vividly illustrated by photographer Mark Neville's *Battle Against Stigma* project. Neville was sent to Helmand in 2011 with the British Forces as an official war artist. Suffering from PTSD himself, and struggling to adapt upon his return, Neville partnered with Jamie Hacker Hughes, an expert in veteran mental health, to develop a book that offers not only a visual exploration of life in the spaces of war, but also includes, in a separate volume, some of the vast number of e-mails and messages from soldiers, their families and friends, and organisations, in response to Neville's work. The book, as well as Neville's photographs and a documentary film form an exhibition intended to "encourage a cultural shift amongst the U.K. population, MOD and government that will remove the stigma of talking about military mental health," according to the website for the project. Neville's work, and the response to it, suggest that campaigns such as "Don't Bottle it Up" are not quite as effective in eradicating stigma as the Army might hope.

While TRiM and the Don't Bottle it Up campaign are aimed at treating mental health issues, the Army has also developed strategies to prevent the onset of mental health problems. In the case brought against the MoD in the early 2000s, it was argued by the defence that it was not possible to prepare soldiers for the emotional impact of combat. But since then, the MoD and the Army have undertaken several initiatives to improve the mental and emotional 'resilience' of troops. Among these is OP SMART (Optimising Performance through Stress Management and Resilience Training), a programme designed to build mental resilience and strength along with physical strength in Army training. OP SMART is part of initiatives designed to "empower individuals and leaders in maintaining mental wellbeing rather than needing to seek help."[56] OP SMART, along with the mandatory Annual Mental Fitness Brief, is designed to ensure that "personnel are always working toward the top levels of mental fitness."[57]

On the surface, it appears as if the Army's emotional regime has begun to shift to acknowledge and deal with intense emotions and psychological damage. However, Harriet Gray argues that TRiM is part of "moves towards the reframing of combat and its harms as individualised, and thus as *private* experience, rather than an issue of national politics."[58] By relegating the powerful emotions and affective responses that might be generated by combat to symptoms that must be managed or eliminated by the individual, TRiM is part of systems that obviate what might be learned from those responses, according to Gray. Because fear and other intense emotions generated by combat are framed as problems to be managed by individuals, they are effectively excised from broader political debates around the consequences of conflict and whether the operations were necessary in the first place.[59] The language of the publicity campaign around Don't Bottle it Up similarly emphasises individual responsibility in managing intense, unwanted emotions.

The BBC, for example, describes "Don't Bottle it Up" as aimed at "persuading servicemen and women not to ignore mental health problems, in a job where many expect themselves to be 'strong.'"[60] There is no mention of the pressure that the Army might place on individuals to be 'strong' through resiliency training, or of the political circumstances that might create stressors in the first place. In the corporate setting, 'resilience' has come under criticism for eliding corporate responsibility by pushing the responsibility for failures to adapt or bounce back from situations created by organisations onto individuals.[61] The rhetoric around these initiatives in the Army is very much focused on the management, control and harnessing of difficult or unwanted emotions rather than their expression, folding into the 'culture of toughness' without disrupting it too radically. There is additionally no mention of fear in OP SMART or in the MoD's strategy documents. It is like a background hum in the rhetoric, behind terms like 'stress', suggesting that it is remains an outlaw emotion for the British Army, and one that is difficult to address directly. It would be interesting to see whether fear registers at all in the official reports of more recent operations in Iraq and Afghanistan. Charles Addison, a young rifleman serving in Afghanistan, describes how even in debriefings, "all mention of fear is excised with a surgeon's precision," which suggests to me that fear continues to be erased as a matter of course in official reports too.[62]

In addition to these internal measures, the Army has begun making moves to adjust its public image. In a recruitment campaign begun in 2017, the British Army began working hard to project the image of itself as an organisation that supported and welcomed a diverse range of people and emotional qualities. The "This is Belonging" campaign for television, radio and digital media, developed with creative agency Karmarama, attempted to shift the image of the British soldier as white, male, and stereotypically stoic and unemotional, to a more inclusive and diverse perspective of military personnel and life. One of the short films released as part of the campaign shows a patrol standing by respectfully to allow a Muslim member to pray. In another film a patrol follows the lead of a black female soldier. Other films in the same campaign attempted to readjust the image of the Army's emotional regime. In "Still Playing the Joker," a soldier plays a prank on a sleeping comrade in a film that suggests the cheeriness of the British squaddie is still an important attribute. But "Expressing my Emotions" makes room for a kind of emotion more usually thought of as unwanted in the Army. In this video, a soldier on operations opens a letter from home containing a tea bag, which he holds up to his nose, becoming tearful at what is presumably the smell of home, before a younger member of the squad offers him some boiling water to make a cup of tea. Another, this time an animated short, asks "What if I get Emotional in the Army?". The voice of a male soldier explains how he thought joining the Army would be "a thousand times worse" than the emotional restrictions imposed on men by society in general, and "that any sign of emotion would be a sign of weakness" that would be "ripped out" of soldiers. The piece ends reassuringly, with the soldier realizing that "no-one is a machine" in the Army, with the suggestion that no-one is treated like a machine either. The campaign implies that the Army's emotional regime is more expansive even than that of general British society, and that the Army makes room for emotions not usually thought of as welcome in the military, such as sadness. Fear, however, is not addressed. The campaign faced criticism from some quarters. "Touchy-feely political correctness has absolutely no role whatever in the British Army," according to Sir Nicholas Sloan, grandson of Winston

Churchill, who warned that changing the Army's approach to recruitment and training could lead to "pale imitations of what is actually required."[63] Major General Tim Cross, also retired, noted that the Army was "not going to be soft and we are not going to be nice to people."[64] Jennifer Mathers points out that these comments are indicative of "who these critics think are the right sort of soldiers: men who will show a stiff upper lip in any circumstances."[65]

It seems like common-sense to expect that the Army needs to avoid being 'soft' and 'nice' and maintain a 'culture of toughness,' given that a large part of its remit involves sending people out to fight. The idea is so pervasive that it is hard to shift. Even the judge in the 2000 case against the MoD accepted that toughness was necessary.[66] But we should remind ourselves that common-sense, through Gramscian perspectives, is historically contingent, and although individual, intimately related to social and cultural context.[67] Because of its relationship to broader society, 'common sense' is inherently ideological. As Robert Eccleshall points out, it is part of ideological processes that render perceptions of life and experience "serviceable by channelling them into a coherent but partial view of society."[68] The idea that 'toughness' is essential to the British Army is part of a coherent but partial view of culture in the military. 'Toughness' in this context is associated with a stereotypical construct of masculinity defined by emotional control, competitiveness, physical strength, fearlessness and combativeness.[69] Clare Duncanson has argued convincingly that the attachment to this particular brand of masculinity in the British Army had serious consequences for how wars were fought in Afghanistan and Iraq by contributing to a valorisation of combat and therefore affecting strategy and decision-making. There are broader issues at stake too, as "valorizing 'tough' attitudes and approaches and discrediting peaceful ones" contributes to the "perpetuation of militarism and war."[70] But Duncanson identifies evidence of a different kind of masculinity being performed in the conflicts in Iraq and Afghanistan, based on "relations of care, empathy, equality and mutual respect," which she terms "peacebuilder masculinity."[71] The Army is gradually coming to the understanding that conceptualising toughness as inherently male and associated with qualities of aggression, emotional reticence, etc, excludes, or ignores, an entire spectrum of emotional and mental attributes that are as valuable, if not more, in armed conflict.

As the character of battlefields change and the Army is increasingly required to develop an "awareness of local and regional politics, law, human persuasion, behaviour and culture, supplemented by a broad range of experiences,"[72] the narrow idea of toughness that has been associated with the Army's emotional regime for the last hundred years is not just outdated, it is a liability. The importance of drawing on a much more developed range of emotions is surfacing in the Army's discourse on leadership. In *The Habit of Excellence*, an officially sanctioned treatise on leadership in the Army, Lt Col Langley Sharp outlines how emotional awareness, not only of those they command, but also of themselves, is essential for leaders in the Army. Good leaders "develop the empathy to see their leadership as others experience it [...] They are humble and willing to change."[73] Leaders are required not only to model the traditional values of "courage, respect or integrity" but are also expected to "be the communicator and translator of what these mean across different contexts, and to individuals with different outlooks."[74] Yet Sharp was required to defend the idea that the inclusion of attributes such as empathy, humility and respect would lead to a "softening" of leadership in the Army, suggesting that the translation of this approach into reality is still meeting with resistance.[75] In 2021, The British Army undertook a radical transformation of its structures and operations under the title "Future Soldier." The Army aims to "become more lethal, agile and expeditionary" and to be "an army equipped with the right culture and leadership to sustain our reputation and modern foundation."[76] But in order to transform effectively, the Army needs to find better ways of acknowledging that emotion – in commanders, soldiers and civilians – is one of the core elements of increasingly messy and complex operating environments. Until the Army finds some way of fully, and officially, accounting for the role played by emotion in conflicts of all kinds, it will only ever have a partial understanding of what conflict is, and how wars should be waged.

Similarly, it is easy to believe that it is 'common-sense' to think that rational structures and systems of organisation should be implemented to control and manage warfare and those who fight it. The idea of making a living from warfighting was an aspect of military life across the world long before the industrial era,[77] but as Chapter 1 and 2 made clear, war was conceived of, and organised, as 'work' at the same time as the battlefield became industrialised. It is only fairly recently, however, that historians of labour have begun examining the implications of conceiving of military life as work.[78] There are a range of 'jobs' advertised on the British Army's recruitment pages, of which only a few might be directly involved in fighting, but the core purpose of the Army is to fight, and the British Army describes its operational effectiveness through the concept of "Fighting Power."[79] One of the most fundamental aspects of 'work' in the Army is that soldiers need to be able and ready to kill, a skill not easily transferable into the civilian world of labour but rationalised in the structures that describe military roles through the language of corporate recruitment. The Infantry Soldier, according to the Ministry of Defence's recruitment website, is an "exciting, varied role" in which individuals will be prepared to "protect the nation, prevent conflict, fight the nation's enemies and deal with disaster at home or overseas." The bureaucratic systems organising the labour of warfighting are now so embedded that they seem reasonable, and the ideological and political issues associated with what soldiers might be asked to do are smoothed over in the process. I am not suggesting that we do not need armies, or that soldiers should not fight, but that by transforming warfighting into work, we have folded conflict and militarism into everyday practices and have therefore obscured, or made difficult, the possibility of critiquing why we might need to fight in the first place.

In addition to organisational structures, the development of reporting practices, of communication systems, of strategy and doctrine have all been designed to "impose order over chaos, to exert control where it most threatens to elude, and to find predictability in the midst of uncertainty."[80] Again, these might seem common-sense approaches to a complex and sometimes chaotic phenomenon, but we should be questioning what processing armed conflict through rational systems has facilitated. Recent British Army doctrine concedes that chaos is inevitable in conflict, "no matter how much information" there might be available, but it goes beyond attempting to impose order on chaos, however, by pointing out that chaos "presents opportunities for the bold to seize."[81] It acknowledges that violence "can result in bloodshed, destruction and human suffering" but argues for the effective application of violence "at the right time and place."[82] Horror, chaos, bloodshed and violence have always been part of warfare, but we should recognise that there is something terrible, in the true sense of the word, in rationalising their use as part of state-endorsed actions as appropriate and effective responses, and in conceptualising the roles played by soldiers as no different from any other kind of work. Exactly what constitutes the "right time and place" for the application of state-sanctioned violence is a difficult question that in the Twenty-first Century is becoming increasingly unclear, as battlefields become battlespaces with no clear temporal or spatial boundaries. We should be questioning far more rigorously what the rationalisation of war has allowed us to tolerate as a society in the past, and what it will allow us to accept in the future.

According to John Law there is a politics at work in the crafting of coherence from chaotic events.[83] The restrictions imposed by the structures of rational controls in both official reports and in academic arguments are of course useful. They have provided insights into the appalling scale and scope of global conflicts, but in the process, their cool calculations and reports of facts and figures have perhaps distracted us from being appalled. Processes both within and outside of the British Army that mobilise rationalist ideologies tend to repress or render invisible any measure or real acknowledgement of conflict's affective power, of the devasting impact of modern warfare on human and animal bodies, and on the globe we inhabit. If we do not at least acknowledge the processes that attempt to reduce war to a rational phenomenon in the documents that form the basis of the Army's operational procedures and that are central to the historiography of Britain's past and future conflicts, we run the risk of reinforcing them. Even worse, as we move into an uncertain future in which catastrophic climate change might increase the risk of conflict over resources, we run the risk of allowing such processes to obscure our understanding of what armed conflict really means for us and for the world we live in.

Notes

1 British Army doctrine distinguishes between the nature of conflict and its character. The nature of conflict involves the core principles of adversarial human interactions occurring within changing land environments. The character of conflict, however,

212 Conclusion

changes due to variations in the contexts in which those conflicts occur. British Army, Land Warfare Development Centre, *Land Operations*, Army Doctrine Publication AC 71940 (2017), 1.
2. Ministry of Defence (MoD), *Land Forces Standing Order No. 1120* (Second Revise), May 2009, 1.
3. MoD, *LFSO* 1120, 1.
4. MoD, *LFSO* 1120, 1.
5. Terry Cook, "Electronic Records, Paper Minds: The Revolution in Information Management and Archives in the Post-Custodial and Post-Modernist Era," *Archives and Manuscripts* 22, no. 1 (1994): Footnote 5, 321.
6. Cook, "Electronic Records," Footnote 5, 321, emphasis in original.
7. MoD, *LFSO* 1120, Enclosure 2, 7.
8. David Dery, "'Papereality' and Learning in Bureaucratic Organizations," *Administration and Society* 29, no. 6 (1998): 677–689.
9. Matt Bardo and Hannah O'Grady, "Did UK Special Forces Execute Unarmed Civilians?," *BBC Panorama*, 1 August 2020.
10. Bardo and O'Grady, 2020. For a summary of the ICC Prosecutor's report into this case, as well as allegations levelled by the BBC of a cover-up, see Patrick Butchard, "UK War Crimes in Iraq: The ICC Prosecutor's Report," House of Commons Library, *Insight*, 15 January 2021.
11. MoD, *LFSO* 1120, Enclosure 2, 3.
12. MoD, *LFSO* 1120, Enclosure 2, 4.
13. MoD, *LFSO* 1120, Enclosure 2, 4.
14. MoD, *LFSO* 1120, Enclosure 2, 4.
15. MoD, *LFSO* 1120, Enclosure 2, 5.
16. General Staff, *Field Service Regulations, Part II: Organisation and Administration*, 1909 (London: HMSO, Reprinted, with Amendments, 1913), 176.
17. MoD, *LFSO* 1120, Enclosure 2, 5.
18. David Holbrook, *Flesh Wounds* (1966, Gloucestershire: Spellmount Limited, 2017), 219.
19. Geoff Nunberg, "After Years of Restraint, a Linguist says 'Yes!' to the Exclamation Point," *Npr.org*. 13 June 2017.
20. Michel De Certeau, *The Practice of Everyday Life*, trans. Steven Rendell (Berkeley: University of California Press, 1984), 144.
21. Francis X. Blouin and William G. Rosenberg, *Processing the Past: Contesting Authorities in History and the Archives* (Online Edition, Oxford Academic Online, 2011), 154.
22. Susan Brayne, Karen Levy and Bryce Newell, "Visual Data and the Law," *Law & Social Inquiry* 43, no. 4 (2018): 1151.
23. Brayne, Levy and Newell, "Visual Data," 1149.
24. Quoted in Steven Morris, "Judges Quash UK Marine Alexander Blackman's Murder Conviction," *The Guardian*, 15 March 2017.
25. The Right Honourable Sir William Gage, *The Report of the Baha Mousa Inquiry*, Volume 1, HC 1452-1 (London: The Stationery Office, 2011), 139–142.
26. MoD, *LFSO* 1120, 1.
27. Andrew Hoskins, "Digital Records Take Something Precious from Military History," *The Conversation*, 4 February 2015. https://theconversation.com/digital-records-take-something-precious-from-military-history-36328.
28. Hoskins, "Digital Records."
29. MoD *LFSO* 1120, 6.
30. Robert Foley, "Learning War's Lessons: The German Army and the Battle of the Somme 1916," *Journal of Military History* 75 (2011), 473.
31. General Headquarters, American Expeditionary Forces, General Orders, no. 196, 5 November, 1918 (Washington D.C.: U.S. Army Center of Military History, 1992): 516–519.

32 General Headquarters, AEF, General Orders no. 196, 516.
33 For a discussion of lessons learned by the American Expeditionary Forces (1997), see Kenneth Hamburger, *Learning Lessons in the American Expeditionary Forces* (United States Army Center of Military History, 1997). For a similar analysis of the German Army and for investigations into the development of doctrine and the use of reporting see Christian Stachelbeck, "'Lessons learned' in WWI: The German Army, Vimy Ridge and the Elastic Defence in Depth in 1917," *Journal of Military and Strategic Studies* 18, no. 2 (2017): 118–135; Tony Cowan, "The Introduction of New German Defensive Tactics in 1916–1917," *British Journal for Military History* 5, no. 2 (2019): 81–99; Foley, "Learning War's Lessons".
34 Christopher Lawrence, "U.S. Army Record Keeping," (blog), Dupuy Institute, 6 February 2017.
35 Christopher Lawrence, *War by Numbers: Understanding Conventional Combat* (University of Nebraska Press, 2017), 146.
36 Joint Staff Secretariat Information Management Division, *Assessment of United States Forces – Iraq Records and Records Management Activities*, White Paper for the DOD CIO, 5.
37 Richard W. Stewart, "Army Operational Records, Data Collection, and Readiness" (AAMH-ZC, February 20, 2009), 5.
38 Conrad Crane qtd in ProPublica, "Lost to History: Missing War Records Complicate Benefit Claims by Afghanistan Veterans," *ProPublica*, 9 November 2012.
39 Joint Staff Secretariat Information Management Division, *Assessment*, 2.
40 Joint Staff Secretariat Information Management Division, *Assessment*, 2.
41 Forward to MoD, *Land Operations*, Army Doctrine Publication AC 71940 (Warminster, Land Warfare Development Centre, 2017), 3.
42 Jon Lindsay, *Information Technology and Military Power* (Itaca NY: Cornell Scholarship online, 2021), 7.
43 Elizabeth Hunt, Simon Wessely, Norman Jones, Roberto J. Rona and Neil Greenberg, "The Mental Health of the UK Armed Forces: Where Facts meet Fiction," *European Journal of Psychotraumatology* 5, no. 1 (2014).
44 Jamie Hacker Hughes and Simon Wessely, "The MoD PTSD Decision: a Psychiatric Perspective," *Occupational Health Review* 122 (July/August 2006): 22.
45 Hacker Hughes and Wessely, "The MoD PTSD Decision," 22.
46 Hacker Hughes and Wessely, "The MoD PTSD Decision," 21.
47 Hacker Hughes and Wessely, "The MoD PTSD Decision," 25.
48 Hacker Hughes and Wessely, "The MoD PTSD Decision," 25.
49 Clare Dyer and Sarah Boseley, "War Veterans Lose Trauma Claim Case," *The Guardian*, 22 May 2003.
50 Hacker Hughes and Wessely, "The MoD PTSD Decision," 23.
51 Hacker Hughes and Wessely, "The MoD PTSD Decision," 23.
52 BBC, "Ex Soldier Wins Stress Damages," *BBC News Channel*, 29 July 2005.
53 A response to a Freedom of Information Request from 2018 revealed that from April to March 2017, the Army had received a total of 1,441 claims for PTSD through the AFCS, for which it paid out around £14 million, and had dealt with 27 claims in common law, for which it had paid out a total of £5.46 million in compensation. Ministry of Defence, Defence Statistics (Health) Ref: FOI2018/12175 (28 October 2018).
54 Lord Dennis Stevenson and Paul Farmer, *Thriving at Work: A Review of Mental Health and Employers* (Department for Work and Pensions and Department of Health and Social Care, 26 October 2017), 5.
55 Ministry of Defence, *People Mental Health and Wellbeing Strategy 2017–2022*, 22 June 2022, 30.
56 Ministry of Defence, *People*, 28.

214   Conclusion

57 Ministry of Defence and Leo Docherty MP, "Mandatory Annual Mental Health Training Launched Across the Armed Forces," Gov.UK, Defence and Armed Forces (10 October 2021).
58 Harriet Gray, "The Trauma Risk Management Approach to Post-Traumatic Stress Disorder in the British Military: Masculinity, Biopolitics and Depoliticisation," *Feminist Review* III, no. 1 (2015): 117.
59 Gray, "The Trauma Risk," 119–120.
60 Caroline Wyatt, "War Veterans 'Don't Need to Cope Alone,'" *BBC News*, Health, 10 October 2011.
61 Jessica Del Pozo, "The Dark Side of Resilience," (blog) *Psychology Today*, 27 November 2021. https://www.psychologytoday.com/us/blog/being-awake-better/202111/the-dark-side-resilience.
62 Charles Addison, *On Dusty Plains: Memoirs of a Rifleman in Afghanistan* (Independently Published, 2021), 75.
63 Quoted in Forces.net, "Army is 'No Place for Touchy Feely Political Correctness,'" News, 25 January 2018.
64 Matthew Weaver, "Army Accused of Political Correctness in Recruitment Campaign," *The Guardian*, 10 January 2018.
65 Jennifer Mathers, "The British Army's Belonging Campaign Finally Recognises that Masculinity has Changed," *The Conversation*, 18 January 2018. https://theconversation.com/the-british-armys-belonging-campaign-finally-recognises-that-masculinity-has-changed-90259.
66 Hacker Hughes and Wessely, "The MoD PTSD Decision," 23.
67 Antonio Gramsci, *Selections From the Prison Notebooks*, eds. Quentin Hoare and Geoffrey Nowell Smith (London: Lawrence & Wishart, 1971), 769.
68 Robert Eccleshall, "Ideology as Commonsense," *Radical Philosophy* RP025 (Summer 1980): 3. https://www.radicalphilosophyarchive.com/commentary/ideology-as-commonsense.
69 For a sample of some of the widespread discussions on the complex relationship between masculinity and military identities, see Paul Higate, *Military Masculinities: Identity and the State* (London: Praeger 2003);
    Ramon Hinojosa, "Doing Hegemony: Military, Men and Constructing a Hegemonic Masculinity," *The Journal of Men's Studies* 18, no. 2 (2010): 179–194; Claire Duncanson, *Forces for Good?: Military Masculinities and Peacebuilding in Afghanistan and Iraq* (Basingstoke: Palgrave Macmillan, 2013); Rebecca Tapscott, "Militarized Masculinity and the Paradox of Restraint: Mechanisms of Social Control Under Modern Authoritarianism," *International Affairs* 96, no. 6 (2020): 1565–1584.
70 Duncanson, *Forces for Good*, 144.
71 Duncanson, *Forces for Good*, 161.
72 Ministry of Defence, "Strategic Trends Programme: Future Operating Environment 2035," First Edition (2015): 31.
73 Langley Sharp, Lieutenant Colonel, *The Habit of Excellence: Why British Army Leadership Works* (London: Penguin Business, 2021), 85.
74 Sharp, *The Habit*, 232.
75 Marco Giannangeli, "British Army gets Emotional to Make 'Generation Z' Fit to Fight," *Express*, 19 September, 2021.
76 Ministry of Defence, British Army, *Future Soldier Guide*, 25 November 2021.
77 Erik-Jan Zürcher, ed., *Fighting for a Living: A Comparative Study of Military Labour 1500–2000* (Amsterdam University Press, 2013).
78 See, for example, see the special edition on "Labor and the Military" in *International Labor and Working-Class History* 2011 and Samuel Fury Childs Daly, "War as Work: Labor and Soldiering in History," *International Labor and Working-Class History* (2022): 1-6, for a brief overview of some of the literature on this topic.
79 MoD, *Land Operations*.

80 Antoine Bousquet, *The Scientific Way of Warfare: Order and Chaos on the Battlefields of Modernity* (London: Hurst Publishers, 2009), 10.
81 MoD, *Land Operations*, 1–2.
82 MoD, *Land Operations*, 1–2.
83 John Law, *After Method: Mess in Social Science Research* (New York: Routledge, 2004), 93.

Bibliography

Primary material: The National Archives (TNA), Kew

Branches and Services: Director of Printing and Stationery Service. WO95-81-4.
Cabinet Office and Predecessors: Historical Section: Registered Files (HS and other Series). CAB103.
Committee on the Work of Psychologists and Psychiatrists in the Services. CAB21/914.
D.D.M.S. Army Group. WO177/316.
Morale of the Army. WO277/16. TNA. Kew.
Prideaux, Frances et al. "Neurosis in War Time." 3 July, 1939. PIN15/2401. TNA. Kew.
Psychiatric Service in Operational Theatres1945, WO32/1150. TNA. Kew.
Psychological Experiments. WO199/799. TNA. Kew.
War Office Meetings. WO163-151. TNA. Kew.
War Office Morale Committee: Reports. WO32/15772. TNA. Kew.
War Office. *Instructors' Handbook on Fieldcraft and Battle Drill.* 1942.
War Office. *First World War and Army of Occupation War Diaries.* 1914–1922. WO 95.
War Office. *War Diaries, Second World War.* 1939–1946. WO166-179.

Primary material (other)

British Army. Land Warfare Development Centre. *Land Operations.* Army Doctrine PublicationAC 71940, 2017.
Gage, William(The Right Honourable Sir). *The Report of the Baha Mousa Inquiry.* Volume 1. HC 1452-1451. London: The Stationery Office, 2011.
General Headquarters. American Expeditionary Forces. General Orders. No. 196. (Washington, D.C.: U.S. Army Center of Military History, 1992). https://history.army.mil/html/books/023/23-22/CMH_Pub_23-22.pdf.
General Staff. *Field Service Regulations, Part I: Operations.* 1909. London, HMSO, Reprinted, with Amendments, 1913.
General Staff. *Field Service Regulations, Part II: Organisation and Administration.* 1909. London, HMSO, Reprinted, with Amendments, 1913.
General Staff. *Field Service Regulations Vol. I: Organization and Administration.* London: HMSO, 1930, Reprinted with Amendments, 1939.
General Staff. *Field Service Regulations Vol. II: Operations – General.* London: HMSO, 1935.
General Staff. War Office. *Training and Manoeuvre Regulations.* London: HMSO, 1913.

Joint Staff Secretariat Information Management Division. *Assessment of United States Forces – Iraq Records and Records Management Activities*. White Paper for the DOD CIO. https://www.esd.whs.mil/Portals/54/Documents/FOID/Reading%20Room/Other/12-F-0679_Assessment_of_United_States_Forces-Iraq_Records_and_Record_Management_Activities.pdf.

Ministry of Defence. Land Forces Standing Order No 1120 (Second Revise). May2009. http://webarchive.nationalarchives.gov.uk/20120215220454/http://www.bahamousainquiry.org/linkedfiles/baha_mousa/module_4/mod_4_witness_statem/exhibit_kedb/miv003708.pdf.

Ministry of Defence. *Land Operations*. Army Doctrine Publication AC 71940. Warminster, Land Warfare Development Centre, 2017. https://assets.publishing.service.gov.uk/government/uploads/system/uploads/attachment_data/file/605298/Army_Field_Manual__AFM__A5_Master_ADP_Interactive_Gov_Web.pdf.

Ministry of Defence. *Defence People Mental Health and Wellbeing Strategy 2017–2022*. 22 June, 2022. https://assets.publishing.service.gov.uk/government/uploads/system/uploads/attachment_data/file/689978/20170713-MHW_Strategy_SCREEN.pdf.

Ministry of Defence. Defence Statistics (Health). Ref: FOI2018/12175 (28 October, 2018). https://assets.publishing.service.gov.uk/government/uploads/system/uploads/attachment_data/file/767112/12175.pdf.

Ministry of Defence. *Future Soldier Guide*. 25 November, 2021. https://www.gov.uk/government/publications/future-soldier-transforming-the-british-army.

Ministry of Defence and Leo Docherty MP. "Mandatory Annual Mental Health Training Launched Across the Armed Forces." Gov.UK. Defence and Armed Forces (10 October, 2021). https://www.gov.uk/government/news/mandatory-annual-mental-health-training-launched-across-the-armed-forces.

Ministry of Defence. "Strategic Trends Programme: Future Operating Environment 2035." First Edition. 2015. https://www.gov.uk/government/publications/future-operating-environment-2035.

Office of War Information. Advance Release for Tuesday Morning Papers. July 28, 1942. X1232. OWI 152.

Pitman & Sons. *A Manual of the Typewriter: A Practical Guide to Commercial, Literary, Legal, Dramatic and all Classes of Typewriting Work*. London, 1893.

Public Record Office Reports. Second Report of the Deputy Keeper of Public Records, vol. 32, 1841.

Public Record Office Reports. Fourth Report of the Deputy Keeper of Public Records, vol. 47, 28 February, 1843, 474.

Public Record Office Reports. Fifth Report of the Deputy Keeper of the Public Records, vol. 41, 1844, 553.

Public Record Office Reports. Tenth Annual Report of the Keeper of Public Records on the Work of the Public Record Office, vol. 45, 1968–68, 370.

Public Record Office Reports. Thirteenth Report of the Deputy Keeper of the Public Records, Appendix, vol. 21, no. 1498, 1852.

Public Record Office Reports. Thirtieth Report of the Deputy Keeper of the Public Records, vol. 26, 1868–69, 4165.

Public Record Office Reports. Thirty-First Annual Report of the Keeper of Public Records, 20th Century House of Commons Sessional Papers, 1989, HC 635.

Public Record Office Reports. Thirty-Sixth Annual Report of the Deputy Keeper of the Public Records, vol. 65, 1875, C.—1301.

Public Record Office Reports. Fortieth Annual Report of the Keeper of Public Records, 20th Century House of Commons Sessional Papers, 1998, HC 615.

Public Record Office Reports. Forty-First Annual Report of the Deputy Keeper of the Public Records, vol. 38, 1880, C.2658.
Public Record Office Reports. Fifty-fourth Annual Report of the Deputy Keeper of the Public Records, vol. 48, 1893, C.7079.
Public Record Office Reports. Fifty-Eighth Annual Report of the Deputy Keeper of the Public Records, vol. 48, 1897, C.8543.
Public Record Office Reports. Sixty-Second Annual Report of the Deputy Keeper of the Public Records, vol. 33, 1901, Cd.617.
The National Archives. *Annual Report and Accounts of The National Archives 2018–19*. HC 2401. https://cdn.nationalarchives.gov.uk/documents/the-national-archives-annual-report-and-accounts-2018-19.pdf.
The National Archives. *Archives for Everyone 2019–2023*. https://www.nationalarchives.gov.uk/about/our-role/plans-policies-performance-and-projects/our-plans/archives-for-everyone.
The National Archives. *Archives for the 21st Century in Action: Refreshed, 2012–2015*. https://silo.tips/download/archives-for-the-21st-century-in-action-refreshed.
The National Archives. *Archives Inspire: The National Archives Plans and Priorities 2015–19*. https://cdn.nationalarchives.gov.uk/documents/archives-inspire-2015-19.pdf.
The National Archives. "Archives Unlocked: Releasing the Potential: Brochure 2017." https://cdn.nationalarchives.gov.uk/documents/archives/Archives-Unlocked-Brochure.pdf.
The National Archives. "Digital Cataloguing Practices at The National Archives." March2017. https://cdn.nationalarchives.gov.uk/documents/digital-cataloguing-practices-march-2017.pdf.
The National Archives. "How to Look for Records of British Army War Diaries 1914–1922." https://www.nationalarchives.gov.uk/help-with-your-research/research-guides/british-army-war-diaries-1914-1922.
Southborough et al. (The Right Honourable Lord). *Report of the War Office Committee of Enquiry into 'Shell-Shock.'* London, HMSO, 1922.
Stevenson (Lord) Dennis and Paul Farmer. "Thriving at Work: A Review of Mental Health and Employers." Department for Work and Pensions and Department of Health and Social Care. 26 October, 2017. https://www.gov.uk/government/publications/thriving-at-work-a-review-of-mental-health-and-employers.
Stewart, Richard. "Army Operational Records, Data Collection, and Readiness." AAMH-ZC, 20 February, 2009. http://www.propublica.org/documents/item/510007-stewart-paper and http://s3.documentcloud.org/documents/510007/stewart-paper.pdf.

Secondary sources

Addison, Charles. *On Dusty Plains: Memoirs of a Rifleman in Afghanistan*. Independently Published, 2021.
Agostinho, Daniela, Sovleig Gade, Nanna Bonde Thystrup, and Kristin Veel. "Introduction: Materialities of War, Digital Archiving, and Artistic Engagements." In *(W) Archives: Archival Imaginaries, War, and Contemporary Art*. Edited by Daniela Agostinho, Sovleig Gade, Nanna Bonde Thystrup, and Kristin Veel. London: Stenberg Press, 2021. xi–xxxi.
Åhäll, Linda and Thomas Gregory. "Introduction: Mapping Emotions, Politics and War." In *Emotions, Politics and War*. Edited by Linda Åhäll and Thomas Gregory. London and New York: Routledge, 2016. 1–14.

Ahrenfeldt, Robert. *Psychiatry in the British Army in the Second World War*. New York: Routledge, 1958.
Allen, Emma. "Our Website: A Design Journey." (Blog) TNA, 16 September, 2013, https://blog.nationalarchives.gov.uk/our-website-a-design-journey.
Allport, Alan. *Browned Off and Bloody-Minded: The British Soldier Goes to War 1939–1945*. New Haven, CT: Yale University Press, 2015.
Anderson, Luvell and Ernie Lepore. "Slurring Words." *Noûs* 47, no. 1 (2013): 25–48. doi:10.1111/j.1468-0068.2010.00820.x.
Angie, Amanda D., Shane Connelly, Ethan P. Waples and Vykinta Kligyte. "The Influence of Discrete Emotions on Judgement and Decision-Making: A Meta-Analytic Review." *Cognition and Emotion* 25, no. 8 (2011): 1393–1422. doi:10.1080/02699931.2010.550751.
Ashbrook, Harry. "Men Learn to Kill without 'Hate.'" *Sunday Mirror*. Sunday Pictorial. 24 May, 1942. British Newspaper Archive.
Bailey, Jonathan. "The First World War and the Birth of the Modern Style of Warfare." In *The Dynamics of Military Revolution 1300–2050*. Edited by MacGregor Knox and Williamson Murray. Cambridge: Cambridge University Press, 2001. 132–153.
Bardo, Matt and Hannah O'Grady. "Did UK Special Forces Execute Unarmed Civilians?" *BBC Panorama*. 1 August, 2020. https://www.bbc.co.uk/news/uk-53597137.
Baron, Alexander. *From the City, From the Plough*. London: Jonathan Cape, 1948.
Bazerman, Charles. "Introduction." In *Handbook of Research on Writing: History, Society, School, Individual, Text*. Edited by Charles Bazerman. New York: Routledge, 2013. 1–4.
BBC. "Ex Soldier Wins Stress Damages." *BBC News Channel*. 29 July, 2005. http://news.bbc.co.uk/1/hi/wales/4725455.stm.
Beaumont, Roger. *War, Chaos and History*. Westport CT: Praeger, 1994.
Beckett, Ian, Timothy Bowman and Mark Connelly. *The British Army and the First World War*. Cambridge: Cambridge University Press, 2017.
Beeching, Wilfred A. *The Century of the Typewriter*. Bournemouth: British Typewriter Museum Publishing, 1974.
Beevor, Antony. *D-Day: The Battle for Normandy*. London: Random House, 2009.
Bell, Amy. "Landscapes of Fear: Wartime London, 1939–1945." *Journal of British Studies* 48, no. 1 (2009): 153–175. doi:10.1086/592386.
Beniger, James. *The Control Revolution: Technological and Economic Origins of the Information Society*. Cambridge MA: Harvard University Press, 1986.
Bird, Cindy. "How I Stopped Dreading and Learned to Love Transcription." *Qualitative Inquiry* 11, no. 2 (2005): 226–248. doi:10.1177/1077800404273413.
Bishop, Alan and Mark Bostridge, editors. *Letters from a Lost Generation: First World War Letters of Vera Brittain and Four Friends: Roland Leighton, Edward Brittain, Victor Richardson, Geoffrey Thurlow*. London: Abacus, 2004.
Blouin Jr., Francis X., and William G. Rosenberg. *Processing the Past: Contesting Authorities in History and the Archives*. Online edition, Oxford Academic, 2011. doi:10.1093/acprof:oso/9780199740543.001.0001.
Bogacz, Ted. "War Neurosis and Cultural Change in England, 1914–22: The Work of the Committee of Enquiry into 'Shell-Shock.'" *Journal of Contemporary History* 24, no. 2 (1989): 227–256.
Bolter, Jay David. *Writing Space: Computers, Hypertext, and the Remediation of Print*. 2nd Ed. Mahwah, NJ: Lawrence Erlbaum Associates, 2000.
Bolter, Jay David and Grusin, Richard. *Remediation: Understanding New Media.*. Cambridge, MA: MIT Press, 1999.

Bond, Brian. *British Military Policy Between the Two World Wars*. Oxford: Clarendon Press, 1980.
Bourke, Joanna. *Dismembering the Male: Men's Bodies, Britain and the Great War*. London: Reaktion Books, 1996.
Bourke, Joanna. "The Emotions in War: Fear and the British and American Military, 1914–45." *Historical Research* 74, no. 185 (2001): 314–330.
Bourke, Joanna. *An Intimate History of Killing: Face-to-Face Killing in Twentieth Century Warfare*. London: Granta Books, 2000.
Bourne, John. "The British Working Man in Arms." In *Facing Armageddon: The First World War Experience*. Edited by Hugh Cecil and Peter Liddle. London: Pen and Sword Select, 1996. 336–352.
Bousquet, Antoine. *The Scientific Way of Warfare: Order and Chaos on the Battlefields of Modernity*. London: Hurst Publishers, 2009.
Bowlby, Alex. *Recollections of Rifleman Bowlby, Italy, 1944*. London: Leo Cooper, 1969.
Bowman, Timothy. *The Edwardian Army: Recruiting, Training, and Deploying the British Army, 1902–1914*. Oxford: Oxford University Press, 2012.
Brayne, Susan, Karen Levy and Bryce Newell. "Visual Data and the Law." *Law & Social Inquiry* 43, no. 4 (2018): 1149–1163. doi:10.1111/lsi.12373.
A British Officer. "The Literature of the South African War, 1899–1902." *The American Historical Review* 12, no. 2 (January1907): 299–321.
Broad, Roger. *The Radical General: Sir Ronald Adam and Britain's New Model Army*. Stroud: Spellmount, 2013.
Brookes, Barbara and James Dunk. "Introduction: Bureaucracy, Archive Files, and the Making of Knowledge." *Rethinking History* 22, no. 3 (2018): 281–288.
Butchard, Patrick. "UK War Crimes in Iraq: The ICC Prosecutor's Report." House of Commons Library. *Insight*. 15 January, 2021. https://commonslibrary.parliament.uk/uk-war-crimes-in-iraq-the-icc-prosecutors-report.
Cantwell, John. *The Public Record Office, 1838–1958*. London: HMSO, 1991.
Caplan, Paul. "London 2012: Distributed Imag(in)ings and Exploiting Protocol." *Journal of Media and Communication* 2, no. 2 (September 2010): 24–39.
Caplan, Paul. "What is a JPEG? The Invisible Object You See Every Day." *The Atlantic*. 24 September, 2013. https://www.theatlantic.com/technology/archive/2013/09/what-is-a-jpeg-the-invisible-object-you-see-every-day/279954.
Cassiodorus. *Institutiones*. Translated by James W. Halpern and Barbara Halpern. Undated. https://faculty.georgetown.edu/jod/inst-trans.html.
Chesher, Chris. "Neither Gaze nor Glance, but Glaze: Relating to Console Game Screens." *Scan Journal* 4, no. 2 (2007). http://scan.net.au/scan/journal/print.php?j_id=11&journal_id=19.
Chen, Anna. "In One's Own Hand: Seeing Manuscripts in a Digital Age." *DHQ: Digital Humanities Quarterly* 6, no. 2 (2012). http://www.digitalhumanities.org/dhq/vol/6/2/000138/000138.html.
Clark, Michael J. "The Rejection of Psychological Approaches to Mental Disorder in Late Nineteenth-Century British Psychiatry." In *Madhouses, Mad-Doctors, and Madmen*. Edited by Andrew Scull. Philadelphia: University of Pennsylvania Press, 1981. 271–312.
Cockburn, James. "Teaching Soldiers to Hate: Moderator's Protest." *Aberdeen Journal*. 5 May, 1942. Editorial. British Library Newspapers. link.gale.com/apps/doc/JE3229241050/BNCN?u=exeter&sid=bookmark-BNCN&xid=b743dfcd, accessed 4 November, 2021.

Collini, Stefan. "The Idea of 'Character' in Victorian Political Thought." *Transactions of the Royal Historical Society* 35 (1985): 29–50. https://www.jstor.org/stable/3679175.

Cook, Terry. "Electronic Records, Paper Minds: The Revolution in Information Management and Archives in the Post-Custodial and Post-Modernist Era." *Archives and Manuscripts* 22, no. 1 (1994): 300–328. https://publications.archivists.org.au/index.php/asa/article/view/8433.

Cook, Terry. "What Is Past Is Prologue: A History of Archival Ideas Since 1898, and the Future Paradigm Shift." *Archivaria* 43 (February1997): 17–63. https://archivaria.ca/index.php/archivaria/article/view/12175.

Cooper, Christine, Jonathan Tweedie, Jane Andrew and Max Baker. "From 'Business-Like' to Businesses: Agencification, Corporatization, and Civil Service Reform under the Thatcher Administration." *Public Administration* 100 (2022): 193–215. doi:10.1111/padm.12732.

Copp, Terry and Bill McAndrew. *Battle Exhaustion: Soldiers and Psychiatrists in the Canadian Army, 1939–1945*. Montreal: McGill-Queen's University Press, 1990.

Cowan, Tony. "The Introduction of New German Defensive Tactics in 1916–1917." *British Journal for Military History* 5, no. 2 (2019): 81–99. ISSN: 2057-0422.

Craig, Barbara. "What are the Clients? Who are the Products? The Future of Archival Public Services in Perspective." *Archivaria* 31 (1990): 135–141.

Craig, Norman. *The Broken Plume: A Platoon Commander's Story, 1940–45*. London: Imperial War Museum, 1982.

Crouth, Jason and Peter Leese, editors. *Traumatic Memories of the Second World War and After*. Basingstoke: Palgrave Macmillan, 2016.

Daily Express. "War 'Hate' Training Attacked." *Daily Express*. 22 May, 1942. www.historic-newspapers.co.uk.

Dale, Margaret. "Learning Organisations." In *Managing Learning*. Edited by Christopher Mabey and Paul Iles. London: Thomson Learning, 1994. 22–33.

Daily, Samuel Fury Childs. "War as Work: Labor and Soldiering in History." *International Labor and Working-Class History* (2022): 1-6. doi:10.1017/S0147547922000035.

Darwin, Charles. *The Expression of the Emotions in Man and Animals*. London: John Murray, 1872.

Dawson, Graham. *Soldier Heroes: British Adventure, Empire and the Imagining of Masculinities*. London and New York: Routledge, 1994.

Dawson, John D'arcy. "Getting Ready for the Day." *Aberdeen Journal*. 20 October, 1942. British Library Newspapers, link.gale.com/apps/doc/JA3238644210/BNCN?u=exeter&sid=bookmark-BNCN&xid=c2d874f5.

Day, Ronald. *The Modern Invention of Information: Discourse, History and Power*. Southern Illinois University Press, 2001.

De Certeau, Michel. *The Practice of Everyday Life*. Translated by Steven Rendell. Berkeley: University of California Press, 1984.

Del Pozo, Jessica. "The Dark Side of Resilience." *Psychology Today*. 27 November, 2021. https://www.psychologytoday.com/us/blog/being-awake-better/202111/the-dark-side-resilience.

Delaney, Douglas E., Mark Frost, and Andrew L. Brown, editors. *Manpower and the Armies of the British Empire in the Two World Wars*. Ithaca, New York: Cornell University Press, 2021. http://www.jstor.org/stable/10.7591/j.ctv16kkwzj.

Derrida, Jacques. "Archive Fever: A Freudian Impression." *Diacritics* 25, no. 2 (Summer, 1995): 9–63.

Dery, David. "'Papereality' and Learning in Bureaucratic Organizations." *Administration and Society* 29, no. 6 (1998): 677–689.

DeVere Brody, Jennifer. *Punctuation: Art, Politics, and Play*. Durham and London: Duke University Press, 2008.

Diaconita, Mihai. "New Feedback Form for Our Research Guides." (Blog) TNA: Behind the Scenes, Technology and Innovation, 11 January, 2019. https://blog.nationalarchives.gov.uk/feedback-form-research-guides.

Dickens, Charles. "The Adventures of the Public Records." *Household Words* 1, no. 17 (July1850): 396–399.

Dixon, Thomas. *From Passions to Emotions: The Creation of a Secular Psychological Category*. Cambridge: Cambridge University Press, 2003.

Dixon, Thomas. *Weeping Brittania: Portrait of a Nation in Tears*. Oxford: Oxford University Press, 2015.

Donaldson, Peter. *Remembering the South African War: Britain and the Memory of the Anglo-Boer War, from 1899 to the Present*. Liverpool: Liverpool University Press, 2013.

Downes, Stephanie, Andrew Lynch and Katrina O'Loughlin. "Introduction – War as Emotion: Cultural Fields of Conflict and Feeling." In *Emotions and War: Medieval to Romantic Literature*. Edited by Stephanie Downes, Andrew Lynch and Katrina O'Loughlin. New York: Palgrave Macmillan, 2015. 1–23.

Doyle, Peter. "'Kitchener's Mob': Myth and Reality in Raising the New Army, 1914–15." In *Redcoats to Tommies: The Experience of the British Soldier from the Eighteenth Century*. Edited by Kevin Linch and Matthew Lord. Woodbridge: Boydell & Brewer, 2021. 58–82.

Dressler, Virginia. "Archive as Medium." *Preservation, Digital Technology & Culture* 47, no. 2 (2018): 45–53. doi:10.1515/pdtc-2018-0002.

Duff, Wendy and Catherine Johnson. "Accidentally Found on Purpose: Information-Seeking Behavior of Historians in Archives." *Information, Community, Policy* 72, no. 4 (2002): 472–496. JSTOR. http://www.jstor.org/stable/40039793.

Duff, Wendy and Verne Harris. "Stories and Names: Archival Description as Narrating Records and Constructing Meanings." *Archival Science* 2 (2002): 263–285. doi:10.1007/BF02435625.

Duffy, Ellie. "National Archives in London, UK by AOC." *Architectural Review*. 17 March, 2022. https://www.architectural-review.com/awards/w-awards/national-archives-in-london-uk-by-aoc.

Dundee Courier. "'Viewyness' in War-Time." *Dundee Courier and Advertiser*. 7 May, 1942. British Library Newspapers, link.gale.com/apps/doc/JE3229241212/BNCN?u=exeter&sid=bookmark-BNCN&xid=1dc0fe76.

Dyer, Clare and Sarah Boseley. "War Veterans Lose Trauma Claim Case." *The Guardian*. 22 May, 2003. https://www.theguardian.com/society/2003/may/22/themilitary.publichealth.

Eccleshall, Robert. "Ideology as Commonsense." *Radical Philosophy* RP025 (Summer 1980): 2–3. https://www.radicalphilosophyarchive.com/commentary/ideology-as-commonsense.

The Economist. "Typewriters." *The Economist*. 12 June, 1943.

Ede, Jeffery. "The Public Record Office and its Users." *Archives* 8, no. 40 (1968): 185–192.

Edmonds, Brigadier-General SirJames E. *History of the Great War: Military Operations in France and Belgium 1915*, Vol. ii. London: Macmillan and Co. Limited, 1936.

Edmonds, Brigadier-General SirJames E. *Military Operations in France and Belgium 1918*. London: Macmillan and Co. Limited, 1935.

Edwards, Jane and Martin Lampert, editors. *Talking Data: Transcription and Coding in Discourse Research*. Hillsdale, NJ: Lawrence Erlbaum, 1993.

Elkins, Caroline. "Looking beyond Mau Mau: Archiving Violence in the Era of Decolonization." *The American Historical Review* 120, no. 3 (2015): 852–868. *JSTOR*, https://www.jstor.org/stable/26577260, accessed 10 July, 2022.

Emerson, Lori. *Reading Writing Interfaces: From the Digital to the Bookbound*. Minneapolis, MN: University of Minnesota Press, 2014.

Empire. Typewriter advert. *The Economist*. 18 December, 1897.

Empire. Typewriter advert. *The Times*. 1 April, 1943.

Ericson, Timothy. "'Preoccupied with our own Gardens': Outreach and Archivists." *Archivaria* 31. (1990): 114–121.

Ernst, Wolfgang. "Archives in Transition: Dynamic Media Memories." In *Digital Memory and the Archive*. Edited by Jussi Parikka. Minneapolis: University of Minnesota Press, 2012. 95–101.

Evans, Tim and Ray Moore, "The Use of PDF/A in Digital Archives: A Case Study from Archaeology," *International Journal of Digital Curation* 9, no. 2 (2014): 132–138. doi:10.2218/ijdc.v9i2.267.

Farge, Arlette. *The Allure of the Archives*. Translated by Thomas Scott-Railton. Originally published as *Le Goût de l'archive*, Editions du Seuil, 1989. New Haven: Yale University Press, 2013.

Federico, Annette. *Engagements with Close Reading*. New York: Routledge, 2016.

Fineman, Stephen. "Emotions and Organisational Control." In *Emotions at Work: Theory, Research and Applications for Management*. Edited by Roy Payne and Carly Cooper. Chichester: Wiley & Sons, 2001. 219–237.

Foley, Robert. "Learning War's Lessons: The German Army and the Battle of the Somme 1916." *Journal of Military History* 75 (2011): 471–504.

Folsom, Ed. "Database as Genre: The Epic Transformation of Archives." *PMLA: Publications of the Modern Language Association of America* 122, no. 5 (October 2007): 1571–1579.

Forces.net. "*Army is 'No Place for Touchy Feely Political Correctness*" News. 25 January, 2018. https://www.forces.net/news/army-no-place-touchy-feely-political-correctness.

Foucault, Michel. *Society Must be Defended: Lectures at the Collége de France, 1975–76*. English Series editor Arnold I. Davidson. Translated by David Macey. New York: Picador, 2003.

Fowler, H.W. *A Dictionary of Modern English Usage*. London: Oxford University Press, 1926.

Fox, Aimée. *Learning to Fight: Military Innovation and Change in the British Army, 1914–1918*. Cambridge: Cambridge University Press, 2017.

Fraser, David. *And We Shall Shock Them: The British Army in the Second World War*. London: Cassell & Co, 1983.

French, David. "Doctrine and Organization in the British Army, 1919–193." *The Historical Journal* 44, no. 2 (2001): 497–515. *JSTOR*. http://www.jstor.org/stable/3133617.

French, David. *Military Identities: The Regimental System, the British Army, and the British People c.1870–2000*. Oxford: Oxford University Press, 2005.

French, David. *Raising Churchill's Army: The British Army and the War against Germany 1919–1945*. Oxford: Oxford University Press, 2001.

French, David. "Sir James Edmonds and the Official History: France and Belgium." In *The First World War and British Military History*. Edited by Brian Bond. Oxford: Oxford University Press, 1991. 69–86.

Fuller, J.F.C. (Colonel). *The Foundations of the Science of War*. London: Hutchinson and Co, 1926.

Giannangeli, Marco. "British Army gets Emotional to Make 'Generation Z' Fit to Fight." *Express*. 19 September, 2021. https://www.express.co.uk/news/uk/1493410/British-Army-generation-z-lt-col-langley-sharp-book.

Giddens, Anthony. *The Nation State and Violence*. Cambridge University Press, Cambridge, 1985.

Gillespie, Tarleton, Pablo J. Boczkowski, and Kirsten A. Foot. "Introduction." In *Media Technologies: Essays on Communication, Materiality, and Society*. Edited by Tarleton Gillespie, Pablo J. Boczkowski, and Kirsten A. Foot. Cambridge, MA: MIT Press Scholarship Online, 2014. doi:10.7551/mitpress/9780262525374.003.0001.

Gitelman, Lisa. *Always Already New: Media, History and the Data of Culture*. Cambridge, MA: MIT Press, 2006.

Gitelman, Lisa. *Paper Knowledge: Toward a Media History of Documents*. Durham and London: Duke University Press, 2014.

Gitelman, Lisa. *Scripts, Grooves and Writing Machines: Representing Technology in the Edison Era*. Stanford, CA: Stanford University Press, 1999.

Glover, Edward. *The Psychology of Fear and Courage*. Harmondsworth, Middlesex: Penguin, 1940.

Godfrey, Simon. *British Army Communications in the Second World War: Lifting the Fog of Battle*. London: Bloomsbury, 2013.

Goldman, Emily. "Introduction: Information Resources and Military Performance." *Journal of Strategic Studies* 27, no. 2 (2004): 195–219. doi:10.1080/0140239042000255896.

Gramsci, Antonio. *Selections From the Prison Notebooks*. Edited by Quentin Hoare and Geoffrey Nowell Smith. London: Lawrence & Wishart, 1971.

The Graphic. "The Public Record Office." *The Graphic*. 27 October, 1900.

Graves, Robert. *Goodbye to All That: An Autobiography*. London: Jonathan Cape, 1929.

Gray, Harriet. "The Trauma Risk Management Approach to Post-Traumatic Stress Disorder in the British Military: Masculinity, Biopolitics and Depoliticisation." *Feminist Review* III, no. 1 (2015): 110–123. doi:10.1057/fr.2015.23.

Gray, J. Glenn. *The Warriors: Reflections of Men in Combat*. 1959. 2nd Revised Ed. Lincoln NE: University of Nebraska Press, 1998.

Grayson, Richard. "Life in the Trenches? The Use of Operation War Diary and Crowdsourcing Methods to Provide an Understanding of the British Army's Day-to-Day Life on the Western Front." *British Journal for Military History* 2, no. 2 (2016): 160–185. ISSN 2057-0422.

Green, Andrew. *Writing the Great War: Sir James Edmonds and the Official Histories, 1915–1948*. London and Portland, OR: Frank Cass, 2003.

Griffith, Paddy. *Battle Tactics of the Western Front: The British Army's Art of Attack, 1916–18*. Yale: Yale University Press, 1994.

Griffiths, Paul and Andrea Scarantino. "Emotions in the Wild: The Situated Perspective on Emotion." In *Cambridge Handbook of Situated Cognition*. Edited by Philip Robbins and Murat Aydede. Cambridge: Cambridge University Press, 2008. 437–453.

G.S.O. *G.H.Q. (Montreuil-Sur-Mer)*. London: Philip Allan & Co., 1920.

Hacker Hughes, Jamie and Simon Wessely. "The MoD PTSD Decision: A Psychiatric Perspective." *Occupational Health Review* 122 (July/August 2006): 21–28.

Hall, Brian N. "The British Army, Information Management and the First World War: Revolution in Military Affairs." *Journal of Strategic Studies* 41, no. 7 (2018): 1001–1030. doi:10.1080/01402390.2018.1504210.

Hall, Brian N. *Communication and British Operations on the Western Front*. Cambridge: Cambridge University Press, 2017.

Hall, Nigel. "The Materiality of Letter Writing: A Nineteenth Century Perspective." In *Letter Writing as a Social Practice*. Edited by David Barton and Nigel Hall. Amsterdam and Philadelphia: John Benjamins Publishing Company, 2000. 83–108.

Ham, Gerald. "Archival Strategies for the Post-Custodial Era." *The American Archivist* 44, no. 3. (Summer1981): 207–216.

Hamburger, Kenneth. *Learning Lessons in the American Expeditionary Forces*. United States Army Center of Military History, 1997. https://history.army.mil/html/books/024/24-1/CMH_Pub_24-1.PDF.

Hart, Basil Liddell. *The British Way in Warfare*. London: Penguin, 1932.

Headrick, Daniel. *When Information Came of Age: Technologies of Knowledge in the Age of Reason and Revolution, 1700–1850*. Oxford: Oxford University Press, 2000.

Hedger, Joseph. "Meaning and Racial Slurs: Derogatory Epithets and the Semantics/Pragmatics Interface." *Language & Communication* 33 no. 3 (2013): 205–213. doi:10.1016/j.langcom.2013.04.004.

Hedstrom, Margaret. "Archives, Memory, and Interfaces with the Past." *Archival Science* 2 (2002): 21–43. doi:10.1023/A:1020800828257.

Heidegger, Martin. *Parmenides*. Translated by Andre Schuwer and Richard Rojcewicz. Bloomington, IN: Indiana University Press, 1992.

Hellbeck, Jochen. "The Diary between Literature and History: A Historian's Critical Response." *The Russian Review* 63, no. 4 (2004): 621–629. JSTOR, http://www.jstor.org/stable/3663983.

Henderson, G.F.R. *The Science of War: A Collection of Essays and Lectures, 1891–1903*. London: Longmans Green, 1912.

Herbert, Alan. *The Secret Battle*. London: Methuen & Co, 1919.

Herrera, Geoffrey L. "Inventing the Railroad and Rifle Revolution: Information, Military Innovation and the Rise of Germany." *Journal of Strategic Studies* 27, no. 2 (2004): 243–271. doi:10.1080/0140239042000255913.

Hiatt, Mary. *The Way Women Write*. New York: Teacher's College Press, 1977.

Higate, Paul. *Military Masculinities: Identity and the State*. London: Praeger, 2003.

Hinojosa, Ramon. "Doing Hegemony: Military, Men and Constructing a Hegemonic Masculinity." *The Journal of Men's Studies* 18, no. 2 (2010): 179–194. doi:10.3149/jms.1802.179.

Hohmann, Jessie. "The Treaty 8 Typewriter: Tracing the Roles of Material Things in Imagining, Realising, and Resisting Colonial Worlds." *London Review of International Law* 5, no. 3 (2017): 371–396. Hoke, Donald. "The Woman and the Typewriter: A Case Study in Technological Innovation and Social Change." *Business and Economic History* 8 (1979): 76–88. JSTOR. https://www.jstor.org/stable/23702593.

Holbrook, David. *Flesh Wounds*. First published 1966. Gloucestershire: Spellmount Limited, 2017.

Hom, Christopher. "Perjoratives." *Philosophy Compass* 5. no. 2 (2010): 164–185. doi:10.1111/j.1747-9991.2009.00274.x.

Hookway, Branden. *Interface*. Cambridge, MA: MIT Press, 2014.

Hornsby, Jennifer. "Meaning and Uselessness: How to Think about Derogatory Words." *Midwest Studies in Philosophy* 25, no. 1 (2001): 128–141. doi:10.1111/1475-4975.00042.

Hoskins, Andrew. "Digital Records Take Something Precious from Military History." *The Conversation*. 4 February, 2015. https://theconversation.com/digital-records-take-something-precious-from-military-history-36328.

Howard, Philip. "Records Held in Most Efficient Repository." *The Times*. 14 October, 1977. The Times Digital Archive, link.gale.com/apps/doc/CS287670606/TTDA?u=exeter&sid=bookmark-TTDA&xid=3108a3b.

Hunt, Elizabeth, Simon Wessely, Norman Jones, Roberto J. Rona and Neil Greenberg. "The Mental Health of the UK Armed Forces: Where Facts meet Fiction." *European Journal of Psychotraumatology* 5, no. 1 (2014). doi:10.3402/ejpt.v5.23617.

Imperial War Museum. "Voices of the First World War: Training for War." N.d. https://www.iwm.org.uk/history/voices-of-the-first-world-war-training-for-war.

Isherwood, Ian. *Remembering the Great War: Writing and Publishing the Experiences of World War I*. London: I.B. Tauris, 2017.

Jaggar, Alison. "Love and Knowledge: Emotion in Feminist Epsitemology." *Inquiry* 32, no. 2 (1989): 151–176. doi:10.1080/00201748908602185.

Janes, Andrew. "*A Series of Unfortunate Events*." (Blog) TNA. 6 February, 2014. https://blog.nationalarchives.gov.uk/series-unfortunate-events.

Janzen, Jenneka. "Pondering the Physical Scriptorium." (Blog) *medievalfragments*. 25 January, 2013. https://medievalfragments.wordpress.com/2013/01/25/pondering-the-physical-scriptorium.

Jenkinson, Hilary. "British Archives and the War." *The American Archivist* VII, no. 1 (January1944): 1–17.

Jenkinson, Hilary. *A Manual of Archive Administration*. Revised Ed. London: Percy Lund, 1937.

Johnson, Steven. *Interface Culture: How New Technology Transforms the Way we Create and Communicate*. New York: Basic Books, 1997.

Jones, Edgar and Simon Wessely. *Shell Shock to PTSD: Military Psychiatry from 1900 to the Gulf War*. Hove and New York: Psychology Press, 2005.

Jones, Edgar. "War and the Practice of Psychotherapy: The UK Experience 1939–1960." *Medical History* 48 (2004): 493–510.

Jünger, Ernst. *Feuer und Blut*. Magdeburg, 1925.

Kocsis, Andrea. "The Challenges of Working on the Operation War Diary Records." (Blog). The National Archives. 6 April, 2022. https://blog.nationalarchives.gov.uk/the-challenges-of-working-on-the-operation-war-diary-records.

Kwakkel, Erik. "Where are the Scriptoria?" (Blog) *medievalfragments*. 5 November 2013. https://medievalfragments.wordpress.com/2013/11/05/where-are-the-scriptoria.

Keegan, John. *The Face of Battle: A Study of Agincourt, Waterloo and the Somme*. London: Penguin, 1978.

Kirschenbaum, Matthew. *Track Changes: A Literary History of Word Processing*. Cambridge, MA: Harvard University Press, 2016.

Kittler, Friedrich. *Gramophone, Film, Typewriter*. Translated by Geoffrey Winthrop-Young and Michael Wutz. Stanford, CA: Stanford University Press, 1999. First published 1986 in German by Brinkmann & Bose (Berlin).

Klindt, Marco. "PDF/A Considered Harmful for Digital Preservation." In *Proceedings of iPres – 14th International Conference on Digital Preservation*. Kyoto, Japan. 25–29 September, 2017. https://ipres2017.jp/wp-content/uploads/15.pdf.

Kratz, Jessie. "The 'Roots' of Genealogy at the National Archives." (Blog) U.S. National Archives. 22 February, 2019. https://prologue.blogs.archives.gov/2019/02/22/the-roots-of-genealogy-at-the-national-archives.

Lapadat, Judith and Anne Lindsay. "Transcription in Research and Practice: From Standardization of Technique to Interpretive Positionings." *Qualitative Inquiry* 5, no. 1 (1999): 64–86. doi:10.1177/107780049900500104.

Larsson, Erika. "Feeling the Past: an Emotional Reflection on an Archive." *Journal of Aesthetics and Culture*. 12 (2020). doi:10.1080/20004214.2020.1810476.

Law, John. *After Method: Mess in Social Science Research*. New York: Routledge, 2004.

Lawes, Aidan. *Chancery Lane: The Strong Box of the Empire*. London: PRO Publications, 1996.

Lawrence, Christopher. *War by Numbers: Understanding Conventional Combat*. University of Nebraska Press, 2017.

Lawrence, Christopher. "U.S. Army Record Keeping." (Blog) Dupuy Institute. 6 February, 2017. http://www.dupuyinstitute.org/blog/2017/02/07/logistics-in-war.

Leed, Eric J. *No Man's Land: Combat and Identity in World War I*. Cambridge: Cambridge University Press, 1979.

Levine, Philippa. *The Amateur and the Professional: Antiquarians, Historians, and Archaeologists in Victorian England, 1838–1886*. Cambridge and New York: Cambridge University Press, 1986.

Lin, Maggie. "Between the lines: The story of Courier." *Medium*. 25 February, 2019. https://medium.com/@plin14/between-the-lines-the-story-of-courier-760e5311cf6d.

Lindsay, Jon R. *Information Technology and Military Power*. Ithaca and London: Cornell University Press, 2021. Cornell Scholarship Online, 2021. doi:10.7591/cornell/9781501749568.003.0001.

Lord, Matthew. *British Concepts of Heroic 'Gallantry' and the Sixties Transition: The Politics of Medals*. New York: Routledge, 2021.

Lyons, Martyn. *The Typewriter Century: A Cultural History of Writing Practices*. Toronto, Buffalo and London: University of Toronto Press, 2021.

Mabbs, Alfred. "The Public Record Office and the Second Review." *Archives* 8, no. 40 (1968): 180–184.

MacKeith, Stephen. "Lasting Lessons of Overseas Military Psychiatry." *Journal of Mental Science* 92, no. 388 (July, 1946): 542–550. doi:10.1192/bjp.92.388.542.

Martin, Henri-Jean. *The History and Power of Writing*. Translated by Lydia G. Cochrane. Chicago: University Press of Chicago, 1994.

Martin, Leonard, David Ward, John Achee and Robert Wyer. "Mood as Input: People have to Interpret the Motivation Implications of their Moods." *Journal of Personality and Social Psychology* 64, no. 3 (1993): 317–326. doi:10.1037/0022-3514.64.3.317.

Massumi, Brian. *Parables for the Virtual: Movement, Affect, Sensation*. Durham and London: Duke University Press, 2002.

Mathers, Jennifer. "The British Army's Belonging Campaign Finally Recognises that Masculinity has Changed." *The Conversation*. 18 January, 2018. https://theconversation.com/the-british-armys-belonging-campaign-finally-recognises-that-masculinity-has-changed-90259.

McAllister, Lauren, Jane Callaghan and Lisa Fellin. "Masculinites and Emotional Expression in U.K. Servicemen: 'Big Boys Don't Cry?'" *Journal of Gender Studies* 28, no. 3 (2019): 257–270. doi:10.1080/09589236.2018.1429898.

McGann, Jerome. "Database, Interface, and Archive Fever." Special issue, *PMLA* 122, no. 5 (October 2007): 1588–1592. *JSTOR*. https://www.jstor.org/stable/25501805.

McGrady, Michael. "Abbreviation and Identification: Cataloguing War Diaries 1939-46." (blog). *TNA*, 25 November, 2021. https://blog.nationalarchives.gov.uk/abbreviation-and-identification-cataloguing-war-diaries-1939-46.

McLuhan, Marshall. *Understanding Media: The Extensions of Man*. London and New York: Routledge, 2001.

Medical Correspondent. "Battle Shock." *The Times*, 25 May, 1915. The Times. Digital Archive. link.gale.com/apps/doc/CS185140409/GDCS?u=exeter&sid=GDCS&xid=0bb77e5c.

Meyer, Jessica. *Men of War: Masculinity and the First World War in Britain*. London: Palgrave Macmillan, 2009.

Min, Kyongho, William H. Wilson and Yoo-Jin Moon. "Typographical and Orthographical Spelling Error Correction." Paper presented at Second International Conference on Language Resources and Evaluation (LREC'00). Athens, Greece, 2000. https://aclanthology.org/L00-1169.

Mitcham, Samuel Jr., and Friedrich von Stauffenberg. *The Battle of Sicily: How the Allies Lost their Chance for Total Victory*. Mechanicsburg, PA: Stackpole Books, 2007.

McGrattan, Matt. "Technical Discovery: Project Alpha." (Blog) TNA. 19 December, 2019. https://blog.nationalarchives.gov.uk/technical-discovery-project-alpha.

Mcluhan, Marshall. *Understanding Media: The Extensions of Man*. Cambridge, MA: MIT Press, 1994.

Morris, Steven. "Judges Quash UK Marine Alexander Blackman's Murder Conviction." *The Guardian*. 15 March, 2017. https://www.theguardian.com/uk-news/2017/mar/15/alexander-blackman-royal-marine-a-judges-quash-murder-conviction.

Natzio, Georgina. "British Army Servicemen and Women 1939–45: Their Selection, Care and Management." *The RUSI Journal* 138, no. 1 (1993): 36–43.

Nesmith, Tom. "Seeing Archives: Postmodernism and the Changing Intellectual Place of Archives," *The American Archivist* 65, no. 1 (Spring–Summer, 2002): 24–41. JSTOR. https://www.jstor.org/stable/40294187.

Noakes, Lucy. "Communities of Feeling: Fear, Death, and Grief in the Writing of British Servicemen in the Second World War." In *Total War: An Emotional History*. Edited by Lucy Noakes, Claire Langhamer, and Claudia Siebrecht. Oxford: British Academy, 2020. British Academy Scholarship Online, 2020. doi:10.5871/bacad/9780197266663.003.0007.

Norton-Taylor, Richard. "Pardons for Executed Soldiers Become Law." *The Guardian*. 9 November, 2006.

Nunberg, Geoff. "After Years of Restraint, a Linguist says 'Yes!' To the Exclamation Point," *Npr.org*. 13 June, 2017. https://www.npr.org/2017/06/08/532148705/after-years-of-restraint-a-linguist-says-yes-to-the-exclamation-point?t=1660734117469.

Obama, Barack. *A Promised Land*. New York: Random House, 2020.

Onoto Pen Advert. *Illustrated London News*. 16 December, 1916.

Orin, Andy. "Behind the App: The Story of Notepad++." *Lifehacker*. 17 June, 2015. https://lifehacker.com/behind-the-app-the-story-of-notepad-1711936108.

Our Own Reporter. "Army Training in Hate and Blood to Cease." *Aberdeen Journal*, 25 May, 1942, 2. British Library Newspapers, www.gale.com/apps/doc/JA3238634133/BNCN?u=exeter&sid=bookmark-BNCN&xid=f873a1f5.

Overy, Richard. *The Bombing War: Europe 1939–1945*. London: Allen Lane, 2013.

Petroski, Henry. *The Pencil: A History of Design and Circumstance*. London: Faber, 1990.

Palazzo, Albert. *Seeking Victory on the Western Front: The British Army and Chemical Warfare in World War I*. Lincoln, NE: University of Nebraska Press, 2000.

Picot, Geoffrey. *Accidental Warrior: In the Front Line from Normandy till Victory*. Lewes: Book Build, 1993. Kindle.

Place, Timothy. *Military Training in the British Army, 1940–1944 – from Dunkirk to D-Day*. London: Frank Cass, 2000.

Plakins Thornton, Tamara. *Handwriting in America: A Cultural History*. New Haven and London: Yale University Press, 1996.

Postman, Neil. *Building a Bridge to the 18th Century: How the Past can Improve our Future*. New York: Vintage Books, 1999.

ProPublica. "Lost to History: Missing War Records Complicate Benefit Claims by Afghanistan Veterans." *ProPublica*. 9 November, 2012. https://www.propublica.org/article/lost-to-history-missing-war-records-complicate-benefit-claims-by-veterans.

Pugh, Joseph. *Information Journeys in Digital Archives*. (EngD Thesis, University of York, 2017). https://etheses.whiterose.ac.uk/20663/1/Proofed%20Corrected%20thesis.pdf.

Punch. "The Typewriter." *Punch* 201, no. 5237 (July1941): 74. Punch Historical Archive.

Raghunathan, Rajagopal and Yaacov Trope. "Walking the Tightrope Between Feeling Good and Being Accurate: Mood as a Resource in Processing Persuasive Messages." *Journal of Personality and Social Psychology* 83, no. 3 (2002): 510–525. doi:10.1037/0022-3514.83.3.510.

Ramsay, Debra. *American Media and the Memory of World War II*. New York: Routledge, 2015.

Ramsay, Debra. "Liminality and the Smearing of War and Play in Battlefield I." *Games Studies: International Journal of Computer Games Research* 20, no. 1 (2020). http://gamestudies.org/2001/articles/ramsay.

Ramsay, Debra. "Tensions in the Interface: The Archive and the Digital." In Hoskins, *Digital Memory Studies*, 280–302.

Reddy, William M. *The Navigation of Feeling: A Framework*. Cambridge: Cambridge University Press, 2001.

Rees, John R. (Brigadier). *The Shaping of Psychiatry by War*. London: Chapman and Hall, 1945.

Rees, John R. (Brigadier). "Three Years of Military Psychiatry in the United Kingdom." *British Medical Journal* 1, no. 4278. (2 January, 1943): 1–6. https://www.ncbi.nlm.nih.gov/pmc/articles/PMC2282055.

Remington. Typewriter advert. *The Daily Mail*. 1 January, 1937.

Rentetzi, Maria. "The Epistemology of the Familiar: A Hymn to Pandora." In *Boxes: A Field Guide*. Edited by Susanne Bauer, Martina Schlünder and Maria Rentezi, 443–458. Manchester: Manchester Mattering Press, 2020.

Richards, Frank. *Old Soldiers Never Die*. First published 1933. New edition, Sussex: Naval and Military Press, 2009.

Riles, Annelise. *The Network Inside Out*. Ann Arbor: University of Michigan Press, 2001.

Robertson, Craig. *The Filing Cabinet: A Vertical History of Information*. University of Minnesota Press, 2021.

Rosenwein, Barbara H. "Worrying about Emotions in History." *The American Historical Review* 107, no. 3 (2002): 821–845. doi:10.1086/ahr/107.3.821.

Runge, Laura. "Beauty and Gallantry: A Model of Polite Conversation Revisited." *Eighteenth-Century Life* 25, no. 1 (Winter 2001): 43–63. Project Muse. https://muse.jhu.edu/article/10535.

Rubin, Donald and Kathryn Greene. "Gender-Typical Style in Written Language." *Research in the Teaching of English* 26, no. 1 (1992): 7–40. JSTOR. http://www.jstor.org/stable/40171293.

Samuels, Martin. "Doctrine for Orders and Decentraliztion in the British and German Armies, 1885–1935." *War in History* 22, no. 4 (2015): 448–477. JSTOR, http://www.jstor.org/stable/26098448.

Sargant, William and Eliot Slater. "The Acute War Neuroses." *The Lancet*. July1940. https://wellcomecollection.org/works/ph7xeaq5.

Saul, David. *100 Days to Victory: How the Great War was Fought and Won*. London: Hodder and Stoughton, 2013.

Scheer, Monique. "Are Emotions a Kind of Practice (and is That What Makes Them Have a History)? A Bourdieuian Approach to Understanding Emotion." *History and Theory* 51, no. 2 (2012): 193–220.

Schön, Donald. "Generative Metaphor: A Perspective on Problem-Setting in Social Policy." In *Metaphor and Thought*. Edited by Andrew Ortony. Cambridge: Cambridge University Press. 137–163.

Schlünder, Martina. "The Generative Possibilities of the Wrong Box." In Bauer, Schlünder and Rentetzi, *Boxes: A Field Guide*. 27–36.

Sellen, Abigail and Richard Harper. *The Myth of the Paperless Office*. Cambridge, MA: MIT Press, 2003.

Seltzer, Mark. *Bodies and Machines*. London: Routledge, 1992.

Shapira, Michal. *The War Inside: Psychoanalysis, Total War, and the Making of the Democratic Self in Postwar Britain*. Cambridge: Cambridge University Press, 2013.

Sharp, David. "Shocked, Shot and Pardoned." *The Lancet* 368, no. 9540 (September 16, 2006). doi:10.1016/S0140-6736(06)69395-1.

Sharp, Langley (Lieutenant Colonel). *The Habit of Excellence: Why British Army Leadership Works*. London: Penguin Business, 2021.

Shephard, Ben. "'Pitiless Psychology': The Role of Prevention in British Military Psychiatry in the Second World War." *History of Psychiatry* 10 (1999): 491–524.

Shephard, Ben. *A War of Nerves: Soldiers and Psychiatrists, 1914–1994*. London: Pimlico, 2002.

Showalter, Dennis E. "Information Capabilities and Military Revolutions: The Nineteenth-Century Experience." *Journal of Strategic Studies* 27, no. 2 (2004): 220–242. doi:10.1080/0140239042000255904.

Simkins, Peter. *Kitchener's Army: The Raising of the New Armies, 1914–16*. Manchester and New York: Manchester University Press, 1988.

Sloan, Geoffrey. "Military Doctrine, Command Philosophy and the Generation of Fighting Power: Genesis and Theory." *International Affairs (Royal Institute of International Affairs 1944–)* 88, no. 2 (2012): 243–263. JSTOR. http://www.jstor.org/stable/41428604.

Smith, Melvin. *Awarded for Valour: A History of the Victoria Cross and the Evolution of British Heroism*. Basingstoke and New York: Palgrave Macmillan, 2008.

Special Correspondent with the Army. "The New Battle Drill." *The Times*. 25 November, 1941. The Times Digital Archive, www.gale.com/apps/doc/CS85539193/TTDA?u=exeter&sid=bookmarkTTDA&xid=01abd47e.

Special Correspondent with the Army. "Realistic Army Training." *The Times*, 7 April, 1942. The Times Digital Archive, www.gale.com/apps/doc/CS34945671/TTDA?u=exeter&sid=bookmark-TTDA&xid=983cb578.

Springhall, John. "The Boy Scouts, Class and Militarism in Relation to British Youth Movements." *International Review of Social History* 16, no. 2 (1971): 125–158. JSTOR, http://www.jstor.org/stable/44581664.

Stachelbeck, Christian. "'Lessons learned' in WWI: The German Army, Vimy Ridge and the Elastic Defence in Depth in 1917." *Journal of Military and Strategic Studies* 18, no. 2 (2017): 118–135. ISSN: 1488-1559X.

Steedman, Carolyn. *Dust*. Manchester: Manchester University Press, 2001.

Stiff, Paul, Paul Dobraszczyk and Mike Esbester. "Designing and Gathering Information: Perspectives on Nineteenth-Century Forms" in Weller, *Information History*, 57–88.

Stoler, Ann. *Along the Archival Grain: Epistemic Anxieties and Colonial Common Sense*. Princeton, NJ: Princeton University Press, 2008.

Swartz, Sally. "Asylum Case Records: Fact and Fiction." *Rethinking History* 22, no. 3 (2018): 289–301. doi:10.1080/13642529.2018.1487096.

Sylvester, Christine. *War as Experience: Contributions from International Relations and Feminist Analysis.* London: Routledge, 2013.

Sylvester, Christine. "War Experiences/War Practices/War Theory." *Millennium: Journal of International Studies* 40, no. 3. (2012): 483–503. doi:10.1177/0305829812442211.

Tapscott, Rebecca. "Militarized Masculinity and the Paradox of Restraint: Mechanisms of Social Control Under Modern Authoritariansm." *International Affairs* 96, no. 6 (2020): 1565–1584. doi:10.1093/ia/iiaa163.

Taylor, Nick. "The Return of Character: Parallels Between Late-Victorian and Twenty-First Century Discourses." *Sociological Research Online* 23, no. 2 (2018): 399–415. doi:10.1177/1360780418769679.

Terraine, John, editor. *General Jack's Diary: War on the Western Front 1914–1918.* London: Cassell, 2001.

The Times. "In Chancery Lane." *The Times.* 21 January, 1926. 17. The Times Digital Archive, www.gale.com/apps/doc/CS286988853/TTDA?u=exeter&sid=bookmark-TTDA&xid=e0071cd5.

Tilley, Susan. "'Challenging' Research Practices: Turning a Critical Lens on the Work of Transcription." *Qualitative Inquiry* 9, no. 5 (2003): 750–773. doi:10.1177/1077800403255296.

Tredinnick, Luke. "Rewriting History: The Information Age and the Knowable Past." In Weller, *Information History*, 175–198.

Truss, Lynne. *Eats, Shoots & Leaves: The Zero Tolerance Approach to Punctuation.* London: Fourth Estate, 2009.

Vallée, Richard. "Slurring and Common Knowledge of Ordinary Language." *Journal of Pragmatics* 61 (2014): 78–90. doi:10.1016/j.pragma.2013.11.013.

Vanderbilt, Tom. "Courier, Dispatched." *Slate.* 20 February, 2004. https://slate.com/human-interest/2004/02/goodbye-to-the-courier-font.html.

Von Xylander, Cheryce. "Cardboard. Thinking the Box." In *Research Objects in their Technical Setting.* Edited by Alfred Nordmann, Bernadette Bensuade Vincent, Sacha Loeve and Astrid Schwartz. London: Routledge, 2017. 166–182.

Walker, Rob. "The Inside Story of How the Lowly PDF Played the Longest Game in Tech." *Marker.* Everyday Design Icons. 14 January, 2021. https://marker.medium.com/the-improbable-tale-of-how-the-lowly-pdf-played-the-longest-game-in-tech-d143d2ba9abf.

The War Illustrated. "The Dauntless Courage of a Highland Laddie, Brutal Cowardice of a Baffled Hun Officer." *The War Illustrated.* 5 February, 1916. https://archive.org/details/TWI1916pt1/page/588/mode/2up?q=%22dauntless+courage%22.

The War Illustrated. "The Fear of Being Afraid." *The War Illustrated.* The Observation Post. 26 January, 1916. xciv. https://archive.org/details/TWI1916pt1/page/n113/mode/2up?q=fear.

Waterman's Pen Advert. *Daily Mail.* 9 November, 1917.

Weaver, Matthew. "Army Accused of Political Correctness in Recruitment Campaign." *The Guardian.* 10 January, 2018. https://www.theguardian.com/uk-news/2018/jan/10/army-accused-of-political-correctness-in-recruitment-campaign.

Weber, Max. *Sociological Writings.* Edited by Wolf Hydebrand. New York: Continuum, 2006.

Weller, Chas. *The Early History of the Typewriter.* La Porte, IN: Chase & Shepherd, Printers, 1918.

Weller, Toni, editor. *Information History in the Modern World: Histories of the Information Age*. New York: Palgrave Macmillan, 2011.

Werner, Marta. "Writing's Other Scene: Crossing and Crossing Out in Emily Dickinson's Manuscripts." *Text* 17. (2005): 197–221. *JSTOR*. https://www.jstor.org/stable/30227822.

Wershler-Henry, Darren. *The Iron Whim: A Fragmented History of Typewriting*. Toronto: McClelland and Stewart, 2005.

Wierzbicka, Anna. "Talking about Emotions: Semantics, Culture, and Cognition." *Cognition and Emotion* 6, no. 3–4 (1992): 285–319. doi:10.1080/02699939208411073.

Wyatt, Caroline. "War Veterans 'Don't Need to Cope Alone.'" *BBC News*. Health. 10 October, 2011. https://www.bbc.co.uk/news/health-15239045.

The Yost, Typewriter Advert. *The Times*. 10 December, 1895.

Zemon Davis, Natalie. *Fiction in the Archives: Pardon Tales and Their Tellers in Sixteenth-Century France*. Stanford, CA: Stanford University Press, 1987.

Zieger, Susan. *The Mediated Mind: Affect, Ephemera and Consumerism in the Nineteenth Century*. New York: Fordham University Press, 2018.

Žilinčík, Samuel. "Strategy and the Instrumental Role of Emotions." *Real Clear Defense: The Strategy Bridge* (25 September, 2018). https://thestrategybridge.org/the-bridge/2018/9/25/strategy-and-the-instrumental-role-of-emotions.

Zürcher, Erik-Jan, editor. *Fighting for a Living: A Comparative Study of Military Labour 1500–2000*. Amsterdam University Press, 2013.

Index

Adam, R., Lt.-Gen 100, 133n170
affect 9, 11, 16, 19, 196, 200, 207, 211; in archives 136, 137, 140, 155, 165–166, 167, 169; in First World War Unit War Diaries 26, 32, 40, 49, 53, 54, 58; in Second World War Unit War Diaries 115–116
Allport, A. 98, 113
Antconc 46, 171, 175, 182
APSS *See* Army Printing and Stationery Services
archival description 15, 16, 138, 156–158, 164, 169, 197
archival grain 138, 139–140, 149, 150, 152, 153, 155, 157, 169
archiving 5, 14, 141, 147, 148–149, 152, 183 *see also* archival description; *respects des fonds*
Army Form C.2118: 7, 9, 12, 16, 17, 25–26, 33, 160, 166; in the First World War 33–36, 39–40, 42, 46, 47, 49, 50–55, 58, 60, 63; in the Second World War 81, 87, 103–104, 105, 107–108, 110–111, 114–115, 116, 117, 119, 120, 126; in current conflicts 195–196
Army Form C.2119: 81, 103, 194
Army Printing and Stationery Services 33, 34, 36, 85

Baron, A. 113
battle exhaustion 88, 91, 95, 108–109; *see also* shell shock
battle schools 96, 99; see also blood and hate training
Beeching, W. 82, 84
blood and hate training 76, 96–99, 101; see also battle schools
boche *see* bosche

Blouin, F. 13, 136, 139, 141, 142, 153, 154, 156, 163, 198
Bogacz, T. 90, 92, 93
Bolter, J.D. 12, 37, 160, 174
bosche 111–112
Bourke, J. 10, 48, 124
Bowlby, A. 113
bureaucracy: and archival description 156–157; and the British Army 4–5, 27–30, 31, 33–36, 42, 46, 47, 57, 58, 62–64, 74, 78–79, 100, 194–197, 203, 210; and paperwork 4–5, 7, 25, 138, 140–143, 164; and The Public Record Office 138, 139, 140–141, 143, 144, 183; in the 19th Century 4–5, 27–29, 183

cardboard box 4, 157, 159, 163–165, 167, 169, 197
character: and the British Army in the First World War 43, 45; and the British Army in the Second World War 78, 89–95, 97, 99, 101, 125; of war 193, 209, 211n1
Cheshire Regiment 17, 38, 48, 58, 105, 108, 109, 111, 115, 116
close reading 11, 18, 104
Cook, T. 148–149, 188n105, 193
Copp, T. 91, 94, 95, 131n128
Craig, B. 149, 150, 151
Craig, N. 102–103, 107, 112, 113

De Certeau, M. 27, 184, 197
Derrida, J. 13, 15
Dery, D. 6, 28, 194
DeVere Brody, J. 53, 54, 115
Directorate of Personnel Selection 100–101

234 Index

doctrine: in the First World War 25, 29–30, 201; in the Second World War 74, 77, 78, 96, 124, 125, 203; in contemporary conflicts 203, 210–211, 211n1; *see also* Field Service Regulations

documentation 4–5, 9–11, 14, 54, 136, 139, 141–143, 156, 159–160, 170, 183, 184, 197, 198–199; and war 1, 3, 17, 18, 47, 60–61, 78, 81, 86, 87, 100, 143–144, 147, 195, 196; study of 3, 6–7

Downes, S. 10, 11, 40, 42, 53

emotion: and national identity 42–43, 45–46, 61, 74, 95–99, 102, 112, 124; and war 9–12, 40, 42, 44, 53, 88, 90, 193, 199, 203–210; as practice 10–12, 26, 40–41, 45–46, 50, 51, 53–54, 56–57, 58, 64, 104, 107–109, 112, 115; emotional engineering 75–76, 87–103; history of 41–42; in the archive 155, 165–166; observable traces of 10–12, 45, 46, 49, 53, 64, 104; outlaw emotions 48, 50, 88, 108, 115, 208; performance of 11, 43, 45, 46, 51, 53, 56, 87, 91, 101–102, 107, 109, 111, 117, 120, 123 *see also* emotives; emotional regime; stiff upper lip

emotional regime 42; and the British Army in the First World War 41–51, 53, 56, 58, 202; and the British Army in the Second World War 75–76, 87–103, 109, 111, 112, 115, 124; and the British Army in current conflicts 206–209

emotives 10–11, 171, 178, 182; in First World War Unit War Diaries 46–53, 56, 58, 61, 64; in Second World War Unit War Diaries 76, 101, 104, 107–115, 117, 123, 124; *see also* emotion

Esher Report 29

Farge, A. 15, 16, 17, 153, 155, 161, 163, 165, 167

Field Service Regulations 1, 25, 28, 145, 161, 193–194, 195; in the First World War 30–33, 34, 38, 47, 49, 50, 52, 53, 55, 56, 59, 60; in the Second World War 74, 75, 76–82, 96, 103, 104, 118, 125; *see also* doctrine

Fineman, S. 42, 43, 75, 102

Foucault, M. 5, 35
fountain pen 37–38, 84, 164
Fox, A. 2, 30, 32, 66n40, 77
Freedom of Information Act 149
French, D. 3, 44, 57, 60, 74, 76, 77, 78, 94, 127n15, 131n125
FSR *see* Field Service Regulations

gallantry: in First World War Unit War Diaries 51–52, 61; in Second World War Unit War Diaries 114–115
General Service Corps 100–101
Gitelman, L. 2, 7, 15, 28, 34, 35, 75, 84, 87, 125, 136, 138, 160, 175
Goldman, E. 6, 80
Green, A. 60–61, 62, 71n204
Grigg Committee Report 144–145
Grusin, R. 160, 174
GSC *See* General Service Corps

Hall, B. 3, 6, 8, 23, 24, 26, 31
Herbert, A. 73–74
Historical Section of the Committee of Imperial Defence 59–61, 80, 143
history 1, 9, 13, 15, 16, 18, 19, 31, 53, 63, 163, 198, 200, 201; and the Public Record Office 140, 141–143, 145, 149, 151; and The National Archives; 139, 150–152, 158, 167, 169, 183, 197; and Unit War Diaries 2, 3, 18, 24, 31, 40, 47, 59–61, 63, 79–80, 106, 124, 126, 196; as profession 5, 141–142; military 2, 9–10, 29, 44, 59, 63, 94, 123; Official 2, 9, 26, 59–62, 63, 114, 193; regimental 44, 52, 56–57
Holbrook, D. 109, 110, 196

indelible pencil 2, 8, 12, 19, 25–26, 38, 46, 64, 164, 192, 196
industrialisation 4, 5, 23, 24, 27, 29, 163; and war 1, 5, 17, 23–24, 25, 28–30, 37, 44–45, 48, 63, 74–75, 77, 100–101, 115, 124, 193, 197, 210
information: history of 4–5, 6–7, 27–28, 34, 164, 183; management in the British Army 2–3, 5–6, 12, 19, 23–25; 27, 31–33, 34–36, 40, 63–64, 74, 76–81, 193–196, 203

Jenkinson, H. 13, 144, 147
Joint Photographic Experts Group *see* JPEG
JPEG 168

Index

Kittler, F. 7, 82, 83, 84

Land Forces Standing Order (1120) 193–195, 199, 201
linguistic analysis 10, 11, 12, 18, 22n71, 26, 40, 76, 111–112
Lynch, A. 10, 11, 40, 42, 53

McAndrew, B. 91, 94, 95, 131n128
Mcluhan, M. 7, 81, 163, 174
mediation 3, 15, 17, 24, 136, 138, 157; of Unit War Diaries 3, 5, 8, 10, 17–19, 24, 25, 33, 58, 63, 107, 125, 126, 169, 197, 198, 201

narration *see* narrative
narrative 9, 11, 16, 28, 31, 178, 184; in archives 141, 142, 151, 152, 155, 157–158, 161, 169, 170, 188n108; in current conflicts 194, 195, 197, 201, 203; in First World War Unit War Diaries 40, 46, 51, 52, 55–59, 60, 62, 64; in Second World War Unit War Diaries 80–81, 92, 104, 106, 110, 112, 116, 117–123, 125, 126
North Staffordshire Regiment 17, 35, 40, 54, 55, 105, 106, 108, 110, 112, 119
Notepad++ 176–177, 182, 190n166
Nottinghamshire and Derbyshire Regiment *see* Sherwood Foresters

O'Loughlin, K. 10, 11, 40, 42, 53
Operation War Diary 18, 161–162, 189n123
Operational Record Keeping 192, 193, 194, 197
Operational Records 192, 193, 194, 195, 196, 197, 198–201
OR *see* Operational Records
ORK *see* Operational Record Keeping
orthographical errors 106, 125

papereality 6, 28, 194
Parachute Regiment 17
PDF *see* Portable Document Format
Picot, G. 98, 113
plain text format 18, 162, 171, 172, 172, 177, 181, 182
Portable Document Format 6–7, 16, 159–162, 168, 174, 175–176, 178, 182, 184
pre-printed (blank) form 6, 7, 33–34, 35, 38, 196

PRO *see* Public Record Office
Public Record Office 4, 14, 15, 74, 151, 153–154, 183; history of;138–149; *see also* The National Archives
Public Records Act: (1838) 140, 146; (1958) 145; amendments to 145

RASC *see* Royal Army Service Corps
reading spaces 12–16, 39, 116; of The National Archives 3, 126, 137–138, 152–159, 165–170
Reddy, W. 10, 42, 46
Report of the War Office Committee on 'Shell Shock' 75, 88, 90–95, 96, 98, 99, 130–131n119, 204–205; *see also* shell shock
respects des fonds 156–157; *see also* archival description
Robertson, C. 4, 163, 164
Rosenberg, G. 13, 136, 139, 141, 142, 153, 154, 156, 163, 198
Royal Army Service Corps 85–86

Scheer, Monique 10, 41, 46, 53, 51, 68n103, 104
Shapira, M. 88, 90
shell shock 87–88, 89, 130n116; in First World War Unit War Diaries 48; in Second World War Unit War Diaries 108; *see also* battle exhaustion; Report of the War Office Committee on 'Shell Shock'
Sherwood Foresters 17, 39, 40, 47, 50, 108–109, 112, 113, 117
Showalter, D. 3, 24
South Staffordshire Regiment 17, 47, 50, 51, 52, 53, 55–58, 61, 102, 105, 106, 112, 114, 117–119, 254
Steedman, C. 1, 15, 153, 163, 183, 184
stiff upper lip 42, 48, 50, 92, 96, 206, 209
Stoler, A. 136, 138, 139, 140, 184
Swartz, S. 9, 16, 18, 153, 170
Sylvester, C. 9, 10, 15, 138

The National Archives 13, 14, 16, 17, 18, 26, 38, 126, 136–139; history of 149–152; *see also* the Public Records Office; reading spaces

TMP *see* Typewriter Mechanics Pool
TNA *see* The National Archives
transcription 18, 138, 162, 167, 170–183

Trauma Risk Management Programme 206–207
Tredinnick, L. 6, 27, 169, 170
TRiM *see* Trauma Risk Management Programme
txt. *see* plain text format
typewriter 2, 8, 19, 81–82, 144, 159, 164, 176, 177, 180, 182, 196; history of 82–85; in the First World War 8, 26, 36–37; in the Second World War 8, 12, 64, 75–76, 85–87, 103, 104–107, 115, 117, 124, 125, 196–197
Typewriter Mechanics Pool 85–86
typographic errors (typos) 104–107, 125, 168, 171, 181

War Office 30, 86, 143, 147, 157
War Office Selection Boards 101
Weber, M. 27, 28
Weller, T. 4, 27–28
Welsh Guards 17, 39, 47, 48, 49, 50, 56, 110, 112–113, 116, 120–123, 166
Wershler-Henry, D. 81–82, 83, 85, 104
Worcestershire Regiment 17, 49, 50
Wozbees *see* War Office Selection Boards
writing spaces 3, 9, 14, 36, 39, 40, 41, 137, 138, 152, 166, 171, 173, 192, 196; definition of 12; in the First World War 26, 34, 38, 39, 46, 55, 58, 64, 202; in the Second World War 75, 76, 103, 105, 106, 115, 116, 124, 126, 167

Printed in the United States
by Baker & Taylor Publisher Services